THE OXFORD ENCYCLOPEDIA OF THE CIVIL WAR

THE OXFORD ENCYCLOPEDIA OF THE CIVIL WAR

William L. Barney

OXFORD
UNIVERSITY PRESS

For all the teachers and students from whom I have learned so much,
and above all, for Elaine, who made it all so special.

Oxford University Press

Oxford University Press, Inc., publishes works that further
Oxford University's objective of excellence
in research, scholarship, and education.

Oxford   New York
Auckland   Cape Town   Dar es Salaam   Hong Kong   Karachi
Kuala Lumpur   Madrid   Melbourne   Mexico City   Nairobi
New Delhi   Shanghai   Taipei   Toronto

With offices in
Argentina   Austria   Brazil   Chile   Czech Republic   France   Greece
Guatemala   Hungary   Italy   Japan   Poland   Portugal   Singapore
South Korea   Switzerland   Thailand   Turkey   Ukraine   Vietnam

Published by Oxford University Press, Inc.
198 Madison Avenue, New York, New York 10016
www.oup.com

The first edition of this book was published in hardcover as *The Civil War and Reconstruction:*
A Student Companion (Oxford University Press, 2001).

Oxford is a registered trademark of Oxford University Press

Library of Congress Cataloging-in-Publication Data

Barney, William L.
   The Oxford encyclopedia of the Civil War / William L. Barney.
      p. cm.
   Rev. and updated ed. of: The Civil War and Reconstruction, 2001
   Includes index.
   ISBN 978-0-19-978201-7 (pbk. : alk. paper)
   1. United States—History—Civil War, 1861–1865—Encyclopedias. 2.
Reconstruction (U.S. history, 1865–1877)—Encyclopedias.   I. Barney,
William L. Civil War and Reconstruction.   II. Title.

E468.B319 2011
973.703—dc22   2010045461

ISBN 9780199782017

1 3 5 7 9 8 6 4 2

Printed in the United States of America on acid-free paper

CONTENTS

PREFACE

More than 150 years after the start of the Civil War, Americans are as fascinated as ever with that agonizing struggle that remains as the watershed in American history. U.S. victory in the war established the permanence of the Union and ended the institution of slavery that had been so central to the social and economic history of the prewar South and indeed the nation as a whole. As embodied in the three great constitutional amendments that came out of the war—the 13th freeing the slaves, the 14th granting the freed population national citizenship, and the 15th barring race as a factor in denying the vote—the war also sparked efforts to create a more equal nation that continue into the present. These momentous results came at the terrible cost of more than 620,000 dead Americans, a figure that easily dwarfs the number of lives lost in any other American war. The conflict also spread economic misery and ruin across much of the former Confederate States of America.

Few areas of American life were left untouched by the war, and debates over its causes, battles, leaders, and meaning still attract the interest and often the passions of Americans more than any other topics in our history. The entries in this book speak to these debates and reveal the war in all its complexity. Arranged alphabetically, the entries provide both seasoned readers and those new to the Civil War ready information on all phases of the conflict from the battlefields to the home fronts.

The battles and major personalities of the war dominate the entries. It was the outcome of battles as influenced by the individual decisions of generals and politicians that most fundamentally shaped the course of the war and set in motion its social and economic consequences. For example, the military stalemate that set in during 1862 was the single most important factor in President Abraham Lincoln's redefinition of Union war aims to embrace the emancipation of the slaves. As the military tide turned against the Confederacy in 1863, the government of President Jefferson Davis made ever-greater demands on its citizens that worsened morale on the Confederate home front. Declining civilian morale in turn undercut the broad base of popular support that Confederate armies needed to achieve victories on the battlefields.

In addition to the war years of 1861–65, the entries also cover the buildup of sectional tensions to the outbreak of war, and efforts during Reconstruction to define the meaning of the war and the terms of Northern victory. Reflecting the importance of slavery as the root cause of the war, many entries deal with its impact on key legislation, compromises, and the political parties that were increasingly sectionalized by the issue.

Once the guns of war were silenced in the spring of 1865, new political battlefields opened, centering on the readmission of former Confederate states to the Union and the issues of whether African Americans, the former slaves, were to be granted equality in the preserved Union. These debates shaped the crisis of Reconstruction from 1865 to 1877. The entries here focus on the major actors in this period, the new laws and constitutional amendments that were passed, and the shifting fortunes of Southern whites and blacks as they grappled with the unprecedented changes that were transforming the society of the South.

The ongoing interest of historians and the general public in the Civil War produced the vast published research upon which this book rests. Central to much of this recent research has been a broadening of scholarship beyond its traditional emphasis on battles and military campaigns to a new concern with the active role played by civilians, women, and African Americans in the epic struggle that reshaped American government and society. The entries thus touch upon a wide spectrum of American experiences during the Civil War era, and if they convey the richness and vitality of the newer research on the war, this volume will have succeeded in its main goal.

THE OXFORD ENCYCLOPEDIA OF THE CIVIL WAR

Abolitionism

Abolitionism emerged in the 1830s as a radically new phase in the antislavery movement. Rejecting gradualism and the colonization of freed slaves abroad, the abolitionists demanded immediate emancipation without payment to slaveowners. Rather than accepting the dominant white view of African Americans as an inferior caste that could never be integrated as equals in American society, they called for an end to racial discrimination.

The abolitionists drew inspiration from the wave of evangelical revivals known as the Second Great Awakening. At the core of abolitionism was the religious argument that slavery was an unmitigated sin and that all Americans who refused to make an immediate moral commitment to end slavery were implicated in that sin. William Lloyd Garrison was the chief propagandist for the movement, but it was the young minister Theodore Dwight Weld who first gained converts for abolitionism in the rural heartland of the North. Weld preached abolitionism as he would a revival, and in his words, he always approached slavery "as preeminently a moral question, arresting the conscience of the nation."

For all their moral fervor and sophisticated use of the latest advances in print technology to spread their message, the abolitionists failed to convert more than a small minority of whites to their position. Most Northern whites were either indifferent or violently opposed to a movement which they viewed as a threat to national peace, white supremacy, and the jobs and profits generated by slave labor for the Northern economy. Even most Northern churches kept themselves apart from the abolitionist crusade. As for Southern whites, nearly all of them denounced the abolitionists as deranged outsiders whose fanatical ideas would touch off slave revolts. They bitterly rejected the charge that slavery per se was a sin and denied the abolitionists freedom of the press and use of the mails throughout the South. In Congress, Southerners pushed for and got a gag rule between 1836 and 1844 that prevented any discussion of abolitionist petitions in the House of Representatives.

By 1840, when abolitionism split into Garrisonian and anti-Garrisonian camps, the movement appeared to have been a failure. Moral suasion—the religious effort aimed at convincing white Americans to renounce the twin sins of slavery and racism—had not worked. Yet, in fact, the abolitionists had accomplished the indispensable task of breaking through the apathy of silence regarding slavery. They had built a network of 1,000 local antislavery societies in the North; added white voices to the black ones that had always fought for the immediate end of slavery; and frightened the South into supporting measures that violated the liberties of white Americans to petition and freely express their views.

Once Northern whites began to

Founded in 1833, the American Anti-Slavery Society called for the immediate abolition of slavery by sponsoring lectures and meetings, organizing and sending signed antislavery petitions to Congress, printing and distributing propaganda, and publishing journals such as the American Anti-Slavery Almanac.

view the slave South as a threat to their own freedoms, the conditions were in place for building a political coalition of antislavery Northerners. This coalition grew into a Northern majority by the 1850s as more Northern whites became convinced that the spread of slavery into the federal territories was an unconscionable threat to their interests. To be sure, their antislavery principles lacked the urgent sense of moral fervor and commitment to racial equality that lay at the heart of abolitionism, but the ongoing abolitionist crusade predisposed Northerners to expect the worst from Southern intentions. As confirmed by the runaway success of Harriet Beecher Stowe's antislavery novel *Uncle Tom's Cabin,* the Northern public was embracing an antislavery position that had been all but unthinkable a generation earlier. By refusing to back down on the moral issue of slavery, the abolitionists were instrumental in forging an image of the antislavery North that ultimately provoked the South to secede.

SEE ALSO
Colonization; Douglass, Frederick; Emancipation; Free-labor ideology; Garrison, William Lloyd; Reform; Stowe, Harriet Beecher; Thirteenth Amendment

FURTHER READING
Goodman, Paul. *Of One Blood: Abolitionism and the Origins of Racial Equality.* Berkeley: University of California Press, 1998.
McKivigan, John R. *The War against Proslavery Religion: Abolitionism and the Northern Churches, 1830–1865.* Ithaca, N.Y.: Cornell University Press, 1984.
Stewart, James Brewer. *Holy Warriors: The Abolitionists and American Society,* Rev. ed. New York: Hill & Wang, 1996.

Absenteeism

Absenteeism refers to soldiers listed on the military rolls but not available for

duty. It includes desertion but is not synonymous with it. Many, perhaps most, soldiers who went AWOL, or absent without leave, intended to return to their units. Nonetheless, rates of absenteeism correlate closely with an army's disciplinary cohesiveness and the willingness of its soldiers to see the war through to the end. Whereas absenteeism remained manageable in Union armies throughout the war, it soared to disastrously high proportions in Confederate armies in the last two years of the war.

Perhaps indicative of the greater resistance of rebel soldiers to discipline, absenteeism in the Confederate ranks was always higher than in Union forces. For example, in June 1862, the figures stood at 30 percent for the rebels and 20 percent for the federals. By the end of 1863, at which point the Union rate stabilized at around 30 percent, the Confederate rate had reached 40 percent—and it kept climbing. Major defeats at Gettysburg, Vicksburg, and Chattanooga had clearly sapped Confederate fighting morale. By the fall of 1864, rebel armies were melting away fast, as over half of the soldiers failed to report for duty. By the early spring of 1865, only two in five still remained with their units. One of those who stayed, Private Luther Mills of North Carolina, explained what was happening when he wrote home from the Petersburg trenches in March 1865: "It is useless to conceal the truth any longer. Most of our people at home have become so demoralized that they write to their husbands, sons, and brothers that desertion *now* is not *dishonorable.*"

SEE ALSO
Desertion

FURTHER READING
Beringer, Richard E., Herman Hathaway, Archer Jones, and William N. Still, Jr. *Why the South Lost the Civil War.* Athens: University of Georgia Press, 1986.

Adams, Charles Francis

UNION DIPLOMAT

- Born: August 18, 1807, Boston, Mass.
- Political parties: Whig, Free Soil, Republican
- Education: Harvard College, A.B., 1825
- Government service: Massachusetts House of Representatives, 1841–44; Massachusetts Senate, 1844–45; U.S. House of Representatives, 1859–61; U.S. minister to England, 1861–68
- Died: November 21, 1886, Boston, Mass.

Although he fought in no battles, Charles Francis Adams scored a major victory for the Union by his success as U.S. minister to England in securing British neutrality during the Civil War. His wartime service in London was the high point of his distinguished public career.

Born into a New England family renowned for the statesmen that it produced, Adams spent much of his youth in Russia and England, where his father, John Quincy Adams, held diplomatic assignments. Upon graduating from Harvard, he joined the Massachusetts bar and then entered politics as a Whig. Strongly opposed to the spread of slavery, he broke with the more conservative wing of his party in 1848 and ran for Vice President on the Free Soil ticket. Elected to Congress in 1858, Adams led the Republican efforts in the House during the secession crisis to devise compromises that would keep the border states from defecting to the Confederacy. He resigned his seat on May 1, 1861, to take up his post as minister to England.

Adams brought superb credentials to his assignment. As the Boston *Evening Transcript* noted back in

March 1861: "Diplomacy and statesmanship run in his blood and have occupied no small portion of the studies of his life." Apart from his education and training, he had learned much of the English character from the childhood years he had spent in England with his father. Most importantly, he knew how to combine tact with firmness in dealing with his English counterpart, Foreign Minister Lord John Russell. Thus, while never yielding any point of principle in the Union position regarding nonrecognition of the Confederacy, he presented that position in as conciliatory a manner as possible. Repeatedly, he toned down the bellicose language in the dispatches he received from Secretary of State William Henry Seward before relaying their contents to Lord Russell.

During the *Trent* affair, the crisis in Anglo-American relations provoked in the fall of 1861 by the Union navy's seizure of two Confederate diplomats from a British ship in the Caribbean, Adams feared that a war with England was imminent. As he wrote from London to his son in December 1861: "It has given us here an indescribably sad feeling to witness the exultation in America over an event which bids fair to be the final calamity in this contest." He advised that the Union should stand on its "honorable record" as the defender of neutral rights at sea and release the diplomats, a move that helped defuse the crisis.

The second great crisis in Anglo-American relations came in the summer of 1863 over the building of Confederate rams in English shipyards. This time,

A tireless advocate of the Union cause while U.S. minister to Great Britain, Charles Francis Adams played a key role in maintaining British neutrality during the war.

Adams took a hard line. He lodged bitter protests and threatened war if the British government allowed the release of the Laird rams, two oceangoing ironclad ships built for the Confederacy by the Laird shipyards in Liverpool. The ministry did retain them, a decision that Adams's son Henry praised as "the crowning stroke of our diplomacy."

After returning to the United States in 1868, Adams served on the arbitration board that settled the *Alabama* claims, the monetary compensation sought by the United States for Union shipping losses inflicted by Confederate raiders built in England. He remained active in the Republican party as a liberal reformer until his death.

SEE ALSO

Alabama claims; Great Britain; Laird rams; *Trent* affair

FURTHER READING

Duberman, Martin B. *Charles Frances Adams, 1807–1886.* Boston: Houghton Mifflin, 1961.

Alabama claims

The general name for claims by the United States upon Great Britain for damages inflicted on Union shipping by British-built Confederate raiders, the *Alabama* claims strained Anglo-American relations in the years just after the Civil War. Three Confederate ships—the *Alabama, Shenandoah,* and *Florida*—accounted for the bulk of these claims. The settlement of the claims in 1872, largely on U.S. terms, set an important precedent for the arbitration of international disputes.

The United States pressed for damages of $19 million. When the British refused to pay any of the claims, bellicose Americans, led by Senator Charles Sumner of Massachusetts, threatened to take Canada in retaliation. Civil unrest in the prairie provinces of Canada and the outbreak of the Franco-Prussian War in 1870 prompted a more conciliatory British response. Above all, the British did not want to find themselves in a war in which the United States turned the tables and allowed an enemy of Britain to build commerce raiders in U.S. shipyards.

The breakthrough in the negotiations came in the Treaty of Washington of 1871. The British offered an apology for releasing the Confederate raiders and agreed to arbitration of the U.S. claims by an international tribunal. Citing the British government for a failure to exercise "due diligence" to prevent the rebel raiders from heading out to sea, the tribunal awarded the United States $15.5 million. The British paid those claims in 1873, opening the way for the two nations to submit other disputes to arbitration.

SEE ALSO

Naval warfare; Semmes, Raphael

FURTHER READING

Cook, Adrian. *The Alabama Claims: American Politics and Anglo-American Relations, 1865–1872.* Ithaca, N.Y.: Cornell University Press, 1975.

Anaconda Plan

The Union needed an offensive strategy to win the Civil War, and in the spring of 1861 President Abraham Lincoln turned to Winfield Scott, his general-in-chief, for military advice. Scott's response was a plan that emphasized applying economic pressure against the Confederacy rather than waging a war of outright conquest. Northern newspapers, reflecting the widely held belief that a bold Union offensive would quickly defeat the Confederacy, scorned Scott's strategy as the "Anaconda Plan," an overly passive approach that would give the rebel states time to consolidate their strength and raise an army. Cartoonists had a field day in depicting Scott's plan as a giant anaconda futilely trying to squeeze the economic life out of the Confederacy.

For all the ridicule that it provoked, Scott's plan was fundamentally sound. It contained three elements: the creation of a large eastern army to defend Washington, D.C., and pin down rebel forces in Virginia; the blockading of the Confederate coast from the Atlantic through the Gulf of Mexico to cut off the area's economic lifeline; and the sending of a joint Army-Navy expedition down the Mississippi River to cordon off the Trans-Mississippi Confederacy, effectively splitting the Confederacy in two. Designed, in Scott's words, "to envelop the insurgent states and bring them to terms with less bloodshed than any other plan," this three-pronged approach laid down the main features of Union strategy throughout the war.

Far more so than most of his contemporaries, Scott grasped the difficulties the Union would face in trying to conquer the Confederacy by force. He dismissed as foolish the talk of a short, bloodless war. Himself a Virginia Unionist, he wanted to spare the South from the devastation and bitterness of a protracted war. He hoped that his plan would eliminate the need for such a war. Once the blockade had taken effect and the Union had gained control of the Mississippi, he was confident that Southern whites would recognize the futility of secession and voluntarily

General Winfield Scott's Anaconda Plan called for a Union thrust down the Mississippi River, combined with a naval blockade that would seal off the Confederate economy from the outside world.

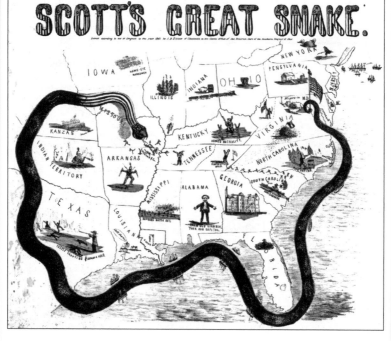

agree to reenter the Union.

Without a doubt, Scott overestimated the extent of Union sentiment in the South. But he correctly predicted at the onset of the war that any Union invasion would rally Southern whites behind the Confederacy and force the Union into waging a war of conquest. As he had feared all along, the North soon lost patience with his strategy of economic envelopment. Against Scott's advice, Lincoln issued the orders in late June 1861 for a federal advance against the Confederates at Manassas, Virginia. The ensuing battle of First Bull Run committed both sides to the armed conflict that Scott wanted to avoid.

SEE ALSO
Blockade; Scott, Winfield

FURTHER READING
Elliott, Charles Winslow. *Winfield Scott: The Soldier and the Man.* New York: Macmillan, 1937.

Anthony, Susan B.

ABOLITIONIST AND FEMINIST

- *Born: February 15, 1820, Adams, Mass.*
- *Education: district schools; private academy*
- *Public service: organizer, New York's Woman's State Temperance Society, 1852; cofounder, Woman's National Loyal League, 1863; president, National Woman Suffrage Association, 1892–1900*
- *Died: March 13, 1906, Rochester, N.Y.*

Susan B. Anthony was a reformer who blended abolitionism and feminism in a radical program seeking full equality for American blacks and women. She was a leading force behind the Woman's

National Loyal League, which mobilized public opinion in the North behind a constitutional amendment freeing all the slaves.

Raised in a reform-minded Quaker family that moved to upstate New York when she was six, Anthony received the best education that her father could afford. Before moving permanently to Rochester in 1850 and committing herself to reform causes, she taught female students at the Canajoharie Academy from 1846 to 1849. Her chance meeting with Elizabeth Cady Stanton in 1851 deepened her involvement in feminism and forged a partnership that shaped much of the 19th-century's women's rights movement.

Although never as fluid or commanding a speaker as Stanton, Anthony brought a steely resolve to her advocacy of unpopular causes. Her courage when threatened by a hostile mob of anti-abolitionists was extraordinary. Calling for no compromise with slavery, she organized a lecture tour of upstate New York in January 1861. Shortly after she was burned in effigy by a mob in Syracuse, she faced down an angry crowd in nearby Auburn by declaring: "Why, boys, you're nothing but a *baby mob*. You ought to go to Syracuse, and learn how to do it, and also learn how to get before the Grand Jury."

Like other abolitionists, Anthony decried the refusal of President Abraham Lincoln to move against slavery at the beginning of the Civil War. As long as slavery existed, she insisted that the full promise of the American Revolution could never be realized. But once black Americans achieved emancipation, she wrote in a draft for a speech in 1862, "then might we boast the just government for which the Fathers of seventy-six fought & bled & died; *but, failed to live.*" Although heartened by the Emancipation Proclamation, she viewed it only as a preliminary step. The decree left slavery in the loyal border states untouched and aroused no groundswell of public support in favor of total emancipation. These concerns prompted Anthony to join with Stanton in establishing the Woman's National Loyal League in 1863.

Whereas Stanton provided the guiding principles for the league, Anthony planned its strategy, raised funds, and supervised the local agents who directed the petition campaign. For what amounted to a full-time job, she received a weekly salary of $12. Only by cutting her expenses through a boarding arrangement with the Stanton family was she able to support herself during the war. Still, her enthusiasm never waned. "We, the League," she wrote fellow abolitionist Samuel May in September 1863, "are *alive* and planning a most vigorous prosecution of *our war* of *ideas*—not bullets & bayonets."

Although the league was a resounding success in rallying mass support that influenced Congress to pass the 13th Amendment in early 1865, it did not achieve its goal of securing political equality for women. Contrary to the expectations of many female abolitionists, Congress did not recognize their work on behalf of emancipation with the conferral of the vote. A petition campaign spearheaded by Anthony in 1865–66 failed to have woman suffrage included as part of the 14th Amendment. In 1869 radical feminists followed Anthony and Stanton into the National Woman Suffrage Association. Winning the vote for women was now the overriding objective or Anthony's life, and she fought for that cause virtually until the day of her death.

SEE ALSO

Emancipation; 14th Amendment; Stanton, Elizabeth Cady; Suffrage; 13th Amendment

FURTHER READING

Barry, Kathleen. *Susan B. Anthony: A Biography of a Singular Feminist.* New York: New York University Press, 1988.
Venet, Wendy Hamand. *Neither Ballots nor Bullets: Women Abolitionists and the Civil War.* Charlottesville: University Press of Virginia, 1991.

Antietam

On September 17, 1862, the Confederate Army of Northern Virginia under Robert E. Lee and the Union Army of the Potomac under George B. McClellan clashed along the banks of Antietam

Union general George B. McClellan's uncoordinated attacks at Antietam badly mauled but did not destroy Robert E. Lee's army.

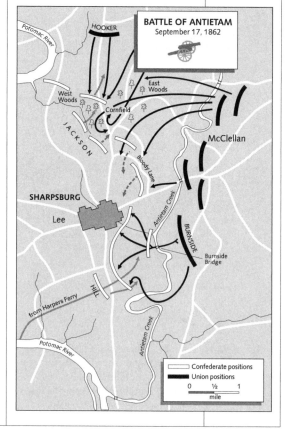

BATTLE OF ANTIETAM
September 17, 1862

HOOKER

Potomac River

West Woods

East Woods

Cornfield

JACKSON

McClellan

Bloody Lane

SHARPSBURG

Lee

Antietam Creek

BURNSIDE

Burnside Bridge

HILL

from Harpers Ferry

Potomac River

Antietam Creek

☐ Confederate positions
■ Union positions

0   ½   1
mile

Creek near the town of Sharpsburg, Maryland. The ensuing battle marked the single bloodiest day of the war. In savage fighting that lasted from dawn to dusk, nearly 25,000 Confederate and Union soldiers were killed or wounded. A Wisconsin officer who lived through the terror of that day described Antietam as "a great, enormous battle—a great tumbling together of all heaven and earth—the slaughter on both sides was enormous."

Lee's decision to move north into Union-held Maryland after his victory at Second Bull Run in August 1862 set in motion the military movements that climaxed in the carnage at Antietam. Rather then passively hold a defensive line in central Virginia, an area already stripped clean of food and provisions, Lee wanted to seize the initiative in the war. By pushing north into enemy territory, he hoped to rally pro-Confederate sympathizers in Maryland; disrupt Union rail connections to the west; shift the war zone away from Virginia's hard-pressed farmers; and gain access to desperately needed supplies for his army. Above all, Lee was seeking an opportunity to win a decisive victory over a Union army on Northern soil. Such a victory might convince Great Britain and France to grant official diplomatic recognition to the Confederacy and even force a demoralized North to accept the futility of continuing the war. As Lee bluntly stated in an 1868 interview, "I went into Maryland to give battle."

Singing "Maryland, My Maryland," Lee's troops began crossing the Potomac River on September 4. After his army concentrated at Frederick, Maryland, Lee divided his forces in order to seize the Union garrison at Harpers Ferry and thus maintain his communications to the South through the Shenandoah Valley. By an incredible stroke of fate, Lee's orders for splitting up his army fell

into the hands of McClellan after two Union soldiers found them discarded in a field near Frederick. McClellan's army was barely a day's march from Lee's scattered forces, but McClellan moved slowly, a delay that allowed Lee just enough time to reunite the bulk of his army along Antietam Creek.

Once Lee learned that Harpers Ferry had fallen to the Confederates and that General Thomas "Stonewall" Jackson's six divisions would soon join him, he decided to make his stand at Antietam. Opposing him was an army of some 80,000 men, more than twice the size of his own forces, but Lee had supreme confidence in his veteran troops and his ability to outfox McClellan.

McClellan's battle plan called for charges first against the Confederate left, then the right, and finally a breakthrough in the weakened Confederate center. The fatal flaw in this plan was that it squandered the Union's numerical superiority in a series of piecemeal attacks. As a result, Lee was able to shift his defenders and seal off—though just barely—Union advances.

The battle began at dawn when Union General Joseph Hooker slammed his corps against Lee's left. The fighting spilled over into the Confederate center

A place of worship for the pacifist German Baptist Brethren, the whitewashed Dunker Church was a focal point of some of the fiercest fighting at Antietam. The fire of Union batteries tore holes in the building and overwhelmed the Confederate artilleryman posted there.

and roared back and forth through woods, across a cornfield, and along a sunken road soon known as "Bloody Lane." Of the slaughter in the cornfield, Hooker wrote: "every stalk of corn in the northern and greater part of the field was cut as closely as could have been done with a knife, and the slain lay in rows precisely as they had stood in their ranks a few moments before."

By midmorning the Confederate center was decimated, and a sustained Union assault would have smashed through it. Although he had 24,000 fresh troops in reserve, McClellan held them back and failed to order an attack. He allowed the focus of the battle to shift to the Confederate right, where his commander, General Ambrose Burnside, was stymied by a few hundred Confederate troops and unable to force a crossing of Antietam Creek until midafternoon. Confederate reinforcements under General A. P. Hill arrived in time to block Burnside's tentative advance, and the battle ground to a halt.

McClellan lost a chance for a decisive victory at Antietam. However, he did force Lee, whose army suffered grievous losses of 25 percent in killed and wounded, to retreat to Virginia. Most significantly, Lincoln claimed Antietam as the Union victory he had been waiting for to issue the preliminary Emancipation Proclamation on September 22, 1862.

SEE ALSO

Armies; Burnside, Ambrose; Hooker, Joseph; Jackson, Thomas "Stonewall"; Lee, Robert E.; McClellan, George B.; Preliminary Emancipation Proclamation; Second Bull Run.

FURTHER READING

Gallagher, Gary W., ed. *The Antietam Campaign.* Chapel Hill: University of North Carolina Press, 1999.
McPherson, James M. *Crossroads of Freedom: Antietam.* New York: Oxford University Press, 2002.
Sears, Stephen W. *Landscape Turned Red: The Battle of Antietam.* New York: Warner Books, 1985.

Appomattox campaign

This was the final campaign for Robert E. Lee's Army of Northern Virginia. Forced to evacuate Richmond on the night of April 2, 1865, Lee tried to find an escape route to the west that would enable him to move his army, now reduced to 35,000 men, southward into North Carolina. There, he could join forces with the Confederate army of Joseph E. Johnston. Anticipating Lee's objective, Union General Ulysses S. Grant aggressively countered in a relentless pursuit that blocked any move to the south by Lee's retreating forces. Finally, surrounded and vastly outnumbered, Lee reluctantly agreed to surrender at Appomattox Courthouse on April 9.

Grant had more than 100,000 troops to call on in the pursuit. Having just captured Petersburg and Richmond, their spirits were understandably high. "We are after Lee, and we are going to have him," jotted Colonel Elisha Hunt Rhodes of the Second Rhode Island Infantry in his diary on April 3. Two days later he noted that everywhere "we see proof of the demoralized condition of Lee's troops. We shall catch him if we keep on, and when we do the war will end."

That same day, April 5, Union cavalry under General Philip H. Sheridan cut Lee's intended southward line of retreat along the Danville and Richmond Railroad. Lee now pushed due west in a desperate effort to reach Lynchburg, the only remaining rail connection to the south and Johnston's army. But on April 6, the swarming federals caught up with and smashed Lee's rear guard under General Richard S.

Ewell. In the fighting at Sayler's Creek the Confederates lost 6,000 men, one-quarter of Lee's remaining force, and much of their wagon train of supplies.

On April 7, Grant sent a formal note to Lee urging him to surrender. When Lee responded the following day with an offer to undertake talks leading to the "restoration of peace"—a politically loaded phrase that raised issues about which neither Grant, nor any other Union general, had any authority to negotiate—Grant concluded that Lee still hoped to escape. Any such hope, however, was dashed when Sheridan's cavalry, backed up by two Union corps, blocked Lee's path at Appomattox Courthouse. Lee did order one final charge at Appomattox, but his depleted troops were thrown back and surrounded. After rejecting a suggestion from a staff officer that the Confederates disperse and retreat into the interior to fight as guerrillas—a strategy that Lee feared would subject Virginia to savage Union reprisals and devastation—Lee accepted the inevitable. "There is nothing left for me to do but go and see General Grant, and I would

rather die a thousand deaths," he said.

Lee met with Grant on the afternoon of April 9 in the parlor of the brick home of William McLean, one of the few remaining white civilians in Appomattox Courthouse. Having moved to Appomattox after his original residence near Manassas was shelled during First Bull Run, McLean now found that the war had caught up with him once again.

Grant's terms were generous. Once they laid down their arms, Lee's men would be paroled and allowed to return to their homes, where they were "not to be disturbed by the United States authorities so long as they observe their paroles, and the laws in force where they may reside." This stipulation was of tremendous significance, for it meant that the rebel soldiers were not to be prosecuted as traitors. After exempting the small arms, horses, and personal baggage of the Confederate officers from the surrender, Grant gave in to Lee's gentle prodding by also permitting enlisted men who claimed ownership of horses and mules to retain them for use on their farms. When informed that

Lee's starving troops had subsisted on parched corn for the past several days, Grant immediately ordered rations for 25,000 men to be sent across the lines.

In a formal ceremony on April 12, about 26,000 Confederates surrendered at Appomattox. It had been four years to the day after the firing on Fort Sumter had triggered the Civil War.

SEE ALSO
Ewell, Richard S.; Grant, Ulysses S.; Johnston, Joseph E.; Lee, Robert E.; Petersburg campaign; Sheridan, Philip H.

FURTHER READING
Henderson, Robert. *The Road to Appomattox.* New York: John Wiley, 1998. Marvel, William. *A Place Called Appomattox.* Chapel Hill: University of North Carolina Press, 2000.

Armies

Armies were the largest organized units of land forces employed by each side. The Union organized 16 armies and the Confederacy about 23. An estimated 2.1 million men fought in Union armies, as opposed to about 800,000 in rebel forces. (See the accompanying table for the fluctuating size of the armies over the course of the war.)

Armies generally took their name from the military department in which they operated, but the Union tended to name theirs after rivers and the Confederacy after states, or portions thereof. For example, the Union had the Army of the Potomac and the Army of the Tennessee, whereas their Confederate counterparts were the Army of Northern Virginia and the Army of Tennessee.

The armies were nearly identical in their organizational structure. Infantry, about 80 percent of all troops, were the

COMPARATIVE SIZE OF THE ARMIES		
Date	Union	Confederate
End of 1861	575,917	326,768
End of 1862	918,191	449,439
End of 1863	860,737	464,646
End of 1864	959,460	400,787

standard combat arm. A total of 10 companies, each with an official strength of 100 men, made up a regiment, the basic infantry unit. Each of the states recruited their own regiments, and volunteers were identified by their state regimental number—for example, the 4th Alabama or the 20th Maine Volunteers. Two or more regiments comprised a brigade, and two or more brigades a division. In the very largest armies, divisions were grouped into corps.

The cavalry, making up about 15 percent of combat troops (slightly higher in Confederate armies), followed a similar organizational chart. Except for those stationed in permanent fortifications, the 5 percent or so of troops in the artillery were organized for field service into batteries, units of four to six cannons accompanied by horse-drawn wagons of ammunition.

Both sides raised their mass armies virtually from scratch. The only army at the outbreak of the secession crisis was the professional or regular U.S. Army. At 16,000 men, it was tiny compared to the numbers that would fight in the Civil War. In large measure because of its slave laborers who could produce food crops and be pressed to serve in war-related industries, the Confederacy was able to mobilize a higher percentage of its available (white) military manpower. Somewhere between 75 and 80 percent of all Southern white males of military age served in Confederate armies. The comparable figure for the Union was about 55 percent. The vast majority of these soldiers were volunteers: 94 percent in the Union armies and 82 percent in the Confederate. Especially in the early stages of the war, most soldiers fought because they wanted to.

SEE ALSO

Absenteeism; Black soldiers; Casualties; Command structure; Conscription; Desertion; Officers; Recruiting bounties; Soldiers, profile of; Southern Union soldiers

FURTHER READING

Crute, Joseph H., Jr. *Units of the Confederate States Army.* Midlothian, Va.: Derwent Books, 1987.
Shannon, Fred A. *The Organization and Administration of the Union Army, 1861–1865.* Cleveland: Arthur H. Clark, 1928.

Artillery

About 5 percent of all troops in the Civil War consisted of artillery. Despite recent advances in rifled cannon, the smoothbore Napoleon (named after the French emperor in the 1850s) was the standard artillery piece in both armies.

Military theory called for field artillery to play both an offensive and defensive role in land warfare, but in practical terms the vastly extended range of the new rifles made the use of the artillery effective only in a defensive capacity. Artillery batteries simply could not advance close enough to blast a hole in a defensive line. This was the painful lesson learned at Gettysburg by the Confederates who followed General George E. Pickett in what became immortalized as Pickett's charge. While the massive Confederate artillery barrage barely dented the federal line, Union cannon mowed down the attacking rebels.

Napoleons, both 6- and 12-pounders, were particularly well suited to the enhanced defensive role of the artillery. They could fire any kind of projectile. When loaded with case (shells that sprayed out lead balls) or

Stationed in the fall of 1864 at Fort Brady on the north side of the James River, the 1st Connecticut Artillery protected the Union supply base at City Point, Virginia, from an attack by Confederate gunboats.

canister (tin cans that scattered iron slugs or golf-ball-sized shot called grape), they laid down an antipersonnel fire that was deadly at short and medium ranges. The effect on attacking troops was akin to walking into the barrel of an exploding shotgun.

Rifled cannon had a greater range and accuracy than the smoothbores, but technological problems slowed their deployment. Rifling grooves into a smoothbore design added a tremendous strain that often resulted in the barrel of the gun blowing up. Unreliable fuses limited the effectiveness of rifled artillery intended for long-range use, and it was difficult to train crews in the handling of these more technologically sophisticated guns. With its greater industrial capacity and larger pool of scientific talent, the Union more easily overcame these problems than the Confederacy. Indeed, the Confederacy obtained most of its artillery either through seizure during the secession crisis or by subsequent capture of Union pieces. Eventually, the proportion of rifled artillery in the Union army rose to 50 percent, a level that was considerably higher than the 30 percent for the Confederacy.

As opposed to land warfare, artillery often favored the attackers in naval engagements. Equipped with new shell guns firing a hollow projectile that exploded into shrapnel, Union warships had a more effective weapon than the solid cannon balls of past naval armaments. These guns inflicted heavy damage on many of the coastal forts seized by the Confederacy in the winter and spring of 1861. Mounted on steam-powered ships, they gave the Union a decided advantage in its offensive operations.

SEE ALSO
Rifles; Tactics

FURTHER READING
Hazlett, James C., Edwin Olmstead, and M. Hume Parks. *Field Artillery Weapons of the Civil War*. Newark: University of Delaware Press, 1983.
Ripley, Warren. *Artillery and Ammunition of the Civil War*. New York: D. Van Nostrand Reinhold, 1970.

Atlanta campaign

The Union campaign that resulted in the capture of Atlanta on September 2, 1864, dispelled the war weariness that had settled over the North in the summer of 1864 and virtually ensured the reelection of President Abraham Lincoln in the fall election. In strategic terms, the fall of Atlanta deprived the Confederacy of a major transportation and industrial center that was vital to the continued logistical support of Southern armies. However measured, this campaign dealt a crushing blow to the Confederacy and its chances for survival.

The campaign lasted for four months and stretched over the 100-mile corridor between Chattanooga and Atlanta. It began on May 4 when General William T. Sherman wheeled his huge force of 110,000 men out of Chattanooga toward the mountains of northern Georgia. Opposing the federals was a Confederate army of 45,000 men (soon reinforced to 60,000) commanded by General Joseph E. Johnston. Although clearly outnumbered, Johnston's Army of Tennessee had the advantage of operating from well-fortified positions in a mountainous terrain that prevented any coordinated Union offensives.

Johnston hoped to defeat Sherman by luring him into making disastrous frontal assaults, but Sherman refused to take the bait. In a deft series of flanking movements, Sherman continually bypassed strong rebel positions and

threatened to cut Johnston's line of communications back to Atlanta along the Western and Atlantic Railroad. First at Dalton, and then at Resaca, Cassville, and Allatoona Pass, Johnston was forced to withdraw. After some sharp skirmishes at Dallas and New Hope Church in late May, Johnston moved back to Marietta, barely 20 miles north of Atlanta. Sensing that a breakthrough was now possible, Sherman ordered a frontal assault on June 27 against the Confederate center anchored on Kennesaw Mountain. Like nearly all such attacks in the war, this one failed. As Union General Oliver O. Howard later wrote: "Our losses in this assault were heavy indeed, and our gain was nothing. We realized now, as never before, the futility of direct assaults upon intrenched lines already well prepared and well manned."

Sherman now returned to his turning movements and by mid-July backed Johnston's army into the inner defenses of Atlanta. On July 17 Confederate president Jefferson Davis made the controversial decision to relieve Johnston of command. Convinced that Johnston,

with whom he had feuded throughout the war, did not have the stomach for an all-out defense of Atlanta, Davis replaced him with John Bell Hood, an aggressive general whom Davis fully expected to attack the invading federals.

Hood was the fighter that Davis wanted, but his appointment simply hastened the fall of Atlanta. Hood quickly went on the offensive in the battles of Peachtree Creek on July 20, Atlanta on July 22, and Ezra Church on July 28. His men fought heroically. Giles Smith, the commander of a Union division at the Battle of Atlanta, said of the rebel charge: "In the impetuosity, splendid abandon, and reckless disregard of danger with which the rebel masses rushed against our line of fire, of iron and cold steel, there has been no parallel during the war." Still, the results of the attacks were devastating to Hood's army. Within a week Hood lost 20,000 men and was reduced to a fighting strength of 35,000.

After such losses, Hood was forced to go back on the defensive. As Sherman began to extend his lines around Atlanta in an encircling movement,

Under orders from Union General William Tecumseh Sherman to "Let the destruction be so thorough that not a rail or tie can be used again," Union work crews rip up railroad tracks at Atlanta.

Hood countered by sending his cavalry north in an effort to cut Sherman's supply line on the railroad leading back to Chattanooga. Sherman, however, had prepared for such a threat by detailing troops and repair crews to guard and maintain the railroad. Hood's cavalry raids accomplished little.

The last battle in the campaign was fought at Jonesboro on August 30. Sherman sent the bulk of his army south of Atlanta to strike at the Montgomery and Atlanta Railroad, Hood's major line of communications. Once he learned that the Confederate attack at Jonesboro had failed to dislodge the federals advancing on the railroad, Hood had no choice but to evacuate Atlanta. After destroying supplies and factories of military value, Hood moved out of the city on September 1. Leading elements of Sherman's army entered the city the next day.

Each side lost about 35,000 men in the campaign that gave the Union its single most decisive victory of the war. The crippled war economy of the Confederacy never recovered from the loss of Atlanta. Union morale soared upon news of Sherman's victory, and Lincoln easily won reelection two months later.

SEE ALSO

Davis, Jefferson; Hood, John Bell; Johnston, Joseph E.; Lincoln, Abraham; Sherman, William T.

FURTHER READING

Castell, Albert. *Decision in the West: The Atlanta Campaign of 1864.* Lawrence: University Press of Kansas, 1992.
McMurry, Richard M. *Atlanta 1864: Last Chance for the Confederacy.* Lincoln: University of Nebraska Press, 2000.
Mitchell, Margaret. *Gone With the Wind.* New York: Macmillan, 1936.

Banking

SEE National Banking Acts

Banks, Nathaniel P.

UNION GENERAL AND POLITICIAN

- *Born: January 30, 1816, Waltham, Mass.*
- *Political parties: Democrat, Know-Nothing, Republican*
- *Education: sporadic schooling in lower grades*
- *Military service: U.S. Army: major general, volunteers, 1861–65*
- *Government service: Massachusetts House of Representatives, 1849–52; U.S. House of Representatives, 1853–57, 1865–73, 1875–79, 1889–91; governor of Massachusetts, 1858–61; Massachusetts Senate, 1874; U.S. marshal, 1879–88*
- *Died: September 1, 1894, Waltham, Mass.*

A nonprofessional general whose appointment was based on the political support that he could bring to the Union war effort, Nathaniel P. Banks was far more successful as a politician than as a general. He saw his military career as a springboard to gaining a Presidential nomination from the Republican party, but those hopes were dashed by his ineptitude as a field commander.

The son of a cotton mill superintendent, Banks went to work in his father's mill as a boy. Ambitious and somewhat vain, he learned the machinist trade, taught himself to be an effective public speaker by practicing at a local debating society, and secured admission to the Massachusetts bar in 1839. He tried seven times to win

With his boyish good looks and affable personality, Nathaniel P. Banks was a natural as a politician, but he failed repeatedly as a Union general.

election to the Massachusetts legislature before finally succeeding in 1849. Thereafter, his political rise was rapid. After entering Congress as a Democrat in 1853, he shrewdly aligned himself with shifts in public sentiment by joining first the Know-Nothings and then the rising Republican party. As a moderate Republican, he was elected Speaker of the House of Representatives in 1856 in a bitter contest that broke along North-South lines. He returned to Massachusetts in 1858, where he served as governor before his appointment as a major-general in January 1861.

As a field general, Banks did little right. His lack of military experience first showed itself in the Shenandoah Valley in the spring of 1862. Banks lost 30 percent of his force and immense amounts of supplies when Confederate General Thomas J. "Stonewall" Jackson forced him out of the valley. Banks suffered another defeat at Jackson's hands at Cedar Mountain, Virginia, on August 9, 1862, in the early stages of the Second Bull Run campaign. Banks attacked without keeping a force in reserve, and his troops were driven back when the rebels counterattacked.

Banks replaced Benjamin F. Butler as commander of the Department of the Gulf in the fall of 1862. The Confederate strong point in the area under his command was Port Hudson, Louisiana. Despite a series of costly assaults ordered by Banks, the rebel garrison held out until the spectacular success of Ulysses S. Grant's Vicksburg campaign forced its capitulation on July 9, 1863.

In the spring of 1864, Banks launched his ill-fated Red River campaign. Naively optimistic at the start of the assault—he wired Washington on April 10 that "My fear is that they [the Confederate forces] may not be willing to meet us"—he ended the operation as a confused, badly beaten general whom

his troops sarcastically nicknamed "Napoleon P. Banks." His career as a field commander was over.

After the war, Banks immediately returned to what he did best: winning elective office. With the exception of a brief stint in the Massachusetts Senate and an appointment as U.S. marshall for Massachusetts in the 1880s, he served mainly as a representative in Congress. Declining health forced him into retirement in 1891, and he died a few years later.

SEE ALSO
Red River campaign

FURTHER READING
Hollandsworth, James G., Jr. *Pretense of Glory: The Life of Nathaniel P. Banks.* Baton Rouge: Louisiana State University Press, 1998.

Barton, Clara
UNION NURSE

- *Born: December 25, 1821, North Oxford, Mass.*
- *Education: Clinton Liberal Institute, 1851*
- *Public service: organizer, nursing services for Union soldiers, 1861–64; superintendent of nurses, Army of the James, 1864–1865; director, Friends of the Missing Men of the U.S. Army, 1865–69; president, American Red Cross, 1882–1904*
- *Died: April 12, 1912, Glen Echo, Md.*

Known as "the angel of the battlefields" for her valiant efforts on behalf of wounded Union soldiers, Clara Barton earned an international reputation during the Civil War as a pioneer in the field of women's nursing. She continued her humanitarian work after the war as a founder of the American Red Cross.

The youngest child in a New

Although she was not affiliated with any nursing or relief agency during the war, Clara Barton succeeded in publicizing the need for better medical care for Union soldiers and helped prod Congress into making reforms.

England farm family, Barton began teaching in the district schools of Massachusetts in 1836—one of the few jobs, apart from mill work, open to women. She attended the Liberal Institute in Clinton, New York, in 1851, and then accepted a teaching position in Bordentown, New Jersey. Shortly after she resigned in 1854 in a dispute over her responsibilities, she secured a post as a clerk in the U.S. Patent Office in Washington with the help of her congressman, Alexander De Witt.

Barton's first exposure to Union casualties came at the very outbreak of the war. On April 19, 1861, she greeted a train arriving in Washington with soldiers from the 6th Massachusetts Regiment, which had been attacked by secessionist sympathizers while passing through Baltimore. Recognizing some of the wounded as former schoolmates, she helped bandage their injuries and organized an impromptu relief effort to bring them supplies. The Union Medical Department, as she immediately discovered, was utterly unprepared to deal with any wounded soldiers, even the small number injured in the Baltimore riot.

A committed Unionist—"The patriot blood of my father was warm in my veins," she later wrote—Barton soon plunged into relief work. With no compensation or accreditation, she spent her time and much of her money purchasing and distributing provisions and medical supplies to the huge volunteer army gathering in Washington. Enraged by the stream of unattended wounded soldiers pouring into the city after the Union defeat at the First Bull Run, she vowed to "go to the rescue of the men who fell" and "work for them

and my country." She first visited field hospitals during the Second Bull Run Campaign in the late summer of 1862 and then battled the army bureaucracy for permission to deliver a wagonload of supplies to the Army of the Potomac. She brought her wagon onto the battlefield at Antietam, where, according to one witness, she "toiled as few men could have done." She experienced the horror of seeing a wounded Union soldier die while she was tending to him.

At Fredericksburg in December and on into the winter of 1862–63, Barton continued her volunteer nursing services for the Army of the Potomac. Sent by the War Department as an unofficial nurse to Hilton Head, South Carolina, in the spring of 1863, she helped organize ambulance service and emergency medical care at the battle of Fort Wagner in July 1863. She was on the Richmond-Petersburg front in 1864 as a matron of a field hospital and a superintendent of nurses. Her war service ended in Andersonville, Georgia, where she accompanied a corps of workmen and clerks who marked the graves of the Union prisoners of war who had died in the notorious Confederate camp there. For four years after the war, she directed a staff charged by Congress with locating missing Union soldiers.

By successfully defying entrenched male bureaucracies and demonstrating that a woman could still be a "lady" while caring for wounded men, Barton was instrumental in opening up the profession of nursing to women. Her greatest leadership, however, came after the war when she was instrumental in the establishment of the American Red Cross. Her service with the International Red Cross in Europe during the Franco-Prussian War in the early 1870s convinced her of the need for such an organization in the United States. Her lobbying and educational work were a key factor in persuading Congress in 1882 to ratify the Geneva Convention of 1864 that had set up the Red Cross. As president of the American branch of the Red Cross from 1882 to 1904, Barton broadened its relief mission to include natural disasters as well as warfare.

SEE ALSO

Medicine; Nurses; Soldier aid societies

FURTHER READING

Burton, David Henry. *Clara Barton: In the Service of Humanity.* Westport, Conn.: Greenwood, 1995.

Oates, Stephen B. *A Woman of Valor: Clara Barton and the Civil War.* New York: Free Press, 1994.

Pryor, Elizabeth Brown. *Clara Barton: Professional Angel.* Philadelphia: University of Pennsylvania Press, 1987.

"Battle Hymn of the Republic"

SEE Howe, Julia Ward

Beauregard, Pierre Gustave T.

CONFEDERATE GENERAL

- *Born: May 28, 1818, Saint Bernard Parish, La.*
- *Education: U.S. Military Academy, B.S., 1838*
- *Military service: U.S. Army: lieutenant, artillery, 1838; lieutenant, engineers, 1838–39; 1st lieutenant, 1839–53; captain, 1853–61; Confederate army: brigadier general, 1861; general, 1861–65*
- *Died: February 20, 1893, New Orleans, La.*

As his colorful nickname of the "Napoleon in Gray" attests, Pierre G. T. Beauregard was one of the most storied Confederate generals. Yet, and in large measure because of his running feud with President Jefferson Davis, his actual combat record was rather meager, and his fabled military abilities never met a true test during the war.

Born into a wealthy French family of sugar planters, Beauregard became fascinated with the great French general Napoleon Bonaparte while attending boarding school in New York City. Against the protests of his family, he insisted on attending West Point, where his excellent academic record gained him a place in the army's elite corps of engineers. After garnering two citations for bravery during the Mexican War, he supervised engineering projects in the 1850s. He had just been appointed superintendent at West Point when Louisiana seceded in January 1861. Having told a Louisiana cadet that he would go along with his native state if it seceded, Beauregard was in no position to protest (although he tried) when relieved of his duties. He resigned from the U.S. Army on February 20 to join the Confederate forces.

Beauregard became the Confederacy's first war hero when, as commander of rebel forces in Charleston, he ordered the successful bombardment of Fort Sumter in April 1861. Hailed as a conquering hero when he was sent to Virginia, he achieved another victory at First Bull Run when his army was reinforced by the troops of General Joseph E. Johnston. Beauregard was now at the pinnacle of his fame, but his grandiose nature, which bordered on conceit, soon got the best of

Vain, flamboyant, and highly skilled at self-promotion, Pierre G. T. Beauregard personified all the dashing qualities of leadership that Southerners expected of their generals. After some early successes, however, his war record as a commander was decidedly spotty.

him. In a report on First Bull Run that was leaked to the press, he claimed that the meddling of President Jefferson Davis had prevented him and his rebel forces from capitalizing on their victory by marching on Washington. Davis retorted by accusing Beauregard of trying "to exalt yourself at my expense," and he transferred his publicity-seeking general to the West.

Second in command in the West to General Albert Sidney Johnston, Beauregard helped plan the Confederate attack at Shiloh, and he took over the army upon the death of Johnston during the fighting on the first day. He telegraphed Richmond that a "complete victory" had been won, only to retreat the next day when faced with a massive federal counterattack. After pledging to defend Corinth, Mississippi, "to the last extremity," he then infuriated Davis by evacuating that key rail junction without a fight on May 30, 1862. When Beauregard took a sick leave a few weeks later, Davis relieved him of his command by claiming that he had left his post without authorization.

Davis was now convinced that Beauregard was an egocentric, boastful mediocrity, and out of wounded pride the general took to referring to the President as "that living specimen of gall and hatred." For most of the remainder of the war, Beauregard was assigned to a relatively minor command in preparing coastal defenses in South Carolina. In April 1864, he returned to Virginia and quite skillfully bottled up a Union army threatening Richmond from the south. His last command was a brief one in the Carolinas under General Joseph E. Johnston.

After the war, Beauregard was active in the politics of reconstructed Louisiana and served as president of two railroads. Still considered a great military leader, he turned down several offers to command foreign armies.

SEE ALSO
First Bull Run; Davis, Jefferson; Shiloh

FURTHER READING
Williams, T. Harry. *P. G. T. Beauregard: Napoleon in Gray*. Baton Rouge: Louisiana State University Press, 1955.

Benjamin, Judah P.
CONFEDERATE POLITICIAN

- *Born: August 6, 1811, St. Croix, Danish West Indies*
- *Political parties: Whig, Democrat*
- *Education: Yale College, 1825–27*
- *Government service: Louisiana House of Representatives, 1842–43; U.S. Senate, 1853–61; Confederacy: attorney general, 1861; secretary of war, 1861–62; secretary of state, 1862–65*
- *Died: May 8, 1894, Paris, France*

Known as the "Brains of the Confederacy" for the suave intelligence that he brought to the Confederate cabinet, Judah P. Benjamin was President Jefferson Davis's most trusted advisor on nonmilitary matters. His closeness to Davis, as well as his Jewish ancestry, made him a favorite target of Davis's opponents, especially late in the war when Benjamin advocated the freeing of slaves who would fight for the Confederacy.

After his parents moved from the West Indies, Benjamin spent his youth first in Charleston and then in Savannah, where he attended the common schools, known today as public elementary schools. He entered Yale at the age of 14 and was a brilliant student, only to leave suddenly during his junior year for reasons that remain a mystery. Settling in New Orleans, he taught school before his admission to the Louisiana bar in 1832. A superb lawyer, he soon amassed a fortune that he invested in a sugar plantation. Entering politics as a Whig, he assumed leadership of the commercial interests of New Orleans in their quest for expanded trading opportunities throughout the Caribbean basin. He switched to the Democratic party in the late 1850s and advocated secession upon the election of Abraham Lincoln.

Famed for his ability as a lawyer, Benjamin was an obvious choice as the first Confederate attorney general. However, his quick intelligence and ability to cut through red tape were wasted in this relatively minor post, and in September 1862, Davis selected him as his second secretary of war. Despite bringing needed order and organization to the War Department, Benjamin soon came under heavy criticism. His political support, though not Davis's friendship, waned as he feuded with touchy generals on matters of protocol. After one such clash with Thomas J. "Stonewall" Jackson, one of Jackson's officers, Thomas R. R. Cobb of Georgia, lashed out: "A grander rascal than this Jew Benjamin does not exist in the Confederacy." As Confederate reversals piled up in the winter of 1861–62, Davis's critics blamed Benjamin for every fault in the administration. Although Benjamin had to be removed, Davis continued to value the Louisianian's friendship and loyalty, and in March 1862, he shifted him to the State Department.

As secretary of state, Benjamin brought a new direction to Confederate diplomacy. Rather than threatening economic reprisals if Britain and France failed to recognize the Confederacy, he emphasized the procurement of loans secured by cotton and the cultivation of a more favorable image for the Confederacy. By 1864 he was proposing Confederate emancipation in return for diplomatic recognition. Ever the pragmatist on the home front as well, he alone in Davis's cabinet came out publicly in favor of arming and freeing the slaves in order to gain the additional soldiers desperately needed to stave off Confederate defeat. "Let us say to every negro who wishes to go into the ranks on condition of being made free—'Go and fight; you are free,'" he proclaimed at a mass meeting in Richmond in February 1865.

Benjamin's call for emancipation produced immediate cries for his ouster from the cabinet. The debate had barely subsided when the Confederacy collapsed. Benjamin gave the slip to his Union pursuers and found a boat on the Florida coast that carried him first to the Bahamas and then to England. He regained his fortune through the cotton trade and became one of England's leading lawyers. A year after he was feted on his retirement by the Bar of England, he died at his home in Paris.

SEE ALSO
Confederate emancipation; Kenner mission

FURTHER READING
Evans, Eli N. *Judah P. Benjamin: The Jewish Confederate*. New York: Free Press, 1988.
Meade, Robert D. *Judah P. Benjamin: Confederate Statesman*. New York: Oxford University Press, 1943.

Bentonville

Bentonville has the distinction of marking the Confederacy's last effort to stop the formidable Union army of General William T. Sherman as it marched north through the Carolinas in the final months of the war. Fought in North Carolina on March 19, 1865, Bentonville was another Confederate defeat, but it threw a scare into Sherman and restored the pride of the soldiers in the shattered remnants of the rebel Army of Tennessee.

Sherman left Savannah on February 1, 1865, and took his huge army of 100,000 men northward into the Carolinas. Wrongly guessing that his objective was either Augusta, Georgia, or Charleston, South Carolina, the Confederates allowed Sherman a virtually free path through the center of South Carolina. Here, Sherman's army destroyed even more resources than in their more famous march through Georgia. Most of Columbia, the capital of South Carolina, went up in smoke on the night of February 17. The Confederates believed that drunken federal soldiers had set the blaze, but Sherman and his defenders pinned the blame on cotton bales set afire by rebel cavalry as it retreated from the city. To Sherman's credit, he assisted his men in putting out the blaze.

The Confederacy finally acted in late February to impede Sherman's uncontested march. On February 22, General Joseph E. Johnston was given command of rebel forces in the Carolinas. Cobbling together an army from the garrison that pulled out of Charleston, a cavalry brigade under General Wade Hampton on leave from Lee's army, and what was left of the Army of Tennessee, Johnston assembled a force of about 20,000 troops in North Carolina. He had far too few men to defeat Sherman's army, let alone the combined force the federals would have once the 30,000 troops of General John M. Schofield marching in from the coast toward Goldsboro linked up with Sherman in mid-March. Johnston had to locate and cripple an isolated wing of Sherman's army before Schofield arrived. If he could do so, he might be able to frustrate Sherman's advance long enough to give the rebel Army of Northern Virginia time to slip by the Union army at Petersburg and come south for a new Confederate offensive.

On March 18, Johnston got the opening he had been waiting for. He learned from Hampton that the two wings of Sherman's army were separated from each other by about a day's march as they headed toward Goldsboro, North Carolina. Contrary to what faulty reconnaissance had led Sherman to believe, Johnston's army was not at Raleigh. Instead, Johnston had concentrated it at Smithfield, midway between Goldsboro and Raleigh, and he was thus poised for a strike against the exposed and unsuspecting left wing of Sherman's army. He ordered an all-out attack at Bentonville for the morning of March 19.

Using Hampton's cavalry as a decoy to draw in the federals, Johnston baited a clever trap for the Union left wing. Indeed, the Union commander, General Henry W. Slocum, later reported that he initially believed "the force in my front consisted only of cavalry with a few pieces of artillery." He soon changed his mind when a rebel deserter (a Union captive who had enlisted in the rebel army to avoid imprisonment) informed him that Johnston's officers had told their men that morning that "'Old Joe' had caught one of Sherman's wings beyond the reach of support, that he intended to *smash* that wing and then go for the other."

The rebel charges at Bentonville were as valiant as any in the war. Particularly for the wasted veterans of the Army of Tennessee, this was a chance for redemption after their humiliating defeats at Franklin and Nashville. And their charges did buckle and briefly open gaps in the Union lines. But the rebel ranks were too thin, and Sherman's veterans were too skilled and cool in erecting defenses. "The assaults were repeated over and over again until a late hour," Slocum noted, "each assault finding us better prepared for resistance."

As the fighting wound down on March 19, the right wing of Sherman's army was rushing toward Bentonville. Johnston spent the next day in erecting a v-shaped defense of entrenchments to protect his army. When night fell on March 20, Sherman had drawn up 60,000 troops against the fewer than 20,000 that still remained with Johnston. Sherman had the opportunity to destroy Johnston's army, but he chose not to take it. Rather than risk an offensive battle, he preferred to avoid needless bloodshed and hurry on to complete the juncture with Schofield. Then he hoped to lead his army triumphantly north to Virginia to take part in the capture of Lee's army.

Johnston slipped away from Bentonville on March 21. His army had suffered 2,600 casualties in the battle, about 1,000 more than its much larger Union foe. Johnston still tried to keep his army intact in the hope that Lee would be able to join him in North Carolina. But Lee was never able to escape the Union Army of the Potomac, and on April 18, Johnston surrendered to Sherman at Durham Station.

SEE ALSO

Johnston, Joseph E.; Sherman, William T.

FURTHER READING

Barrett, John G. *Sherman's March Through the Carolinas.* Chapel Hill: University of North Carolina Press, 1956.

Bradley, Mark L. *Last Stand in the Carolinas: The Battle of Bentonville.* Campbell, Calif.: Savas Woodbury Publishers, 1996.

Hughes, Nathaniel C. *Bentonville: The Final Battle of Sherman and Johnston.* Chapel Hill: University of North Carolina Press, 1996.

Black Codes

The Black Codes were laws passed by Southern state legislatures immediately after the Civil War that defined and reg-

ulated the legal status of the emancipated slaves. The laws were so discriminatory and restrictive that they convinced many Northerners that the federal government needed to take an active role in establishing and protecting black civil rights.

The Black Codes did recognize certain minimal rights of the freed population, mainly the right to acquire and hold property, enter into legal marriages, make contracts, and sue and be sued. At the same time, however, the codes relegated blacks to a separate and inferior legal status. Blacks could not vote, hold public office, serve on juries, own firearms, enlist in the military, or testify in court cases involving whites. Many of the codes also placed restrictions on the right of blacks to assemble in public meetings and move about freely.

What particularly aroused Northern anger were sweeping labor provisions that seemed nothing less than a disguised form of slavery. Vagrancy was defined in such a way as to require all blacks to give proof of gainful employment, usually in the form of an annual labor contract on a neighboring plantation. Local judges (all of whom were white) had the power to fine and arrest blacks without such a contract and hire them out to local planters if they could not pay the fine. Apprenticeship laws gave local white courts complete authority to determine whether black parents were providing adequate support for their children. The courts bound over black children as apprentices, regardless of the parents' wishes, to local planters who were to serve as their "guardians." This practice was especially widespread in the Upper South, where, in some counties, as many as one-quarter of black children were bound over to their parents' former owners as cheap laborers.

Southern whites accepted the legal end of slavery, but most of them regarded the very idea of civil equality between the races as absurd and dangerous. They also had little faith in the ability or willingness of the freed blacks to work without coercive legal controls forcing them to do so. By giving legal expression to these attitudes, the Black Codes confirmed the worst of Northern fears regarding the refusal of the postwar South to take any meaningful step toward racial justice.

The Freedman's Bureau and the army suspended enforcement of the most blatantly discriminatory features of the Black Codes. Meanwhile, the Republican majority in Congress had every reason to conclude that the federal government had to take additional steps to protect the legal rights of the freed slaves.

SEE ALSO

Civil Rights Act of 1866; Freedmen's Bureau; Johnson's Program of Reconstruction

FURTHER READING

Rabinowitz, Howard N. *Race Relations in the Urban South, 1865–1890*. New York: Oxford University Press, 1978.
Wilson, Theodore B. *The Black Codes of the South*. Tuscaloosa: University of Alabama Press, 1965.

Black soldiers

The employment of black troops in Union armies was nearly as revolutionary a step as the Union's decision to make emancipation a war aim. On the eve of the Civil War, white prejudice and legal restrictions barred African Americans from serving in the U.S. Army or the state militias. Yet, by 1865 blacks comprised about 10 percent of the Union armies and nearly one-quarter

of naval enlistments (because the duty was so onerous, the navy had always accepted blacks to maintain adequate numbers of sailors).

When the war broke out, white Northerners almost unanimously agreed that it was to be an exclusively white man's war. The *Indianapolis Journal*, the leading Republican newspaper in Indiana, reflected that sentiment in November 1861, when it expressed the hope that "we may never have to confess to the world that the United States Government has to seek an ally in the negro to regain its authority." Racial slurs depicted blacks as a weak, cowardly race incapable of the courageous self-reliance demanded of the soldier. According to the logic of white supremacy, arming the blacks would not only be a military blunder and a confession of white failure, but it would also imply that blacks had achieved a measure of equality that whites were not yet willing to grant.

From the firing of the first shot, African Americans and their abolitionist allies sensed that the war offered a priceless opportunity for the nation to destroy slavery and for blacks to stake a claim to equality through their military service to the Union. Frederick Douglass, the great black leader, put it best when he said: "Once let the black man get upon his person the brass letters, U.S.: let him get an eagle on his button, and a musket on his shoulder and bullets in his pocket, and there is no power on earth which can deny that he has earned the right to citizenship." Precisely because so many whites agreed with Douglass's logic, Northern governors and the War Department initially rejected all offers of black volunteers. Moreover, the use of black troops early in the war might well have cost the Union the support of the slave states in the Border South.

The first glimmer of a change in

federal policy came in July 1862, when Congress passed a revised Militia Act authorizing the enrollment of blacks into military service. In the context of his emerging emancipation policy, President Abraham Lincoln was also now considering the use of black troops. His Emancipation Proclamation on January 1, 1863, specifically linked the two in stating that, henceforth, the Union military would accept freed slaves "to garrison forts, positions, stations, and other places, and to man vessels of all sorts in said service." The war had developed into a stalemate, and Lincoln justified these extraordinary Union policies on grounds of military necessity.

Although the first Union black troops were mustered into service in the fall of 1862, recruitment did not begin in earnest until the spring of 1863. The heaviest enlistment drives were in the Mississippi Valley and the sea islands along the Georgia and South Carolina coasts, the federally occupied areas with the largest concentrations of slaves. Union recruiters often used heavy-handed tactics, but blacks generally welcomed the chance to fight for their freedom and that of their families. "In Secesh times I used to pray the Lord for this opportunity to be released from bondage and to fight for my liberty," said Solomon Bradley of South Carolina, "and I could not feel right so long as I was not in the regiment."

Much to the surprise of most whites, blacks quickly proved their worth as combat soldiers in such battles as Port Hudson (May 27, 1863), Millikin's Bend (June 7, 1863), and Fort Wagner (July 18, 1863). For the most part, however, blacks were used primarily for garrison and rear-guard duty. Their main role was to free up white troops for combat service, and they were often stationed in districts where yellow fever and malaria had decimated the white soldiers. Such assignments, combined with poor medical care, explain why blacks had a much higher mortality rate than white soldiers.

The heroic charge of the black troops in the 54th Massachusetts Regiment at Fort Wagner, South Carolina, in July 1863 provided the climactic moment in the 1989 motion picture Glory, *which re-created the story of the regiment and its commander, Colonel Robert Gould Shaw.*

In addition to running a greater risk of dying in the war, black troops also had to confront discrimination in terms of pay and access to officers' commissions. Until June 1864, when Congress equalized military salaries, white privates were paid $13 a month and given a clothing allowance of $3.50, whereas blacks received $10 a month and had $3 deducted in advance for clothing. With very few exceptions, the army reserved officers' commissions in the segregated black regiments for whites, a policy designed to raise white morale by providing opportunities for rapid advancement. On top of this second-class treatment in the Union army, black soldiers also faced the threat of reenslavement or mistreatment if captured by the Confederates.

In the North, free blacks enlisted at a rate three times higher than that of whites. Within the South, the highest enlistment rates among former slaves occurred in the loyal border states that had been exempted from the Emancipation Proclamation. Enrollment in the Union army brought freedom to these soldiers and their families.

About 180,000 blacks served in the Union army, and four fifths of them had been slaves when the war began. As Lincoln and other Northern whites came to recognize, the Union could win the war only by freeing and arming the slaves. Black soldiers played a vital role in the Union victory, and their combat record influenced whites after the war to take the first steps toward racial equality.

SEE ALSO

Casualties; Emancipation; Emancipation Proclamation

FURTHER READING

Berlin, Ira, et al., eds. *Freedom: A Documentary History of Emancipation, 1861–1867; Series 2: The Black Military Experience.* New York: Cambridge University Press, 1982.

Cornish, Dudley Taylor. *The Sable Arm: Negro Troops in the Union Army, 1861–1865.* New York: Longmans, Green, 1956.
Glatthaar, Joseph T. *Forged in Battle: The Civil War Alliance of Black Soldiers and White Officers.* New York: Free Press, 1990.
Smith, John David, ed. *Black Soldiers in Blue: African American Troops in the Civil War Era.* Chapel Hill: University of North Carolina Press, 2002.

Black suffrage

The vast majority of whites before the Civil War did not believe that African Americans were entitled to any civil rights except those that an individual state might wish to confer. As for the basic *political* right of voting, which was under the exclusive jurisdiction of the states, blacks could vote on equal terms with whites only in New England (with the exception of Connecticut). It took the massive changes wrought by the Civil War to create the opening that made possible the passage in 1870 of the 15th Amendment, which granted blacks the right to vote.

Northern free blacks and their abolitionist allies led the drive for black suffrage in the prewar years. Although they received some support from anti-slavery Republicans, the nearly unanimous opposition of Democrats blocked all efforts in the North to extend black voting beyond New England. Then, white attitudes began to change during the Civil War. By 1865, as a direct consequence of wartime emancipation and black military service, a clear majority of Republicans favored some form of black suffrage. Senator Charles Sumner of Massachusetts, a leading Republican radical, was their chief spokesman. He insisted that black suffrage had now become absolutely necessary so that the emancipated slaves could protect their

These three freedmen are having an avid political discussion on a Richmond street corner. African Americans turned to politics in an effort to protect their gains under Radical Reconstruction.

freedom. The cornerstone of any black equality before the law, he argued, had to rest on blacks having voting power.

Despite the firm commitment of Republican radicals to black suffrage, the party moved cautiously on the issue. As Joseph A. Geiger, an Ohio Republican, wrote Senator John Sherman of Ohio: "It is apparent to any sensible man that its [black suffrage's] agitation will do harm." The problem was the unrelenting opposition of the Democrats and their success in cutting into the Republican vote by appealing to white prejudice. Despite very strong Republican backing, voters in Connecticut, Wisconsin, and Minnesota in 1865 all rejected amendments to their state constitutions extending the vote to blacks. Similar referenda in 1867 also failed in Ohio and Kansas.

Although Iowa and Minnesota consented to black suffrage in 1868, the major breakthrough came in the South, not the North. In 1867 Congress mandated that the 10 former Confederate states that had rejected the 14th Amendment place black suffrage in new state constitutions as a precondition for readmission to the Union. In order to protect this extraordinary basis for the voting rights of freedmen, a precedent that could easily be overturned by Democratic state governments in the future, the Republicans placed black suffrage in the Constitution with the 15th Amendment. By so doing, they also enfranchised the considerable black population living in Southern states that had not undergone Reconstruction and the much smaller number of blacks who still lacked the right to vote in 11 Northern states. The *National Anti-Slavery Standard* well summarized the rationale behind the 15th Amendment when it declared in 1868 that "No reconstruction at the South will be safe and enduring which does not give the negro a national guarantee that he shall not be deprived of the ballot under the shield of 'State Sovereignty.'" And, it tellingly added: "Nor should the invidious distinctions now made against the blacks in the North be long allowed to continue."

SEE ALSO

15th Amendment; Military Reconstruction Act of 1867

FURTHER READING

Dykstra, Robert A. *Bright Radical Star: Black Freedom and White Supremacy on the Hawkeye Frontier.* Cambridge, Mass.: Harvard University Press, 1993.
McPherson, James M. *The Struggle for Equality: Abolitionists and the Negro in the Civil War and Reconstruction.* Princeton, N.J.: Princeton University Press, 1964.

Blair, Montgomery

UNION POLITICIAN

- *Born: May 10, 1813, Franklin County, Ky.*
- *Political parties: Democrat, American, Republican, Democrat*
- *Education: U.S. Military Academy, B.S., 1835*
- *Military service: brevet lieutenant, artillery, 1835–36*
- *Government service: U.S. district attorney for Missouri, 1839–41; mayor of St. Louis, 1842–43; judge, court of common pleas in St. Louis, 1845–49; U.S. solicitor general, 1855–58; U.S. postmaster general, 1861–64; Maryland House of Delegates, 1878–79*
- *Died: July 27, 1883, Silver Spring, Md.*

A member of Lincoln's cabinet from the key border state of Maryland, Montgomery Blair represented a powerful political family that was instrumental in the founding of the Republican party in

both Maryland and Missouri. Distrusted by Republican radicals for his conservative approach to slavery, he was forced out as postmaster general in 1864. During Reconstruction he returned to his former political home in the Democratic party.

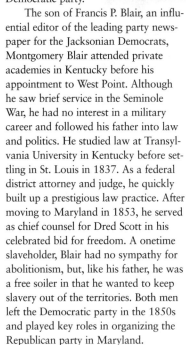

The son of Francis P. Blair, an influential editor of the leading party newspaper for the Jacksonian Democrats, Montgomery Blair attended private academies in Kentucky before his appointment to West Point. Although he saw brief service in the Seminole War, he had no interest in a military career and followed his father into law and politics. He studied law at Transylvania University in Kentucky before settling in St. Louis in 1837. As a federal district attorney and judge, he quickly built up a prestigious law practice. After moving to Maryland in 1853, he served as chief counsel for Dred Scott in his celebrated bid for freedom. A onetime slaveholder, Blair had no sympathy for abolitionism, but, like his father, he was a free soiler in that he wanted to keep slavery out of the territories. Both men left the Democratic party in the 1850s and played key roles in organizing the Republican party in Maryland.

Blair's political connections and the critical need of President Lincoln to have a border-state representative in his cabinet gained him the position of postmaster general in March 1861. Ironically, given his generally conservative political views, Blair initially was the only member of Lincoln's cabinet to

Postmaster General in Lincoln's cabinet, Montgomery Blair belonged to a powerful family of border-state Unionists whose support Lincoln carefully cultivated during the war.

favor unequivocally the reinforcement of Fort Sumter. As Secretary of the Navy Gideon B. Welles recorded in his diary, Blair's "indignation that any idea of abandoning Sumter should be entertained or thought of was unbounded."

Blair supported a vigorous prosecution of the war and artfully used the political patronage at his disposal to support Lincoln's position within the party, especially against the more radical elements led by Secretary of the Treasury Salmon P. Chase. Still, he was the most conservative cabinet member when it came to emancipation. He opposed Lincoln's decision on emancipation in the summer of 1862 on the grounds that a political backlash in the North would deprive the Republicans of the control of Congress. He was, as reported by Chase, "afraid of the influence of the Proclamation on the Border States and on the Army."

The opposition of radical Republicans induced Blair to make a standing offer to Lincoln that he would resign whenever the President thought best. Lincoln took him up on that offer in September 1864. Blair resigned as part of a political deal in which John C. Frémont, the third-party candidate of a splinter faction of radical Republicans, withdrew from the Presidential race.

The Reconstruction policy of the congressional Republicans was far too radical for Blair. He, along with the rest of the Blair political clan, returned to the Democratic fold in opposition to Republican policies that enfranchised the freedmen and, in border states such as Maryland, attempted to deprive white rebel sympathizers of the vote. After providing legal counsel to Samuel F. Tilden, the Democratic candidate in the disputed Presidential election of 1876, Blair won a seat in the Maryland legislature, where he vainly tried to re-open the controversial settlement of the

1876 election that resulted in a victory for the Republican candidate, Rutherford B. Hayes. Shortly before his death, he unsuccessfully ran for Congress.

SEE ALSO
Dred Scott decision; Emancipation Proclamation

FURTHER READING
Smith, William E. *The Francis Preston Blair Family in Politics.* 2 vols. New York: Macmillan, 1933.

Bleeding Kansas

Violence between pro- and antislavery factions exploded on the Kansas frontier in the mid-1850s following the passage of the Kansas-Nebraska Act. As popularized by the Republican party, "Bleeding Kansas" symbolized for many Northerners the ruthless efforts of Southerners to force slavery into the territories.

Although most of the settlers moving into Kansas were interested primarily in acquiring land of their own, the settlement of the territory quickly became enmeshed in the struggle over slavery reopened by the Kansas-Nebraska Act in the spring of 1854. The doctrine of popular sovereignty pitted slavery and free-soil advocates in a bitter competition to see who could dominate the territorial government. Senator David Atchison of Missouri headed the proslavery forces. For him, Southern control of Kansas would "carry slavery to the Pacific Ocean; if we fail we lose Missouri, Arkansas, and Texas and all the territories; the game must be played boldly." He played the game by organizing Missourians to cross into Kansas and stuff ballot boxes. Antislavery Yankees, who had been sent to Kansas by the New England Emigrant Aid Society, spearheaded

LIBERTY, THE FAIR MAID OF KANSAS—IN THE HANDS OF THE "BORDER RUFFIANS".

the effort to win Kansas for free labor.

A pro–Southern Democratic administration in Washington recognized a territorial legislature that proslavery men had carried through fraudulent tactics. Once this legislature passed laws that criminalized any criticism of slavery in Kansas, violence was inevitable. It was at its worst in the spring of 1856, when a band of Missourians sacked Lawrence, the center of the free-soil camp in Kansas, and the abolitionist John Brown retaliated by murdering five presumably proslavery settlers.

Sporadic fighting continued until 1859. By then, a free-soil majority, aided by a sympathetic Congress, had succeeded in turning back an attempt to bring Kansas into the Union under a proslavery Constitution. In January 1861, Kansas entered the Union as a free state.

SEE ALSO

Brown, John; Kansas-Nebraska Act

FURTHER READING

Etcheson, Nicole. *Bleeding Kansas: Contested Liberty in the Civil War Era.*

Lawrence: University Press of Kansas, 2004.

Rawley, James A. *Race and Politics: "Bleeding Kansas" and the Coming of the Civil War.* Philadelphia: J. B. Lippincott, 1969.

Blockade

On April 19, 1861, just six days after the Union garrison surrendered at Fort Sumter, President Abraham Lincoln proclaimed a naval blockade of the Confederacy. The goal, as reported by Union Secretary of the Navy Gideon B. Welles in his annual report for 1861, was the "closing of all the insurgent ports along a coast of more than 3,000 miles." With the Union capture in January 1865 of Fort Fisher, and with it the port of Wilmington, North Carolina, that goal was largely achieved. The Union blockade had grown steadily tighter throughout the war and was a major, though not in itself decisive, cause of the Confederate defeat.

The Union established four blockading zones—two for the Atlantic Ocean and two for the Gulf of Mexico—and supplied the more than 600 ships that eventually made up the blockading squadron out of huge depots set up in Beaufort, North Carolina, Port Royal, South Carolina, and Pensacola, Florida. The thorniest logistical problem that had to be overcome was the need for 5,000 tons of coal per week for the steamships in the squadron. For the sailors in the squadron, the chief problem was boredom. On average, only once or twice a month did the thrill of chasing a blockade runner break the monotony of performing repetitive shipboard tasks while subsisting on stale water and an unappetizing fare of moldy biscuits, beans, and salt pork. Little wonder that a coal shoveler stationed off Charleston pleaded with his captain: "Give me a discharge, and let me go home. I am a poor weak, miserable, nervous, half-crazy boy."

Measured by the percentage of blockade runners captured or destroyed, the Union blockade was not particularly successful. Five out of six vessels (though only one out of two by the early months of 1865) successfully ran the blockade during the war. As late as 1864, the Confederacy was able to export through the blockade nine-tenths of the cotton consigned to foreign purchases. On the other hand, when measured by the sharp decline in the *volume* of Confederate trade, the blockade was an undoubted success. Some 8,000 ships moved in or out of Confederate ports during the war, mostly involved in intracoastal trade, compared to 20,000 vessels in the four years immediately preceding the war. In terms of the tonnage of goods, Confederate wartime trade fell to one-third of the South's prewar figures in the late 1850s. This falloff in trade, especially for consumer goods, contributed to the wartime shortages that drove up prices in the Confederacy's ruinous bout of runaway inflation.

From a strategic standpoint, the greatest impact of the blockade was in denying the Confederacy access to the heavy industrial equipment, such as railroad machinery and rolling stock, it needed to maintain its deteriorating rail network. Confederate railroads broke down or were captured faster than they could be repaired or replaced. As the railroads crumbled, civilian morale and military effectiveness declined in the face of bottlenecks and delays in the movement of essential goods and supplies.

Although Confederate naval strategy never assigned top priority to breaking the blockade, the growing economic

This ship stationed off the entrance to the Charleston harbor was part of the vastly enlarged Union navy that made the Union blockade more effective as the war progressed.

pressure exerted by the blockade was a significant element in the Union's overall victorious strategy. It choked off the normal channels of Southern trade, worsened the financial and supply problems of the Confederacy, and helped cripple rebel railroads.

SEE ALSO

Blockade runners; Fort Fisher; Lincoln, Abraham; Naval warfare; Welles, Gideon B.

FURTHER READING

Browning, Robert M., Jr. *From Cape Charles to Cape Fear: The North Atlantic Blockading Squadron during the Civil War*. Tuscaloosa: University of Alabama Press, 1993.
Browning, Robert M., Jr. *Success Is All That Was Expected: The South Atlantic Blockading Squadron during the Civil War*. Washington, D. C.: Brassey's Inc., 2002.
Jones, Virgil C. *The Civil War at Sea: The Blockaders*. New York: Holt, Rinehart, & Winston, 1960.
Surdam, David G. *Northern Naval Superiority and the Economics of the American Civil War*. Columbia: University of South Carolina Press, 2001.

Blockade runners

Driven by patriotism and especially the lure of high profits, blockade running was a mainstay of the Confederate war effort. Blockade runners brought in from Europe some 400,000 rifles, 60 percent of the Confederacy's supply. They accounted for one-third of the lead needed for the production of bullets, three-fourths of the raw materials that went into the manufacture of gunpowder, and nearly all the paper for cartridges. The lifeline of supplies kept open by the blockade runners also included most of the cloth and leather used for uniforms and military accoutrements. Most of the consumer goods they carried were of light weight and small bulk, quasi-luxury items that could fetch a high price.

The most successful blockade-running vessels were steam-propelled ships specially outfitted to evade the Union blockaders. Painted gray for low visibility, burning smoke-free anthracite coal to avoid detection, constructed with a shallow draft for maneuverability, and equipped with powerful boilers for speed, these steamers could slip past or outrun nearly all pursuers. Their names—*Let Her Be, Let Her Rip, Banshee, Beauregard,* and *The Dare* for example—were often as colorful and dashing as the exploits of their crews. About 300 of these fast steamers ran the blockade on round trips between Southern and foreign ports. They completed 1,000 of their 1,300 runs—a success rate of more than 75 percent.

Fortunes were made in running the blockade. Two trips recouped the cost of purchasing and outfitting a blockade runner. After that, the profits were immense. Cotton could be purchased in the Confederacy for 6 to 8 cents a pound and then resold in Europe for more than 50 cents a pound. Markups were about as high for the luxury items such as silks and perfumes that the blockade runners preferred to bring back on their return voyages. By one estimate, blockade runners had banked $20 million in profits by the end of 1863.

Attracted by the profit potential, the British supplied most of the capital, as well as the crews, for the blockade runners. Larger British firms, aside from financing voyages, sent cargoes by regular freight to blockade-running stations in the Caribbean, most notably Nassau and Bermuda. Here, the blockade runners picked up supplies for distribution to entry ports in the Confederacy. The main ports that remained open for most of the war were Charleston and Wilmington. W. C. Corsan, a British steel merchant visiting the Confederacy, noted of Charleston in 1862, "The truth is, that

Although equipped with a hundred pounder rifle gun, this Confederate blockade runner was unable to avoid capture by the Union army.

the business caused by these sales of blockade-goods formed almost the whole business of the city. It was a very large trade, filled the hotels with strangers, and employed many porters, draymen, and other labourers." As for Wilmington, Union secretary of the navy Gideon B. Welles was grumbling in his diary as late as August 1864 that "Wilmington seems to be almost an open port." Both these ports withstood federal attacks until February 1865.

Apart from steamers operated by the Confederate Ordnance Bureau and by individual states, private entrepreneurs had a free hand in blockade running until the Confederate government began to nationalize the trade in early 1864. New measures announced in February and March prohibited the importation of most goods not deemed essential for the war effort, required special authorization from President Jefferson Davis for exporting such cash staples as cotton, and reserved for the use of the Confederate government half of the cargo space on blockade runners. Confronted with growing shortages of food and supplies as more and more of its territory and resources were lost to advancing federal armies, the Confederate government reacted by nationalizing

the flow of foreign trade in order to gain greater access to wartime necessities from the outside. Despite bitter criticism, the controls took hold, and increased shipments of foreign goods helped the Confederacy stave off defeat for another year.

The blockade runners were vital to the Confederate war effort. Their success early in the war bought the Confederacy time in which to build an industrial base for their own military production. Late in the war, and under regulations that converted them into a virtual arm of the Confederate government, the blockade runners brought in the essential supplies that could no longer be gathered internally from the shrinking area of rebel-held territory.

SEE ALSO
Blockade; Great Britain; Naval warfare

FURTHER READING
Cochrane, Hamilton. *Blockade Runners of the Confederacy.* Indianapolis: Bobbs-Merrill, 1958.
Horner, David L. *The Blockade Runners: True Tales of Running the Yankee Blockade off the Confederate Coast.* New York: Dodd, Mead, 1968.
Wise, Stephen R. *Lifeline of the Confederacy: Blockade Running During the Civil War.* Columbia: University of South Carolina Press, 1988.

Booth, John Wilkes

LINCOLN'S ASSASSIN

- *Born: May 10, 1838, near Baltimore, Md.*
- *Education: private academies*
- *Occupation: Shakespearean actor, 1855–64*
- *Died: April 26, 1865, near Bowling Green, Va.*

Driven by the conviction that Abraham Lincoln was a murderous tyrant, John Wilkes Booth mortally wounded the U.S. President on the evening of April 14, 1865, at Ford's Theatre in Washington. The assassination elevated the martyred Lincoln into the ranks of America's greatest heroes and branded Booth as the American Judas whose very name became synonymous with infamy.

Booth's British parents migrated to the United States in 1821, and his father, Junius Brutus Booth, gained renown as America's most celebrated tragic actor. The young Booth left school after his father's death in 1852 and soon followed his father and older brothers into the theater. After playing in stock productions in Philadelphia for a year, he joined the company of the Richmond Theatre in 1858 and became a great favorite of his Southern audiences. By 1861 he was a star of the first rank, earning on his tours $20,000 a year, a princely income for that time.

As a member of an elite Richmond militia regiment, Booth witnessed John Brown's execution in 1858. He identified passionately with the Southern cause and believed, as he wrote in 1864 in a letter that he left with his sister in Philadelphia, that "This country was formed for the *white* and not for the black man." In the same letter, he repeated his long-held view that Lincoln's election had been a

declaration of war against Southern institutions and liberties and that "the abolitionists *were the only traitors* in the land."

Although he did not fight for the Confederate cause, Booth served it with his talent and money. His public fame enabled him to circulate among Union officials and soldiers and gather information that he relayed to Confederate authorities. He also smuggled items such as quinine behind rebel lines. In the summer of 1864, the Confederate secret service recruited him for a mission to kidnap Lincoln and bring him to Richmond where he was to be held hostage for the release of Confederate prisoners of war. Abandoning his acting career, he threw himself into the project and rounded up co-conspirators.

In addition to these rewards for the capture of John Wilkes Booth and his accomplices, federal authorities offered large cash payments for the apprehension of President Jefferson Davis and certain of his "agents" initially suspected of having plotted to assassinate Lincoln.

For six months, Booth plotted to seize Lincoln, but the opportunity never quite presented itself. At some point, most likely in early April 1865, he resolved to kill the President instead. What apparently triggered his decision was Lincoln's announcement, in his final speech on April 11, that he favored limited black suffrage. Upon hearing this, Booth reportedly told a companion: "That means nigger citizenship. Now, by God! I'll put him through."

Upon learning that Lincoln would be attending Ford's Theatre on April 14, Booth moved quickly. He gathered his co-conspirators and assigned them high-ranking Union officials to assassinate. Although nothing came of these plans except a savage stabbing of Secretary of State William Henry Seward, Booth carried out his leading role. Slipping undetected into the theater, he shot Lincoln through the back of the head and escaped after leaping from Lincoln's box onto the stage.

Aided by an accomplice, David Herold, Booth fled south along a pre-arranged escape route. Slowed by a leg broken by his fall onto the stage at Ford's Theatre, the assassin was cornered after 20 days of flight in an abandoned tobacco barn less than 100 miles from Washington. Herold surrendered, but Booth refused to give up. He lived only a few hours after being shot, probably by Sergeant Boston Corbett. As he lay dying, he pleaded with the Union soldiers, "Tell Mother I die for my country."

SEE ALSO

Secret service

FURTHER READING

Rhodehamel, John and Louise Taper, eds. *"Right or Wrong, God Judge Me": The Writings of John Wilkes Booth.* Urbana: University of Illinois Press, 1997.
Steers, Edward. *Blood on the Moon: The Assassination of Abraham Lincoln.* Lexington: University Press of Kentucky, 2001.

Border South

The northernmost tier of slave states running eastward from Missouri to Delaware, the Border South was a stronghold of Unionism in the election of 1860. During the Civil War, this part of the South provided the strategic key to the Union's conquest of the Confederacy.

Slavery was in decline throughout the Border South after 1830. In each of these five states—Delaware, Maryland, Virginia, Kentucky, and Missouri—the percentage of slaves in the total population dropped between 1830 and 1860. Slavery was gradually losing out because of its incompatibility with major structural changes that were occurring in the economy of the region. Wheat was replacing or competing with tobacco as the major cash crop, and urban economies were shifting to manufacturing. Both of these changes favored free labor over slavery.

Economically, as well as geographically, the Border South was caught in the middle between the North and South. Still, its growing ties to the Northern economy and the unmistakable weakening of slavery had ominous implications for the defenders of slavery in the Lower South. "Those border States can get along without slavery," noted Senator Alfred Iveson of Georgia during the secession crisis. "Their soil and climate are appropriate to white labor; they can live and flourish without African slavery; but the cotton States cannot."

After providing John Bell and Stephen A. Douglas, the centrist candidates in the election of 1860, with their strongest support in the slave states, the Border South hung back from following

The strategic location of the Border South made it indispensable for Lincoln's government to retain this region within the Union.

BORDER SOUTH

the Lower South out of the Union. Its politicians desperately tried to patch together some compromise to reunite the nation. When those efforts collapsed and war broke out in April 1861, Virginia was the only border state to secede. The success of Abraham Lincoln's administration in holding within the Union the remaining states of the region marked a crucial first step in forging the eventual Union victory.

The loyal border states (including the new Union state of West Virginia, formed in 1863 from a section of Virginia that had not wanted to secede) were the strategic pivot around which the Civil War turned. Control of Missouri enabled the Union to secure the upper Mississippi River, maintain contact with

Kansas and the Pacific Coast, and protect the lower Midwest from Confederate harassment. A Unionist Kentucky guaranteed the Union open access to the Ohio River, its chief logistical means for supplying its western armies, and provided a staging area for invasions of the mid-South through Tennessee. West Virginia straddled a critical rail link between the Midwest and the East. Had Maryland seceded, Washington would have been encircled by rebel territory and, in all likelihood, the North would have had to abandon it.

In addition to their strategic importance, these states had substantial economic and manpower reserves that helped tip the military balance to the Union. They supplied the Union with

250,000 white and black soldiers, significantly more than double the number they furnished the Confederacy. They contained more than half of the factory capacity of the slave South, one-third of its corn production, and one-fifth of its livestock. Lincoln was scarcely exaggerating when he informed Congress in March 1862 that permanent Union control of these states "substantially ends the rebellion."

Given the centrality of the Border South to the entire Union war effort, Lincoln used whatever combination of military force and political persuasion was necessary to keep these states out of the Confederacy. It was here that he was most likely to sanction military arrests and the closing down of pro-secessionist newspapers. He also refused to proclaim emancipation as a war aim until he was convinced that these states were firmly bound to the Union. The Unionist-Republican parties he carefully nurtured in the Border South did not long survive the coming of peace, but Lincoln had won the greater prize of enlisting the northernmost slave states in the war against the Confederacy.

SEE ALSO

Election of 1860; Emancipation; Secession; Slavery; Southern Union soldiers

FURTHER READING

Freehling, William W. *The Reintegration of American History: Slavery and the Civil War.* New York: Oxford University Press, 1994.

Bragg, Braxton
CONFEDERATE GENERAL

- *Born: March 22, 1817, Warrenton, N.C.*
- *Education: U.S. Military Academy, B.S., 1837*
- *Military service: U.S. Army: lieutenant, 1837–46; 1st lieutenant, 1846; captain, 1846; major, 1846; lieutenant*

colonel, 1847–56; Confederate army: brigadier general, 1861; major-general, 1862–65
- *Died: September 27, 1876, Galveston, Tex.*

Perhaps because of chronic migraine headaches, Braxton Bragg had a dyspeptic personality that resulted in his quarreling with practically everyone. His unpopularity among both his officers and his troops hampered his effectiveness as commander of the Army of Tennessee and overshadowed his considerable strengths as an administrator and strategic planner.

Bragg attended the Warrenton Male Academy and secured an appointment to West Point, where he graduated near the top of his class in 1837. After serving in the Seminole War and on the frontier, he distinguished himself in the Mexican War as an artillery officer. He left the army in 1856 to run a Louisiana sugar plantation that he purchased with funds provided by his wealthy wife.

Widely viewed as one of the best officers who had served in the U.S. Army, Bragg had an enviable military reputation at the start of the war. His first command was on the Gulf Coast between Pensacola and Mobile, where he organized Confederate defenses. In February 1862, he was ordered north from the Gulf with 10,000 troops to join General Albert Sidney Johnston's rebel army in Kentucky. Although Bragg did not perform particularly well at Shiloh, President Jefferson Davis put him in charge of the Army of Tennessee in June 1862.

Bragg led a brilliantly conceived invasion of Kentucky in the late summer of 1862, only to be forced to withdraw after the battle of Perryville. Hampered by his faulty troop dispositions and by a command structure divided between himself and General Edmund Kirby Smith, he allowed the federals to regain the initiative. In the aftermath of Perryville, John Buie, one of his soldiers, wrote: "Genl. Bragg…still commands this army, though everybody seems to have lost all confidence in him since his Ky. Raid." Bragg's army was turning against him, and the bloody but indecisive battle of Stones River at the end of the year saw rebel morale slip further.

Bragg almost redeemed himself at Chickamauga in September 1863, but he missed an opportunity to deliver a knockout blow and, much to the disgust of his officers, failed to pursue the retreating Union army. Two months later at Chattanooga, Ulysses S. Grant badly outmaneuvered Bragg and routed his army in a crushing Union victory. In vain Bragg had tried to rally his troops by shouting, "Here is your commander." "Here's your mule!" was their derisive response as they kept on retreating.

Chattanooga cost Bragg his command, and he spent most of the final year of the war in Richmond as a military advisor to Davis. After serving in the Carolinas Campaign in the winter of 1865, he accompanied Davis as he attempted to escape capture following the loss of Richmond. A civil engineer in Alabama after the war, Bragg later moved to Texas.

SEE ALSO

Bragg's Kentucky invasion; Chattanooga Campaign; Chickamauga; Stones River

FURTHER READING

Connelly, Thomas Lawrence. *Autumn of Glory: The Army of Tennessee, 1862–1865.* Baton Rouge: Louisiana State University Press, 1971.
Hallock, Judith. *Braxton Bragg and Confederate Defeat.* Vol. 2. Tuscaloosa: University of Alabama Press, 1991.
McWhiney, Grady. *Braxton Bragg and Confederate Defeat.* Vol. 1. New York: Columbia University Press, 1969.

Bragg's Kentucky invasion

As Confederate forces under General Robert E. Lee were invading Maryland in September 1862, another Confederate offensive was getting under way in Kentucky. Conceived by General Braxton Bragg, commander of the Army of Tennessee, this invasion aimed at clearing middle Tennessee of federal troops and reclaiming Kentucky for the Confederacy.

After Corinth, Mississippi, fell to federal forces in late May 1862, the huge Union army in the West was divided between two major commands. General Ulysses S. Grant was in charge west of the Tennessee River, and to the east, General Don Carlos Buell commanded the Army of the Ohio with orders to advance on Chattanooga. Grant needed time to concentrate his scattered troops in western Tennessee, and Buell edged toward Chattanooga at a snail's pace. This near-immobility of the Union armies gave Bragg an opportunity to make a swift move and catch the federals off guard.

In late July, Bragg began sending 30,000 of his infantry on a 775-mile journey by rail that would take them south to Mobile, then northeast to Atlanta, and finally to Chattanooga. This was an unprecedented strategic use of the rail network, and it opened the way into Tennessee and Kentucky for the Confederates. Having swung around Buell's army, Bragg now planned a joint offensive with General Edmund Kirby Smith, who had an independent command over rebel forces in east Tennessee. Bragg was to move north from Chattanooga and Smith from Knoxville, and together they would defeat Buell's army and perhaps drive as far north as the Ohio River.

Smith moved first. On August 14 he headed north across the Cumberland Plateau with 21,000 men, and on September 2 they occupied Lexington, Kentucky. Pushing north out of Chattanooga in late August, Bragg's army of 30,000 marched parallel and about 100 miles to the west of Smith's advance. By mid-September, Bragg was in central Kentucky and in a position to block Buell's retreat back to Louisville along the Louisville and Nashville Railroad. However, after first relishing the prospect of a battle, Bragg decided that he should first unite with Smith's army. He turned away from Buell and headed east to Lexington for a meeting with Smith. Along the way he dispersed his troops to gather badly needed supplies and to recruit Kentuckians into his army. But appeals to Southern pride failed to attract many recruits. As Smith wrote Bragg on September 18, "The Kentuckians are slow and backward in rallying to our standard. Their hearts are evidently with us, but their blue-grass and fat-grass are against us."

By turning east to Lexington, Bragg had left open the road to Louisville for Buell's army. Buell promptly took that road, and his army, reinforced to 60,000 men, reached Louisville on September 29. After immediately receiving orders to attack Bragg or lose his command, Buell finally went on the offensive. Feinting with part of his army toward Frankfort, the Kentucky state capital where Bragg and Smith were attending the inauguration of their newly installed Confederate governor, Buell moved most of his forces against the still-dispersed elements of Bragg's army well to the south of Frankfort.

As scattered Confederate units began to concentrate in response to Buell's offensive, a Union corps searching for water clashed on October 7 with 16,000 rebels along a tributary of the Chaplin River at Perryville. Mistakenly believing that the main Union offensive was aimed at Frankfort, Bragg ordered General Leonidas P. Polk, the Confederate commander at Perryville, to attack what in fact were the lead elements of the bulk of Buell's army. Despite briefly overrunning an inexperienced division of federals on October 8, Polk's outnumbered troops likely would have suffered a major defeat had it not been for an acoustic shadow—a phenomenon in which topographical and climatic conditions muffle and localize the sounds of battle. A Union staff officer who accidentally stumbled onto the battle later recalled: "At one bound my horse carried me from stillness into the uproar of battle." Buell and the entire right wing of his army were unaware that a battle was being fought until late in the afternoon. As a result, more than half of the Union forces never fought, and the Confederates were able to organize an orderly retreat.

Measured in terms of casualties, Perryville was not a major battle. The Union lost only 4,200 men and the Confederacy 3,400. Still, it brought an end to Bragg's Kentucky invasion. Bragg lacked a secure line of supplies needed to allow him to stay in Kentucky very long without massive support from Kentuckians themselves. Having failed to gain that support, he now withdrew back into middle Tennessee. After a promising beginning, the Kentucky invasion turned out to be just a raid with no strategic benefit for the Confederacy.

SEE ALSO
Bragg, Braxton; Buell, Don Carlos; Polk, Leonidas P.; Smith, Edmund Kirby

FURTHER READING
McDonough, James Lee. *War in Kentucky: From Shiloh to Perryville.* Knoxville:

University of Tennessee Press, 1994.
Noe, Kenneth W. *Perryville: This Grand Havoc of Battle*. Lexington: University Press of Kentucky, 2001.

Breckinridge, John C.

CONFEDERATE GENERAL AND POLITICIAN

- *Born: Jan. 15, 1821, near Lexington, Ky.*
- *Political party: Democrat*
- *Education: Centre College, B.A., 1839; College of New Jersey (Princeton), 1839; studied law, Transylvania University, 1840*
- *Military service: U.S. Army: major, 3rd Kentucky Volunteers, 1847–48; Confederate army: brigadier general, 1861–62; major-general, 1862–65*
- *Government service: Kentucky House of Representatives, 1849–51; U.S. House of Representatives, 1851–55; U.S. Vice President, 1857–61; U.S. Senate, 1861; Confederacy: secretary of war, 1865*
- *Died: May 17, 1875, Lexington, Ky.*

The unsuccessful Presidential candidate of the Southern Democrats in 1860, John C. Breckinridge sided with the Confederacy once his native state of Kentucky declared its allegiance to the Union in September 1861. After a solid record as a Confederate general, he retired from politics during the Reconstruction period.

Born into one of Kentucky's most distinguished political families, Breckinridge received a superb education before embarking on a career in law. After briefly practicing in Iowa, he settled in Lexington in 1845. Although he saw no combat as a volunteer officer in the Mexican War, he was able to use his war record as a springboard into politics. After a term in the Kentucky legislature, where he opposed efforts to introduce a plan of gradual emancipation, he was elected to Congress. Running on the Democratic ticket with James Buchanan in 1856, he became the youngest man ever to serve as Vice President.

A moderate states' rights Democrat, Breckinridge reflected the divided sectional loyalties of his border state of Kentucky. He insisted he was not a secessionist while campaigning for the Presidency in 1860 and favored compromise proposals during the winter of 1860–61 that might have delayed or prevented secession. However, as a U.S. senator he opposed all efforts to coerce the seceded states back into the Union once the Civil War broke out. He later justified his stand by declaring to his fellow Kentuckians: "I would have blushed to meet you with the confession that I had purchased for you exemption from the perils of the battlefields and the shame of waging war against your Southern brethren by hiring others to

A passable general at best, John C. Breckinridge was more valuable to the Confederacy as a symbol of its resolve to claim Kentucky for the Southern cause.

do the work you shrank from performing." Soon after the Kentucky legislature committed to the Union, he left the state under threat of military arrest and volunteered for service in the Confederate army. In December 1861, the U.S. Senate stripped him of his seat.

Breckinridge proved to be a competent, though not a notable, Confederate general. Following a brigade command in central Kentucky, he led the Reserve Corps at Shiloh and assisted in the defense of Vicksburg. After failing to storm Union-held Baton Rouge in the summer of 1862, he joined Braxton Bragg's Army of Tennessee and led, much against his wishes, the last and disastrous Confederate attack at Murfreesboro on January 2, 1863. He commanded his division in all the major western battles of 1863 before receiving his first territorial command in the spring of 1864. As head of a department in western Virginia, he was victorious at the battle of New Market on May 15, 1864, and then took part in Jubal A. Early's raid on Washington. After a final tour of duty in the West in late 1864, he joined Jefferson Davis's cabinet in February 1865, as the last Confederate secretary of war.

Breckinridge followed Davis in his flight from Richmond before slipping away and escaping to Cuba from the Florida coast. Living in Cuba, England, and Canada, he did not return to the United States until 1869, when the federal government dropped legal charges against him. He resumed his law practice in Kentucky and became heavily involved in promoting railroads. Complications after major surgery hastened his death in 1875.

SEE ALSO
Border South; Election of 1860

FURTHER READING
Davis, William C. *Breckinridge: Statesman,* *Soldier, Symbol.* Baton Rouge: Louisiana State University Press, 1974.
Heck, Frank Hopkins. *Proud Kentuckian: John C. Breckinridge, 1821–1875.* Lexington: University Press of Kentucky, 1976.

Brown, John
ABOLITIONIST

- *Born: May 9, 1800, West Torrington, Conn.*
- *Education: lower grades and some studying for the ministry*
- *Occupation: tanner, farmer, shepherd*
- *Died: December 2, 1859, Charlestown, Va. (now W. Va.)*

A failure in nearly every pursuit that he tried, John Brown was nonetheless a catalyst in the coming of the Civil War. His fantastic attempt to spark a slave uprising in his raid on the Harpers Ferry armory in October 1859 enflamed sectional tensions to a fever pitch. Following his execution two months later, abolitionists hailed him as a martyr to the antislavery cause, and more and more Southerners feared for their safety within the Union.

The son of a stern, unbending Calvinist father, Brown moved in 1805 with his family to the Western Reserve District of Ohio, an early center of antislavery activity. At the age of eight he suffered the grievous loss of his mother when she died in childbirth. An indifferent student, he quit school and went to work at his father's tannery. While rounding up cattle and delivering them to army outposts that had contracted with his father for beef during the War of 1812, he witnessed the savage beating of a slave boy in a frontier cabin. He later claimed that the incident made him "a most *determined* foe" of slavery.

By the afternoon of October 17, local militia, soon joined by U.S. regular troops, were attacking John Brown and his band at Harpers Ferry. Whether knowingly or not, Brown had led his men into a trap.

After joining his father's Congregational Church in 1816, Brown briefly studied for the ministry at an academy in Connecticut before an eye infection and lack of funds forced him to return home. He set up his own tannery following his marriage in 1820 and then struck out with his growing family in 1826 for a fresh start in northwestern Pennsylvania. Growing debts and declining business fortunes resulted in his return to the Western Reserve in 1835, thus setting a pattern of frequent moves and recurring economic failures that characterized his adult life. By the time that he and five of his sons took up land claims in Kansas in 1855, he had failed in 20 ventures in six different states.

The one consistent element in Brown's life was his stand against slavery. Although not a member of an abolitionist society, he participated actively in the Underground Railroad, which provided safe havens for fugitive slaves, and passionately believed that slavery was an unconscionable sin. Once caught up in the turmoil over slavery on the Kansas frontier, he quickly found a violent outlet for his antislavery convictions. On May 24, 1856, three days after proslavery Missourians had ransacked the free-soil town of Lawrence, Brown and a party of six men (four of whom were his sons) murdered five Southern settlers along the Pottawatomie River. Driven out of Kansas at the end of the year, he resurfaced in the East. After trying for three years, he finally convinced a group of six abolitionists to fund his scheme of seizing the federal armory at Harpers Ferry, Virginia, and distributing weapons to slaves for a guerrilla war against the slaveholders.

Utterly convinced in his Calvinist soul that he was God's appointed agent for unleashing divine wrath against the sin of slavery, Brown led 19 men (including 5 blacks) into Harpers Ferry on the evening of October 16, 1859. After gaining his major objectives—the arsenal and the rifle works—he inexplicably sat back and waited while federal and Virginia troops snapped shut the trap in which he had placed himself and his followers. After U.S. Marines stormed his position on October 18, 10 of Brown's men lay dead or dying, and 4 more had been captured along with Brown.

During his trial and execution by Virginia authorities, a strange calm descended on Brown. Poised and self-assured, he rejected the pleadings of friends that he adopt an insanity defense. He claimed full responsibility for his actions and insisted that he had but carried out God's will. A savage fiend in the eyes of Southerners, he became for the abolitionists a saint in the holy war against slavery. He welcomed and seemingly anticipated his martyrdom. In a note that he wrote on the morning of his execution, he declared: "I, John Brown, am now quite *certain* that the crimes of this *guilty, land: will* never be purged away, but with Blood." It was an unerringly accurate prophecy.

SEE ALSO
Abolitionists

FURTHER READING
Finkelman, Paul, ed. *His Soul Goes Marching On: Responses to John Brown and the Harpers Ferry Raid.* Charlottesville: University Press of Virginia, 1995.
McGlone, Robert E. *John Brown's War against Slavery.* New York: Cambridge University Press, 2009.
Oates, Stephen B. *To Purge This Land with Blood: A Biography of John Brown.* New York: Harper & Row, 1970.

Brown, Joseph E.
CONFEDERATE POLITICIAN

- *Born: April 15, 1821, Long Creek, S.C.*
- *Political parties: Democrat, Republican*
- *Education: Yale Law School, 1846*
- *Government service: Georgia Senate, 1849–50; Georgia circuit judge, 1855–57; governor of Georgia, 1857–61; chief justice, Georgia Supreme Court, 1868–70; U.S. Senate, 1880–91; Confederacy: governor of Georgia, 1861–65*
- *Died: November 30, 1894, Atlanta, Ga.*

An extreme proponent of states' rights, Joseph Brown was the most caustic of all Confederate governors in his criticism of the centralizing policies of the Confederate government in Richmond. Combined with his extensive program of economic relief to Georgia's soldier families and its poor, his stand on behalf of Georgia's sovereignty kept him in power throughout the war.

Born into a Scotch-Irish farming family that moved to northern Georgia when he was a child, Brown spent most of his youth working as a day laborer on his father's farm. After attending private academies and teaching school, he drew on the assistance of a patron for a year's study at Yale Law School. Upon returning to Georgia, he established a solid law practice before winning a seat in the Georgia Senate as a States' Rights Democrat. Anxious to build up his personal fortune, he invested in real estate, mining ventures, and slaves and then returned to politics in 1857 when a deadlocked Democratic convention nominated him for governor. Once elected, he revealed his political genius for striking a dramatic pose that appealed both to common whites and the planter elite. He stridently defended the right of Southerners to take their slaves into the federal territories and attacked the Georgia banks for misusing the people's money when they lacked reserves of gold to redeem their banknotes during the financial panic of 1857. A strong supporter of secession, he made a special appeal to nonslaveholders to join with the planters in leaving the Union.

Brown's Southern nationalism placed the needs and rights of individual states over those of the central government. Jealously guarding his prerogatives as governor, he first clashed with President Jefferson Davis over the appointment of army officers and the control of state-supplied weapons. Their most acrimonious disputes concerned national conscription and the suspension of the writ of habeas corpus. In both instances Brown accused Davis of creating a military despotism that, as the governor put it, was "subversive of [Georgia's] sovereignty and at war with all the principles for the support of which Georgia entered into this revolution."

Brown's attacks on Davis were popular in Georgia, and they served as an outlet for the civilian discontent that built up as the demands of the war effort impoverished much of the state's population. Brown responded to the plight on the home front by eventually shifting over half of the state's budget to relief. He funded this aid through high taxes that placed the major fiscal burden onto the rich. He justified these taxes to the legislature in 1864 by declaring that since the poor "have generally paid their part of the cost of this war in military service, exposure, fatigue and blood, the rich, who have been in a much greater degree exempt from these, should meet the money demands of the Government."

Following his brief imprisonment by federal authorities at the end of the war, Brown returned to his law practice in Atlanta and then stunned his former political allies by joining the Republican party in 1867. He was amply rewarded for his party reversal with the presidency of the Western and Atlantic Railroad Company and the post of chief justice of the state supreme court. As the Republican party in Georgia collapsed, he jumped back to the Democrats in 1871 and concluded his remarkable political career as a very wealthy U.S. senator. He died in semiretirement.

SEE ALSO
States' rights

FURTHER READING
Parks, Joseph H. *Joseph E. Brown of Georgia.* Baton Rouge: Louisiana State University Press, 1976.

Buchanan, James
15TH PRESIDENT OF THE UNITED STATES

- *Born: April 23, 1791, near Mercersburg, Pa.*
- *Political party: Democrat*
- *Education: Dickinson College, B.A., 1809*
- *Military service: volunteer of dragoons, 1812*
- *Government service: Pennsylvania House of Representatives, 1814–16; U.S. House of Representatives, 1821–31; minister to Russia, 1832–33; U.S. Senate, 1834–45; U.S. secretary of state, 1845–49; minister to Great Britain, 1853–56; President of the United States, 1857–61*
- *Died: June 1, 1868, near Lancaster, Pa.*

An inconsistent leader, James Buchanan had an ill-fated Presidency that saw first the sectional breakup of his Democratic party and then the initial collapse of the Union. Although he believed that secession was illegal, he also felt that he had

Although in reality very wealthy from his law practice, Presidential candidate James Buchanan appears in this 1856 cartoon as a poor, shabby politician trying to win the favor of the South by scheming to annex Cuba as a slave state.

no power under the Constitution to prevent it. As a result, he failed to hold the country together during the secession winter of 1860–61.

Born into a marginally prosperous Scotch-Irish family, Buchanan used his talents as a lawyer and politician to amass a considerable fortune. After graduating at the top of his class at Dickinson College, he entered the Pennsylvania bar in 1812 and began practicing law in Lancaster. His one great love, Anne Carolina Coleman, died in 1819 after her family broke off the engagement, and he remained a bachelor throughout his life. Pouring his energies into politics, he abandoned the dying Federalist party and emerged as a leading Jacksonian Democrat in Pennsylvania. In the absence of a wife and family, he grew closest to the Southern politicians with whom he associated during his long career in Congress. Cementing these bonds were Buchanan's pro-Southern positions on states' rights, slavery, and territorial acquisitions for the South. He roundly denounced the abolitionists and offered but the mildest criticism of slavery.

Mentioned several times as a Democratic Presidential candidate, Buchanan finally received his party's nomination

A SERVICEABLE GARMENT—
OR REVERIE OF A BACHELOR.

in 1856. Apart from his strength in Pennsylvania and his acceptability to Southern Democrats, he had the additional advantage of having been out of the country serving as minister to Great Britain during the bitter infighting over the Kansas-Nebraska Act. Although he ran poorly in the North, he won the election by sweeping all of the slave states but Maryland.

Convinced that the Union was in real danger and that the Republicans and their abolitionist allies were the sole source of the threat to national stability, Buchanan committed his administration to eliminating the issue that had given birth to the Republican party—the status of slavery in the territories. Shortly after his election, he wrote that his goal was "to arrest, if possible, the agitation of the slavery question at the North, and to destroy sectional parties. Should a kind Providence enable me to succeed in my efforts to restore harmony to the Union, I shall feel that I have not lived in vain."

Surely, Providence did not shine on Buchanan or his administration. His pro-Southern sympathies were so apparent that he unwittingly fed Northern fears that a "Slave Power Conspiracy" of Southerners was on the verge of spreading slavery throughout the nation and of crushing Northern liberties in the process. His support of the proslavery *Dred Scott* decision backfired when Northerners vowed to keep slavery out of the territories regardless of the Supreme Court's ruling. By throwing all the resources of his office behind an unsuccessful effort to bring Kansas into the Union as a slave state under the fraudulent Lecompton Constitution, he defied the northern wing of his party and forced Stephen A. Douglas, the most powerful Northern Democrat, into open opposition. The ensuing sectional split in the party continued to fester until it provoked the walkout of the Southern Democrats at the national convention of the Democrats in 1860.

Buchanan was a lame-duck President when the secession crisis erupted in late 1860. He forfeited any possibility that he could serve as a sectional com-promiser when he publicly placed all the blame for the crisis on the Republicans and asked for additional concessions to the South. Believing that he was constitutionally powerless to stop secession, his overriding objective was to prevent a civil war and leave the crisis for the Republicans to resolve when President-elect Abraham Lincoln took office in March 1861. His boldest action was the sending of a relief ship, the *Star of the West,* to Fort Sumter in January. When the ship was fired upon, he arranged an unofficial compromise by which he agreed to abandon attempts at reprovisioning the fort in return for a pledge from South Carolina authorities to respect the status quo.

His reputation destroyed by the time he left the Presidency, Buchanan was an unpopular figure in the North during the Civil War. He supported the Union war effort but opposed the Republicans on emancipation. As late as the fall of 1864, he held out the hope that "a frank and manly offer to the Confederates that they might return to the Union just as they were before they left it, leaving the slavery question to settle itself, might possibly be accepted." He spent his retirement managing his finances and writing *Mr. Buchanan's Administration on the Eve of the Revolution,* a defense of his administration that was published in 1866. He died at his beloved Wheatlands estate from a severe cold.

SEE ALSO
Bleeding Kansas; *Dred Scott* decision; Secession

FURTHER READING
Baker, Jean. *James Buchanan.* New York: Times Books, 2004.
Klein, Philip Shriver. *President James Buchanan: A Biography.* University Park: Pennsylvania State University Press, 1962.
Smith, Elbert B. *The Presidency of James Buchanan.* Lawrence: University Press of Kansas, 1975.

Buell, Don Carlos

UNION GENERAL

- *Born: March 23, 1818, Lowell, Ohio*
- *Education: U.S. Military Academy, B.S., 1841*
- *Military service: U.S. Army: lieutenant, 1841–46; 1st lieutenant, 1846–61; brigadier general, 1861; major-general, 1862–64*
- *Died: November 19, 1898, Airdrie, Ky.*

Don Carlos Buell never lived up to his prewar reputation as one of the best generals in the U.S. Army. A superb organizer who kept a tight rein on his troops, he was too cautious and methodical as a field commander to make the bold decisions necessary for a successful campaign. Politically hampered by his affiliation with the Democratic party and his opposition to turning the war into a crusade against slavery, he failed to gain the full confidence of the Lincoln administration and was relieved of command in October 1862.

Raised on a farm in Indiana, Buell received an appointment to West Point, where he graduated 32nd in a class of 52. After serving in the Mexican War, he transferred to staff duty in the adjutant general's department. Called east from San Francisco at the outbreak of the war, he helped train volunteers in the fledging Army of the Potomac in the summer of 1861.

Buell received his first major command in November 1861 as head of the Department of the Ohio with responsibility for federal operations in Kentucky and Tennessee. Aided by Ulysses S. Grant's successful drive against Forts Henry and Donelson, Buell met little resistance as he occupied Bowling Green, Kentucky, and Nashville, Tennessee, in February 1862. Ordered to unite with Grant's army, he arrived at Shiloh on April 6 just in time to help turn back the rebel attack and convert the battle into a Union victory.

Despite the immense supply problems that he faced in attempting a campaign against Chattanooga in the summer of 1862, Buell came under sharp criticism from his superiors in Washington for dallying while Confederates under General Braxton Bragg were concentrating troops for an invasion of Kentucky. Buell's stress on preparedness over fighting was also costing him the support of his soldiers. "He is inaugurating the dancing-master policy: 'By your leave, my dear sir, we will have a fight, that is, if you are sufficiently fortified; no hurry; take your own time,'" wrote John Beatty, a disgruntled Union colonel.

After temporarily being relieved of command on September 30, Buell did mount an offensive to force Bragg out of Kentucky. However, his failure to pursue Bragg's army after the battle of Perryville on October 8 sealed his fate. Political pressure from the Republican governors in the Midwest, combined with the long-held feeling that Buell was too lenient on Southern civilians and too hesitant to fight rebel armies, led to his replacement by General William S. Rosecrans on October 24.

After a formal investigation into his handling of the Tennessee and Kentucky campaigns, Buell resigned from the army on June 1, 1864. In his postwar civilian career, he was president of the Green River Iron Company and a government pension agent from 1885 to 1889.

SEE ALSO

Bragg's Kentucky invasion; Shiloh

FURTHER READING

Engle, Stephen D. *Don Carlos Buell: Most Promising of All.* Chapel Hill: University of North Carolina Press, 1999.

Burnside, Ambrose E.
UNION GENERAL

- *Born: May 23, 1824, Liberty, Ind.*
- *Education: U.S. Military Academy, B.S., 1847*
- *Military service: U.S. Army: lieutenant, 1847–51; 1st lieutenant, 1851–53; colonel, 1st Rhode Island Volunteers, 1861; brigadier general, 1861; major-general, 1862–65*
- *Died: September 13, 1881, Bristol, R.I.*

Forever associated with the disastrous federal charges at Fredericksburg, Ambrose E. Burnside was a competent corps commander who lacked the ability and confidence to command an army. He was, Ulysses S. Grant recalled in his memoirs, "an officer who was generally liked and respected." Grant added that "[i]t was hardly his fault" that he was ever placed in command of the Army of the Potomac. After the Fredericksburg debacle, Burnside held subordinate positions in Ohio, Tennessee, and Virginia.

Burnside was a partner in a tailor's shop in Liberty before his appointment to West Point. He served primarily in garrison duty during the Mexican War and then was posted to the western frontier. Following his resignation from the army in 1853, he settled in Rhode Island and manufactured firearms. At the outbreak of the war, he raised a company of three-month volunteers and then commanded a brigade at First Bull Run. In the winter and spring of 1862, he led a successful expedition against the North Carolina coast and established a Union beachhead in the eastern part of the state. He returned to Virginia in the summer of 1862 with reinforcements for the Army of the Potomac.

Despite his uninspired leadership of the Union left wing at Antietam, Burnside was offered the command of the Army of the Potomac when President Abraham Lincoln decided to replace

Union General Ambrose E. Burnside became forever identified with this narrow bridge across Antietam Creek when he inexplicably squandered an opportunity to crush the weak Confederate position on the other side during the battle of Antietam.

General George B. McClellan in November 1862. According to General C. P. Buckingham, a staff officer of the War Department, Burnside initially "declined the command. Among other objections, he urged his want of confidence in himself." Advised by McClellan to take the command, Burnside reluctantly accepted. Unfortunately for the army, Burnside's negative assessment of his own capabilities was an accurate one, and he persisted with his offensive against the impregnable rebel position at Fredricksburg long after any chance for its success had vanished.

Removed from command in January 1863 after the humiliating "Mud March"—an abortive effort to move the army through a quagmire of mud—Burnside went west as head of the Department of the Ohio. He cracked down on rebel sympathizers in the Midwest and arrested Clement L. Vallandigham, an outspoken Peace Democrat. In the fall he assisted in the defense of Knoxville. Returning to the East in 1864, he commanded the IX Corps during Grant's Virginia Campaign. Made the scapegoat for the Union failure in the Petersburg mine assault, he was again relieved of command.

Burnside resigned from the army in 1865 and had a successful postwar career as a director in railroad and industrial pursuits. He served three terms as the governor of Rhode Island before his election to the U.S. Senate in 1874. He was still a senator at the time of his death.

SEE ALSO

Antietam; Fredericksburg; Petersburg campaign

FURTHER READING

Marvel, William. *Burnside.* Chapel Hill: University of North Carolina Press, 1991.

Butler, Benjamin F.

UNION GENERAL AND POLITICIAN

- *Born: November 5, 1818, Deerfield, N.H.*
- *Political parties: Democrat, Republican, Democrat-Greenback*
- *Education: Waterville (now Colby) College, A.B., 1838*
- *Military service: U.S. Army: brigadier general, Massachusetts Volunteers, 1861; major-general, volunteers, 1861–65*
- *Government service: Massachusetts House of Representatives, 1853; Massachusetts Senate, 1859; U.S. House of Representatives, 1867–75; 1877–79; governor of Massachusetts, 1883*
- *Died: January 11, 1893, Washington, D.C.*

A general who owed his appointment to President Abraham Lincoln's need to cultivate support from northern Democrats, Benjamin F. Butler had a genius for fomenting controversy. His actions as military commander of Union-occupied New Orleans made him hated throughout the South. Although an ineffective general, he was a shrewd politician who emerged as one of the staunchest supporters of the freed slaves.

Raised by his widowed mother, Butler was a bright, ambitious student who was admitted to the Massachusetts bar in 1840 after graduating from college. He quickly built up a very successful practice in criminal law. Politically, he was a conservative, pro–Southern Democrat who served in both houses of the Massachusetts legislature in the 1850s. Despite his support for John C. Breckinridge, the Southern rights candidate in the Presidential election of 1860, he was firmly committed to the Union once Fort Sumter fell.

Butler had a flair for attracting

attention to himself, and he did so at the very start of the war. In Philadelphia, while commanding the 8th Massachusetts regiment en route to Washington in April 1861, Butler learned that the rail lines south to Washington had been cut by rebel sympathizers. He commandeered a steamboat, transported his men by water to Annapolis, Maryland, and then organized the mechanics among his troops to repair the rail line to Washington. Sent ahead by Butler, the 7th New York arrived in the capital on April 24 and lifted the threat of a rebel blockade of the city. On May 13, Butler occupied Baltimore and neutralized pro-Confederate activity.

By late May 1861, Butler commanded Fortress Monroe in tidewater Virginia. Immediately faced with the problem of what to do with escaped slaves who made it behind Union lines (official Union policy early in the war called for returning fugitive slaves to their owners), he hit upon the ingenious solution of declaring the fugitives contraband of war—that is, enemy property liable to seizure. Butler's stand was pop-

ular in the North, and it set a precedent followed by most other Union generals.

After taking part in the successful invasion of Hatteras Inlet in August, Butler was put in charge of Union-occupied New Orleans in the spring of 1862. There, he became known as the "Beast of New Orleans" for his order decreeing that any woman who insulted federal officers or soldiers was to be "regarded and held liable to be treated as a woman of the town plying her avocation"—a prostitute, in other words. Enraged, President Jefferson Davis responded to this apparent defaming of Southern white womanhood by ordering that in the event of Butler's capture, "the officer in command of the capturing force do cause him to be immediately executed by hanging."

Despite its notoriety, Butler's command in New Orleans was generally as temperate as it was firm, and he made a real effort to provide for the city's white poor and its growing numbers of fugitive slaves. Relieved in December 1862, he spent the remainder of the war holding a series of ineffective, if not bungled,

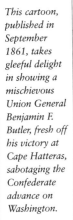

This cartoon, published in September 1861, takes gleeful delight in showing a mischievous Union General Benjamin F. Butler, fresh off his victory at Cape Hatteras, sabotaging the Confederate advance on Washington.

commands in North Carolina and Virginia. He was incompetent as a combat general, but his political influence was so great that Lincoln felt compelled to keep him in the field through the end of 1864.

Butler's postwar political career was as controversial as his wartime record. He began as an outspoken radical Republican and played a prominent role in the impeachment proceedings against President Andrew Johnson. However, he soon broke with his party over financial issues and switched back to the Democrats as an advocate of greenbacks and workers' rights. He unsuccessfully ran for the Presidency on the Greenback-Labor ticket in 1884.

SEE ALSO
Contrabands; Fugitive slaves

FURTHER READING
Trefussee, Hans L. *Ben Butler: The South Called Him Beast!* New York: Twayne Publishers, 1957.
West, Richard S. *Lincoln's Scapegoat General: A Life of Benjamin F. Butler, 1818–1893.* Boston: Houghton Mifflin, 1965.

Calhoun, John C.
SOUTHERN POLITICIAN

- *Born: March 18, 1782, Abbeville County, S.C.*
- *Political party: Democratic-Republican*
- *Education: Yale College, B.A., 1804; Tapping Reeve Law School, 1805*
- *Government service: South Carolina House of Representatives, 1809–10; U.S. House of Representatives, 1811–16; U.S. secretary of war, 1817–24; Vice President, 1825–32; U.S. Senate, 1833–44, 1845–50; U.S. secretary of state, 1844–45*
- *Died: March 31, 1850, Washington, D.C.*

The most influential and innovative of Southern politicians who articulated states' rights doctrines, John C. Calhoun cast a long shadow over the Civil War. After his death in 1850, Southern fire-eaters molded his ideas into a full-blown ideology of secession.

Born into a prosperous, Scotch-Irish family of slaveholders in the South Carolina upcountry, Calhoun received a superb education in private academies. Following his graduation from Yale College, he attended law school in Connecticut, read law in Charleston, and set up practice near his boyhood home. He quickly tired of the law and entered politics in 1809 as a state representative from his local district of Abbeville. Two years later, he was in Congress as a "War Hawk" demanding sterner measures against British violations of American rights. This nationalist phase continued through his tenure as secretary of war when he supported legislation to strengthen the Union through a national bank, a mildly protective tariff, and improved transportation facilities.

By the mid-1820s, Calhoun was abandoning nationalism for states' rights. He viewed the success of Northern manufacturers in obtaining ever greater tariff protection from Congress as a sign that the sectional balance of power was shifting to the North. He felt that a high tariff was an unequal and unconstitutional tax on the agrarian South in that it benefited only the North and forced Southern planters and farmers to pay more for the manufactured goods that they needed. His greatest fear was that the growing numerical

John C. Calhoun brought an unflinching intensity to his defense of Southern rights.

majority in the North would soon dominate the federal government and convert it into a consolidated system of power that directly threatened the minority interests of the South. Acting on that fear, he formulated a constitutional argument that gave individual states the right to nullify a federal law.

Although President Andrew Jackson defeated the challenge of the South Carolina nullifiers, Calhoun remained a committed Southern sectionalist. After resigning as Vice President and entering the U.S. Senate, he declared in the mid-1830s that his goal was "to turn back the Government to where it commenced its operations in 1789..., to take a fresh start, a new departure, on the State Rights Republican tack." What made this effort to check the power of the national government all the more urgent was the rise of Northern abolitionism in the 1830s, a movement Calhoun was convinced would soon take over the government and emancipate the slaves.

As a fervid defender of Southern rights, Calhoun remained active on the national stage until virtually the day of his death. As secretary of state in the last months of John Tyler's presidency, he defended on proslavery grounds the proposed annexation of Texas and insisted that it was necessary for the security of the South within the Union. When the ensuing Mexican War led, contrary to Calhoun's wishes, to the annexation of a large chunk of former Mexican territory, he bitterly denounced Northern attempts to keep slavery out of that territory. In his last public speech, delivered in March 1850, he warned that the Union was doomed unless the North consented to a constitutional amendment that would allow the South as a section to veto national legislation that threatened its interests. For Calhoun, the sectionally balanced federal republic of 1787 had become "a

great national consolidated democracy" that outnumbered Southerners might soon be forced to leave.

Calhoun always stopped short of calling for secession, but the radical Southern politicians who competed in the 1850s for his mantle of leadership found in his ideas all the constitutional ammunition they needed to make a case for the South to leave the Union. For these politicians, secession was the only way to protect slavery, the most sensitive of all Southern interests.

SEE ALSO

Abolitionism; Fire-eaters; Nullification; States' rights

FURTHER READING

Niven, John. *John C. Calhoun and the Price of Union: A Biography.* Baton Rouge: Louisiana State University Press, 1988.
Peterson, Merrill D. *The Great Triumvirate: Webster, Clay, and Calhoun.* New York: Oxford University Press, 1987.

Cameron, Simon

UNION POLITICIAN

- Born: March 8, 1799, Lancaster County, Pa.
- Political parties: Democrat, Know-Nothing, Republican
- Education: sporadic schooling in lower grades
- Government service: U.S. Senate, 1845–49, 1857–61, 1867–77; U.S. secretary of war, 1861–62; U.S. minister to Russia, 1862
- Died: June 26, 1889, Donegal Springs, Pa.

One of the strongest party bosses of the 19th century, Simon Cameron proved inept as the Union's first secretary of war. When he prematurely raised the politically explosive issue of arming freed slaves in late 1861, he became even more of a liability to the Lincoln administration. Forced out and sent to Russia as U.S. minister, he returned to the United States within a year and resumed his successful political career as head of the Republican party machine in Pennsylvania.

His father's business failures forced the young Cameron to make his own way. After serving as a printer's apprentice, he entered the newspaper trade in his native Pennsylvania. Adept at securing political patronage, he parlayed his skills as a journalist into the role of a party insider in the Jacksonian movement. In the 1830s, he amassed his first fortune as a banker and contractor for canals and railroads. His questionable handling of monetary claims held by the Winnebago Indians gained him the derisive nickname of "The Great Winnebago Chief."

By 1845 Cameron's political influence was great enough to win him a seat in the U.S. Senate as James Buchanan's successor. After his support of protective tariffs cost him the backing of the Buchanan wing of the Pennsylvania Democrats, Cameron rebuilt his political base in the 1850s by switching first to the Know-Nothing party and then to the Republican party. His party machine controlled Pennsylvania's votes at the 1860 Republican convention, and Cameron pledged those votes to Lincoln in return for a cabinet post—secretary of war.

Any head of the war department would have faced a herculean task in bringing order to the mushrooming of Union forces from 16,000 regular troops to 500,000 volunteers within the space of a year. Cameron, however, compounded the problem by placing political considerations above prudent administrative decisions. Secretary of the Navy Gideon B. Welles captured this side of the Pennsylvanian when he noted in his diary: "His party tools he never forgets, so long as they are faithful in his cause and interest, and he freely gives his time, labor, and money to assist them. He is accurate and sharp, but has no enlarged view or grasp of mind; is supple as well as subtle and resorts to means which good men would shun." Some of those "means" consisted of overloading military traffic on the Pennsylvania railroads in which Cameron had a financial interest.

Most of Cameron's problems as secretary of war were ones of omission. He failed to rein in recruiting by individuals and irregular groups. He provided Northern governors with no guidance in the organization of regiments or selection of officers. His handling of government contracts was so slipshod that corruption became a byword for doing business with the federal government.

By the time a House investigatory committee censured Cameron's management as secretary of war in mid-1862, Cameron had long since been posted to Russia. Lincoln eased him out in January 1862 after Cameron, in an apparent bid to win the political support of antislavery Republicans, had attempted to place a long passage in his annual department report advocating the emancipation and arming of Confederate slaves.

Cameron returned to the U.S. Senate in 1867, where he remained until he retired in 1877 after securing assurances from the Pennsylvania legislature that it would elect his son to fill his seat. His patronage machine in Pennsylvania outlived his death in 1889 and survived as a force in Pennsylvania politics until 1921.

SEE ALSO
Stanton, Edwin McMasters

FURTHER READING
Bradley, Erwin Stanley. *Simon Cameron, Lincoln's Secretary of War: A Political Biography.* Philadelphia: University of Pennsylvania Press, 1966.

Cannon

SEE Artillery

Carolinas campaign

SEE Bentonville

Casualties

About 620,000 soldiers lost their lives in the Civil War, a death toll that would be proportionately equivalent to six million in the America of today. The tally of Union dead was 360,000, and the most common estimate for the Confederacy is 260,000. (Many of the records concerning the Confederate numbers were lost or destroyed.) As many Americans died in this war as the combined total in all other American wars through Vietnam.

The casualty lists include deaths from all causes. Disease was the major killer, and actual combat-related deaths were about one-third of the total. The deadly firepower of rifled muskets against massed, frontal assaults accounted for most of the battlefield deaths. Indeed, the bayonet, the weapon of choice in military doctrine for close-order fighting, inflicted fewer than 1 percent of battlefield wounds.

Battle losses mounted with frightening speed when large armies clashed. More Americans, for example, were killed in a day's fighting at Shiloh than had died of battle wounds in the entire Mexican War. The Union army suffered nearly 1,000 casualties per minute in its assault at Cold Harbor. During the war about 60 Union regiments, and an even greater number of Confederate ones, lost more than 50 percent of their men

in a single engagement. As the war dragged on, many soldiers took the precaution of making out their own "identification tags" before they went into battle. On scraps of paper or cloth pinned to their tunics, they jotted down their names, next of kin, and home addresses.

A Confederate soldier stood a one-in-eight chance of being killed in action, odds that were double those for his Union counterpart. Even more dangerous was the position of a Confederate general. Nearly one in five rebel generals was killed or mortally wounded in battle, more than twice the rate of Union generals. Generals were expected to lead their men, not direct them from the rear, and Johnny Rebs (a nickname

The desire of families to bring their dead soldiers home for burial sparked the rise of modern embalming practices.

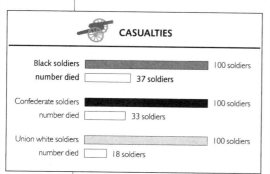

CASUALTIES

Black soldiers	100 soldiers
number died	37 soldiers
Confederate soldiers	100 soldiers
number died	33 soldiers
Union white soldiers	100 soldiers
number died	18 soldiers

The odds of a white Union soldier dying in the war were much lower than those for a black or Confederate soldier.

for Confederate soldiers) especially demanded that their generals should set an example of courage for them.

Garrison duty was the assignment of most Union black soldiers, and correspondingly their odds of dying in battle were sharply lower than those for white soldiers in either army. However, they were far more likely to suffer from disease. As a result, the overall mortality rate of blacks was 40-percent higher than that of white Union soldiers.

Two in five black, one in three Confederate, and nearly one in five Union soldiers died in the war. In the spring of 1861, few observers ever imagined that the war's toll would be so high or that mourning would soon loom large in the nation's culture.

SEE ALSO

Black soldiers; Disease; Rifles; Tactics

FURTHER READING

Faust, Drew Gilpin. *This Republic of Suffering: Death and the American Civil War.* New York: Knopf, 2008.
Livermore, Thomas L. *Numbers and Losses in the Civil War in America, 1861–65.* Boston: Houghton Mifflin, 1900.

Causes of the Civil War

Slavery, as Abraham Lincoln often noted, was the root cause of the Civil War. Tensions over slavery dated back to the contradictory nature of the American Revolution of 1776 that resulted in a republic simultaneously committed to freedom for whites and bondage for blacks. By 1860 those tensions had become so polarized along sectional lines that the North and South lacked any common ground on which to compromise on the issue.

The American Revolution produced both the world's leading model of political democracy and one of its greatest slaveholding powers. Freedom for whites existed side by side with enslavement for African Americans, who amounted to some 20 percent of the population when the United States won its independence from Britain. The U.S. Constitution, crafted at Philadelphia in 1787, also embodied this profound paradox when it recognized the right of a state to regulate slavery within its boundaries.

Slavery became a sectional institution within a generation of the Revolutionary War, as all of the states north of Maryland undertook gradual programs of emancipation. Slavery had always been a minor adjunct to the Northern economy, and revolutionary principles of liberty and equality inspired these emancipation efforts. Thus, by the early 19th century, slavery was almost exclusively confined to the South, home to more than 90 percent of American blacks. And, just as the North was abandoning slavery, the invention of the cotton gin in the 1790s and rising demand in English textile factories for raw cotton were making slaveholding an increasingly attractive economic option for more and more Southern whites. Economic conditions now stimulated the westward expansion of slavery throughout the southeastern United States, and an explosion in cotton production wedded the Southern economy to slavery.

As the North and South grew farther apart in their patterns of social and economic development, the South's share of political power began slipping. From a rough balance of power with the North in 1790, the South held only 42 percent of the seats in the House of Representatives by 1820. This decline became all the more worrisome to Southerners when the North attempted to force emancipation upon Missouri when it applied for admission as a slave state in 1820. For the first time, Southern politicians threatened secession. After bitter debates, the sections agreed on the Missouri Compromise of 1820, the heart of which was the drawing of a line through the Louisiana Purchase Territory that prohibited slavery north of the latitude 36°30' and allowed it to the south.

Soon after the Missouri controversy came the enactment of protective tariffs that Southerners insisted unfairly and unconstitutionally favored Northern manufacturers over Southern planters. This issue precipitated the sectional crisis of 1832–33, in which John C. Cal-houn of South Carolina held that a state could nullify federal legislation that it determined violated its interests.

Quickly overshadowing tariffs as a divisive sectional issue was the abolitionist movement that sprang up in the North in the 1830s. Inspired by Northern evangelical Protestantism and a belief in the right of African Americans to be treated as co-equal citizens, abolitionists denounced slavery as an abominable national sin and urged all Americans to begin the work of emancipation immediately. Skillful at spreading their message, the abolitionists launched a major propaganda campaign in the mid-1830s and deluged Congress with antislavery petitions.

Although initially provoking almost as much opposition in the North as in the South, the abolitionists continued their unrelenting condemnation of slavery. Most important, the agitation of the slavery issue by the abolitionists predisposed many Northerners to see in the admission of the slave republic of Texas in 1845 and the outbreak of the Mexican War in 1846 the work of a

This 1856 Republican cartoon accuses the Democrats of forcing slavery on the free-soil settlers of Kansas. As Northerners increasingly feared that an aggressive South threatened their liberties, sectional hostilities intensified.

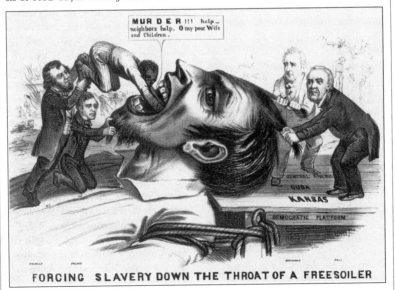

MURDER!!! help— neighbors help. O my poor Wife and Children.

GENERAL PIERCE
CUBA
KANSAS
DEMOCRATIC PLATFORM

FORCING SLAVERY DOWN THE THROAT OF A FREESOILER

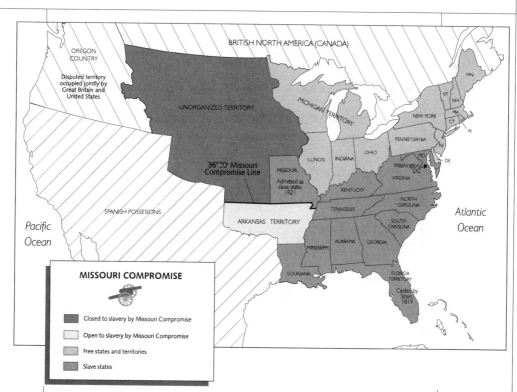

MISSOURI COMPROMISE

- Closed to slavery by Missouri Compromise
- Open to slavery by Missouri Compromise
- Free states and territories
- Slave states

"Slave Power"—a conspiracy of slave-holders intent on spreading slavery throughout new regions in the West and thereby depriving Northern farmers and workers of the opportunity to settle the West for their social and economic advancement. When Northern congress-men rallied behind the Wilmot Proviso in 1846 in an attempt to bar slavery from any territories gained in the Mexi-can War, enraged Southerners formed their own sectional bloc and forced the ultimate defeat of the legislation. The issue of the expansion of slavery had moved to center stage in U.S. politics and would continue to dominate it through the 1850s.

By the middle of the 19th century, the North and South differed far more profoundly than they had at the birth of the Union that brought them together. As a result of industrialization, urban-ization, and immigration, the free states were growing and evolving more rapidly than the overwhelmingly agrar-ian states of the slave South. A new middle class in the North was embrac-ing reforms that many Southerners saw as a threat to the stability of a slave society.

Most ominously for slaveholders, a Northern majority was forming that viewed slavery as a moral wrong that should be set on the road to extinction. Northerners now saw slavery as a bar-baric relic from the past, a barrier to secular and Christian progress that con-tradicted the ideals of the Declaration of Independence and degraded the free-labor aspirations of Northern society. Most of these antislavery Northerners, however, continued to denounce the abolitionist minority as reckless agita-tors who endangered the safety of the

The Missouri Compromise of 1820 drew a line that was critical in main-taining sectional peace for the next 30 years.

*The compari-
son of freedom
versus slavery
detailed at the
bottom of this
map indicates
how by the
1850s Ameri-
cans were
dividing the
Union into two
very distinct,
and perhaps
antagonistic,
regions.*

Union. Pointing out that the Constitution protected slavery in the states, they wanted only to keep slavery out of the territories, not to stamp it out altogether. Still, even this position posed a real threat to Southern values and interests. Arguing that the territories were the common property of all the states and that slavery needed to expand onto fresh land in order to survive, Southerners insisted on what they deemed their constitutional right to carry slaves into the territories. The result was a decade of sectional strife that culminated in secession.

All efforts to reach a settlement on the issue of slavery in the territories—the Compromise of 1850, the Kansas-Nebraska Act, the *Dred Scott* decision—soon broke down and fed the fires of sectional discord. The issue energized the formation of the Republican party in the North around the core principle of blocking the expansion of slavery. The major Protestant denominations had already split into sectional wings in the 1840s over the slavery issue, and only the Democrats now remained as a major national institution that represented the interests of both sections.

Once Democratic unity shattered during the administration of James Buchanan (1857–61) and John Brown's raid rattled sectional nerves, the stage was set for the Republican triumph under Abraham Lincoln in 1860 and the Southern reaction. Rather than accept Republican rule, Southern radicals immediately launched a campaign for secession that climaxed in the outbreak of the Civil War.

SEE ALSO

Abolitionism; Compromise of 1850; *Dred Scott* decision; Kansas-Nebraska Act;

Nullification; Secession; Slavery; Wilmot Proviso

FURTHER READING

Levine, Bruce. *Half Slave and Half Free: The Roots of Civil War.* New York: Hill & Wang, 1992.

Morrison, Michael A. *Slavery and the American West: The Eclipse of Manifest Destiny and the Coming of the Civil War.* Chapel Hill: University of North Carolina Press, 1997.

Pressly, Thomas J. *Americans Interpret Their Civil War,* 2nd ed. New York: Collier Books, 1962.

Reid, Brian Holden. *The Origins of the American Civil War.* New York: Addison Wesley Longman, 1996.

Cavalry

The most glamorous army unit in the Civil War, the cavalry nonetheless played only a minor combat role. Outnumbered by a factor of four or five by infantry troops and often operating in heavily wooded terrain, cavalry rarely could launch a massed attack. When soldiers on horseback did attack, the firepower of rifled musketry backed up by artillery forced them to dismount before they could begin fighting. As a result, both sides used their cavalry primarily for scouting, screening, and raiding.

Confederate cavalry was far superior to its Union counterpart in the first two years of the war. As a result of the high value that Southern culture placed on horsemanship, the Confederate army had the advantage of drawing on cavalrymen who required little formal training. Moreover, unlike the Union army, Confederate cavalry troops had to supply their own mounts. They chose personal favorites and early in the war rode circles around Union cavalry struggling with government-issued stock.

By 1863 the cavalry branches of the two armies were about equal in their performance. On one hand, the Union had gradually built up the numbers and skills of its cavalry and was equipping

President and Mrs. Lincoln attended this review of the cavalry of the Army of the Potomac in April 1863. A newspaper reported that "our Chief Magistrate could not but have felt a thrill of pride as he looked over the sea of bayonets, the blue coats, and the determined faces."

its best units with seven-shot repeating carbines, weapons that significantly increased their firepower. Union commanders, especially in the West, had also learned from the success of Confederate General Nathan B. Forrest that cavalry could be used as highly mobile raiders and as dismounted troopers. On the other hand, the attrition of the war was depleting the Confederacy of its best cavalry officers and horses. The once-magnificent Confederate cavalry suffered an irreversible decline as it ran out of replacements for its killed, wounded, or diseased horses. The usable service of the average cavalry mount was less than six months, and the agricultural and military demand for horses in the South far outstripped the supply. Moreover, simply providing hay and other feed for the cavalry horses placed a huge burden on a Confederate rail system that was already overburdened.

As the war drew to a close, the outnumbered and outgunned Confederate cavalry was increasingly no match for its Union opponents. Under the leadership of such commanders as Generals Philip H. Sheridan and James H. Wilson, the Union was now employing its cavalry with devastating effectiveness as a mobile strike force. The use of cavalry as an offensive spearhead was a revolutionary new tactic that the Confederacy was powerless to combat.

SEE ALSO
Raids; Sheridan, Philip H.; Stuart, James Ewell Brown ("Jeb")

FURTHER READING
Carter, Samuel. *The Last Cavaliers: Confederate and Union Cavalry in the Civil War.* New York: St. Martin's Press, 1979.
Oates, Stephen B. *Confederate Cavalry West of the River.* Austin: University of Texas Press, 1961.
Starr, Stephen Z. *The Union Cavalry in the Civil War.* 3 vols. Baton Rouge: Louisiana State University Press, 1979–85.

Chancellorsville

Often called Robert E. Lee's masterpiece, Chancellorsville was fought May 1–4, 1863, in a densely wooded area 10 miles west of Fredericksburg, Virginia. Outnumbered nearly two to one, Lee waged an almost perfect battle in which he completely confused his Union counterpart, General Joseph Hooker.

Hooker replaced Ambrose E. Burnside as commander of the Army of the Potomac on January 25, 1863. An excellent administrator, he restored the Union army to fighting trim after its morale had sunk in mid-January when Burnside sent troops on a march that bogged down in a sea of mud. Hooker developed a superb plan for catching Lee in a pincer movement designed to crush the Confederates between the two large wings of the Army of the Potomac. Aware that Lee's troop strength was down to 60,000 once two rebel divisions under General James Longstreet were dispatched to North Carolina on a supply-gathering mission, Hooker moved skillfully in late April to take advantage of his numerical superiority.

After first sending Union cavalry under General George Stoneman to disrupt Lee's rail connections with Richmond, Hooker moved half of his army some 20 miles upriver from the Union base at Falmouth. These troops crossed the Rappahannock River at Kelly's Ford and by May 1 were joined by two additional corps in the vicinity of Chancellorsville, a tiny crossroads settlement. Meanwhile, Hooker's other 47,000 troops were attacking Lee's forces at Fredericksburg with the goal of pinning Lee down and diverting his attention from Hooker's grand flanking movement to

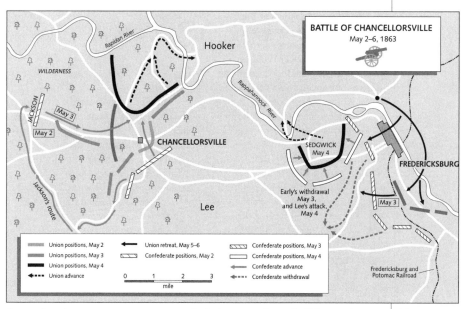

the north and west.

Lee, threatened both in his front and rear, was in a critical position. Hooker was certain that Lee would withdraw toward Richmond to establish a new defensive line. Instead, Lee divided his army and went on the offensive. Leaving behind a small screening force of 10,000 men at Fredericksburg, he redeployed his remaining 45,000 to the west to take on Hooker's much larger army.

Hooker was virtually assured a victory had he only acted forcefully on May 1. However, after tentatively sending his five corps eastward, he drew back when rebel skirmishers contested the advance. Hooker now made the fatal mistake of positioning his army for a defensive battle and surrendering the initiative to Lee. Informed by his cavalry that Hooker's extreme right wing was "up in the air"—that is, in an isolated position with no natural protection—Lee undertook his most daring gamble of the war. He further divided his army by sending 25,000 troops under General Thomas J. "Stonewall"

Jackson on a long, daylight march over forest trails around the front of Hooker's army.

When Jackson's men rushed out of the woods in the late afternoon of May 2 and hit the 11th Corps under General Oliver O. Howard, the Union right caved in. As later described by John L. Collins of the 8th Pennsylvania Cavalry, "the seething, surging sea of humanity broke over the feeble barrier [of Union defenders], and General Howard and his officers were carried away by main force with the tide." Jackson pushed the attack for the next two hours. Upon returning from a reconnaissance mission, he was accidentally shot by Confederate pickets, a wound that would cost him his life on May 10.

After Lee sprang his surprise assault on the Union right, Hooker could think only of saving his army. He positioned his corps into a defensive shell and thereby freed up Lee to send reinforcements eastward to check the advance of the Union force under General John Sedgwick that had overrun

Thomas "Stonewall" Jackson's daring march at Chancellorsville turned what appeared to be a certain defeat for General Robert E. Lee's outnumbered Confederate army into a surprising victory.

the Confederate defenders at Fredericksburg. On May 4, a now-outnumbered Sedgwick withdrew across the Rappahannock. Hooker followed on May 5 when he abandoned his strong fortifications and ordered a full retreat for the Army of the Potomac.

As Hooker later admitted, he simply lost his nerve at Chancellorsville. Darius N. Couch, one of his generals, explained what had happened: "Hooker expected Lee to fall back without risking battle. Finding himself mistaken, he assumed the defensive, and was outgeneraled and became demoralized by the superior tactical boldness of the enemy." Still, the 17,000 Union casualties were proportionately fewer than the 13,000 suffered by the Confederates (amounting to about 20 percent of Lee's troop strength). And the loss of Jackson, Lee's boldest corps commander, was irreplaceable for the Confederacy.

SEE ALSO

Burnside, Ambrose E.; Hooker, Joseph; Jackson, Thomas J.; Lee, Robert E.; Longstreet, James.

FURTHER READING

Bigelow, John. *The Campaign of Chancellorsville: A Strategic and Tactical Study.* New Haven, Conn.: Yale University Press, 1910.
Furgurson, Ernest B. *Chancellorsville, 1863: The Souls of the Brave.* New York: Knopf, 1992.
Sears, Stephen W. *Chancellorsville.* Boston: Houghton Mifflin, 1996.

Chase, Salmon P.

UNION POLITICIAN

- *Born: January 13, 1808, Cornish, N.H.*
- *Political parties: Whig, Liberty, Free-Soil, Free-Soil Democrat, Republican*
- *Education: Dartmouth College, A.B., 1826*
- *Government service: U.S. Senate, 1849–55, 1861; governor of Ohio, 1855–59; U.S. secretary of the*
treasury, 1861–64; chief justice of the United States, 1864–73
- *Died: May 7, 1873, New York, N.Y.*

The most committed antislavery member of President Abraham Lincoln's cabinet, Salmon P. Chase pushed for emancipation, the arming of freed slaves, and equal rights for African Americans. "The American blacks must be called into this conflict," he wrote in April 1863, "not as cattle, not now, even as contrabands, but as men."

Chase was only nine when his father died, and his mother, perhaps now burdened by financial problems, sent him to Ohio to be raised by an uncle. After graduating from Dartmouth and gaining admittance to the bar in 1829, he moved to Cincinnati and acquired a national reputation for defending fugitive slaves who had escaped across the Ohio River. For Chase, slavery was "a curse, a reproach, a blight, an evil, a wrong, a sin," and opposition to the institution shaped and defined his political career. As an antislavery politician, he popularized the idea in the North that the Constitution embodied a principle of universal freedom and recognized slavery only as a local institution under the control of individual states.

By 1860 Chase was the acknowledged leader of the antislavery wing of the Republican party and a candidate for the party's Presidential nomination. But his politics were too radical, and he had to settle for the post of secretary of the Treasury. Despite his lack of financial experience, he was bold and able as the nation's chief fiscal officer. Most of the war's immense cost was met by borrowing, and at Chase's insistence, the federal bonds needed to pay for the war were sold primarily by popular subscription and not through private bankers. Sales of the most successful bond issue totaled $400 million, and Chase proudly reported in December 1863, "The history of the world may be searched in vain for a parallel case of popular financial support to a national government."

Chase was instrumental in establishing a national banking system to replace the hodgepodge of state banks that had proved unable to meet the Treasury's fiscal needs. The chief virtue of the new system was its provision for a uniform national currency. With great reluctance, Chase also supported the issuing of greenbacks, paper money accepted as legal tender that was backed only by the government's promise to pay. Although he feared that the greenbacks would lead to runaway inflation, he recognized that they were necessary as a war measure that would enable the Treasury to pay all its bills. A series of new internal taxes, including the first federal income tax, rounded out his fiscal program.

Chase's political ambitions continued to center on gaining the Presidency, and in early 1864 he unsuccessfully challenged Lincoln for the Republican Presidential nomination. In the midst of a dispute over Treasury patronage, Lincoln accepted Chase's resignation in June 1864. With his reelection safely out of the way, Lincoln then placated his party's radical wing by appointing Chase as chief justice of the United States in December 1864.

Before his death from a paralytic stroke, Chase reorganized the federal courts in the postwar South and presided over the impeachment trial of President Andrew Johnson. In Supreme Court decisions regarding Reconstruction policy, he carefully avoided challenging the political prerogatives of the congressional Republicans.

SEE ALSO
Greenbacks; Legal Tender Act of 1862; National Banking Act of 1863; Taxation

FURTHER READING
Blue, Frederick J. *Salmon P. Chase: A Life in Politics*. Kent, Ohio: Kent State University Press, 1987.
Niven, John. *Salmon P. Chase: A Biography*. New York: Oxford University Press, 1995.

Chattanooga campaign

The campaign that resulted in permanent Union control of Chattanooga had its origins in the federal defeat at Chickamauga in late September 1863. After the Union army fled to Chattanooga, Braxton Bragg, the victorious Confederate commander at Chickamauga, moved his army to the high ground east and south of the city and tried to starve out the federals by cutting their supply lines. But Bragg mismanaged both the siege and the disposition of his troops. A reinforced Union army took advantage of these errors, and in the battles of Lookout Mountain and Missionary Ridge on November 24–25, 1863, it routed Bragg's forces and solidified its control of the gateway city to the Confederate heartland in Georgia.

Chattanooga, the hub of three railroads that crisscrossed the Confederacy, was a vital strategic center that the Union was determined to hold at all costs. Once William S. Rosecrans, the defeated federal commander at Chickamauga, had allowed his army to be bottled up in Chattanooga, the Union high command rushed reinforcements to him. From the Army of the Potomac

Built by Union army engineers in late 1863, this railroad bridge at Whiteside, Tennessee, was a critical link that funneled supplies into Chattanooga, the base for the federal move into Georgia. The tents in the foreground are the camp for the guard detachment of Union troops.

came 20,000 troops under General Joseph Hooker, and an additional 17,000 men arrived from Memphis and Vicksburg. Of equal significance, President Abraham Lincoln, who likened Rosecrans's inactivity to the dazed response of "a duck hit on the head," reorganized the Union command structure in the West. After Lincoln elevated Ulysses S. Grant to the overall command of the western armies, Grant went to Chattanooga and replaced Rosecrans with General George H. Thomas as the head of the Army of the Cumberland.

While the Union was moving to regain the momentum in Chattanooga, Bragg frittered away his initial advantage. He was caught by surprise on October 27 when an amphibious Union attack overran a small Confederate force at Brown's Ferry, downriver from Chattanooga. Once a pontoon bridge was erected across the Tennessee River at this point, "the cracker line," as the soldiers soon called it, funneled ample supplies to the federal forces. Aware now that he had no immediate hope of capturing Chattanooga, Bragg sent

15,000 troops under General James Longstreet on an expedition to retake Knoxville in east Tennessee. This move reduced Bragg's force to 40,000 troops and gave the Union army, reinforced by mid-November to 70,000 men, the opportunity to assume the offensive.

Grant launched his offensive in late November. Four divisions under General William T. Sherman were to make the main attack against the rebel right at the northern end of Missionary Ridge. In support of Sherman, secondary attacks were ordered against the Confederate left on Lookout Mountain and the center along Missionary Ridge. In the Battle of Lookout Mountain on November 24, Hooker's federals rolled up the rebel position, and the troops led by Thomas seized Orchard Knob, a low ridge that afforded a staging area for further Union assaults against the Confederate center. But Sherman's attack ran into stiff resistance and made little headway.

By midafternoon on November 25, Sherman's offensive was verging on failure. Concerned that the Confederates might shift troops from their center to launch a counterattack against Sherman, Grant ordered Thomas to take the first line of rebel defenders at the base of Missionary Ridge. The result was the most surprisingly successful attack of the entire war. Contrary to their orders, Thomas's men did not stop at the foot of the ridge but continued to charge up the ridge itself. "There was a halt of but a few minutes, to take breath and to re-form lines," recalled General Joseph S. Fullerton, of the Army of the Cumberland; "then, with a sudden impulse, and without orders, all started up the ridge. Officers, catching their spirit, first followed, then led."

The charging federals made it all the way to the top of Missionary Ridge. Bragg's engineers had blundered badly when they placed the Confederate lines at the topographical (or highest) crest of the ridge and not at the military crest, the highest point that allowed an unobstructed line of fire. As a result, Confederate fire was ineffective, and the federals gained confidence as they scrambled up the slope and veered off into ravines to outflank pockets of Confederate resistance. Panic swept through the rebel ranks, and Bragg's entire army began a retreat to the southeast.

In addition to his 6,700 casualties at Chattanooga, Bragg had completely lost the confidence of his troops. He was soon relieved of command. The Union forces lost 5,800 men in the campaign that avenged their defeat at Chickamauga and set the stage for their invasion of Georgia.

SEE ALSO

Bragg, Braxton; Chickamauga; Grant, Ulysses S.; Hooker, Joseph; Longstreet, James; Rosecrans, William S.; Sherman, William T.; Thomas, George H.

FURTHER READING

Cozzens, Peter. *The Shipwreck of Their Hopes: The Battles for Chattanooga.* Urbana: University of Illinois Press, 1994.

McDonough, James Lee. *Chattanooga—A Death Grip on the Confederacy.* Knoxville: University of Tennessee Press, 1984.

Chesnut, Mary
CONFEDERATE AUTHOR

- *Born: March 31, 1823, Mount Pleasant, near Camden, S.C.*
- *Education: tutored at home; Madame Talvande's French School for Young Ladies*
- *Died: November 22, 1886, Camden, S.C.*

The author of the most widely acclaimed Confederate diary, Mary Chesnut was a member of the South Carolina aristocracy. She spent much of the war in Richmond among the Southern political and social elite, and her wartime journal remains unequaled for the emotional immediacy that it imparts to the Confederate war effort.

Born into a rich family, Chesnut married into even greater wealth. Raised within a family that had numerous connections to other planter dynasties, she benefited from an excellent private education that trained her for the life of a cultivated Southern belle. In 1840, she married James Chesnut, a lawyer-planter who had inherited a plantation that encompassed five square miles near Camden, South Carolina. While her husband served in the U.S. Senate in the late 1850s, she became friends with Jefferson and Varina Davis, a friendship that deepened during the Civil War.

Chesnut began writing her diary early in the war, and she expanded her wartime jottings into a substantially longer account that she was still working on at the time of her death in the 1880s. The final version presented a vast panorama of characters drawn from all walks of Southern life, although the emphasis remained on the high society of Richmond and South Carolina that Chesnut knew so well.

A committed secessionist, Chesnut nonetheless viewed the possibility of a sectional war with a sense of foreboding. Part of that dread derived from her inability to fathom the thoughts or intentions of her slaves. "Not by one word or look can we detect any change in the demeanor of these negro servants [slaves]," she noted in April 1861, when the harbor guns of Charleston were blasting away at Fort Sumter. "Are they stolidly stupid or wiser than we are, silent and strong, biding their time?" she asked. Adding to these concerns over the slaves' reaction to the war was her guilt over what she called the "*monstrous* system" of slavery, a moral indictment that she kept confined to her diary and never allowed to emerge as a challenge to the institution itself.

Chesnut also doubted from the very beginning whether the South's male leaders were up to the task of building and defending a nation. "One of the first things which depressed me," she recalled of her reaction to South Carolina's secession, "was the kind of men put in office at this crisis, invariably some sleeping deadhead long forgotten or passed over. Young and active spirits ignored, places for worn-out politicians seemed the rule—when our only hope is to use *all* the talents God has given us." But many of those talents, as she acidly relates, were squandered by a male ruling class consumed by its vanities and jealousies. Although she strongly defended Jefferson Davis's leadership, she concluded that clashing male egos doomed his efforts. By so doing, she made clear her resentments against male domination—"There is no slave, after all," she wrote, "like a wife."

At war's end, Chesnut and her husband were refugees lacking enough hard currency even to pay passage to a ferryman as they fled across the Southern landscape. The war wiped out James Chesnut's vast fortune, and Mary's marketing of butter and eggs was their main source of income in the postwar period. Her diary and fictional pieces remained unpublished during her lifetime. She died unaware that she had written one of the masterpieces of Civil War literature.

SEE ALSO
Literature

FURTHER READING
De Credico, Mary A. *Mary Boykin Chesnut: A Confederate Woman's Life.* Madison, Wis.: Madison House, 1996.
Woodward, C. Vann, ed. *Mary Chesnut's Civil War.* New Haven, Conn.: Yale University Press, 1981.

Chickamauga

Fought on September 19–20, 1863, near Chickamauga Creek in the mountainous terrain of north Georgia, Chickamauga was the bloodiest two-day battle of the war. Casualties totaled more than 34,000 men in a battle that saw the Confederacy squander a splendid opportunity to smash the Union Army of the Cumberland and achieve a decisive strategic victory in the West.

The troop movements that culminated at Chickamauga began in late June 1863. Ever since the battle of Murfreesboro at the start of the year, the Army of the Cumberland under General William S. Rosecrans and the Confederate Army of Tennessee under General Braxton Bragg had been frozen in position in the middle of Tennessee.

The military lines became fluid when Rosecrans initiated a movement on June 23 that shifted his army to the south and west around Bragg's right flank. Known as the Tullahoma Campaign, Rosecrans's maneuvers threatened to cut off Bragg's line of communications and thereby forced the Confederates to retreat back to Chattanooga. Then, after a pause of six weeks, Rosecrans succeeded also in maneuvering Bragg out of Chattanooga.

Having lost Chattanooga on September 9, Bragg pulled his army back to La Fayette, Georgia, some 25 miles to the south. The retreat was an orderly one, and the alarmed Confederate high command began funneling reinforcements to Bragg, the largest of which were two divisions under General James Longstreet sent from the Army of Northern Virginia. While Bragg's army was regrouping and growing, Rosecrans mistakenly assumed that the Confederates were in a headlong retreat. An overconfident Rosecrans divided his army and allowed its three corps to become widely separated along a 40-mile front as it passed through gaps in the Georgia mountains. Bragg was now in a position to destroy Rosecrans's army piecemeal.

First on September 11, and again on September 13, Bragg issued orders to attack isolated units of the Union army. But the orders were vague, and Bragg's generals had grown tired of his tendency to scapegoat subordinates for his own misjudgments in command. On both occasions, Bragg's corps commanders hesitated and thus gave the federals time to slip away and reconcentrate.

Despite these missed opportunities, Bragg almost dealt Rosecrans's army a devastating blow at Chickamauga a week later. Reinforced now to nearly 70,000 men against the Union's 58,000, Bragg attacked on September 19 with

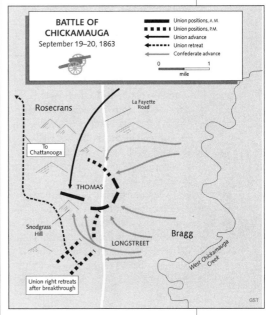

superior numbers—a rare advantage for a Confederate general. Throughout the day, Bragg pressed against the federal left or northern flank in an effort to seize the La Fayette Road and block any Union retreat to Chattanooga. The fighting was heavy but indecisive.

When Bragg resumed the attack on the following morning, Rosecrans made a nearly fatal mistake. He detached a brigade to shore up his threatened position on the left—but in so doing inadvertently opened a large gap on the right side of the Union army. Before that gap could be filled, Longstreet sent 20,000 Confederates pouring through it. "The deep Confederate lines suddenly appeared," recalled Union General Gates P. Thruston. "The woods in our front seemed alive. On they came like an angry flood...; resistance only increased the multitude."

Longstreet's shattering advance spread panic through the Union right, and the entire position crumbled. Upon hearing the news, Rosecrans concluded

Only the defensive stand anchored by General George H. Thomas's troops saved the Union army from a disastrous defeat at Chickamauga.

that all was lost. Soon, one-third of the Union army, including Rosecrans, was fleeing back to Chattanooga. All that saved the Union army from a disastrous rout was Bragg's refusal to rush reinforcements to Longstreet and the determined resistance put up by General George H. Thomas, the corps commander on the Union left flank. Thomas rallied his men around Snodgrass Hill, staved off repeated rebel attacks, and bought the Union army the time it needed to retreat safely to Chattanooga.

The Confederates had clearly won at Chickamauga, but their failure to destroy Rosecrans's army made their victory an empty one. "Whatever blunders each of us in authority committed before the battles of the 19th and 20th, and during their progress," later wrote General Daniel H. Hill, one of Bragg's commanders at Chickamauga, "the great blunder of all was that of not pursuing the enemy on the 21st." Bragg had lost 18,000 men, or 30 percent of his army, and yet had gained little after such huge casualties.

SEE ALSO
Bragg, Braxton; Longstreet, James; Rosecrans, William S.; Thomas, George H.

FURTHER READING
Cozzens, Peter. *This Terrible Sound: The Battle of Chickamauga.* Urbana: University of Illinois Press, 1992.
Tucker, Glen. *Chickamauga: Bloody Battle in the West.* Indianapolis, Ind.: Bobbs-Merrill, 1962.

Churches

Speaking of secession in the spring of 1860, Thomas R. R. Cobb of Georgia asserted, "This revolution has been accomplished mainly by the Churches."

In turn, Northern churches had been instrumental in the opposition of most Northerners to this "revolution." In the North, as well as the South, the churches gave a religious meaning to the growing sense of distinctive sectional identities that coalesced into the Union and Confederate causes.

During the secession crisis, thousands of evangelical ministers enthusiastically supported the cause of their respective sections. In a typical exhortation in the North, the Reverend A. L. Stone of Boston called upon citizens to "strike for Law and Union, for country and God's great ordinance of Government." The Reverend James H. Thornwell of South Carolina urged Southerners to secede even though "our path to victory may be through a baptism of fire." Benjamin M. Palmer, a Presbyterian minister in New Orleans, became the most noted religious orator for secession when 50,000 pamphlets broadcast his Thanksgiving Day sermon of November 29, 1860. "If [the South] has the grace given her to know her hour," Palmer proclaimed, "she will save herself, the country, and the world."

Once the war began, the churches were in the forefront of support for the Union or the Confederacy. They bolstered civilian morale by converting the war into a holy cause. They distributed Bibles and religious tracts to the soldiers, provided military chaplains, and served as centers of voluntary action. Particularly in the Confederacy, the churches were a major resource for the war effort. They furnished bells to be melted down for the armaments industry, carpets to be cut into cloth, and pew cushions to be used as hospital beds. Ministers eagerly turned piety to patriotic purposes by responding to the calls of President Jefferson Davis to lead days of fasting and prayer.

As the tide of war turned in the

Union's favor, Northern Protestants were ever more convinced that God had willed a Union victory for the regeneration of the American people and the advent of His kingdom on earth. Methodist Bishop Gilbert Haven prophesied in 1864 that God had prepared the United States to "renew and unite the world." Triumphant in Christ, a united United States would make "wars cease to the end of the earth, the millennial glory rest upon the world-republic and universal liberty, equality, and brotherhood bring universal peace."

Conversely, Confederate military reverses resulted in Southerners doubting whether God was on their side. In searching for a theological reason for God's disfavor, many religious leaders concluded that perhaps slavery and the Confederacy were, after all, not compatible. This soul-searching generally did not lead to a renunciation of slavery as a sin, but rather a cataloguing of sins committed by slaveholders who had failed in their religious duties of Christian stewardship. Nonetheless, religious doubts now plagued the war effort and contributed to Confederate defeat.

SEE ALSO
Religion

FURTHER READING
Goen, C.C. *Broken Churches, Broken Nation: Denominational Schisms and the Coming of the American Civil War.* Macon, Ga.: Mercer University Press, 1985.
Moorhead, James H. *American Apocalypse: Yankee Protestants and the Civil War.* New Haven: Yale University Press, 1978.
Noll, Mark A. *The Civil War as a Theological Crisis.* Chapel Hill: University of North Carolina Press, 2006.
Silver, James W. *Confederate Morale and Church Propaganda.* New York: W. W. Norton, 1967.

Civil liberties

SEE Habeas corpus, suspension of

Civil Rights Act of 1866

Sponsored by Republican Senator Lyman Trumbull of Illinois, the Civil Rights Bill of 1866 marked the first attempt to define under law the rights of American citizenship. In April 1866, Congress overrode President Andrew Johnson's veto of the bill and enacted it into law, the first time that a significant piece of legislation had ever survived a Presidential veto.

The broad purpose of the bill was to give statutory meaning to the freedom conferred on the slaves in the 13th Amendment. More specifically, the bill was a response to the *Dred Scott* Supreme Court decision of 1857, which had ruled that blacks were not American citizens, and the Southern Black Codes of 1865, which denied legal

A stubborn Andrew Johnson drags the Freedman's Bureau and civil rights legislation into the thicket of his Presidential vetoes in this 1866 illustration from a leading Northern newspaper.

THE CRUEL UNCLE AND THE VETOED BABES IN THE WOOD.

equality to the recently freed slaves. In addition, the bill also struck down several discriminatory laws in the North.

The bill defined all persons born or naturalized in the United States (except Native Americans) as citizens and nationalized the principle of equality before the law by extending its protection to all citizens. Cases in which any citizen was deprived of the full enjoyment of rights of person and property on account of race were to be transferred from state to federal courts. This represented an unprecedented extension of federal power into legal areas that had always been the exclusive concern of individual states. Still, the bill fell short of revolutionizing federal-state relations, for federal intervention would be triggered only by discriminatory state legislation. As Trumbull explained, the bill "will have no operation in any state where the laws are equal." Nor did the bill call for black suffrage or any form of social integration.

A unified Republican Party passed the bill on March 13, 1866, only to be shocked two weeks later when Johnson vetoed it. For Johnson, the bill was an unconstitutional invasion of states' rights and a "stride towards centralization, and the concentration of all legislative powers in the national Government." On the other hand, nearly all Republicans agreed with the *Springfield* (Illinois) *Republican* when it said of the party's obligation to offer legal protection to African Americans: "The party is nothing, if it does not do this—the nation is dishonored if [Johnson] hesitates in this." After the Civil Rights Bill became law, the Republicans incorporated a strengthened version of it into the 14th Amendment.

SEE ALSO

Congressional Reconstruction; 14th Amendment; 13th Amendment

FURTHER READING

Belz, Herman. *A New Birth of Freedom: The Republican Party and Freedmen's Rights, 1861–1866.* Westport, Conn.: Greenwood Press, 1976.

Cleburne, Patrick R.

CONFEDERATE GENERAL

- *Born: March 17, 1828, County Cork, Ireland*
- *Education: studied apothecary in Ireland; read law in Helena, Ark., 1850–56*
- *Military service: Confederate army: captain, 1st Arkansas State Troops, 1861; colonel, 15th Arkansas Volunteers; brigadier general, 1862; major-general, 1862–64*
- *Died: November 30, 1864, Franklin, Tenn.*

Nicknamed the "Stonewall Jackson of the West" for his gallantry and aggressiveness, Patrick R. Cleburne was one of only two foreign-born officers to attain the rank of major-general in the Confederate army. After compiling a superb combat record in the western theater, he stirred up controversy in January 1864, when he prepared a circular letter to the Confederate Congress calling for the eventual emancipation of all slaves who remained loyal to the Confederacy and the arming of some of those slaves into combat units.

Cleburne studied for a druggist's degree in his native Ireland but failed the language requirement for licensing. He then enlisted in the British 41st Regiment on Foot and served for three years before purchasing his discharge and emigrating to the United States in 1849. He landed in New Orleans and soon made his way to Helena, Arkansas, where he prospered as a druggist and lawyer. Identifying strongly with his adopted South, he organized a volunteer company, the Yell Rifles, in the spring of 1861 and participated in the capture of the federal arsenal in Little Rock when Arkansas seceded.

Transferred to Kentucky in the fall of 1861, Cleburne revealed a flair for leadership that earned him a promotion to brigadier general in March 1862. His first combat action was at Shiloh, where he distinguished himself on both days of the battle by rallying his troops to throw back federal counterattacks. Wounded at the battle of Richmond during General Braxton Bragg's Kentucky Campaign, he recovered in time to take part in the battle of Perryville, where he was wounded a second time.

In 1863 Cleburne emerged as one of the best division commanders in the Army of Tennessee. His troops idolized him for the bravery that he showed in leading charges at Murfreesboro and Chickamauga. He successfully covered the Confederate retreat from Chattanooga in November 1863, when his stand at Ringgold Gap saved the army's artillery and wagon train.

In January 1864, Cleburne became the first Confederate officer to go on record publicly with a call for arming and freeing the slaves. His proposal, he insisted, offered the Confederacy its only hope of replenishing its exhausted armies and thereby winning its political independence. "As between the loss of independence and the loss of slavery, we assume that every patriot will freely give up the latter—give up the negro slave rather than be a slave himself," he proclaimed. But his call for emancipation and black regiments was too heretical for most Southern whites, and the Confederate Congress did not seriously consider it until early 1865 when the Confederacy was on the verge of utter collapse.

Although subjected to heavy criticism for his stand on ending slavery, Cleburne continued to perform brilliantly in the Army of Tennessee until his death in the battle of Franklin in November 1864. After telling a subordinate at Franklin, "If we are to die, let us die like men," he had two horses shot out from under him before he charged ahead on foot. He died when a Union bullet pierced his heart. He was one of six Confederate generals killed in that battle.

SEE ALSO
Black soldiers; Confederate emancipation

FURTHER READING
Symonds, Craig L. *Stonewall of the West: Patrick Cleburne and the Civil War.* Lawrence: University Press of Kansas, 1997.

Cold Harbor

SEE Grant's Virginia campaign

Colonization

Until well into the Civil War, the colonization abroad of African Americans struck many whites as the most practical solution for the end of slavery and America's white-defined racial "problem." Organized white support for colonization dated back to the founding of the American Colonization Society in 1816 and was not formally abandoned until the society disbanded in 1892.

The basic premise behind colonization was the belief that white prejudice would never permit blacks to live as equals in American society. From the establishment of the United States in 1787, most whites feared that a general emancipation of the slaves would lead either to a race war or a debasement of the white race through intermarriage with blacks. For the white reformers who founded the American Colonization Society, the only way to end slavery and maintain racial peace was through a program of gradual emancipation accompanied by the removal of blacks from the United States.

Some African Americans always supported colonization as a means of escaping American racism and the persecution of the black race. In 1815, Paul Cuffe, a black Quaker shipowner from Massachusetts, sponsored the first settlement of American blacks in Africa when he sailed with 38 colonists to Sierra Leone. A clear majority of free African Americans, however, rejected the whole notion of colonization, especially once it became identified with the white elite who directed the American Colonization Society. These blacks identified themselves as Americans who had every right to enjoy the blessings of liberty. In protest meetings held in their churches, they denounced the central assumption of the white colonizers that blacks were unfit to live as free citizens in the United States.

Before the outbreak of the Civil War, the efforts of the American Colonization Society succeeded in settling no more than 10,000 blacks in Liberia, its colony in West Africa that declared its political independence in 1847. These numbers were pitifully small compared to the ballooning of America's slave population to more than 4 million by 1860. Still, the attraction of colonization persisted.

Early in the Civil War, President Abraham Lincoln, who had long supported colonization, pushed for the expatriation of blacks as part of his original program of gradual, compensated emancipation. In response to Lincoln's prompting, Congress appropriated funds for colonization in April 1862, when it emancipated the slaves in Washington, D.C. It provided an additional $500,000 in colonization funding in July 1862, when it freed slaves in the hands of Union military forces.

In an effort to make emancipation palatable to whites in the Border South and to relieve Northern whites' fears of a mass exodus of former slaves out of the South into the North, Lincoln pushed throughout 1862 and 1863 for the voluntary removal of blacks to government-sponsored colonies in Central America and the Caribbean. Little came of these efforts. Most blacks viewed Lincoln's plan as a blatant concession to white prejudice and a contrived attempt to avoid establishing a just, national policy for blacks. The colonies, set up in Panama and on an island off the coast of Haiti, soon collapsed in a morass of fraud and disease.

To Lincoln's credit, he stopped promoting the colonization of African Americans when the failure of that policy became obvious. In its place, he began to accept the need for a broader, more egalitarian vision of the United States in which the federal government would take the first necessary steps toward racial justice. He was the first President to welcome a delegation of black leaders to the White House and the first to recommend some form of black suffrage. Most important, the Union war effort that he successfully led resulted in black emancipation, citizenship, and voting rights. Those gains at least offered the hope that future talk of black colonization would be out of the question.

Joseph Jenkins Roberts, a free black born in Virginia, emigrated to Liberia in 1829 under the auspices of the American Colonization Society. He established a successful export business and, in 1847, was elected as Liberia's first president.

SEE ALSO

Abolitionism; Emancipation

FURTHER READING

Burin, Eric. *Slavery and the Peculiar Solution: A History of the American Colonization Society.* Gainesville: University Press of Florida, 2005.

Staudenraus, P. J. *The African Colonization Movement, 1816–1865.* New York: Columbia University Press, 1961.

Vorenberg, Michael. "Abraham Lincoln and the Politics of Black Colonization." *Journal of the Abraham Lincoln Association* 14, No. 2 (Summer 1993): 23–45.

Command structure

Both the Union and the Confederate armies began the Civil War with a rudimentary command structure that differed little from the organizational system that had evolved in the small prewar U.S. Army. With the brief exception of the Mexican War, military units had been no larger than a regiment (about 1,000 men), and the staff system in place at the outbreak of the Civil War was adequate only for a small-unit army. No military staff existed to advise the Union or Confederate President as commander in chief. Winfield Scott was the general in chief of Union armies, but his office had no standing in law, and he had neither a staff to direct nor an army to command.

Through a process of improvisation that President Abraham Lincoln shrewdly encouraged, the Union created an approximation of a modern system of command by 1864. The War Board, established by Secretary of War Edwin M. Stanton in March 1862, functioned like a general staff by deliberating on strategy and coordinating logistical details. In reviving the rank of lieutenant general for Ulysses S. Grant in February 1864, Congress intended Grant to act as general in chief and authorized President Lincoln to appoint Grant as commander of all U.S. armies. At the same time, a new command office, the chief of staff, was established. General Henry W. Halleck, the first chief of staff, served as military advisor to the President and channeled information between Lincoln and Grant. The result was an efficient chain of command that brought greater unity and direction to the overall war effort.

The Confederate command structure initially was almost identical to the Union's. Probably as a result of his feuding while secretary of war (1853–57) with General in Chief Winfield Scott, President Jefferson Davis dispensed with the post altogether. He relied at first for strategic advice upon a strengthened adjutant general and his secretaries of war. Then he instituted a major reform in March 1862 by placing General Robert E. Lee in charge of "the conduct of military operations in the armies of the Confederacy." Until he assumed field command of the Army of Northern Virginia in June 1862, Lee functioned as a chief of staff and provided Davis with valuable advice. Although Davis appointed the unpopular Braxton Bragg to Lee's former post in February 1864, he lacked a chief of staff for most of the war and never did create a formal structure at his Richmond headquarters to assist him in planning military operations and formulating strategy. A desperate Confederate Congress elevated Lee to the command of all rebel armies in February 1865, but by then it was far too late to reverse Confederate military fortunes.

SEE ALSO

Davis, Jefferson; Halleck, Henry W.; Lee, Robert E.; Lincoln, Abraham

FURTHER READING

Hattaway, Herman, and Archer Jones. *How the North Won: A Military History of the Civil War.* Urbana: University of Illinois Press, 1983.

Vandiver, Frank E. *Rebel Brass: The Confederate Command System.* Baton Rouge: Louisiana State University Press, 1956.

Committee on the Conduct of the War

Organized in December 1861 and continued through the remainder of the war, the Committee on the Conduct of the War was a congressional investigative body dominated by radical Republicans. It kept up constant pressure for the vigorous prosecution of a Northern war effort aimed at overthrowing slavery.

The committee's origins lay in the impatience of antislavery Republicans with the slow pace of Union armies in the first year of the war. The stinging defeat of a Union reconnaissance force at Ball's Bluff, Virginia, on October 21, 1861, spurred congressional Republicans when they met in December to appoint a joint committee to investigate "the conduct of the present war." Proslavery Democratic generals were always a favorite target of the committee, and in its first order of business it made Democratic General Charles P. Stone into the scapegoat for the defeat at Ball's Bluff.

Under the hard-driving leadership of its chairman, Republican Senator Benjamin F. Wade of Ohio, the committee was undoubtedly highly partisan and often vindictive, and it ruined the military careers of several conservative Democratic generals. On balance, however, the committee was probably an asset to the Union war effort. Apart from prying into the politics of Union generals, it also investigated the war contracts of army suppliers, medical conditions for wounded Union soldiers, and licenses for trading behind enemy lines. However bullying the tactics were, its hearings exposed much of the corruption that had characterized the Union's early military expenditures and improved the efficiency of the system of military procurement. Most important, the committee prodded and pushed Union commanders to take whatever steps were necessary to win the war. It was in the vanguard for converting the war into one of general emancipation and then into one that the Union would wage using black soldiers.

SEE ALSO
Radicals

FURTHER READING

Tap, Bruce. *Over Lincoln's Shoulder: The Committee on the Conduct of the War.* Lawrence: University Press of Kansas, 1998.

Compromise of 1850

Designed primarily to settle the question of the status of slavery in the territories acquired in the Mexican War, the Compromise of 1850 was only temporarily successful in defusing sectional tensions. Salmon P. Chase of Ohio best captured the tentative nature of the compromise when he noted, "The question of slavery in the territories has been avoided. It has not been settled."

By the time Congress convened in December 1849, the need to reach a political settlement for the territories ceded by Mexico in 1848 had become critical. California, where gold had recently been discovered, was applying

for statehood with a constitution that prohibited slavery. Texas was laying claim to the eastern half of New Mexico and was threatening a military invasion if its claim was rejected. In the rest of the Mexican cession, Mormon settlers in Utah and a free-soil group in New Mexico were organizing governments with wildly overlapping boundaries. Not only did governments have to be established or recognized, but the status of slavery in the territories had to be determined as well. Abolitionist demands to end slave-trading operations in Washington, D.C., and Southern calls for a more stringent fugitive slave law further deepened the sectional division between antislavery Northerners and proslavery Southerners.

Henry Clay, the leader of the Whigs, framed all the sectional grievances into a single omnibus bill that repeatedly failed to win majority support. Stephen A. Douglas, an Illinois Democrat, then took over the measure and divided it into six separate bills. By building a coalition behind each bill, one drawn largely from Northern Democrats and Southern Whigs, he was able to secure passage of what became known collectively as the Compromise of 1850. Its provisions admitted California as a free state; organized the territories of New Mexico and Utah with no explicit reference to slavery; compensated Texas with a partial federal assumption of its public debt in return for its acceptance of a boundary resolution that favored New Mexico; abolished the slave trade in the District of Columbia; and enacted stronger fugitive slave legislation.

Antislavery Northerners and Southerners committed to the expansion of slavery denounced the Compromise of 1850 as a sellout to the other side. And, for all the desperate hopes of moderates that a final settlement had been reached, the issue of slavery in the territories rekindled sectional animosities when Congress organized the Kansas and Nebraska territories in 1854.

SEE ALSO
Fugitive Slave Act of 1850; Kansas-Nebraska Act

FURTHER READING
Hamilton, Holman. *Prologue to Conflict: The Crisis and Compromise of 1850.* Lexington: University of Kentucky Press, 1964.

Compromise of 1877

SEE Election of 1876

Confederate Constitution

The Confederate Constitution was a close replica of the U.S. Constitution. After all, Southerners had long argued that they had no quarrel with the work of the nation's founders, only its perversion by abolitionists and power-hungry political parties such as the antislavery Republicans.

After assembling at Montgomery, Alabama, on February 4, 1861, delegates from the seven states of the Lower South that had launched secession quickly hammered out first a Provisional Constitution and then a permanent one that was unanimously adopted on March 11. They were proud of their work. Howell Cobb of Georgia described the new Constitution as "the ablest instrument ever prepared for the government of a free people."

The changes from the U.S. Constitution primarily reflected the Southern commitment to slavery and states' rights. Thus, the Confederate Constitution expressly forbade Congress from passing any law "denying or impairing the rights of property in negro slaves." It also obligated Congress to enact legislation protecting the property rights of slaveholders in any territories that might

be acquired. Nonetheless, in a significant blow to the South Carolina radicals, the African or foreign slave trade was prohibited.

The Constitution highlighted states' rights by declaring that "each State acting in its sovereign and independent character" was the source of the new government for the Southern people. It dropped the "general welfare" clause used by Alexander Hamilton and others to broaden national authority, prohibited protective tariffs, and denied the Confederate government authority to "appropriate money for any internal improvement intended to facilitate commerce." The states, not Congress, could now initiate constitutional amendments, and they were given the right to impeach Confederate officials living and operating within their borders.

Another goal was to curb the partisan excesses that Southerners believed had corrupted political life in the old Union. With the exception of cabinet members and the diplomatic corps, the President had to show cause for removing civil officers of the executive branch. The purpose here was to prevent the President from using his control of appointive offices to build up a party following inimical to the public good. Even more striking was a provision limiting the President to only one six-year term. With no hope of returning to power, the President presumably would be more motivated to serve the interests of all the people.

For all its emphasis on states' rights, the Confederate Constitution stopped short of endorsing the right of secession or even the doctrine of nullification earlier favored by John C. Calhoun. Its stated purpose was "to form a permanent federal government," and the document left enough room for a nationalist vision of the Confederacy to emerge. When President Jefferson Davis attempted to implement that vision, he touched off the very political bickering that the Confederate Constitution was designed to avoid.

SEE ALSO
Confederate politics; Federalism; Nullification; Secession; States' rights

FURTHER READING
De Rosa, Marshall L. *The Confederate Constitution of 1861: An Inquiry into American Constitutionalism.* Columbia: University of Missouri Press, 1991.
Fehrenbacher, Don E. *Constitutions and Constitutionalism in the Slaveholding South.* Athens: University of Georgia Press, 1989.

Confederate emancipation

During the winter of 1864–65, Confederates engaged in the most open debate over slavery ever aired in the South. That debate culminated in a decision in March 1865 to use emancipated slaves as soldiers in the Confederate army, a decision that would have been utterly unthinkable back in 1861 when the Confederacy was founded to preserve and protect the institution of slavery.

Patrick R. Cleburne, a young, non-slaveholding general in the Army of Tennessee, was the first leading Confederate to argue that the arming and freeing of the slaves had become necessary to gain Confederate independence. In a document that he circulated among his fellow officers in January 1864, he predicted that Confederate defenses would collapse within a year unless slaves were recruited as soldiers. The South was running out of whites for its armies, and already numerically superior Union armies were adding to their strength by arming former Confederate slaves. Slavery, he reasoned, "from being one of our chief sources of strength at the commencement of the war, has now become, in a military point of view, one of our chief sources of weakness." The only recourse for the Confederacy, the only way to enlarge its armies so as to balance the growing numerical size of Union forces, was to arm its own slaves. He was confident that if the slaves were promised their independence, and then armed, they would become loyal Confederates and staunch allies of their former owners. Slavery would again be a source of strength.

Emancipation, of course, was the direct antithesis of the perpetual black bondage that nearly all Southern whites had believed was the fundamental social purpose of the Confederacy. Understandably, President Jefferson Davis not only rejected Cleburne's plan but also attempted to suppress all debate on the subject. Nonetheless, as the Confederate military situation grew increasingly desperate, talk of black soldiers and emancipation could not be stifled. Davis himself cautiously broached the subject when he asked the Confederate Congress in November 1864 for authorization to embark upon a program of gradual, compensated emancipation for up to 40,000 slaves whom he wanted to enlist in the Confederate war effort. He stopped short of calling for black troops but reserved the right to do so if military necessity so dictated.

Davis's November message to Congress forced into the open the debate over arming and freeing the slaves. Many Confederates, especially those in areas not yet overrun by Union armies that brought forced emancipation in their wake, remained horrified at the very idea of sanctioning any emancipation. *"We want no Confederate Government without our institutions,"* thundered the *Charleston Mercury* on January 13, 1865. Howell Cobb of Georgia, a general and politician, insisted that "The day you make soldiers of [slaves] is the beginning of the end of the revolution. If slaves will make good soldiers our whole theory of slavery is wrong—but they won't make soldiers. As a class they are wanting in every qualification of a soldier."

The turning point in the debate came in February 1865, when General Robert E. Lee, the most revered of all Confederates, publicly endorsed employing freed slaves as soldiers. By a very narrow vote on March 13, 1865, the Confederate Congress authorized Davis to call on the states for up to one-fourth of their male slaves "to perform military service in whatever capacity he may desire." No slaveholder was compelled to deliver up slaves, nor was emancipation of those who might serve as soldiers expressly provided. Still, Confederate authorities were prepared to initiate emancipation. On March 23, the War Department adopted regulations that accepted for armed service only those slaves granted freedom by their owners. Two days later, the first black company of ex-slaves formed under the new law.

Thus, in the last days of the war, the Confederacy was on the verge of dismantling slavery in one last, desperate bid to gain its independence. The decision came far too late to affect the outcome of the war or to answer the question of whether large numbers of blacks indeed would have fought for the Confederacy. That the decision was made at all indicates just how driven many Confederates had become in their desire to avoid what they saw as the subjugation of Northern rule. Many die-hard Confederates had openly argued that it was better to free their slaves than to become the slaves of the Yankees.

SEE ALSO
Black soldiers; Slavery

FURTHER READING
Durden, Robert F. *The Gray and the Black: The Confederate Debate on Emancipation.* Baton Rouge: Louisiana State University Press, 1972.
Levine, Bruce. *Confederate Emancipation: Southern Plans to Free and Arm Slaves during the Civil War.* New York: Oxford University Press, 2006.

Confederate paper money
SEE Inflation

Confederate politics

Unlike the Union, the Confederacy formally renounced political parties. Confederates were virtually unanimous in believing that partisanship had corrupted the original intent of the Union and destroyed sectional harmony. They pledged to organize Confederate politics around the ideal of nonpartisan unity. Nevertheless, factionalism soon developed over the extent of Confederate national powers and the proper role of the state governments. As the war dragged on, this factionalism increasingly divided the Confederacy from within. Worse yet from the perspective of the Confederate male elite, Southern politics became more threatening and disruptive as those formally excluded—white women and slaves—mobilized with ever greater defiance in seeking relief from the war's demands.

The first cracks in the veneer of political unity appeared in the spring of 1862. A nearly unbroken run of military reversals that included the Union breakthrough at Forts Henry and Donelson and the capture of New Orleans shook confidence in the military

Seated in the middle of this photograph of a family in black mourning clothes, John Minor Botts of Virginia was an unconditional Unionist who was temporarily jailed in Richmond in 1862 for his opposition to the Confederacy.

strategy of President Jefferson Davis and his administration. Moreover, just as inflation was starting to erode living standards, the Confederate Congress passed two highly controversial acts. The first, in February 1862, authorized Davis to suspend the writ of habeas corpus, and the second, in April, imposed a national draft to raise military manpower. In effect, nonslaveholders would now be forced to sacrifice in a war brought on by the concerns of planters over the safety of their slave property. Drawing upon deeply entrenched values of individual liberty and states' rights, an opposition formed in defense of threatened local interests.

The anti-administration opposition expressed itself in a bewildering variety of factions built around personalities, family ties, prior political loyalties, debates over military strategy, and, above all, the rejection of Davis's leadership. This opposition was all the more divisive and difficult to combat because it was so diffuse and never did gel into an organized political party. By the same token, Davis did not head a party whose institutional ties and appeals to loyalty could unite its supporters and defeat its opponents.

The champions of Davis espoused an ideology of national unity, one that called for political and military centralization as the only means of winning the war and protecting Southern independence. But they increasingly lost ground to administration critics who claimed, as did Governor Joseph E. Brown of Georgia, that Southerners had "more to apprehend from military despotism than from subjugation from the [Northern] army."

Although most Southerners remained committed to the goal of national independence, they delivered a sharp rebuke to the Davis administration in the Confederate congressional elections held in the fall of 1863. The voters favored anti-Davis Whigs, especially those who had initially opposed secession, at the expense of the Democratic-secessionists who had been elected overwhelmingly to the first Confederate Congress in 1861. The anti-Davis tide was strongest in districts of the Confederacy not yet overrun by the Union army. Civilians in these unoccupied areas bore a disproportionate share of the war's costs, for they alone were accessible to Confederate officials. They turned against Davis and his supporters for having failed to end a taxing war.

Although anti-administration politicians were just a few votes short of dominating the second Confederate Congress, Davis maintained a tenuous control until the end of the war. His leadership had not been openly rejected, but it fell far short of resolving the tensions between national centralization and individual liberties that made a mockery of the Confederacy's call for nonpartisan unity.

SEE ALSO

Brown, Joseph E.; Davis, Jefferson; Dissenters; Habeas corpus, suspension of; Inflation; States' rights; Stephens, Alexander H.

FURTHER READING

McCurry, Stephanie. *Confederate Reckoning:*

Power and Politics in the Civil War South. Cambridge: Harvard University Press, 2010.

McKitrick, Eric L. "Party Politics and the Union and Confederate War Efforts." In *The American Party Systems: Stages of Political Development,* ed. William Nisbet Chambers and Walter Dean Burnham. New York: Oxford University Press, 1975.

Rable, George C. *The Confederate Republic: A Revolution Against Politics.* Chapel Hill: University of North Carolina Press, 1994.

Rubin, Anne Sarah. *A Shattered Nation: The Rise and Fall of the Confederacy, 1861–1868.* Chapel Hill: University of North Carolina Press, 2005.

Congressional Reconstruction

Congress always contended that it had a coequal right with the President to determine Reconstruction policy. After nearly reaching a consensus with President Abraham Lincoln in the final months of the Civil War, Congress found itself at an impasse with President Andrew Johnson in the spring of 1866. Over repeated presidential vetoes, Congress finally enacted Reconstruction measures that called for sweeping changes in the civil and political life of the postwar South.

Congressional Republicans had no blueprint for Reconstruction. A few, led by Thaddeus Stevens of Pennsylvania, wanted to revolutionize Southern society by breaking up the estates of the planters and distributing the land in 40-acre parcels to freedmen and impoverished white Unionists. Other radicals, led by Charles Sumner of Massachusetts, pushed for black suffrage, arguing that blacks needed the vote in order to protect their freedom. At the other end of party opinion, a handful of conservatives favored accepting Johnson's plan of Reconstruction, which returned power to the South's traditional ruling elite. Most Republicans occupied a middle position between these two extremes. What united the moderate majority and eventually drove them closer to the radicals was a common conviction that the future safety of the Union required the imposition of political penalties on leading former Confederates and an expanded use of federal power to protect the rights of the freedmen.

The Republicans held more than two-thirds of the seats in Congress at the war's end and easily had enough votes in December 1865 to block the admission of the congressional delegations from Johnson's restored governments in the South. After putting Johnson's

The 38th Congress (1863–65) secured the first major victory of Congressional Reconstruction with approval of the 13th Amendment, which freed the slaves when ratified by the states.

program on hold, the Republicans appointed a Joint Committee of Fifteen on Reconstruction to conduct hearings on conditions in the South. The decision on readmitting the former Confederate states would await its recommendation. Meanwhile, a rift developed with Johnson when the President openly defied the Republican majority in Congress.

In February 1866, Johnson vetoed a bill to extend the life of the Freedmen's Bureau, a federal agency created in 1865 to administer emergency aid to war refugees in the South. A month later, he vetoed a civil rights bill that granted national citizenship and legal protection to the freed slaves. On both occasions, he insisted that any legislation affecting states denied representation in Congress was inherently unconstitutional. The final break came in June 1866, when Johnson announced his opposition to the 14th Amendment, a series of constitutional changes that embodied the North's terms for a more secure and just Union after the war.

Johnson's unbending opposition forced an extraordinary unity on the Republicans. In order for the party to have any say in Reconstruction, it had to close ranks to obtain the two-thirds majority necessary to override a Presidential veto or to pass constitutional amendments. Additional support for the party came when the congressional elections in the fall of 1866 swelled its majorities in Congress. The Republicans interpreted these returns as an endorsement of their stand on the 14th Amendment. Even the *New York Herald,* a former ally of Johnson's, now editorialized that "Mr. Johnson forgets that we have passed through the fiery ordeal of a mighty revolution, and that the preexisting order of things is gone and can return no more—that a great work of reconstruction is before us, and that we cannot escape it."

The problem for the Republicans was finding some mechanism to force Southern acceptance of the 14th Amendment. Tennessee was the only former Confederate state to have ratified the amendment; the other 10 defiantly refused. The Republicans lacked any public support for placing the South under indefinite military rule, and, as a party, they were unwilling to punish former rebels by a wholesale disenfranchisement of Southern whites. They found a way out of their dilemma in the Military Reconstruction Act of March 1867. Black suffrage, to be implemented under temporary military rule, was now added to the ratification of the 14th Amendment as the price of readmission for the 10 rebel states still out of the Union.

The capstone of congressional Reconstruction was the 15th Amendment, which aimed at guaranteeing black male suffrage throughout the nation. When this amendment was ratified in 1870, most Republicans concluded that Reconstruction was over. The party seemingly had met its goals. The Union war dead had been honored in a just peace that recognized their sacrifices; the rebels had been forced to recognize their defeat; and a more perfect Union had been created through an extension of federal powers to embrace legal equality for the freed slaves.

The promise of congressional Reconstruction, however, fell far short of reality for Southern blacks. The gains they made in economic and political democracy rested upon newly formed Republican parties in the South. The old planter elite overturned all these parties by 1877 and once again forced blacks to accept a dependent position in Southern society.

SEE ALSO

Civil Rights Act of 1866; 15th Amendment; 14th Amendment; Freedmen's

Bureau; Johnson's program of Reconstruction; Military Reconstruction Act of 1867; Radicals; Radical Reconstruction in the South; Wartime Reconstruction

FURTHER READING

Brock, W. R. *An American Crisis: Congress and Reconstruction, 1865–1867.* New York: Harper, 1966.

Foner, Eric. *Reconstruction: America's Unfinished Revolution, 1863–1877.* New York: Harper & Row, 1988.

Conscription

Both sides resorted to national conscription, or a draft, in order to shore up the size of their armies once volunteering fell off. The Confederate draft came a year earlier than the Union's and was more difficult to evade. It produced about 18 percent of all the soldiers in the Confederate army as opposed to the 6 percent of Union troops raised by a draft.

In April 1862, the Confederate Congress passed the first comprehensive conscription act in U.S. history. Intended to stimulate volunteering and to prevent the original 12-month enlistees from going home, the act placed in the direct service of the Confederacy all white males between the ages of 18 and 35, except those with special exemptions. The men already in the army were kept in service and had three years added to their original date of enlistment.

For the remainder of the war, the Confederacy tightened its draft by closing loopholes and by extending it to include whites between the ages of 17 and 50. In December 1863, conscripts were prohibited from sending substitutes (that is, hiring someone in their place), and in February 1864, the Congress canceled all previous grants of exemptions and drew a new list that halved the original number of exemptions. Confederate bureaucrats and essential industrial workers comprised most of those still exempted.

To many Southern whites, the Confederate draft violated states' rights and

In New York City and elsewhere in the North, men filed into draft offices in an effort to secure an exemption from the Union draft.

individual liberties. Much of the anger centered on the so-called Twenty Negro law of October 1862, that granted draft exemptions for overseers on plantations with 20 or more slaves. Justified as necessary for maintaining security and increasing food production in plantation districts, these exemptions nonetheless aroused cries of class favoritism toward planters and their sons.

Despite a barrage of criticism, the Confederacy rigorously enforced its draft. Under pressure from its generals to send every fit white male to the front, the War Department felt it had no choice but to exhaust all draftable manpower. Indeed, as early as January 1864, the Conscription Bureau was reporting: "The results indicate . . . that fresh material for the armies can no longer be estimated as an element of future calculation for their increase."

The Union did not implement its draft until the spring of 1863. When it did, Union troops had to quell an explosion of opposition in the New York City draft riots of July 1863, an event that had no parallel in the Confederacy. The Union draft provoked such resistance even though it was more limited in scope than its Confederate counterpart. It was restricted to men between the ages of 20 and 45 and was applied only in districts that had not filled their assigned troop quotas. No Northerner was placed in military service until selected by the draft. In contrast, eligible Southerners were technically part of the army once the Confederate Congress had passed the draft legislation.

The Union held four draft enrollments that called about 250,000 men into military service. About 20 percent of those called refused to appear, and draft-dodging spread as the war dragged on. About two-fifths paid the $300 commutation fee that enabled them to buy their way out of serving until Congress abolished that provision in the summer of 1864. Another one-third hired substitutes. The cost of commutation or hiring a substitute was beyond the reach of most working-class Northerners, whose annual wages were only about $500. Responding to workers' cries of "a rich man's war and a poor man's fight," county and especially urban governments set up draft funds that purchased exemptions for low-income workers. As a result of all these ways to stay out of the draft, the number of men drafted directly into the Union army totaled only 46,000. Still, the draft had served its purpose: prodding men to volunteer as they scrambled to avoid the stigma of conscription.

SEE ALSO

Armies; Recruiting bounties

FURTHER READING

Geary, James W. *We Need Men: The Union Draft in the Civil War.* DeKalb: Northern Illinois University Press, 1991.
Moore, Albert Burton. *Conscription and Conflict in the Confederacy.* New York: Hillary House Publishers, 1963.

Constitutional Union party

Hastily formed in the spring of 1860 by old-line Whigs, the Constitutional Union party presented itself as a conservative alternative to the sectionalized Republican party and the Southern-dominated Democratic party. Viewing agitation over the slavery issue as the greatest threat to national unity, they vowed to take slavery out of politics and unify Americans around a devotion to the Union and the Constitution.

Although they drew support from

financial and textile interests in the Northeast with a direct stake in the Southern economy, the Constitutional Unionists were always strongest in the Upper South. Here, the Whigs retained their party organization and continued to offer a political alternative to the Democrats. Desperately anxious to stave off a dissolution of the Union that would find them, quite literally, in the middle of any armed conflict, these Whigs met with their Northern allies at Baltimore in May 1860 and nominated former Senator John Bell of Tennessee for the Presidency.

Like Bell at age 64 and his running mate, 67-year-old Edward Everett of Massachusetts, the men who lined up behind the Constitutional Union party represented an older generation of Americans, primarily Whig in background, who believed that reckless demagogues in the Republican and Democratic parties were on the verge of breaking up the Union. Convinced that Southern rights were already adequately protected in the Union, they denounced both the Republicans and the Southern Democrats as sectional extremists for refusing to cease agitation of the slavery issue. Yet, by running on what amounted to a nonplatform of the "Constitution, the Union, and the Enforcement of the Laws," the Constitutional Unionists offered only to evade, not resolve, the burning political issue that so concerned the electorate.

Established business and planting interests in the Upper South and their commercial counterparts in Northern cities provided the leadership for the party, and traditionally non-Democratic yeoman farmers in the Upper South turned out in support of Bell. The party carried Virginia, Kentucky, and Tennessee in 1860, but its base of popular support was so narrow that Bell won only 13 percent of the popular vote.

This showing was far too weak for the party to play its hoped-for role of spoiler in the Presidential election by denying any candidate an electoral majority. The Republicans won, and as the Constitutional Unionists had always feared, secession was about to become a reality.

SEE ALSO
Democratic party; Election of 1860; Republican party; Whig party

FURTHER READING
Knupfer, Peter B. *The Union As It Is: Constitutional Unionism and Sectional Compromise, 1787–1861.* Chapel Hill: University of North Carolina Press, 1991.
Parks, John Howard. *John Bell of Tennessee.* Baton Rouge: Louisiana State Press, 1950.

Contrabands

The term "contraband" refers to enemy property liable to seizure in a war. Once Union General Benjamin F. Butler set the precedent in May 1861 of declaring three runaway slaves who made it into his lines at Fortress Monroe in Virginia to be contraband of war, the term stuck as the popular name for slaves who came under federal control during the Civil War.

Through a process of trial and error, a federal contraband policy took shape in 1862 and 1863. It had two goals: relieving Union armies of the responsibility for caring for escaped slaves; and demonstrating to Northern voters that the unraveling of slavery would not result in an exodus of blacks to the North. At the core of this policy was the decision to put the black refugees to work in the South. The army organized labor battalions of blacks for the heavy,

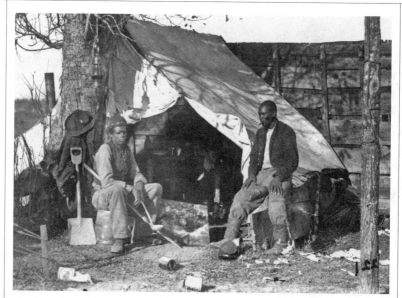

These two African Americans are escaped slaves in Virginia who made their way into Union lines in the fall of 1863. They joined the swelling numbers of contraband laborers who worked for the Union army.

physical work of chopping wood, hauling supplies, and building roads and fortifications. Contraband wages, which were often late in being paid, were one-third to one-fifth of what black laborers could earn in civilian employment. More than 200,000 blacks labored in this underpaid military workforce.

Many more contrabands were put to work growing cotton. Loyal planters and Northern lessees of abandoned lands contracted for contraband laborers from the army commanders. These contracts typically contained few safeguards for the former slaves. Exploitation was flagrant, and in nearly all cases the wages were so low that the freedmen wound up with little more than room and board in return for their labor. The conditions on many of the worst leased plantations approximated slavery.

For all its abuses, the Union policy of reestablishing refugee slaves as a rural workforce in the occupied areas of the South was a success. Returning blacks to the plantations helped free up Union armies to engage in military operations, provided the labor to re-

supply the textile mills of New England with cotton, and convinced at least some doubting Northern whites that black labor could be profitable without the coercive controls of slavery.

The unemployable contrabands—the aged, the sick, children, and their mothers—remained the longest in the contraband camps set up by the Union military. Conditions in these refugee centers were appalling. As in any Civil War encampment, disease was rampant and sanitary standards abysmal. Compounding the medical problems was the weakened state of many of the refugees when they arrived. As noted by John Eaton, a Union military chaplain in Mississippi, the refugees from slavery encompassed "every stage of disease or decrepitude [and were] often nearly naked, with flesh torn by the terrible experiences of their escapes." Northern benevolent societies contributed emergency food and military supplies, but the care provided remained inadequate. The mortality rate in the contraband camps hovered around 25 percent during the war.

The Union army used these contrabands to repair rail track near Murfreesboro, Tennessee, after the battle of Stones River.

The camps remained open until the last months of the war, and eventually upwards of 1 million blacks—a quarter of the slave population in 1860—made it behind Union lines. The refugees streamed in as the Union armies advanced, and they provided much of the labor that kept those armies on the move.

SEE ALSO

Black soldiers; Emancipation

FURTHER READING

Gerteis, Louis S. *From Contraband to Freedman: Federal Policy toward Southern Blacks, 1861–1865.* Westport, Conn.: Greenwood Press, 1973.
Rose, Willie Lee. *Rehearsal for Reconstruction: The Port Royal Experiment.* Indianapolis, Ind.: Bobbs-Merrill, 1964.

Copperheads

SEE Dissenters; Union politics

Cost of the war

The real cost of the Civil War will forever defy exact measurement. How can one place a value on lives lost or shattered and on goods that were never produced because of the war? An estimate prepared in 1869 by David Wells, the Special Commissioner of Revenue, placed the monetary cost of the war at just over $9 billion, a figure that included about $3 billion in Confederate expenditures and losses. A recent computerized analysis puts the cost at $6.6 billion, roughly divided between the Union and Confederacy. Once indirect costs, such as pensions for Union soldiers and interest payments on the swollen national debt, are added, the overall cost more than doubles.

The direct military expenditures of the Union came to $2.3 billion, or 40 times the amount of all federal revenue in 1860. Confederate military spending totaled just over $1 billion. The debt loads of both governments soared as they struggled to raise funds to pay for the utterly unprecedented costs of the war. For example, the federal government spent more money during the war than it had in the entire period from 1789 to 1860. All the money that Southerners invested in Confederate bonds and notes became worthless when it became clear following their defeat that the U.S. government would not pay a cent of the Confederate public debt. Meanwhile, the Union's war costs accumulated as an immense national debt that rose from $65 million in 1860 to $2.6 billion at the end of the war. In per capita terms, the debt increased 37 times over and would not be as high again until World War I. Still, the postwar economy generated enough revenue to allow the Treasury to pay off most of this debt by the 1890s.

Unlike Northerners, Southerners were hit with devastating property losses during the Civil War. The 1860 census listed Southern property valued at $7.2 billion. About a third of this

This Northern cartoon lampoons the ramshackle finances of the Confederacy and the efforts of Jefferson Davis to find a way to pay for the war and control inflation.

figure included slave property, an investment that was wiped out with the Union's policy of emancipation. In addition, the South lost more than 30 percent of its livestock, a prime source of wealth for its nonslaveholders, and farm values fell by one-half. Five years after the war was over, the 1870 census listed Southern property values at barely over $2 billion. Property losses had been immense.

As the postwar South struggled with its legacy of defeat and poverty, its economy continued to lag behind that of the North's. Indeed, not until 1950 would the South's relative share of per capita national income climb back to the 1860 level. This overriding burden of poverty worsened race relations as Southern whites persisted in equating their economic plight with the freedom of the former slaves. One cost of the Civil War that the victorious North never considered paying was that of supplying federal money to assist the South in rebuilding its economy.

SEE ALSO

Casualties

FURTHER READING

Goldin, Claudia and Frank Lewis. "The Economic Cost of the American Civil War." *Journal of Economic History* 35, No. 2 (June 1975): 299–325.

Crittenden-Johnson Resolutions

Passed by the Union Congress just after the federal defeat at First Bull Run in July 1861, the Crittenden-Johnson Resolutions stipulated that the North was waging a limited war whose sole objective was "to defend and maintain the supremacy of the Constitution, and to preserve the Union." Slavery, as well as all the other "rights or established institutions" of the seceded states, was to be left untouched.

In the early stages of the Civil War, the theme of preserving, not changing, the old Union of 1860 was absolutely essential to creating and maintaining Northern unity. By affirming that theme in the Johnson-Crittenden Resolutions, Congress laid out the broadest possible political platform on which all

Northerners could stand in support of the Union war effort. Much of the support of Northern Democrats, and nearly all of the support from Unionists in the loyal border states, was based on the condition that this war was being fought solely to restore the Union as it existed in 1860. The co-sponsors of the resolutions, John J. Crittenden of Kentucky in the House and Andrew Johnson of Tennessee in the Senate, were anxious to put Congress on record declaring that the destruction of slavery was not to be a war objective. Most antislavery Republicans grudgingly voted for the resolutions because they felt they could not yet risk damaging Northern morale and unity by appearing to favor a war against slavery.

The Confederate victory at First Bull Run indicated that the war was likely to be a long, protracted affair, and the initial Republican reaction was to put a premium on preserving Northern unity. As the war dragged on in 1861 with no significant Union victories, public opinion in the North began to shift in favor of taking a harder line on slavery. Antislavery Republicans registered this shift when Congress assembled in December 1861. By reversing their previous votes of support, 53 Republicans defeated a Democratic effort to reaffirm the Resolutions in the House.

By the end of 1861, the war was starting to turn into a crusade against slavery. "God is not on the side of the strongest battalions," argued Moncure D. Conway, a Virginia-born abolitionist. "The strongest battalions are on the side of God." A growing number of Northerners now supported that position.

SEE ALSO
Border South; Emancipation

FURTHER READING
Kirwan, Albert Dennis. *John J. Crittenden: The Struggle for the Union.* 1962. Reprint, Westport, Conn.: Greenwood, 1974.

Davis, Jefferson
CONFEDERATE PRESIDENT

- *Born: June 3, 1808, Christian (now Todd) County, Ky.*
- *Political party: Democrat*
- *Education: Transylvania University, 1821–24; U.S. Military Academy, B.S., 1828*
- *Military service: U.S. Army: lieutenant, 1828–33; 1st lieutenant, dragoons, 1833–35; colonel, 1st Mississippi Rifles, 1846-47*
- *Government service: U.S. House of Representatives, 1845–46; U.S. Senate, 1847–51, 1857–61; U.S. secretary of war, 1853–57; Confederacy: president, 1861–65*
- *Died: December 6, 1889, New Orleans, La.*

"The man and the hour have met!" declared William Lowndes Yancey as Jefferson Davis arrived in Montgomery, Alabama, to assume the presidency of the Confederacy in February 1861. After a brief honeymoon period, Davis failed to capture the hearts of Southern whites, and he increasingly became the scapegoat for Confederate military reversals. He faced a nearly impossible task under wartime conditions in trying to forge the seceded states into an independent nation, and it is doubtful if the South had any soldier-statesman who could have succeeded where he failed.

Like Lincoln, who also was born in south-central Kentucky, Davis spent his youth on the western frontier. The son of an ambitious, slaveholding farmer who eventually settled his family in Wilkinson County, Mississippi, he attended private academies and Transylvania University in Kentucky before enrolling at West Point in 1824. A carefree cadet who was almost expelled for out-of-bounds drinking in a local tavern, he graduated in the bottom half of his class. Posted to frontier duty, he served in the army for seven years before resigning his commission and eloping with Knox Taylor, the daughter of his disapproving commander, Zachary Taylor. The marriage ended in tragedy when his bride of three months died of malaria contracted at Brierfield, Davis's Mississippi plantation. A grief-stricken Davis withdrew into semi-seclusion for the next decade. He read and studied, managed his plantation, and developed a cold, formal reserve that he relaxed only in the presence of women and children.

Davis emerged from his shell in 1845 when he married Varina Howell and entered politics as a states' rights Democrat. Resigning his seat in Congress at the outbreak of the Mexican War to serve as colonel of the 1st Mississippi Rifles, he was lion-ized as a war hero for his exploits at the battle of Buena Vista. Touted as "Colonel Jeff Davis, the Game Cock of the South," he entered the U.S. Sen-ate in 1847, a seat he held until his appointment as sec-retary of war in 1853. As war secre-tary, he was an excellent administra-tor concerned with enlarging and mod-ernizing the army. Upon returning to the Senate, he led the Southern campaign to keep the territo-ries open to slavery.

Davis was a logical choice to head the Confederate government that took shape in the winter of 1860-61. Both his public experience and his military record had been distinguished. A South-ern nationalist, though not a firebrand who had agitated for secession, he com-manded a broad range of support that was needed to bring the Upper South into the Confederacy and knit together political factions. In his inaugural message he insisted that the Confederacy stood on the right of self-government and wanted to leave the Union peacefully.

Davis's decision to order the firing on Fort Sumter eliminated any possibil-ity that secession would be peaceful and forced him into the role of a wartime

As president of the Confederacy, Jefferson Davis became a focal point for North-ern anger and bitterness when war broke out in 1861. He and other Confeder-ate leaders, this cartoon suggests, were traitors who should be hanged.

JEFF DAVIS ON THE RIGHT PLATFORM, *or the last "act of secession".*

president. He threw himself into that role with an unbending dedication that resulted in a further deterioration of his already-poor health. Characteristic of his appearance was this description in May 1861 by William Howard Russell, a British war correspondent: "The expression of his face is anxious, he has a very haggard, care-worn, and pain-drawn look, though no trace of anything but the utmost confidence and the greatest decision could be detected in his conversation."

At least publicly, Davis's confidence in the Confederate cause never wavered. But, in one of his greatest failings as a war leader, he was unable to inspire Southern whites to join him in self-sacrificing devotion to Confederate victory. The nationalizing measures that Davis enacted to raise an army, call up conscripts, and impress private property for military use clashed with traditional Southern values of localism and manly independence. For many Confederates, especially the nonslaveholding farmers in the mountains and hill country, Davis became a tyrant who was stripping away their liberties.

As a military leader, Davis favored a "defensive-offensive," a strategy that called for Confederate armies to assume the defensive while waiting for an opportunity to launch a counterattack against invading Union armies. The strategy was sound but flawed in its execution. Davis dispersed his armies too widely in a futile attempt to protect too much territory and failed to coordinate adequately the departmental structures in which he had divided army commands. Unaided by a general staff, Davis wavered between concentrating military resources in either the eastern or western theaters. As a result, General Robert E. Lee's army lacked the manpower to break out of Virginia and possible chances to reverse Confederate set-

backs in the West were squandered.

Despite denouncing the Emancipation Proclamation as "the most execrable measure recorded in the history of guilty man," Davis came around to backing a limited form of Confederate emancipation in March 1865. This desperate bid to augment depleted Confederate armies with black soldiers who were promised their freedom in exchange for their service came far too late to affect the outcome of the war.

Refusing to accept defeat, Davis fled Richmond when the city fell in April 1865. He hoped to join Confederate forces west of the Mississippi River and rally Southerners to continue the war by guerrilla tactics. Captured near Irwinville, Georgia, on May 10, he was indicted for treason against the United States and imprisoned for two years. No formal charges were pressed, and he was released on parole.

After traveling abroad and writing *The Rise and Fall of the Confederate Government* (1881), an arid defense of his wartime record, Davis quietly spent his last years at Beauvoir, a plantation on the Mississippi coast. The U.S. citizenship that he never sought to reclaim was finally restored to him in the 1970s during the Presidency of Jimmy Carter.

SEE ALSO

Confederate emancipation

FURTHER READING

Cooper, William J., Jr. *Jefferson Davis and the Civil War Era*. Baton Rouge: Louisiana State University Press, 2008.
Davis, Varina. *Jefferson Davis, Ex-President of the Confederate States of America: A Memoir by His Wife*. Baltimore: Nautical & Aviation Publishing Co., 1990.
Davis, William C. *Jefferson Davis: The Man and His Hour*. New York: Harper-Collins, 1991.
Eaton, Clement. *Jefferson Davis*. New York: Free Press, 1977.

Democratic party

Formed between 1824 and 1828 to support the candidacy of Andrew Jackson for the Presidency, the Democratic party succeeded in building the first mass-based political organization in U.S. history. The party's stand in favor of states' rights and individual liberties attracted a broad coalition of voters that enabled the Democrats to play a dominant role in national politics down to the Civil War. Following the division of the party into sectional wings over the slavery issue in the late 1850s, the Democrats entered a period of political decline that was not reversed until the end of Reconstruction in the 1870s.

Proclaiming themselves the friend of the common man and the foe of aristocratic privilege, the Democrats spoke to the fears of workers and backwoods farmers who saw an activist government as a threat to their economic and cultural equality. The party's greatest strength, however, was always in the South. Southerners anxious to defend slavery were particularly drawn to a party that championed the rights of local white majorities to determine their own affairs free from outside interference. Unlike the Whigs, the Democrats railed against the dangers to a traditional agrarian way of life posed by industrialization and urban growth. As strident anti-abolitionists and unabashed white supremacists, the Democrats also seemingly promised the South that slavery and its attendant relationship between blacks and whites would be left undisturbed. Moreover, most Southerners welcomed the Democratic emphasis on an expansionist foreign policy for the opportunities that it offered for slavery to expand.

The issue of slavery's expansion, which was closely linked in the North to Southern control of the federal government, ultimately destroyed Democratic party unity. When Northern Democrats opposed to slavery's expansion introduced the Wilmot Proviso during the

When the Democratic party met in April 1861 for its national convention in Charleston, South Carolina, ardent Southerners packed into the galleries cheered on the delegates who demanded protection for slavery in the federal territories.

Mexican War, the party attempted to close its divisions by first rallying behind the Compromise of 1850 and then introducing the concept of popular sovereignty to resolve the issue of slavery in the territories. Emboldened by the decision of the U.S. Supreme Court in the *Dred Scott* decision, Southern Democrats by the late 1850s were demanding a federal slave code to protect the rights of slaveholders in the territories. When Northern Democrats refused to accept that demand as an official plank in the party's platform for 1860, the Democrats split into two rival party organizations. That split helped pave the way for the Republican victory in 1860, which triggered secession.

In the South, slaveholding Democrats were in the forefront of the secession movement. In the North, most Democrats backed the Union cause once Fort Sumter was fired upon. Although generally supportive of the Union war effort, Northern Democrats opposed the nationalizing measures of the Republicans and denounced emancipation and the 13th Amendment. The Democrats remained harsh critics of Republican policies throughout the Reconstruction period. By the mid-1870s, as a solidly Democratic South began to take shape, the party finally regained the sectional unity and prominence in national affairs that it had lost in 1860.

SEE ALSO

Compromise of 1850; Congressional Reconstruction; *Dred Scott* decision; Election of 1860; Federal Slave Code; Popular sovereignty; Republican party; 13th Amendment; Whig party; Wilmot Proviso

FURTHER READING

Cooper, William J., Jr. *The South and the Politics of Slavery, 1828–1856.* Baton Rouge: Louisiana State University Press, 1978.
Silbey, Joel H. *A Respectable Minority: The Democratic Party in the Civil War Era, 1860–1868.* New York: W. W. Norton, 1977.

Desertion

Desertion rates were about the same in Confederate and Union armies until the last year of the war. By late 1864, the growing desperation of families left behind and the looming inevitability of defeat produced a near epidemic of rebel desertions. For the war as a whole, at least 100,000 Confederate soldiers, or about 13 percent of all enlistments, deserted. Union desertions were around 200,000, or 10 percent of all forces.

Both sides resorted to increasingly harsh measures in an effort to stem losses from desertion. The Civil War saw 500 military executions—more than the combined total of all other previous U.S. wars—and two-thirds of those executions were for desertion. Still, the odds were quite good that the deserter would get away. Apprehension rates in both armies averaged only 20 percent. Families at home aided many Northern deserters by sending them a civilian suit of clothes that made their escape easier.

Southern families encouraged their menfolk to desert by simply writing letters describing their worsening plight as the war dragged on. The Reverend John Paris, while preaching at the execution of 22 rebel deserters in Kinston, North Carolina, in February 1864, blamed Southern women for the terrible spectacle of the execution. An "appeal from home," he said, had caused the men to desert. Quite a change had occurred since the early stages of the war, when Southern wives and daughters had branded desertion as disgraceful.

Much more so than in the North, desertions weakened morale in the South and hampered its war effort.

Confederate deserters and draft dodgers, often combined with local Unionists, controlled ever larger blocs of territory late in the war. Parts of western North Carolina and northern Georgia and Alabama became a no-man's-land where Confederate authority was openly defied. This pressure from its civilian rear hastened the collapse of the Confederacy.

SEE ALSO
Absenteeism

FURTHER READING
Lonn, Ella. *Desertion during the Civil War.* New York: Century, 1928.
Weitz, Mark A. *More Damning than Slaughter: Desertion in the Confederate Army.* Lincoln: University of Nebraska Press, 2005.

Direct tax

Passed by the Confederate Congress in April 1863, the direct tax was a tax-in-kind on agricultural products. The tax amounted to one-tenth of all farm produce. Intended to reduce the need for more inflationary paper currency and to increase the supply of food to Confederate armies, the tax was at best only a qualified success.

The agricultural tithe was both cumbersome to administer and unevenly enforced. Collections under the tax could take place only in areas accessible to the tax agents. As a result, farmers in Virginia, the Carolinas, and Georgia wound up paying nearly all of the tax. Having paid little (if any) taxes before the war, many of these farmers denounced the direct tax as unjust and tyrannical. Far more fair, they argued, would have been a graduated tax on agricultural profits payable in currency.

The distribution of food supplies gathered under the tax placed a tremendous strain on the transportation system of the Confederacy. Tons of supplies spoiled at depots while awaiting shipment to the front. Out of $150 million of provisions collected under the tithe, more than two-thirds never reached the armies. What did get through, however, probably prevented the soldiers from starving.

Although better transportation facilities would have increased the efficiency of the direct tax, the more fundamental problem facing the Confederacy late in the war was a shrinking agricultural base from which to draw food supplies. Even before the direct tax was enacted, the Confederacy had lost prime grain and livestock areas to the Union. Then, in the last two years of the war, Union raiders increasingly targeted food resources. As a result, Lucius B. Northrop, the harassed head of the Confederate Commissary Department, was forced to admit in December 1864, "The idea that there is *plenty for all* in the country is absurd. The efforts of the enemy have been too successful."

SEE ALSO
Impressment Act

FURTHER READING
Todd, Richard Cecil. *Confederate Finance.* Athens: University of Georgia Press, 1954.

Disease

Disease was the scourge of Civil War armies. One in 10 Union soldiers and nearly 1 in 5 Confederate soldiers died from some illness. Disease killed two soldiers in camp for every one that died on the battlefield or in a hospital from a wound.

A burial party at Andersonville Prison, Georgia, places bodies in trenches hastily dug in the summer of 1864 to a depth of only four feet. Deaths from disease were notoriously high in the prison camps for captured soldiers.

Disease struck in two waves. The first was an epidemic of diseases that normally struck during childhood, such as measles and mumps, which broke out as rural recruits were brought together in the central training and distribution camps. Within a year of their formation, regiments typically lost nearly half of their effective strength through illness. Without fresh recruits, regiments tended to vanish as a result of disease within three years, by which time they were consolidated or disbanded. It was no wonder that H. H. Green, a Georgia soldier, wrote home from his first camp: "There some dying every day on either side[;] the death bells ringing in my ears constant[.]"

The second wave of disease—typhoid, smallpox, dysentery, diarrhea, and malaria—debilitated soldiers throughout the war. No one understood the bacteriological origins of disease at that time, and hoards of lice and rats attracted by the spillover from shallow latrines continually reinfected the troops. As a result, nearly every soldier suffered from diarrhea-dysentery. The Union army alone reported 1.7 million cases of this severe intestinal disorder, and the death rate from the disease rose fivefold over the course of the war.

Typhoid and malaria—"camp fevers" to the soldiers—were second only to diarrhea and dysentery in spreading misery and death. Troops stationed in the hot and humid lower Mississippi Valley were especially hard-hit by malaria, an often fatal disease transmitted by mosquitoes. Confederate General Robert E. Lee often cited his concerns over malaria as a reason he did not want to send his eastern troops to the western theater. He had reason to be worried. In large part because of their greater exposure to malaria, the western soldiers in the Union army stood a 43-percent higher chance of dying from disease than those in the eastern theater.

Mortality rates from disease as a percentage of all war deaths for soldiers were lower in the Civil War (61 percent) than the Revolutionary War (73 percent) or the Mexican War (86 percent). This, of course, was of little consolation to Civil War soldiers, who often had more to fear from confinement in a camp or garrison than action on the battlefield.

SEE ALSO

Casualties; Medicine

FURTHER READING

Humphreys, Margaret. *Intensely Human: The Health of the Black Soldier in the Civil War*. Baltimore: Johns Hopkins University Press, 2008.
Steiner, Paul E. *Disease in the Civil War: Natural Biological Warfare in 1861–1865*. Springfield, Ill.: C. C. Thomas, 1968.

Dissenters

Dissenters, those who actively opposed their respective governments in the Union and Confederacy, grew in numbers as the Civil War settled into a prolonged, bloody conflict. Dissent took many forms: opposing war policies on constitutional grounds; refusing to pay taxes; giving aid to the enemy; deserting from military service or enlisting for the other side; and, in the case of the Unionist nonslaveholders who formed the new state of West Virginia, transferring political allegiance to the opposing government. The most common expression of dissent was in support of a peaceful, negotiated end to the war. By the midpoint of the war, peace movements were proliferating in both the Union and the Confederacy, and they temporarily threatened to bring the war to a halt.

Northern peace movements centered in the faction of the Democratic party stigmatized by the Republicans as Copperheads for plotting treason against the Union. Midwesterners of Southern descent, known as the Butternuts, and working-class Catholic immigrants in Northern cities turned decisively against the Union war effort once it was linked to emancipation. Committed to white supremacy and fearful of economic competition from freed slaves, these Democrats decried emancipation as the most revolutionary of the intrusive and unconstitutional changes the Republicans were forcing on American society.

Insisting that they patriotically supported the one, true federal Union of 1860, and not the despotic Union of military subjugation and emancipation favored by the Republicans, the Peace Democrats achieved their greatest success in writing their party's platform in 1864, which called for an end to hostilities and then a restoration of the old Union. They opposed, as Democratic Congressman Clement Vallandigham of Ohio put it, both "the Secessionist Rebellion South, and the Abolition Rebellion, North and West." If only the Republicans would drop their demand for emancipation, they claimed, peace was still possible.

A surge of Union victories in the fall of 1864 undercut the appeal of the Peace Democrats and assured the reelection of President Abraham Lincoln. Meanwhile, Confederate peace movements had already crested and then failed.

This cartoon's caption read: "There once was an old party-Wall quite cracked and just ready to fall; the Copperheads came and completed its shame by sticking their Bills on the Wall." "Copperhead" was a Northern nickname for anyone against the war and in favor of restoring the Union by a negotiated settlement with the South.

"O wicked WALL!"—*Midsummer Night's Dream,* V. 1.

As early as 1861, peace societies emerged in Arkansas among nonslaveholding farmers. Then, as promises of a glorious and short war gave way to the reality of conscription, impressment, inflation, and endless casualties, disenchantment with the war spread. Southerners most alienated from the Confederate government were concentrated in the German-speaking districts of Texas and throughout the upland regions of northern Alabama, Georgia, North Carolina, and eastern Tennessee.

Apart from the Unionists of East Tennessee, opposition to the Confederacy ran deepest in central North Carolina, a region of small farms where Quaker sects had maintained a tradition of religious opposition to slavery. By 1863, it was home to the Heroes of America, a secret society that offered protection and an extensive network of civilian support for Unionists and Confederate draft dodgers and deserters. Despite repeated efforts by military authorities to clamp down on these disloyal Confederates, resistance deepened. The result was a civil war within a civil war.

North Carolina was also home to the strongest peace movement within the Confederacy. Led by Democratic editor William W. Holden, the movement threatened to unseat Zebulon B. Vance in the gubernatorial election of 1864 and call for a convention to take North Carolina out of the Confederacy if a peace settlement could not be reached with the North. Vance cleverly coopted the movement by donning the mantle of peace himself. After branding Holden as the real war candidate for exposing North Carolina to the possibility of a civil war against its Confederate neighbors, he pledged to push for peace once the Confederacy had won a major victory. By convincing the voters that he shared their passion for an honorable peace, he easily won reelection. Subse-quently, he continued to back the war effort. The growing movement for peace represented a genuine concern over the mounting costs and destructiveness of the war. Yet all efforts for peace floundered on the utter incompatibility of the war aims of the Union and Confederacy. Lincoln's government would accept nothing less than the return of the rebel states to the Union. Davis's government would negotiate only on terms that recognized Confederate independence.

SEE ALSO

Confederate politics; Southern Union soldiers; Union politics; War governors

FURTHER READING

Escott, Paul D. *After Secession: Jefferson Davis and the Failure of Confederate Nationalism.* Baton Rouge: Louisiana State University Press, 1978.

Inscoe, John C. and Robert C. Kenzer, eds. *Enemies of the Country: New Perspectives on Unionists in the Civil War South.* Athens: University of Georgia Press, 2001.

Klement, Frank L. *The Limits of Dissent: Clement L. Vallandigham and the Civil War.* Lexington: University Press of Kentucky, 1970.

Weber, Jennifer L. *Copperheads: The Rise and Fall of Lincoln's Opponents in the North.* New York: Oxford University Press, 2006.

Dix, Dorothea L.

NORTHERN REFORMER

- *Born: April 4, 1802, Hampden, Maine*
- *Education: some lower grades*
- *Public service: reformer; superintendent of Union nurses, 1861–65*
- *Died: July 17, 1887, Trenton, N.J.*

A tireless advocate before the Civil War for more humane treatment of the mentally ill, Dorothea Dix supervised female nurses in Union hospitals during the war. More than 3,000 nurses served under her direction, a precedent that hastened the acceptance of women as professional nurses.

Dorothea Dix was once dismissed by George Templeton Strong, the treasurer of the U.S. Sanitary Commission, as "that philanthropic lunatic [who] is disgusted with us because we do not leave everything else and rush off the instant she tells us of something that demands attention"; in fact, she brought a badly needed sense of urgency to the organization of a nursing corps for Union soldiers.

The daughter of an itinerant preacher, Dix had a troubled childhood. Her father drank heavily, her mother was frequently ill, and the family struggled to avoid poverty. Sent at the age of 12 to live with her wealthy grandmother in Boston, she became aware of a world of books and learning. To her grandmother's consternation, she shunned the role of a cultivated belle and instead declared that she wanted to be a teacher and help the poor and needy. After teaching in Worcester, Massachusetts, she returned to Boston and from 1821–34 operated a school for girls in the Dix mansion. Suffering from tuberculosis, she traveled to England in 1836 to recover her health and there learned of the latest reforms for improving the care and treatment of the mentally ill.

Dix's poor health prevented her from resuming teaching when she returned to the United States in 1838, but a legacy from her grandmother's estate left her with the financial independence that made possible a career in humanitarian reform. In the early 1840s she visited every jail and asylum for the poor in Massachusetts and was appalled by the conditions she found. Her *Memorial to the Legislature of Massachusetts* in 1843 shocked public opinion and sparked state reforms in the care of the indigent and insane. Traveling more than 30,000 miles in the next decade, she embarked on a nationwide crusade for state-supported hospitals for the insane. Her efforts resulted in the founding or enlarging of 15 such hospitals.

Dix was in New Jersey when the Civil War started. Rushing to Washington upon hearing that a Baltimore mob had fired upon Massachusetts troops passing through the city, she immediately volunteered her services to the surgeon-general. "I propose," she said, "to organize under the official auspices of the War Department, an Army nursing corps made up of women volunteers." Her persistence—she even visited President Abraham Lincoln to press her cause—and fame as a reformer soon gained her a commission as "Superintendent of United States Army Nurses."

"I never had so few moments for myself," Dix wrote a friend in May 1861, and for the duration of the war, she threw herself into her work. Her standards were high and often inflexible. The only women who should be sent to Washington, she informed a relief association in New York, were "those who are sober, earnest, self-sacrificing, and self-sustained." To protect the reputation of her volunteer corps and promote the professionalism of its efforts, she insisted that all applicants should be over the age of 30 and plain in appearance. Her zeal for efficiency and caring treatment brought her into repeated conflicts with the antiquated and often callous medical bureaucracy. Independent nurses who did not pass through her training were also exposed to her wrath. Although dogmatic and authoritarian, she set standards that helped break down traditional barriers against the entrance of women into military nursing.

Dix continued her reform efforts long after the war was over. She traveled constantly and never did establish a permanent home for herself. Fittingly, she died at a New Jersey hospital in Trenton that she had been instrumental in founding.

SEE ALSO
Medicine; Nurses

FURTHER READING
Gollaher, David. *Voice for the Mad: The*

Life of Dorothea Dix. New York: Free Press, 1995.
Marshall, Helen E. *Dorothea Dix: Forgotten Samaritan.* Chapel Hill: University of North Carolina Press, 1937.

Douglas, Stephen A.

NORTHERN POLITICIAN

- Born: April 23, 1813, Brandon, Vt.
- Political party: Democrat
- Education: sporadic schooling in private academics
- Government service: Illinois state attorney, 1834–35; Illinois House of Representatives, 1836; Register of land office at Springfield, Ill., 1837–40; Illinois secretary of state, 1840; Illinois state judge, 1841–43; U.S. House of Representatives, 1843–47; U.S. Senate, 1847–61
- Died: June 3, 1861, Chicago, Ill.

The most dynamic and forceful Democratic leader to emerge in the mid-19th century, Stephen A. Douglas failed in his bid for the Presidency in 1860 when his party split over the slavery issue. After warning of the danger of disunion during the Presidential campaign, he desperately worked for a sectional compromise once secession began. When those efforts collapsed, he spent the last two months of his life rallying support for the Union cause.

Born of old English stock in New England, the young Douglas accompanied his widowed mother to Ontario County, New York, when she remarried. After attending Canandaigua Academy, he studied law before his ambition to make a name for himself in the growing West took him to Cleveland in 1833. After pushing on to St. Louis, he settled in southern Illinois. Admitted to the Illinois bar in 1834, he opened a law office in Jacksonville and began his rapid rise in the Illinois

Democratic party. The political connections he cultivated as a register of the land office and his work on behalf of Martin Van Buren in the latter's unsuccessful Presidential reelection campaign of 1840 soon made him the most influential Democrat in the state. In 1843 he entered Congress. First as a representative and then as a senator, he remained there for the rest of his life.

Douglas strongly identified with the principles of Jacksonian Democracy, particularly as they seemed to apply to his adopted West. "I have become a *Western* man," he wrote a friend back East in 1833, "[and] have imbibed Western feelings, principles and interests." Like Abraham Lincoln, who became his chief rival in Illinois politics by the late 1850s, Douglas believed that the United States had a mission to set an example of democratic government for the rest of the world to follow. "Our success is the foundation of all their hopes," he told his fellow congressmen in 1848. For Douglas, that success would be measured by the spread of the American people and their democratic institutions of free government across the North American continent. This, he insisted, was the destiny of the United States, and he devoted his political career to making it a reality.

For most of his congressional career, Douglas chaired the Committee on Territories in both the House and Senate. From this powerful position, he championed westward expansion, a transcontinental railroad, and free land for settlers. Central to his program for the West was territorial self-government or, as it was called, popular sovereignty.

The death of Stephen A. Douglas just after the outbreak of the Civil War deprived Northern Democrats of their most forceful and energetic leader. "There can be no neutrals in this war, only patriots— or traitors," he proclaimed a month before he died.

Defining the term as the "right of the people of an organized Territory...to govern themselves in respect to their own internal policy and domestic affairs," he always insisted that it offered the only democratic way of resolving the issue of slavery in the territories.

With the doctrine of popular sovereignty Douglas tried to stake out a middle, national position between sectional extremists on the slavery issue. The tragedy of his career was that popular sovereignty itself became incredibly divisive. Northerners never fully trusted Douglas on the slavery question once many of them accepted the Republican charge that his Kansas-Nebraska Act was a slaveholders' plot to expand slavery at the expense of free labor. When he declared, most notably in his 1858 debates with Lincoln, that regardless of the *Dred Scott* decision by the Supreme Court, territorial settlers could still exclude slavery by not passing the local legislation necessary to protect it, his name became anathema to most Southerners. The bitter opposition of Southerners cost Douglas a united Democratic party in 1860 and destroyed his Presidential bid.

Douglas struggled in vain to save the Union once secession got under way. He backed a constitutional amendment to protect slavery in the states, tried to form a national Union party, and urged Lincoln to abandon Fort Sumter. When hostilities began, he fully supported Lincoln's call for troops. He was uniting Northern Democrats behind the Union cause up to the point of his death from typhoid fever a few weeks after the war started.

SEE ALSO
Dred Scott decision; Election of 1860; Kansas-Nebraska Act; Lincoln-Douglas debates; Popular sovereignty

FURTHER READING
Johannsen, Robert W. *Stephen A. Douglas.* New York: Oxford University Press, 1973.

Douglass, Frederick
ABOLITIONIST

- *Born: around February 1817, Tuckahoe, near Easton, Md.*
- *Education: self-taught*
- *Occupation: editor, lecturer, author*
- *Government service: marshal, District of Columbia, 1877–81; recorder of deeds, District of Columbia, 1881–86; U.S. consul general, Haiti, 1889–91*
- *Died: February 20, 1895, Washington, D.C.*

Following his escape from slavery in 1838, Frederick Douglass was a driving force behind abolitionism. An eloquent speaker and prolific writer, he championed the cause of black liberation and then the recruitment of black troops when the Civil War erupted. He continued his reform efforts after the war as an agitator for black suffrage and civil rights.

The fourth child of a slave mother (his father was an unknown white man), Douglass was born into slavery on the Eastern Shore of Maryland. His mother died when he was a child, and his master sent him to Baltimore to serve as a household slave. His stay in Baltimore was a critical turning point in his life, for it was there that he learned to read and write and to glimpse the possibilities for human freedom offered by the greater range of activities and contacts open to urban slaves as opposed to field hands on a plantation. After an unsuccessful attempt to escape in 1835, he passed himself off in 1838 as a seaman, boarded a train, and made his way to New York City. Of his feelings when he safely arrived, he later wrote: "I suppose I felt as one may imagine the unarmed mariner to feel when he is rescued by a friendly man-of-war from the pursuit of a pirate."

Soon after Douglass's fiancée, a free black, joined him in New York. The couple married and then moved to New Bedford, Massachusetts, where the new husband abandoned the slave name of Bailey given him by his mother for "Douglass," after a heroic character in Sir Walter Scott's poem *Lady of the Lake.* The racial prejudice of local whites prevented him from working as a skilled laborer, and he struggled to support himself and his wife for the next three years. Then, after delivering a powerful speech at an antislavery meeting in 1841, he launched his career as a spellbinding lecturer on the abolitionist circuit. His autobiography, *Narrative of the Life of Frederick Douglass, an American Slave,* became a best-seller when it was published in 1845.

Fearing that the details of his identity and place of residence revealed in his autobiography exposed him to the risk of reenslavement, Douglass sailed to England on a speaking tour. English friends purchased his freedom in December 1846, and upon returning to the United States in 1847, he founded the *North Star,* an abolitionist newspaper that was the first of many journals he was to edit and publish. Now unwilling merely to follow the lead of white abolitionists, he broke with William Lloyd Garrison in 1851 when he publicly denied the Garrisonian reading of the Constitution as a proslavery document. If correctly interpreted, Douglass insisted, "the Constitution is a *glorious liberty document,*" and he called for a political war against slavery. Throughout the 1850s he fought against all forms of legal discrimination as he solidified his position as the foremost black reformer of his day.

Douglass hailed the outbreak of the Civil War as a momentous watershed for African Americans. He immediately sensed, as he wrote in *Douglass's*

Monthly after the fall of Fort Sumter, that the war could lead to "a tremendous revolution in all things pertaining to the possible future of the colored people of the United States." To hasten that revolution, he pressured the Union administration to declare for emancipation and to accept black recruits as combat soldiers. "Men in earnest don't fight with one hand, when they might fight with two," he wrote in the fall of 1861, "and a man drowning would not refuse to be saved even by a colored hand." When black soldiers were accepted, two of his sons were among the first to enlist.

Once emancipation was achieved, Douglass's goals focused on securing equality before the law and full rights of citizenship, including the vote, for the freed population. He aligned himself with the Radical Republicans during Reconstruction and received a number of patronage appointments as a reward for his party loyalty. His denunciation of lynchings in the South was the last reform cause he took up before his death from a heart attack.

SEE ALSO

Abolitionism; Black soldiers; Black suffrage

FURTHER READING

Baker, Houston A., Jr., ed. *Narrative of the Life of Frederick Douglass, an American Slave.* New York: Viking Penguin, 1982.
McFeely, William S. *Frederick Douglass.* New York: W. W. Norton, 1991.
Oakes, James. *The Radical and the Republican: Frederick Douglass, Abraham Lincoln, and the Triumph of Antislavery Politics.* New York: W. W. Norton, 2007.

Before the Lincoln administration committed itself to emancipation, Frederick Douglass tirelessly insisted that "Sound policy, not less then humanity, demands the instant liberation of every slave in the rebel states." He was speaking for all African Americans.

Draft

SEE Conscription

Dred Scott decision

Designed to end the controversy over the status of slavery in the territories, the *Dred Scott* decision of the U.S. Supreme Court in 1857 had exactly the opposite effect. The Court's proslavery ruling infuriated antislavery forces in the North and deepened sectional division within the Democratic party.

Dred Scott was a slave taken by his owner in the 1830s from Missouri into the free state of Illinois and later into the Wisconsin Territory, where slavery had been prohibited by the Missouri Compromise of 1820. After returning to Missouri in 1838 with his master, Scott sued for his freedom in 1846 on the grounds that his residence in a free state and a free territory had made him a free man. Missouri courts first ruled for and then against him. With the assistance of the abolitionists, he took his case to the Supreme Court, headed by Chief Justice Roger Taney of Maryland. The Court reached a decision on March 6, 1857.

Five of the nine justices were Southern Democrats. Joined by a sixth Democrat, Justice Robert Grier of Pennsylvania, they all agreed that Scott was still a slave and that the Missouri Compromise was unconstitutional. Taney wrote the most influential and widely cited opinion. He first declared that "negroes of African descent" could not be citizens of the United States and hence Scott had no legal right to bring suit in a federal court. He went on to argue that slaves were a form of property protected by the Fifth Amendment, which prohibited Congress from denying a citizen the use of his or her property without due process of law. Slavery could not be singled out for exclusion from the territories, and

Moving clockwise from Lincoln in the upper right corner to John Bell, Stephen A. Douglas, and John C. Breckinridge, this cartoon from the campaign of 1860 depicts the four Presidential candidates wrestling with the consequences of the Dred Scott decision. Its negative portrayal of African Americans was typical of American culture as a whole.

thus the Missouri Compromise restriction on slavery was unconstitutional. Taney went on to add, in a blow directed against the popular sovereignty doctrine associated with Stephen A. Douglas, that a territorial legislature likewise had no constitutional power to ban slavery in the territories.

Republicans and Northern Democrats alike assailed the Court's decision. The Republicans charged that this proslavery reading of the Constitution would soon lead to the legalization of slavery in *all* the states. By refusing to support the decision, Northern Democrats alienated the Southern wing of their party, and the stage was set for the breakup of the Democrats in 1860 that paved the way for a Republican victory.

SEE ALSO

Citizenship; Federal slave code; 14th Amendment

FURTHER READING

Fehrenbacher, Don E. *The Dred Scott Case: Its Significance in American Law and Politics.* New York: Oxford University Press, 1978.

Du Pont, Samuel F.

UNION ADMIRAL

- *Born: September 27, 1803, Bergen Point, N.J.*
- *Education: sporadic schooling in lower grades*
- *Military service: U.S. Navy: midshipman, 1815–26; lieutenant, 1826–43; commander, 1843–55; captain, 1855–61; commodore, 1861–62; rear admiral, 1862–65*
- *Died: June 23, 1865, Philadelphia, Pa.*

The first Union naval hero, Samuel F. Du Pont was instrumental in establishing the blockade along the South Atlantic coast. His victory at the battle of Port Royal Sound in November 1861 was the first major success of the Union navy in the war. His reputation suffered, however, when his attack on Charleston in April 1863 resulted in the worst naval defeat for the Union during the war.

The nephew of the founder of the largest gunpowder factory in antebellum America, Du Pont spent most of his youth in Delaware. His grandfather secured him an appointment as a midshipman, and at the age of 14 he saw his first maritime service in the Mediterranean. By the outbreak of the Mexican War, he had risen to the rank of commander. After helping clear the Gulf of California of Mexican ships during that war, he held a variety of administrative posts in the 1850s and was active in promoting naval reform.

As an experienced commander and administrator with 45 years of naval service, Du Pont was a strong choice to head the Blockade Strategy Board put together by Secretary of the Navy Gideon B. Welles in the spring of 1861. Charged with devising an overall strategic plan for the Union navy, the board divided the Confederate coast into four blockading zones and urged that a large, deepwater harbor be seized for each zone to serve as a base for year-long operations. Upon Du Pont's recommendation, the board selected Port Royal Sound, halfway between Savannah and Charleston, as the projected base for the South Atlantic Blockading Squadron, and Du Pont was given command of the joint army-navy expedition that was to capture Port Royal.

Despite a rebel informant who leaked news of the expedition and a gale of near-hurricane force that scattered the federal fleet and drove ashore most of the transports carrying the army troops, Du Pont went ahead with the attack. He won a stunning victory by employing innovative tactics that

Samuel F. Du Pont is second from the left aboard his flagship USS Wabash in 1863. He was the first commander of the Union's South Atlantic Blockading Squadron.

concentrated the fire of his fleet on the stronger of the two rebel forts guarding Port Royal. Once that fort fell, the other had to be abandoned, and the way was open for Union forces to secure the harbor. Du Pont followed up that victory by occupying the sounds along the Georgia coast and seizing Jacksonville and St. Augustine in Florida.

The turning point of Du Pont's naval career came with the Department of the Navy's decision to launch an attack against Charleston in April 1863. Although he felt that his fleet of ironclads needed the backing of 25,000 troops to have any realistic chance of success, he launched the attack without army support. The outer harbor defenses were even stronger than he had feared, and his fleet was hit with three times as many shells as it was able to fire in return. After assessing the damage to his ships, he decided not to renew the battle on the second day. "We have met with a sad repulse," he reported to his chief of staff; "I shall not turn it into a great disaster."

Anxious to deflect criticism from themselves, the officials in the department blamed Du Pont for the Union defeat at Charleston. After agreeing to be relieved of command, he served on boards and commissions for the remainder of the war. His health had been failing for a number of years, and he died shortly after the war.

SEE ALSO
Blockade; Naval warfare

FURTHER READING
Weddle, Kevin J. *Lincoln's Tragic Admiral: The Life of Samuel F. Du Pont.* Charlottesville: University of Virginia Press, 2005.

Early, Jubal A.

CONFEDERATE GENERAL

- Born: November 3, 1816, Franklin County, Va.
- Education: U.S. Military Academy, B.S., 1837
- Military service: U.S. Army: lieutenant, artillery, 1837; 1st lieutenant, 1838; major, 1st Virginia Volunteers, 1847–48; Confederate army: colonel, 1861; brigadier general, 1861–63; major general, 1863–64; lieutenant general, 1864–65
- Died: March 2, 1895, Lynchburg, Va.

Six feet tall, with a long, black beard and a caustic tongue, Jubal A. Early looked and sounded like the fighter that he was. Edward Porter Alexander, a fellow general in Robert E. Lee's Army of Northern Virginia, recalled, "His greatest quality perhaps was the fearlessness with which he fought against all odds & discouragements." Best known for his raid against Washington in July

1864, he suffered a series of decisive defeats in the Shenandoah Valley in the fall of 1864 and was relieved of command in early 1865.

After attending Danville Male Academy in Virginia, Early entered West Point and graduated in the top half of his class. He fought in the Seminole War before resigning his commission in 1838 to study law. Admitted to the bar in 1840, he became a successful lawyer and Whig politician, serving first in the Virginia House of Delegates and then as commonwealth's attorney from 1842 to 1852. He was a major of volunteers during the Mexican War. Although elected as a Unionist delegate from Franklin County during the secession crisis, he promptly followed his native state out of the Union.

Early led a brigade at First Bull Run and in the early stages of the Peninsula campaign before he was wounded at Williamsburg. After returning to duty in the Second Bull Run Campaign, he became a division commander and was active in all the major

Union troops reinforced this bridge and other Union bridges that connected Washington to the Virginia side of the Potomac River when General Jubal A. Early led a Confederate raid that threatened the capital in the summer of 1864.

engagements of the Army of Northern Virginia through the spring of 1864. He took over General Richard S. Ewell's corps in May 1864, and led it at the battle of Cold Harbor.

In June 1864, General Robert E. Lee ordered Early to take his corps to the Shenandoah Valley, drive out the federal forces under General David Hunter, and, if possible, threaten Washington from the rear. Lee hoped that Early, like Thomas "Stonewall" Jackson in the spring of 1862, would panic the authorities in Washington into detaching troops from the huge Union army threatening to encircle Richmond. After pushing Hunter into West Virginia and defeating a hastily thrown-together federal army at Monocacy, Maryland, Early did reach the outskirts of Washington on July 11 in a raid that was a qualified success. Only the arrival of the 6th Corps from the Army of the Potomac at Petersburg prevented a rebel assault on the outer defenses of the Union's capital.

When Early launched another raid into Maryland in late July, Union authorities finally woke up to the need to unify their scattered commands in the Shenandoah Valley into a powerful new department. The commander of that department, General Philip H. Sheridan, had orders to follow Early "to the death." After defeating Early in battles at Winchester and Fisher's Hill in September 1864, Sheridan led a counterattack at Cedar Creek on October 19 that smashed Early's army. Early later remarked of the rebel reversal at Cedar Creek: "The Yankees got whipped. We got scared."

Early's defeats in the Shenandoah Valley cost him the confidence of his troops, and at the end of the war he was without a command. Refusing to surrender, he fled after the war, first to Mexico and then to Canada. He returned to Virginia in 1869, resumed his law practice, and served as the first president of the Southern Historical Society. Fiercely loyal to Lee's memory, Early led the campaign to pin responsibility for the Confederate defeat at Gettysburg on General James Longstreet.

SEE ALSO
Longstreet, James; Sheridan, Philip H.

FURTHER READING
Bushong, Millard K. *Old Jube: A Biography of General Jubal A. Early.* Boyce, Va.: Carr Publishing, 1955.
Gallagher, Gary W. *Jubal A. Early, the Lost Cause, and Civil War History: A Persistent Legacy.* Milwaukee, Wis.: Marquette University Press, 1995.

Election of 1860

The victory of Republican Abraham Lincoln in the Presidential election of 1860 set in motion the events that culminated in secession and the outbreak of the Civil War. For Republicans such as William Cullen Bryant, who rejoiced that "the cause of justice and liberty has triumphed in the late election," the disastrous follow-up to the election could not have been more surprising.

It was an unusual election in that four major candidates were running: John Bell of Tennessee, the candidate of the newly formed Constitutional Union party; Abraham Lincoln, the Republican nominee; and two Democrats, Stephen A. Douglas of Illinois (for the Northern wing of the party) and John C. Breckinridge of Kentucky (for the Southern wing). Despite the lingering effects of an economic downturn in the North in 1858, slavery was the dominant issue in the campaign. As Republican Orville H. Browning reported in August: "It is manifest to all that there is an

A Philadelphia printing shop produced this banner for the Lincoln Republicans during the election of 1860. The parties were adept at drawing upon the graphic arts to promote their candidates.

unusual degree of political interest pervading the country—that people, everywhere, are excited,...and yet, from one extremity of the Republic to the other, scarcely any other subject is mentioned, or any other question discussed...save the question of negro slavery."

On the issue of slavery, each of the candidates had a distinctive position. Although insisting that the federal government had absolutely no right to interfere with slavery in the states where it existed, Lincoln pledged to keep slavery out of the territories. In sharp opposition, Breckinridge endorsed the Southern demand for congressional protection of slavery in the territories. Douglas still clung to the position that the territorial settlers could determine the slavery issue for themselves. Holding that any additional discussion of slavery simply strengthened the hand of disunionists in both sections, Bell limited himself to a declaration of support for the Union and a love of the Constitution.

The emphasis on slavery—or more precisely, the future of slavery and the relatively clear-cut stands on the issue taken by the candidates—contributed to the pronounced sectionalized nature of the voting returns. Lincoln was not even on the ballot in 10 of the slave states, and he and Douglas combined received less than 15 percent of the popular vote in the South. Conversely, they gained 90 percent of the Northern vote. On the other side of the sectional divide, Breckinridge and Bell won 85 percent of the Southern vote.

When the ballots were counted, Lincoln, as seasoned observers had

expected since the late summer, was the winner. Douglas's support was widely scattered, and he carried outright only the state of Missouri. Breckinridge swept the Lower South and Bell ran strongly in the Upper South, but Lincoln gained a clear electoral majority with 40 percent of the popular vote by taking the entire North (except for New Jersey, whose electoral votes he split with Douglas). His staunchest supporters were rural and small-town evangelical Yankees in New England and the upper Midwest. By running exceptionally well among new, younger voters and cutting heavily into the former Know-Nothing vote, he carried the Mid-Atlantic and lower midwestern states lost by John C. Frémont in 1856. Having won the election, he was now to face the greatest crisis that ever confronted any U.S. President.

SEE ALSO
Constitutional Union party; Democratic party; Lincoln, Abraham; Republican party; Secession

FURTHER READING
Gienapp, William E. "Who Voted for Lincoln?" in *Abraham Lincoln and the American Political Tradition,* edited by John L. Thomas. Amherst: University of Massachusetts Press, 1986.
Luthin, Reinhard H. *The First Lincoln Campaign.* Cambridge, Mass.: Harvard University Press, 1944.

Election of 1864

SEE Union politics

Election of 1876

The disputed Presidential election of 1876 resulted in a political settlement by which the Republicans gained the Presidency in return for agreeing to bring Reconstruction to a formal end. The biggest winners were the Southern Democrats, for they were now free to shape the South's racial agenda on their own terms—namely, white supremacy.

Following their stunning setbacks in the congressional elections of 1874, the Republicans scrambled to regroup for the Presidential contest in 1876. Hoping to defuse Democratic attacks of having promoted a bloated, corruption-ridden government under President Ulysses S. Grant, they campaigned on the same themes of reform and retrenchment that the Democrats emphasized. Their candidate was Ohio governor Rutherford B. Hayes, a former Union general who had established a reputation for honesty and efficiency during his tenure as governor. The Democrats countered with Governor Samuel J. Tilden of New York, a wealthy lawyer known to the public for his role in helping break up the notorious Boss Tweed ring in New York City.

The Republicans half expected to lose. The scandals of the Grant administration, growing Northern weariness over Reconstruction and Republican rule in the South, and the political fallout from an economic depression that refused to lift all pointed toward a Democratic victory. As it was, Tilden, who gained a bare majority of the popular vote, initially appeared to have won. Still, as a result of disputed returns from South Carolina, Florida, and Louisiana—the only Southern states where Republican administrations had survived—he was one vote short of the electoral majority needed to claim the Presidency. If all of the disputed returns were counted for Hayes, he would be President.

Throughout the winter of 1876–77, it was unclear just who would be declared President. After complex maneuverings and wild rumors of a possible resumption of sectional violence, Congress finally appointed a 15-member electoral commission to settle the issue. The Republicans still had enough strength in Congress to secure a one-vote majority on the commission. To no one's surprise, the commission, citing fraud and intimidation in the Democratic returns, awarded all the disputed ballots to Hayes and thus proclaimed him President.

Southern Democrats went along with the decision because home rule in racial matters was of greater importance to them than having a Democrat in the White House. Through intermediaries, Hayes confided to Southern Democrats that he would remove the last federal troops from the South and hence deprive the remaining Southern Republican governments of any federal assistance. Vague promises of Republican support for a Southern transcontinental

This Thomas Nast cartoon depicted the widespread relief in the North over the ability of the party managers to reach an agreement that avoided violence in settling the disputed Presidential contest between Rutherford B. Hayes and Samuel J. Tilden in 1876.

railroad and subsidies for the Southern economy were also allegedly made, but the critical feature of what came to be called the Compromise of 1877 was the Republican pledge to stay out of the internal affairs of the South.

The settlement of the election of 1876 brought an end to black aspirations to be treated as legal and political equals in the post–Civil War South. Until well into the 20th century, white Democratic governments largely ignored the constitutional protections of the 14th and 15th amendments as they applied to African Americans.

SEE ALSO

Congressional Reconstruction; Democratic party; 15th Amendment; 14th Amendment; Republican party

FURTHER READING

Holt, Michael F. *By One Vote: The Disputed Presidential Election of 1876.* Lawrence: University Press of Kansas, 2008.
Woodward, C. Vann. *Reunion and Reaction: The Compromise of 1877 and the End of Reconstruction.* Boston: Little, Brown, 1951.

Emancipation

Emancipation began with the countless decisions of individual slaves to seize freedom whenever the opportunity presented itself during the Civil War. By refusing to wait for a cautious Union government to act, they helped force the hand of that government when emancipation emerged as a political possibility in 1862.

President Abraham Lincoln's primary concern in the early stages of the war was to hold together a political coalition of Republicans, War Democrats, and Unionists in the Border South. A premature declaration of emancipation as a war aim would have shattered that coalition and likely cost Lincoln the support he needed to wage the war. Emancipation would become politically feasible only when a majority of Northerners, civilians and military personnel alike, grasped that the Union and slavery were incompatible. Once that point was reached in late 1862, the war assumed an entirely new character.

Congress took the first official step against slavery in August 1861 when it passed the First Confiscation Act, a measure that included slaves among the property used "in aid of the rebellion" that could be seized by Union armies. At the end of the month, General John C. Frémont went considerably further when he invoked martial law to free the slaves of all rebel masters in Missouri. Worried that Frémont's precipitate move would "ruin our rather fair prospect for [keeping] Kentucky [in the Union]," Lincoln countermanded the order.

Despite his rebuff, Frémont had many backers in Congress. Republicans were hearing from their constituents back home that the Union was far too lenient with unrepentant rebels. When Congress assembled in late 1861, it stepped up the pressure on Lincoln to move against slavery. In March 1862, Congress prohibited the army from returning to their owners fugitive slaves who had come behind Union lines. This was a direct refutation of the army's initial policy of enforcing the Fugitive Slave Act of 1850. In April, Congress passed a bill for compensated emancipation in the District of Columbia. In June, Congress prohibited slavery in all federal territories and ratified a treaty with Britain for the joint suppression of the African slave trade. And finally in July, it opened up militia service to blacks and passed a Second Confiscation Act that freed all slaves of rebel masters, regardless of whether they had actually been used to aid the rebellion. (Lincoln doubted the constitutionality of this measure and did little to enforce it.) Frustrated with the continued massive military resistance of the Confederacy, Northern public opinion was growing ever harsher toward slavery.

Lincoln both reflected and guided this antislavery shift in Northern attitudes. As if to signal approval of a harder stand against slavery, he had refused in February 1862 to commute the death sentence of Captain Nathaniel Gordon, a Northern slave trader who was the first and only U.S. citizen ever to be executed under a congressional act of 1819 declaring involvement in the African slave trade a capital offense. In March, Lincoln proposed a program for voluntary and gradual emancipation by the states that included federal compensation of $400 per slave and funds for the colonization abroad of the freed blacks. He aimed this program specifically at the loyal border states. Their acceptance of the plan would end any lingering hope in the Confederacy of ever winning over these slave states, and, Lincoln reasoned, well might bring the war to a rapid end.

The last critical element in converting the North to a policy of emancipation was the army itself. As Union armies advanced into the South, they were met by fleeing slaves who offered their services as workers, scouts, and spies. In the first year of the war, official policy called for the return or exclusion of such slaves. The army was to retain for its own use only those slaves who fell under the technical provisions of the First Confiscation Act. In practice, however, it proved impossible to determine the loyalty of masters or the prior uses to which their slaves had been put. Efforts to sort out the legal entanglements were so time-consuming and dis-

ruptive of military routine that Union commanders followed the path of least resistance and put to work all the able-bodied slaves who entered their lines. Then, as Union forces became increasingly dependent on these laborers and their services, the army acquired a vested stake in emancipation. After all, about the only reliable friends and allies the Union army had found in the occupied South were the slaves themselves. Thus, by their own actions, the fleeing slaves had forced the army to confront the issue of emancipation it initially had tried to ignore.

By July 1862, Lincoln was prepared to abolish slavery by Presidential decree. Representatives from the border states probably removed any lingering doubts in his mind when they informed him on July 12 of their rejection of his plan for voluntary emancipation. Although these states, as well as the Union-occupied areas in the Confederacy as of January 1, 1863, were excluded from the Emancipation Proclamation, Lincoln accurately foresaw that the war would sweep away slavery everywhere. Slavery crumbled in a practical, if not legal, sense in the Border South when slaves rushed off to join the Union army in 1863 and 1864. Very late in the war, Maryland and Missouri provided for emancipation in their state constitutions. In Kentucky and Delaware, legal emancipation would have to wait for the passage of the 13th Amendment in 1865.

SEE ALSO

Black soldiers; Contrabands; Emancipation Proclamation; 13th Amendment

FURTHER READING

Berlin, Ira et al. *Slaves No More: Three Essays on Emancipation and the Civil War.* New York: Cambridge University Press, 1992.
Litwack, Leon F. *Been in the Storm So Long: The Aftermath of Slavery.* New York: Knopf, 1979.

Emancipation Proclamation

Issued on New Year's Day, 1863, by President Abraham Lincoln, the Emancipation Proclamation elevated the Civil War to a new and higher moral level. By declaring "forever free" the slaves in Confederate-held territory, the proclamation gave the Union cause a moral purpose in a war effort that earlier could be criticized as a naked grab for power. It also gave a tremendous emotional boost to friends of the Union at home and abroad and greatly reduced any chance of foreign recognition of the Confederacy.

On July 22, 1862, Lincoln announced to his cabinet his intention to issue a proclamation of general emancipation in the Confederate South. Abolitionists, free blacks, and antislavery members of Congress had been urging him to do so since the start of the war. Worried that that action might cause the Union to lose support in the Border South, he hung back until the failure of the Union offensive against Richmond in June 1862 convinced him that emancipation had now become a war measure essential for achieving Union victory.

Following the shrewd advice of Secretary of State William H. Seward, Lincoln delayed his proclamation until he could peg it to a federal victory. Otherwise, it would appear to be an act of desperation by a defeated government. The battle of Antietam gave him that victory, and on September 22, 1862, he issued a preliminary Emancipation Proclamation. He warned the Confederacy that emancipation would take effect on January 1, 1863, in all the territory it then held. Until then, rebel states were free to reenter the Union with slavery intact. He found no takers.

The final version of the Emancipation Proclamation incorporated some key changes in Lincoln's thinking since the fall. He dropped earlier references to the colonization of freed slaves and monetary compensation for loyal slaveowners. Most significantly, his proclamation now called for enlisting emancipated slaves into the Union military. As

A free American eagle flies front and center of the nation's capitol in this allegorical painting celebrating the Emancipation Proclamation. The goddess of Liberty rides a chariot that is drawn by white horses and flanked by Abraham Lincoln and Union officers on the right, rejoicing blacks on the left.

he noted in March 1863, arming the liberated slaves enabled the North to utilize "the great *available* and yet *unavailed* of, force for restoring the Union."

The dry, legalistic phrases of the Emancipation Proclamation fell far short of a ringing declaration on behalf of human freedom. The abolitionists immediately pointed out that the proclamation freed slaves only in areas where the Union exercised no authority and kept them enslaved in areas that were under effective federal control. Consistent with Lincoln's belief that emancipation was constitutional only under the war powers of the President, the proclamation declared free only those slaves in the Confederacy. It excluded slaves in the loyal states of the Border South and those in the Union-occupied areas of Tennessee, western Virginia (which would become the state of West Virginia that June), southern Louisiana, and Norfolk and Virginia's eastern shore.

However bland its language was, the Emancipation Proclamation signaled that the war had taken an irreversible turn toward a social and economic revolution. For all their disappointment that the proclamation had not freed all the slaves, black Americans embraced it in spontaneous celebrations of joy. Henry M. Turner, a black minister in Washington, was fully justified in writing, "The first day of January, 1863, is destined to form one of the most memorable epochs in the history of the world."

SEE ALSO

Black soldiers; Emancipation; 13th Amendment

FURTHER READING

Franklin, John Hope. *The Emancipation Proclamation.* New York: Doubleday, 1963.
Guelzo, Allen C. *Lincoln's Emancipation Proclamation: The End of Slavery in America.* New York: Simon & Schuster, 2004.

Enforcement Acts

SEE Ku Klux Klan

Evans, Augusta Jane
CONFEDERATE AUTHOR

- *Born: May 8, 1835, Columbus, Ga.*
- *Education: no formal schooling*
- *Occupation: author*
- *Died: May 9, 1909, near Mobile, Ala.*

A fervid Southern patriot, Augusta Evans was the author of *Macaria; or Altars of Sacrifice,* the most popular novel published in the Confederacy. Its stirring depiction of the selfless sacrifice of its heroines to the Confederate cause attracted a wide readership in the North as well, and at least one Union general, George Thomas, went so far as to ban the novel from Union lines.

Born into a prominent but impoverished family, Evans moved with her parents to San Antonio, Texas, and then to Mobile, Alabama, in 1848 as her father vainly tried to rebuild his lost fortune. The library of a wealthy aunt enabled her to escape into a world of books, and in her late teens she embarked on a literary career. Her second novel, *Beulah* (1859), was a commercial success that gained her a national reputation. In *Beulah* she called upon Southern women to be "imperishable monuments of true female heroism" by accepting their duties as wives and mothers to shield Southern civilization from the greed and corruption of an immoral North.

Utterly certain that the North had long been waging a political and cultural war against the South, Evans was a rabid secessionist. Shortly after Alabama seceded in January 1861, she wrote a friend that the time had come for all Southerners to "conquer or perish together; delay is ruinous, suicidal." She rushed to Montgomery to attend President Jefferson Davis's inauguration and to begin cultivating a network of friends among Confederate leaders.

When the war broke out, Evans helped organize the women of Mobile for the city's defense and founded a hospital and then an orphan asylum. Taking time off from her work as a nurse, she traveled throughout the Confederacy visiting battle sites and rallying rebel troops. Still, as she wrote General Pierre G. T. Beauregard in August 1862, she longed to do more for "the consummation of our freedom." The result of that longing was *Macaria,* her patriotic novel that was published in 1864.

Defying the conventions of the domestic novel, *Macaria* was openly partisan in its depiction of divisive sectional issues. It also broke new ground by refusing to present marriage as the only means of women's personal fulfillment. Its three main characters—Russell Aubrey, Electra Gray, and Irene Huntingdon—were all martyrs to the Confederate cause. Russell dies a hero's death on the battlefield just after Irene confesses her love for him. Rejecting loveless marriages, both Irene and Electra find fulfillment through their tireless sacrifices for Confederate victory. As Irene tells Electra when the war begins: "You and I have much to do, during these days of gloom and national trial, for upon the purity, the devotion, and the patriotism of the women of our land, not less than upon the heroism of our armies, depends our national salvation."

Following the Southern surrender, Evans initially hoped to write the definitive history of the Confederacy. Upon hearing that Alexander H. Stephens was working on such a project, she abandoned her plans and turned to the security of a marriage with Lorenzo Madison Wilson, a wealthy Mobile businessman, and a career as the writer of conventional domestic novels. Her postwar fiction barely touched upon the Civil War.

SEE ALSO

Literature

FURTHER READING

Faust, Drew Gilpin. *Mothers of Invention: Women of the Slaveholding South in the American Civil War.* Chapel Hill: University of North Carolina Press, 1996.

Fidler, William P. *Augusta Evans Wilson, 1835–1909.* Tuscaloosa: University of Alabama Press, 1951.

Ewell, Richard S.

CONFEDERATE GENERAL

- *Born: February 8, 1817, Georgetown, Washington, D.C.*
- *Education: U.S. Military Academy, B.S., 1840*
- *Military service: U.S. Army: brevet lieutenant, dragoons (cavalry), 1840; lieutenant, 1840–45; 1st lieutenant, 1845–49; captain, 1849-61; Confederate army: colonel, 1861; brigadier general, 1861–62; major general, 1862–63; lieutenant general, 1863–65*
- *Died: January 25, 1872, Spring Hill, Tenn.*

With a bald head that drooped to one side, a beak-like nose, and bulging eyes, Richard S. Ewell reminded many onlookers of a bird. His eccentricities, such as humming to himself while munching on sunflower seeds when his chronic dyspepsia flared up, added to his reputation as a real character. Still, he was a bold, seasoned fighter who compiled an excellent record as a brigade and division commander. Had he succeeded in driving the federals off Cemetery Hill on the first day's battle at Gettysburg, he would have been remembered as one of the Confederacy's finest generals.

The son of a physician, Ewell was raised in Prince William County, Virginia. After graduating in the top quarter of his class at West Point, he entered the dragoons (cavalry), fought with distinction in the Mexican War, and served almost continuously at frontier outposts in the Southwest. Despite his strong Unionism, he resigned his commission in May 1861 and volunteered for Confederate service.

After leading a brigade at First Bull Run, Ewell excelled as a division commander under the iron-willed generalship of Thomas J. "Stonewall" Jackson during the Shenandoah Valley Campaign in the spring of 1862. Ewell referred to Jackson as "that enthusiastic fanatic" and was often baffled by his orders, but he learned how to adjust to Jackson's relentless pace and led his troops to victories at Winchester and Cross Keys. Ewell also fought under Jackson in the Peninsula Campaign and at Second Bull Run, where a Union shell cost him a leg at Groveton, Virginia, in August 1862.

Ewell returned to duty in May 1863, in charge of part of Jackson's old corps. His wooden leg made it impossible for him to mount a horse, and he had to be strapped into the saddle. Many felt that his wound had dulled his zeal for combat (others, however, cited his recent marriage to the nurse who had supervised his convalescence). Whatever the reason, Ewell was shaky at Gettysburg. General Robert E. Lee's orders gave him more discretion than Jackson's had, and without precise directions Ewell failed to push the Confederate advantage on July 1 and then was overly passive on the following two days in attacks that were supposed to be coordinated with rebel assaults elsewhere along the Union line.

Ewell performed better in the early stages of the Union's Virginia Campaign in the spring of 1864. A fellow officer, Edward Porter Alexander, recalled of the fighting in the "Wilderness," a nearly impenetrable area of woods and underbrush near the Rapidan River, on May 5 that "dear, glorious, old, one-legged Ewell...sat back & not only whipped everything that attacked him but he even sallied out on some rash ones & captured two guns & quite a lot of prisoners." A bad fall from a horse at Spotsylvania later in the month left him unfit for an active field command. After heading the Richmond defenses in the last months of the war, he was captured at Sayler's Creek on April 6, 1865.

Federal authorities detained Ewell in Fort Warren for three months. Upon gaining his parole, he retired to Tennessee, where he died at his farm.

The eccentric Richard S. Ewell was a fine general whose military reputation suffered when set against the exploits of the Confederate corps commander whom he replaced, Thomas "Stonewall" Jackson.

SEE ALSO
Gettysburg

FURTHER READING
Casdorph, Paul D. *Confederate General R. S. Ewell: Lee's Hesitant Commander.* Lexington: University Press of Kentucky, 2004.
Gallagher, Gary W., ed. *The First Day at Gettysburg: Essays on Confederate and Union Leadership.* Kent, Ohio: Kent State University Press, 1992.
Pfanz, Donald C. *Richard S. Ewell: A Soldier's Life.* Chapel Hill: University of North Carolina Press, 1998.

Farragut, David G.

UNION ADMIRAL

- *Born: July 5, 1801, Campbell's Station, Tenn.*
- *Education: sporadic schooling in lower grades and in the U.S. Navy*
- *Military service: U.S. Navy: midshipman, 1810–25; lieutenant, 1825–41; commander, 1841–55; captain, 1855–62; rear admiral, 1862–64; vice admiral, 1864–66; admiral, 1866–70*
- *Died: August 14, 1870, Portsmouth, N.H.*

The first U.S. naval officer to hold the rank of admiral, David G. Farragut was the Union's most famous naval hero. He shot into prominence when he ran his fleet past the Confederate forts guarding the lower Mississippi River and occupied New Orleans in April 1862. The highlight of his Civil War career was his successful assault on Mobile Bay in August 1864.

Although born on the Tennessee frontier, Farragut spent much of his early youth in New Orleans. In 1810, following the death of his mother and the departure of his father for naval service, he was taken in by Commodore David Porter, whose dying father had been cared for in the Farragut household. Porter had promised to serve the young boy as a "friend and guardian." After some schooling in Washington, he entered the U.S. Navy as a midshipman and served under Porter during the War of 1812. At the age of 12 he became the youngest American to ever command a prize ship seized in war.

Naval schoolmasters provided most of Farragut's education, and service in foreign waters helped him acquire fluency in several languages. He gradually rose in rank and commanded blockaders during the Mexican War. Since 1823 he had made his home in Norfolk, Virginia, and when told upon Virginia's secession that Norfolk was no place for a Unionist, he replied, "Well, then, I can live somewhere else." That evening he left with his family for the North.

Despite some initial hesitancy in the Navy Department because of his Southern background, Farragut received the command of the West Gulf Squadron in December 1861, with orders to organize an expedition against New Orleans. When the expedition was temporarily stymied by its inability to reduce the rebel forts guarding the mouth of the Mississippi River, he made the decision on April 24, 1862, that quickly knocked the Confederacy's major seaport out of the war. Contrary to the letter of his orders and the advice of many of his officers, he ordered his fleet to push through the gauntlet of Confederate fire and steam upriver to New Orleans. His bold tactics succeeded, and the city surrendered without a fight on April 25.

Once he had taken New Orleans, Farragut wanted to move immediately against Mobile. Instead he was ordered to operate on the Mississippi River with his oceanic fleet. After opening up the river to Union control as far north as Vicksburg but failing to capture Port Hudson, he returned to the gulf for blockade duty. He finally won approval for the Mobile expedition in the summer of 1864. As the battle raged in Mobile Bay on August 5, Farragut climbed the main rigging of the *Hartford,* his flagship, to gain the best vantage point. While lashed to the rigging, he responded to a warning that a nearby Union ship had just been sunk by a torpedo (a submarine mine) with the words that immortalized him: "Damn the torpedoes! Full speed ahead." Although their primers snapped as the *Hartford* passed over head, the torpedoes failed to explode. Farragut's fleet passed the Confederate forts and dispersed the rebel flotilla.

Apart from his brief command of the James River fleet in early 1865, Farragut saw little active service after his spectacular victory at Mobile. His health was failing and in 1867 he suffered his first heart attack. He died a year later while on an official visit to the Portsmouth navy yard.

SEE ALSO
Naval warfare

FURTHER READING
Duffy, James P. *Lincoln's Admiral: The Civil War Campaigns of David Farragut.* New York: Wiley, 1997.
Lewis, Charles Lee. *David Glasgow Farragut.* 2 vols. Annapolis, Md.: United States Naval Institute, 1941–43.

Federal Slave Code

Building upon the proslavery ruling of the Supreme Court in the *Dred Scott* decision of 1857, Southern Democrats began to push for a federal slave code in the late 1850s. Such a code would consist of federal protection for slavery in the territories.

Proslavery Southerners received a tremendous moral boost when the Supreme Court ruled in *Dred Scott* that the Missouri Compromise was unconstitutional because Congress had no power to prohibit slavery in the territories. Nonetheless, many Southern Democrats felt they had won but an empty victory. The antislavery Republicans rejected the *Dred Scott* decision as one that nationalized slavery, and the Northern Democrats evaded it through the concept of popular sovereignty, which held that only the actual settlers of a given territory had the power to decide on slavery. In his debates with Abraham Lincoln in the fall of 1858, Stephen A. Douglas of Illinois argued in his Freeport Doctrine that a territorial legislature could prohibit slavery by simply not passing the local laws needed to legalize and protect the institution.

In rebutting the Freeport Doctrine, Southern Democrats led by Jefferson Davis of Mississippi argued that the right to carry slaves into the territories that had just been sanctioned by the Supreme Court implied the additional right to claim protection for that property. In February 1859, Davis introduced resolutions in the Senate that called upon the federal government to provide the "needful protection" if it was not forthcoming from the courts. Although utterly unacceptable to Northern congressmen, this demand became an ideological ultimatum that Southern Democrats tried to force on the rest of their party.

When the Democrats met for their national convention at Charleston, South Carolina, in the spring of 1860, the Douglas Democrats refused to write a slave-code plank into their party's platform. This refusal triggered a walkout of delegates from the Lower South. Divided into two sectional wings with each backing its own slate of candidates, the Democrats were unable to prevent the Republicans from winning the Presidency.

SEE ALSO
Dred Scott decision; Election of 1860

FURTHER READING
Bestor, Arthur E. "The American Civil War as a Constitutional Crisis." *American Historical Review* (January 1964): 327–52.
Nichols, Roy F. *The Disruption of American Democracy.* New York: Macmillan, 1948.

Federalism

Federalism is a political concept referring to the sharing of powers between a central government and its local units. In the American system of government, federalism involves the division and sharing of power between the overlapping and often competing layers of government at the national, state, and local levels.

The Union created in the Constitution was not a consolidated national state. Americans profoundly feared centralized power and the coercive authority of a national government that had the legal and political means of directly exerting its will over them. Consequently, the new federal government issued no national currency, barely levied any taxes (and most of these were in the form of tariff duties on imports), and set down no definitive concept of citizenship to establish the primacy of national over state citizenship.

The broad powers granted to the federal government involved the areas of commerce, coinage, foreign policy, and military affairs. Other powers were reserved for the states, which still retained their sovereign capacity to govern the daily lives of their citizens and to determine who could exercise the rights of citizenship. The individual states and their political subdivisions were the source of nearly all the governing authority that impacted on the social and economic welfare of Americans. The result was a diffusion of political power along the lines of federalism.

For most Americans in the pre–Civil War years, this diffusion of power was a positive blessing, a safeguard for their individual liberties. However, the absence of a strong national authority reduced the chances of reaching a peaceful resolution of the slavery issue. The antislavery majority that formed in the North by the mid-19th century lacked the means of exerting its will in the absence of national institutions of government. At the same time, proslavery Southerners seized on the Constitution's ambiguity over the ultimate source of sovereign power and fashioned states'-rights doctrines into a legal rationale for secession. As the sectional conflict over slavery heated up in the 1850s, American federalism produced a political gridlock that heightened frustrations in both the North and South. That deadlock exploded into violence in 1861, and only the emergence of strong, national powers in the victorious Union brought the sections back together.

SEE ALSO
Nationalism; States' rights; Union

FURTHER READING
Finkelman, Paul. *An Imperfect Union: Slavery, Federalism, and Comity.* Chapel Hill: University of North Carolina Press, 1981.

Feminism

SEE Women's rights movement

15th Amendment

The last of the three constitutional amendments that came out of the Civil War, the 15th Amendment declared that "the right of citizens of the United States to vote shall not be denied or abridged by the United States or by any State on account of race, color, or previous condition of servitude." It passed Congress in 1869 and was added to the Constitution the following year when ratified by the states.

Once the Republicans retained the Presidency in the election of 1868, they moved quickly on the suffrage issue. Party idealism—that is, the desire to take a moral stand on behalf of black rights—certainly drove many Republicans to back the nationalization of the black vote, but party expediency was even more important.

The black vote that had given state Republican parties temporary majority control throughout most of the former Confederacy rested upon the extraordinary legislation of 1867 that could be repealed or declared unconstitutional. Once states had been readmitted to the Union, nothing could prevent revived Democratic parties in the South from rewriting their state constitutions to dis-

franchise the freedmen. Moreover, Reconstruction legislation did not apply to the Border South, and here sizable black minorities did not have the vote. In the North, where blacks comprised less than 2 percent of the population, only eight of the 22 states allowed black suffrage. Thus, in acting to extend and guarantee black voting, the Republicans hoped to protect their party's foundation in the Lower South, add new voters in the Upper South, and gain additional support in closely contested Northern states.

The short, precise wording of the 15th Amendment said nothing about using poll taxes, literacy tests, and property qualifications as grounds for denying the vote. Far from an oversight, this omission was intentional. By stopping short of an unequivocal guarantee of the right to vote, sponsors of the amendment picked up needed support

THE RESULT OF THE FIFTEENTH AMENDMENT.

The central scene in this 15th Amendment commemorative print is a celebratory parade led by black troops down Baltimore's Monument Street. The vignettes around the edges include portraits of Abraham Lincoln (top left) and Frederick Douglass (middle right).

from party moderates who insisted that Northern states be left free to shape their own voting standards. The way was thus left open for the massive disfranchisement of Southern blacks in the early 20th century. Moreover, in ignoring the claims of women to the vote, the 15th Amendment perpetuated the disfranchisement of women on the basis of their gender. Angered and disappointed, Susan B. Anthony and Elizabeth Cady Stanton led radical feminists out of the reform coalition that had spearheaded the advancement of the emancipated slaves.

SEE ALSO
Black suffrage; Congressional Reconstruction; Military Reconstruction Act of 1867; Suffrage

FURTHER READING
Gillette, William. *The Right to Vote: Politics and the Passage of the 15th Amendment.* Baltimore: Johns Hopkins University Press, 1969.

Fire-eaters

Contemporaries referred to the most extreme prewar Southern nationalists as "fire-eaters." The image invoked by the term was that of swaggering hotheads intent on breaking up the Union in their defense of slavery and Southern rights. The best-known of these radicals were Edmund Ruffin of Virginia, Robert Barnwell Rhett of South Carolina, and William Lowndes Yancey of Alabama.

The fire-eaters were the ideologues of secession. They identified the ownership of slaves as the most fundamental of all Southern rights and the basis for all Southern white liberties. They warned that any outside interference with slavery would inevitably deprive Southerners of their honor and equality. By the 1840s they were convinced that the political power of the North and its unrelenting attacks on slavery had reached a point where secession offered the only protection for Southern freedoms.

Too doctrinaire and scornful of compromise to hold positions of power in the national political parties, the fire-eaters turned to agitation to spread their message that Southern honor and security demanded separate nationhood. Through speeches, pamphlets, editorials, and committees of correspondence they popularized secession as a constitutional right among the Southern white masses. Comparing themselves with the patriots of 1776, they called upon Southerners to uphold the memory of their liberty-loving ancestors by throwing off the shackles of Northern tyranny.

Although blocked in their secessionist efforts during the sectional crisis over the Compromise of 1850, the fire-eaters played a key role in the secession movement of 1860–61. They were instrumental in the breakup of the national Democratic party over the issue of federal protection of slavery in the territories and relentlessly exploited Southern fears over Abraham Lincoln's election. Having learned from their defeat in 1850, they realized that their efforts would be doomed if they waited for Southern unity before taking decisive action. They now forced the issue through their strategy of separate state secessions. This strategy was a brilliant success, but the fire-eaters were soon shunted aside when more moderate politicians anxious to present an image of restraint and unity began the task of constructing a new Confederate government.

SEE ALSO
Rhett, Robert Barnwell; Ruffin, Edmund; Secession; Yancey, William Lowndes

FURTHER READING

Heidler, David S. *Pulling the Temple Down: The Fire-Eaters and the Destruction of the Union.* Mechanicsburg, Pa.: Stackpole Books, 1994.

Walther, Eric H. *The Fire-Eaters.* Baton Rouge: Louisiana State University Press, 1992.

First Bull Run

On July 21, 1861, two amateur armies fought at Bull Run Creek near the railroad town of Manassas Junction, Virginia, 25 miles southwest of Washington. Called First Bull Run in the North and First Manassas in the South (the Union usually named battles after the nearest river or stream and the Confederacy after the town that served as a base of operations for its troops), the battle was the first major engagement of the war.

By June 1861, an impatient North was demanding that the Union launch an immediate offensive against Confederate positions in northern Virginia. Newspaper editors coined the slogan "Forward to Richmond" and insisted that the rebellion would collapse once a federal army occupied the new capital city of the Confederacy, just 100 miles from Washington. Anxious himself for a show of force against the Confederates, President

Abraham Lincoln ordered General Irvin McDowell, commander of the Union forces around Washington, to advance on the Confederate army of 25,000 men under General Pierre G. T. Beauregard encamped at Manassas Junction. McDowell protested in vain that his troops were too inexperienced for such an offensive. Most of them were three-month volunteers and militia whose enlistments would soon be up. They were, as McDowell put it, "exceedingly raw." Lincoln conceded the point but countered that the Confederate forces were just as green.

Prior to pulling his army of 35,000 men out of Washington on July 16, McDowell had received assurances that a second Confederate army, some 13,000 men under General Joseph E. Johnston in the Shenandoah Valley, would be pinned down and thereby

As he feared, Union General Irvin McDowell expected too much of his raw troops when he ordered them to cross the stream of Bull Run in a series of complicated maneuvers.

prevented from reinforcing Beauregard at Manassas. This was the assignment of General Robert Patterson, whose Union army was stationed near Harpers Ferry. Concerned about the rawness of his own troops, and convinced that he was badly outnumbered by Johnston's forces, Patterson allowed Johnston to slip away. Utilizing the Manassas Gap Railroad, Johnston quickly shifted 11,000 troops to the Bull Run front. The last of these reinforcements reached the battlefield on the afternoon of July 21 just as Union forces were threatening to break through on the Confederate left.

Contrary to his expectations, McDowell faced an army at Manassas nearly equal in size to his. Alerted by Rose O'Neal Greenhow, a wealthy Washington socialite and a Confederate spy, of McDowell's move toward Manassas, the Confederate high command had enough time to concentrate Beauregard's and Johnston's armies while the Union army slowly made its way to Bull Run. Still, McDowell had a sound tactical plan, and he almost achieved victory. After a feinting move against the Confederate right, he surprised Beauregard by throwing the bulk of his forces against the weakly defended Confederate left. Despite a grueling seven-hour march through heavy terrain to get into position for the battle, the federals in the flanking column fought as well as anyone could have expected. They breached the Confederate line and drove the rebels back onto Henry House Hill. (Judith Henry, an aged widow who refused to be moved from her house, was killed by a shell, becoming the first civilian death of the war.) As the federals were pressing their attack, General Thomas J. Jackson rallied the panicky Confederates and established a solid line of defense on the hilltop. Jackson's stand passed into legend when a fellow general, Bernard E. Bee of South Carolina, shouted, "There is Jackson standing like a stone wall! Rally behind the Virginians!" Ever after, Jackson was known as "Stonewall."

The tenacious defense of the Henry House Hill turned the tide of the battle. The arrival of fresh Confederate reinforcements late in the afternoon demoralized the exhausted federals and transformed their defeat into a rout. "We made our way off the field as we would, without order or discipline," recalled Major Abner R. Small of the 16th Maine. Another Union officer later wrote that "no power could have stopped them short of the camps they had left less than a week before."

McDowell's worst fears had been realized, and the way to Washington was apparently open to the Confederates. But the Confederate army was as disorganized in victory as the Union army was in defeat, and neither Johnston nor Beauregard ordered a pursuit to Washington. The Union suffered casualties of about 2,800 men in the fighting, while the Confederacy lost 1,900. These casualties were rather slight by the standards of subsequent battles, but they served notice that the war would not be, as most Americans had expected, a short and relatively bloodless affair. While a jubilant Confederacy basked in the glow of its first major victory, a humiliated Union girded itself for the long struggle ahead.

SEE ALSO
Beauregard, Pierre G. T.; Greenhow, Rose O'Neal; Jackson, Thomas J.; Johnston, Joseph E.; Lincoln, Abraham; McDowell, Irvin; Second Bull Run.

FURTHER READING
Catton, Bruce. *The Coming Fury.* Garden City, N.Y.: Doubleday, 1961.
Davis, William C. *Battle at Bull Run.* Garden City, N.Y.: Doubleday, 1977.

Flags

Civil War soldiers marched into battle with their regimental, state, and national flags carried by a color guard. Communities in the North and South shared the common ritual of presenting a flag to their soldiers as they departed for the war. Sewn by the women of the community, the regimental flag was a powerful symbol of the soldiers' respective nationalities, their homes, and the womenfolk they had pledged to defend and honor.

The original Confederate national flag—the Stars and Bars—so closely resembled the U.S. Stars and Stripes that confusion was inevitable in the smoke of battle. In the fall of 1861, the War Department authorized a new battle flag for the Confederate army. Commonly called the "Southern Cross," it bore a blue cross, studded with 13 white stars, across a background of red. In 1863 the Confederate Congress adopted a new national flag—a white field with the Southern Cross superimposed in the upper right corner. (This is the version of the Confederate flag that caused so much controversy in

the 1990s when it was flown over the State House in Columbia, South Carolina.) At the very end of the war, when it hardly mattered, the Confederate Congress added a red bar to the outer edge of the white field so that the national flag would not look so much like a flag of truce.

For all the symbolism of the national flags, the soldiers most likely formed a deeper emotional attachment to their regimental colors. Each regimental flag bore a progressively longer list of the battles in which the unit had fought, and the colors acquired a sacred stature as the embodiment of the soldiers' valor and courage. Duty in the regimental color guard, which went into battle in the center of the front line, was a source of great pride. It also was an incredibly dangerous assignment. The color guard was the most visible marker of a unit's position and its progress registered the unit's performance. During the early stages of the war, officers directed their men to zero in on the opponent's color guard. "Now, shoot down the colors," recalled the rebel soldier Wayland F. Dunaway of his orders at the battle of Fredericksburg.

This battle flag proclaims the prominent role played by the 1st Arkansas regiment at Chickamauga. The crossed cannon at the flag's center signify that the regiment had captured enemy artillery.

The bars crossing this Confederate regimental flag proudly list the western battles in which the flag was carried.

Long after the war was over, the possession of the enemy's colors was a highly charged political issue. Union veterans bitterly denounced President Grover Cleveland in 1887 when he endorsed a recommendation that the War Department return captured Confederate flags to the South. Cleveland backed off, and most of these flags remained in the North until the early 20th century when they were finally returned to the South.

SEE ALSO
Armies

FURTHER READING
Bonner, Robert E. *Colors and Blood: Flag Passions of the Confederate South.* Princeton, N.J.: Princeton University Press, 2002.
Civil War Battle Flags of the Union Army and Order of Battle. New York: Knickerbocker Press, 1997.
Coski, John M. *The Confederate Battle Flag: America's Most Embattled Emblem.* Cambridge: Belknap Press of Harvard University Press, 2005.
Rollins, Richard, ed. *The Returned Battle Flags.* Redondo Beach, Calif.: Rank and File Publications, 1997.

Forrest, Nathan Bedford

CONFEDERATE GENERAL

- *Born: July 13, 1821, Bedford County, Tenn.*
- *Education: no formal education*
- *Military service: Confederate army: private, cavalry, 1861; lieutenant colonel, 1861–62; colonel, 1862; brigadier general, 1862–63; major-general, 1863–65; lieutenant general, 1865*
- *Died: October 29, 1877, Memphis, Tenn.*

His Union opponents feared and despised Nathan Bedford Forrest more than any other rebel general. An amateur soldier with an intuitive grasp of cavalry warfare and a concept of strategy that he reduced to the phrase, "I always make it a rule to get there first with the most men," Forrest bedeviled Union forces in Tennessee and northern Mississippi for most of the war. Union General William T. Sherman paid him quite a compliment when he declared in 1864: "That devil Forrest [must be] hunted down and killed if it costs 10,000 lives and bankrupts the Federal treasury."

Born into a struggling Tennessee farm family, Forrest escaped poverty by learning how to leverage small amounts of capital into the profitable trading of livestock, land, and slaves. Although lacking in education and social polish—"I never see a pen but what I think of a snake," he once remarked—he grasped that slave trading offered the quickest path to wealth in the plantation South. Memphis was the hub city for his slave-trading business, and by the late 1850s he was a wealthy man with a large plantation in Mississippi.

When Tennessee seceded, Forrest enlisted as a private in the Tennessee Mounted Rifles. His political connections and reputation for reckless bravery soon gained him a commission as a lieutenant colonel in the cavalry. An Alabamian in his command, David C. Kelley, later recalled that Forrest's men soon learned that his "single will, impervious to argument, appeal, or threat...was ever to be the governing impulse in their movements."

After seeing his first combat action on reconnaissance missions in Kentucky, Forrest participated in the defense of Fort Donelson. Refusing to surrender, he led his command out of the fort before the Confederates capitulated. Two months later, while covering the rebel retreat at Shiloh, he was

The fierce-looking General Nathan Bedford Forrest was the Confederate cavalry commander most feared by the Union army.

The killing of African-American soldiers who had surrendered to Nathan Bedford Forrest's troops at Fort Pillow became a battle cry for black federal soldiers who swore revenge for their slain comrades.

seriously wounded. A fast healer, he recovered in time to smash a Union supply depot at Murfreesboro, Tennessee, in June 1862. Keyed to lightning-fast movements that kept the federals guessing and off guard, this was the first of a series of cavalry raids that made Forrest a legend in the western theater.

Assigned to General Braxton Bragg's Tennessee operations in 1863, the strong-willed Forrest unsurprisingly had a falling-out with the acerbic and vacillating Bragg. Forrest secured an independent command in northern Mississippi and western Tennessee and on April 12, 1864, captured the Union garrison at Fort Pillow. Although Union and Confederate accounts differ as to what happened after the rebels overran the fort, the weight of the evidence points to a massacre of the federal black troops after they surrendered.

At Brice's Cross Roads in June and Tupelo, Mississippi, in July, Forrest's aggressive tactics resulted in two spectacular victories that added to his legend. Although his command continued to torment the federals, it was placed under General John Bell Hood in the fall of 1864 and was decimated in Hood's Tennessee Campaign. Forrest's last battle was at Selma, Alabama, in April 1865. The large Union force crushed the rebels, but Forrest killed with his own hand his thirtieth and last federal soldier.

Financially wiped out by the war, Forrest struggled at a number of business pursuits but wound up deeper in debt and litigation. As a founder of the Ku Klux Klan and the supposed perpetrator of the Fort Pillow massacre, he remained a highly controversial, if not notorious, public figure. He died in Memphis, probably of diabetes.

SEE ALSO

Ku Klux Klan

FURTHER READING

Hurst, Jack. *Nathan Bedford Forrest.* New York: Vintage, 1994.
Wills, Brian Steel. *A Battle from the Start: The Life of Nathan Bedford Forrest.* New York: HarperCollins, 1992.

Fort Fisher

Fort Fisher guarded the seaward approach to Wilmington, North Carolina. Situated 20 miles up the Cape Fear River, Wilmington was the most important blockade-running port still in Confederate hands at the beginning of 1865 and the primary conduit for supplies to Robert E. Lee's Army of North Virginia. In a devastating blow to the Confederacy, a Union amphibious operation—the most brilliantly executed of the war—captured Fort Fisher on January 15, 1865.

After paying more attention to Charleston for most of the war, the Union high command in the fall of 1865 finally decided to concentrate on Wilmington. To seize Wilmington, however, required a successful attack on Fort Fisher, the most formidable fort in the Confederacy. Constructed out of packed sand and earth over a log frame, its walls were 25 feet thick and impervious to even direct hits from naval shells. Mounting 47 heavy artillery, the fort had plenty of firepower to punish an invading fleet. Only a massive joint operation, one combining naval and land units, had any chance of taking the fort.

Launched in December 1864, the first Union expedition against the fort failed. After assembling at Hampton Roads, Virginia, a Union fleet of 60 warships commanded by Admiral David Dixon Porter and 6,500 troops under General Benjamin F. Butler moved against the fort. Neither the detonation near the fort on December 24 of a Union ship packed with 215 tons of gunpowder (Butler's idea) nor the subsequent bombardment of 20,000 shells from Porter's fleet seriously damaged the fort. About

2,000 federal troops went ashore north of the fort on Christmas Day, but they were quickly recalled by Butler, who felt upon hearing of the ineffectiveness of the naval bombardment that any assault on the fort would be hopeless. On December 26, Butler sent his expeditionary force back to Norfolk.

On January 13, 1865, a larger and better-coordinated amphibious force loomed off Fort Fisher. A disgusted Ulysses S. Grant had replaced Butler with General Alfred H. Terry and provided him with an infantry force of 8,000 men. At sunrise on January 13, Porter's fleet opened fire. Colonel William Lamb, the Confederate commander at Fort Fisher, recalled seeing at that moment "the most formidable armada the world had ever known.... Suddenly that long line of floating fortresses rained shot and shell, upon fort and beach and wooden hills, causing the very earth and sea to tremble." Unlike the bombardment in December, Porter ordered his gunners to aim at specific targets in the fort. Their firing, the greatest naval barrage of the war, was steady, deliberate, and accurate. Over 50,000 projectiles—some 1.5 million pounds of ordinance—were hurled into the fort, and more than half of its guns were knocked out in three days of shelling.

The firing from the Union warships provided cover for the landing of Terry's troops and artillery. On January 15, Terry's soldiers stormed the western (land) side of the fort while a force of 2,000 sailors and marines distracted the rebel defenders with an attack from the sea side. After close fighting that lasted from three o'clock in the afternoon to ten o'clock in the evening, the fort and its garrison of 2,000 men finally fell. Union forces occupied Wilmington a month later.

When news of the fall of Fort Fisher reached the blockade runners in

Bermuda, the U.S. consul there reported that "business was nearly suspended, and had they known that the Islands were to sink in 24 hours, there could hardly have been greater consternation; the blockade runners and their aiders feel their doom is sealed." And so it was, along with that of the Confederacy. Critically dependent by now on the supplies brought in through Wilmington for its armies, the Confederacy survived for only a few months after the Union victory at Fort Fisher.

SEE ALSO

Blockade; Blockade runners; Butler, Benjamin F.; Naval warfare; Porter, David Dixon

FURTHER READING

Gragg, Rod. *Confederate Goliath: The Battle of Fort Fisher.* New York: HarperCollins, 1991.

Reed, Rowena. *Combined Operations in the Civil War.* Annapolis, Md.: Naval Institute Press, 1978.

Fort Pillow massacre

SEE Forrest, Nathan Bedford

Forts Henry and Donelson

The loss of Forts Henry and Donelson in February 1862 was the first major defeat the Confederacy suffered in the western theater. Located in Tennessee just below the Kentucky border, these forts controlled access from the north to the Tennessee (Henry) and Cumberland (Donelson) rivers, two invasion corridors into the interior of the South for waterborne federal troops. Once these forts

fell, the Confederacy never did regain the strategic initiative in the West.

About 43,000 troops under General Albert Sidney Johnston held the vulnerable Kentucky-Tennessee border for the Confederacy in the winter of 1861–62. Johnston's "long Kentucky line" of 300 miles stretched from Columbus on the Mississippi River to the southeast through Forts Henry and Donelson and then northward to Bowling Green and east to the Cumberland Gap. As his men waited for the expected Union advance, disease and the cold chill of a Kentucky winter took its toll, especially on units from the Deep South. "They had come out to fight the enemies of their country in human shape, but not in the form of fever and pestilence," grimly noted a surgeon in the 22nd Mississippi.

Opposing the Confederates were Union forces of twice their size. However, a balky command structure that divided authority over Kentucky into two separate departments, one headquartered in St. Louis and the other in Louisville, made it difficult for the Union to concentrate its forces and agree on a unified plan of attack. The initiative of a hitherto unknown Union general, Ulysses S. Grant, finally jumpstarted the Union offensive.

Having discovered during a reconnaissance action in late January that Fort Henry was very poorly defended, Grant convinced his superiors to order a joint army-navy expedition against it. A flotilla of Union gunboats under Flag Officer Andrew H. Foote accompanied Grant's invasion force of 15,000 men. On February 6, the undermanned Confederate garrison surrendered after a shelling from Foote's fleet. Flooding from heavy rains had submerged most of the river fort, and resistance was hopeless. Almost immediately, Foote moved upriver (south) to destroy the

Memphis and Ohio Railroad bridge, a key link in the Tennessee rail communications that supplied Johnson's army in Kentucky. While Foote moved farther south into northern Alabama, Grant marched his troops 12 miles to the east for an attack on Fort Donelson.

Upon hearing of the loss of Fort Henry, and knowing that another Union army under General Don Carlos Buell was moving toward Bowling Green, Johnston realized that his defensive line in Kentucky could no longer be held. He pulled back troops from Columbus, abandoned Bowling Green, and sent 12,000 reinforcements to Fort Donelson with orders to hold the fort until the Confederate Army of Kentucky could make good its retreat south of the Cumberland River.

After Grant's army, now increased to 23,000 men, began to surround Donelson on February 13, Foote's fleet, having returned from its raiding mission, tried to batter the fort into submission the following day. The fort's shore batteries heavily damaged the fleet and forced it to turn back. On the following day the Confederates almost escaped the trap that Grant was setting for them. Their senior commander, General John B. Floyd, ordered an attempt at a breakthrough that was on the verge of success when, inexplicably, Floyd lost his nerve and marched his forces back into the fort. Then, as if to highlight his unfitness for command, Floyd announced that he was fleeing the next morning with as many of his Virginia troops as could accompany him on two steamers that were arriving at daybreak. General Gideon J. Pillow, second in command, fled along with Floyd, and General Simon B. Buckner was saddled with the responsibility of surrendering the fort. When Buckner requested terms, Grant replied with a phrase that made him a hero in the North: "No terms except unconditional and immediate surrender can be accepted." On February 16 about 12,500 Confederates surrendered.

Grant's victories at Forts Henry and Donelson forced the Confederates to abandon not only Kentucky but also large chunks of Tennessee. The Confederacy lost Nashville, Tennessee's capital, in late February, and Johnston's army retreated south to Corinth, Mississippi.

SEE ALSO

Buell, Don Carlos; Grant, Ulysses S.; Johnston, Albert Sidney

FURTHER READING

Cooling, Benjamin F. *Forts Henry and Donelson: The Key to the Confederate Heartland.* Knoxville: University of Tennessee Press, 1987.
Horn, Stanley F. *Army of Tennessee.* Indianapolis, Ind.: Bobbs-Merrill, 1941.

14th Amendment

A complex measure that passed Congress in 1866 and was ratified in 1868, the 14th Amendment distilled the Republicans' conception of the meaning of Union victory in the Civil War. It remains one of the most influential amendments added to the Constitution after the original 10 that comprised the Bill of Rights.

Written by the Republican Joint Committee of 15 on Reconstruction, the 14th Amendment served for most Republicans as the North's peace terms for the defeated South. Its first section had the most enduring impact. Modeled after the Civil Rights Act of 1866, it declared that all persons born or naturalized within the United States were citizens of the United States. This section clarified ambiguities over the definition of national citizenship and reversed the *Dred Scott* decision that held that African-Americans were not, and never could be, American citizens. It also altered traditional constitutional relations by giving the federal government the responsibility for protecting rights of citizenship that hitherto had been entrusted to the exclusive jurisdiction of the states.

The other sections dealt more specifically with political issues arising out of the drama of Reconstruction. Section two, which was never applied, provided for a proportional reduction of congressional representation whenever a state denied the vote to a portion of its adult male citizens. Section three, which was the most bitterly criticized in the South, disqualified from state and federal office all individuals who had supported the Confederacy after having taken an oath to uphold the Constitution. Congress could lift this disqualification by a two-thirds vote in both the House and the Senate, but in the meantime the bulk of the South's ruling class was barred from office. The fourth section dealt with the war's cost. It reaffirmed that the Union war debt would be paid in full, repudiated the Confederate war debt, and voided "any claim for the loss or emancipation of any slave." Section five reserved for Congress the power to enforce the provisions of the amendment.

In all likelihood Southern acceptance of the 14th Amendment would have brought Reconstruction to an end with no provision having been made for black suffrage. But only one former Confederate state, Tennessee, ratified the amendment. Frustrated Republicans responded with a more radical program that mandated black suffrage in the other 10 ex-Confederate states. Once black males had the vote in these states, an electoral majority formed in favor of

the 14th Amendment. Upon ratifying the amendment, these states were readmitted to the Union.

SEE ALSO

Citizenship; *Dred Scott* decision; Federalism; Military Reconstruction Act of 1867; Reconstruction

FURTHER READING

Hyman, Harold M. *A More Perfect Union: The Impact of the Civil War and Reconstruction on the Constitution.* New York: Knopf, 1973.
James, Joseph B. *The Framing of the 14th Amendment.* Urbana: University of Illinois Press, 1956.

France

Of the major European powers, France had the greatest stake in a Confederate victory during the Civil War. The French ruler Napoleon III dreamed of creating a vassal empire in Mexico and

Ferdinand Maximilian, a hapless Austrian archduke, paid with his life for allowing Napoleon III to install him as the emperor of Mexico during the Civil War.

perhaps even contesting U.S. control west of the Mississippi River. An independent and friendly Confederacy would act as a necessary counterweight to Union power. Despite his pro-Southern sympathies, Napoleon was enough of a realist not to risk a war against the Union unless Britain first took the lead in recognizing the Confederacy. That recognition never came, and Napoleon's puppet in Mexico, the Archduke Ferdinand Maximilian, soon paid the price for Napoleon's courting of the Confederacy.

Napoleon took his cue in U.S. diplomacy from Henri Mercier, his minister in Washington. Although Mercier favored recognition of the Confederacy from the very start, he cautioned Napoleon to act only in concert with the other European powers. While waiting for the British to intervene on behalf of the Confederacy, Napoleon sent French troops into Mexico in 1862, deposed the government of Benito Juarez, and installed Maximilian as emperor. He could so openly flaunt the American Monroe Doctrine of non-European intervention in the Western Hemisphere because the Union fleet was tied up trying to enforce the blockade against the Confederacy.

By 1863 France and the Confederacy seemed to be on the verge of forging a formal alliance. Each had a common interest in Union defeat, and each supported anti-Juarez warlords in northern Mexico who controlled ports that enabled the Confederacy to evade the Union blockade. The risk of an alliance, one based on a French recognition of the Confederacy in return for a recognition of the French regime in Mexico, was so great that it affected the Union's military strategy in the West.

President Abraham Lincoln insisted on the Red River Campaign in the winter of 1864 in an effort to establish a strong Union presence in Texas as a warning to France to back off. That campaign failed, but the Confederacy suffered a more crippling loss when France continued to withhold recognition. In the end, all the Confederacy received from Napoleon was his assistance in arranging a loan in 1863 from the French banking family of Emile Erlanger and Company. The Erlanger loan temporarily restored Confederate credit in Europe before the Southern military reversals in the summer of 1863.

Free to exert pressure on the French in Mexico once the Confederacy had been defeated, the United States positioned a large military force on the Texas-Mexican border. The last French troops left Mexico in 1867, and the abandoned Maximilian was executed by the followers of Juarez.

SEE ALSO
Great Britain

FURTHER READING
Case, Lynn M. and Warren F. Spencer. *The United States and France: Civil War Diplomacy.* Philadelphia: University of Pennsylvania Press, 1970.

Fredericksburg

The battle of Fredericksburg on December 13, 1862, was a depressing defeat for the Union and one of the easiest victories ever won by General Robert E. Lee's Army of Northern Virginia. Lee's Union counterpart at Fredericksburg, General Ambrose E. Burnside, had taken command of the Army of the Potomac from George B. McClellan on November 7. President Abraham Lincoln, exasperated by McClellan's failure to follow up the Union victory at

Antietam with a vigorous pursuit of Lee's army, turned to a new commander in the hope of launching an offensive against Lee before the winter's rains put an end to active campaigning. Fully aware that he was expected to go on the offensive, Burnside did produce a competent plan of operations. His major blunder, however, was in sticking to that plan long after any chance of its success was gone.

Burnside wanted to cross the Rappahannock River at Fredericksburg, about 50 miles north of Richmond. A successful crossing, if carried out quickly enough, would place Burnside's huge army of 122,000 men between Lee's forces and Richmond. Having lost the initiative to the federals, Lee would have no choice but to rush south to defend Richmond and his supply lines by attacking Burnside's much larger army.

Burnside's plan went well in its early stages. The lead elements of the Army of the Potomac arrived on the north bank of the Rappahannock opposite Fredericksburg on November 17. Lee had been taken by surprise, and only about 500 Confederate soldiers were available to defend Fredericksburg. One corps of Lee's army was more than a day's march away at Culpepper, and the other was off in the Shenandoah Valley. However,

rather than exploiting his advantage by attempting to ford the 400-foot-wide Rappahannock, Burnside threw away the element of surprise and decided to wait until pontoon bridges (temporary bridges supported by a floating structure over the water) arrived. Because of a muddled chain of communications, the promised pontoons did not arrive for a week. This delay gave Lee ample time to concentrate his entire 78,000-man army, most of it on nearly unassailable high ground to the rear of Fredericksburg.

With a stubbornness that bordered on stupidity, Burnside nonetheless went ahead with his original plan of crossing at Fredericksburg. Harassed by Confederate sharpshooters, Union engineers were unable to put down the pontoon bridges until December 11. By the following evening, Union troops had occupied Fredericksburg, and Burnside ordered an attack on Lee's army the next morning.

Once the morning mist burned off, the advancing federal troops presented a grand spectacle to Confederate Lieutenant William M. Owen: "Their bright bayonets glistening in the sunlight made the line look like a huge serpent of blue and steel." Huge gaps soon appeared in that line and others of the attacking federals. Although Burnside sent one Union corps against the Confederate

In the middle of this scene of Fredericksburg is the courthouse steeple used by the Union's Signal Corps to relay information on Confederate troop movements to General Ambrose Burnside.

right to the south of Fredericksburg, he directed most of the Union charges against the Confederate left in the belief that this was the weakest link in the rebel position. He was tragically mistaken. The Confederates had anticipated a major attack aimed at the hilly slopes to the west of Fredericksburg. Lee had this approach so well covered that Edward Porter Alexander, his chief of ordinance, was able to report before the battle, "A chicken could not live on that field when we open [fire] on it."

The Confederates, standing six-deep in a sunken road behind a stone wall at the base of Marye's Heights, easily repulsed every federal charge—six in all. Confederate General James Longstreet noted of the slaughter: "The dead were piled sometimes three deep, and when morning broke, the spectacle that we saw upon the battle-field was one of the most distressing I ever witnessed." Incredibly, Burnside's officers had to talk him out of renewing the Union attacks on December 14.

More than 12,000 Union soldiers fell at Fredericksburg; Confederate casualties numbered about 5,000. When news of the defeat reached the North, a deep gloom settled over the Union war effort. Critics on all sides angrily cited Fredericksburg as conclusive evidence of the incompetence and failure of the Lincoln administration in fashioning a winning strategy for the war.

SEE ALSO

Antietam; Burnside, Ambrose E.; Jackson, Thomas J.; Lee, Robert E.; Longstreet, James; McClellan, George B.

FURTHER READING

Gallagher, Gary W., ed. *The Fredericksburg Campaign: Decision on the Rappahannock*. Chapel Hill: University of North Carolina Press, 1995.
O'Reilly, Francis. *The Fredericksburg Campaign: Winter War on the Rappahannock*. Baton Rouge: Louisiana State University Press, 2003.

Free blacks

Just under 10 percent of all African Americans were free on the eve of the Civil War, and their numbers were about evenly divided between the North and South. Wherever they lived, however, free blacks faced legal restrictions and a wall of white prejudice that relegated them to the lowest rungs of American society. The Civil War brought an end to slavery but not to the notions of white superiority that continued to deny African Americans their full rights of citizenship.

Laws at all levels of American government in the pre–Civil War period confronted free blacks with a host of legal restrictions. Federal statutes dating back to the 1790s denied citizenship to black immigrants and barred blacks from serving in the militia. As of 1860, only four states in New England allowed blacks to vote on the same terms as whites. Nearly all the states barred free blacks from testifying against whites in court cases and serving on juries. Many states, especially the newer ones in the West, prohibited the entry of blacks or else required them to post a heavy bond as a guarantee of "good behavior." Free blacks faced discrimination in jobs, housing, and access to education. Former President James Madison summarized white attitudes when he wrote in 1820 that free blacks "are every where regarded as a nuisance, and must really be such as long as they are under the degradation which public sentiment inflicts on them."

White prejudice and restrictions helped bind together the African-American community, as free blacks relied on their own resources to organize churches, schools, fraternal orders, and mutual-aid societies. Black churches became the focal point of their community life and the centers from which they launched their attack on slavery. By the 1840s, black leaders were raising their voices at African-American conventions for an immediate end to slavery and the degraded status forced upon all blacks. "Rise, brethren, rise! Strike for freedom or die slaves," exhorted New Yorker David Ruggles in 1841. This increased militancy led to open defiance of the Fugitive Slave Act of 1850 by Northern blacks and their bold assistance of fugitive slaves as they sought freedom in the North or in Canada.

Free blacks played a critical role in bringing the sectional crisis over slavery to a climax in 1860–61, and they welcomed the war as an opportunity to destroy slavery. When the federal government finally allowed free blacks in the summer of 1862 to enlist in Union armies, they did so at a rate three times higher than that of Northern whites. This contribution to Union victory, along with that of the former slaves who joined the Union army, accelerated the drive for a constitutional guarantee of black freedom that was achieved in the 13th Amendment of 1865.

The goals of national citizenship and equality before the law that had seemed so distant in 1860 received constitutional enactment in the 14th Amendment of 1867 and black suffrage came in the 15th Amendment of 1870. A gigantic step had been taken on the road to black equality. But it was only a step. White attitudes of black inferiority remained entrenched, and Northern whites soon tired of trying to give meaning and protection to constitutional expressions of black equality. The promise of Reconstruction soon faded, and across the nation whites forced African Americans once again back into a subordinate position in American society.

SEE ALSO

Abolitionism; Black soldiers; Black suffrage; Colonization; Impressed laborers

FURTHER READING

Berlin, Ira. *Slaves Without Masters: The Free Negro in the Antebellum South.* New York: Pantheon, 1974.
Horton, James O. and Lois E. Horton. *In Hope of Liberty: Culture, Community, and Protest among Northern Free Blacks.* New York: Oxford University Press, 1997.
Litwack, Leon F. *North of Slavery: The Negro in the Free States, 1790–1860.* Chicago: University of Chicago Press, 1961.

Unless they could immediately produce their freedom papers, free blacks in the South such as this man were liable to seizure as slaves.

Free-labor ideology

The free-labor ideology summarized the worldview of the enterprising Northerners who joined the Republican party in the 1850s. At the core of this ideology was the belief that only a society based on free labor could offer individuals opportunities for social and economic advancement.

"The great idea and basis of the Republican Party," proclaimed Republican Richard Yates of Illinois in 1860, "is free labor. . . . To make labor honorable is the object and aim of the Republican Party." This commitment to free labor was simultaneously an affirmation of the glories of Northern society and a condemnation of social conditions in the slave South.

Slavery, in the minds of Republicans, produced a rigid, hierarchical society divided between haughty slaveowners, powerless slaves, and degraded poor whites. "It *is* impossible for any manual labor to be considered honorable, while it is almost exclusively performed by slaves, and is thereby made a badge of slavery," asserted Senator James Dixon of Connecticut in a typical Republican charge. Slavery, by enabling a small master class to monopolize economic life and by reducing most whites to poverty and ignorance through the ruinous competition of unpaid, compulsory labor, doomed the South in Republican eyes to economic backwardness and social misery.

The free-labor North, in direct contrast for the Republicans, promoted and rewarded individual initiative and ambition. No class held unlimited power over another. The incentives of higher wages offered to free labor drove the

economy forward toward ever greater prosperity. Hardworking, self-disciplined workers could achieve upward social and economic mobility. For the Republicans, Northern society did not harbor any permanent class of laborers. "The man who labored for another last year," claimed Abraham Lincoln, "this year labors for himself, and next year he will hire others to labor for him." In fact, a permanent working class was forming in Northern cities by the 1850s, but the Republicans insisted that free homesteads in the West would act as a safety valve to keep chances for economic independence open.

The nearly unbounded faith of Republicans in the benefits of free labor was the prime source of their opposition to the spread of slavery into the territories. They feared that the introduction of slavery would degrade all forms of labor, choke off avenues for individual betterment, and place power in the hands of an arrogant, slaveholding elite. Their free-labor ideology also enabled them to identify the Union

Capital and labor are personified as a businessman and a worker shaking hands. According to free-labor ideology, the interests of capital and labor complemented each other, and free and equal competition allowed workers to become employers themselves.

cause during the Civil War with the universal yearnings of workers for a better life. President Abraham Lincoln eloquently made this connection when he addressed Congress in July 1861: "On the side of the Union, [the Civil War] is a struggle for maintaining in the world, that form and substance of government, whose leading object is, to elevate the condition of men—to lift artificial weights from all shoulders... to afford all, an unfettered start, and a fair chance, in the race of life."

SEE ALSO
Republican party

FURTHER READING
Foner, Eric. *Free Soil, Free Labor, Free Men: The Ideology of the Republican Party before the Civil War.* New York: Oxford University Press, 1970.

Freedmen's Bureau

The first federal agency ever created to deal with problems of social and eco-nomic welfare, the Freedmen's Bureau operated from 1865 to 1869. It played a major role in shaping labor relations in the postwar South.

Congress created the Freedmen's Bureau in March 1865 to administer relief for up to one year after the war to white refugees and freed slaves in the South. The War Department staffed the bureau and initially provided it with funds. As suggested by its official title, the Bureau for Refugees, Freedmen, and Abandoned Lands, the bureau was not intended to deal exclusively with blacks or to limit itself solely to the problem of relief. In fact, it dispensed more relief in the form of food and clothing to whites than it did to blacks. Moreover, in the first year of its existence, it oversaw some 850,000 acres of confiscated and abandoned land in the South that had come under the military control of the federal government. The bureau was authorized to assign this land in 40-acre plots to freedmen and loyal refugees for a rental period of up to three years, after which the lessees had the option to buy the plot at its appraised value. However, late in the summer of 1865, President Andrew Johnson ordered the return of

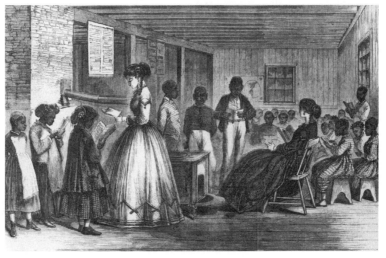

Many of the teachers who staffed the schools set up by the Freedmen's Bureau were young women from the North.

seized and abandoned land to all previous owners who had been pardoned. As a result, blacks lost their best opportunity for acquiring land with federal assistance.

The passage of the Black Codes and reports that Southern whites were enforcing a disguised form of slavery for the freed population convinced Congress of the need to continue the bureau and expand its jurisdiction. In July 1866, it overrode Johnson's veto and placed freedmen's affairs under the national jurisdiction of the bureau through 1868. Funded with a budget of $6.9 million, the bureau now had authorization to rent and repair schools and hospitals as well as furnish rations and clothing. The act also empowered agents of the bureau, most of whom were officers on loan from the army, to adjudicate labor disputes and provide a court of last resort for blacks who were systematically being denied their rights in Southern courts. The bureau helped to restore order to the chaotic labor situation, and, white protests notwithstanding, its rulings on the sanctity of written contracts were evenhanded and often favored planters.

After a year's extension in 1868, the bureau's funding ran out in 1869. It had spent a third of its budget on schools, assisted in the enrollment of more than 100,000 black students, and funded more than 100 hospitals. Despite these positive accomplishments in supervising the transition of blacks to freedom, Congress persisted in viewing the bureau as an emergency measure and refused to convert it into a permanent agency with a civilian staff.

SEE ALSO
Black Codes

FURTHER READING
Bentley, George R. *A History of the Freedmen's Bureau.* New York: Octagon Books, 1974.

Frémont, John C.
UNION GENERAL AND POLITICIAN

- *Born: January 21, 1813, Savannah, Ga.*
- *Political parties: Democrat, Republican*
- *Education: College of Charleston, 1829–31*
- *Military service: lieutenant, topographical engineers, 1838–46; major, California volunteers, 1846; lieutenant colonel, mounted rifles, 1846–48; major general, 1861–64*
- *Government service: U.S. Senate, 1850–51; territorial governor of Arizona, 1878–83*
- *Died: July 13, 1890, New York City, N.Y.*

A romantic figure whose fame exceeded his accomplishments, John C. Frémont took the unprecedented step in the summer of 1861 of issuing an emancipation proclamation in his military district of Missouri. Following the revocation of his decree by President Abraham Lincoln, Frémont compiled a very spotty military record in Missouri and the Shenandoah Valley before unsuccessfully running for the Presidency in 1864.

Frémont's parents, a French émigré dancing teacher and a Richmond housewife, eloped in 1811 and settled in Savannah, Georgia. His father died in 1818 and his widowed mother moved to Charleston, South Carolina, where Frémont gained a benefactor in a wealthy lawyer who paid for his schooling. Although expelled from the College of Charleston, he was able in 1838 to gain a commission in the prestigious Topographical Engineers Corps through his friendship with Joel R. Poinsett, a leading South Carolina Democrat. In 1841 he gained another political ally when he married Jessie Benton, the daughter of Missouri's most powerful politician, Thomas Hart Benton.

In the 1840s Frémont led a series of exploratory missions across the Trans-Mississippi West that won him popular fame as "The Pathfinder." He played a controversial role in the conquest of California that climaxed in his court-martial for disobeying an order from General Stephen W. Kearney. Resigning to avoid dismissal, he then served a brief term as senator from California and led two more expeditions to the West before securing the Presidential nomination of the new Republican party in 1856. A popular hero with no tainted political record to defend, he ran a surprisingly strong second to President-elect James Buchanan.

Frémont's continued support from antislavery Republicans resulted in his appointment at the outbreak of the Civil War as commander of the Department of the West, with headquarters in St. Louis. When he arrived in St. Louis in July 1861, he faced the divided political loyalties of a slave state and a deteriorating military situation. His problems worsened when he began feuding with the Blair family, the leaders of the Missouri Republican party. Then, completely on his own initiative, he issued a proclamation on August 30, 1861, freeing the slaves of all Missourians who resisted federal authority. All he offered President Lincoln as an explanation was the vague argument, "I have been compelled to move fast and act with my best judgment as the occasion rose." Justifiably fearful that any emancipation policy would drive the loyal border states, and especially Kentucky, out of the Union, Lincoln quickly countermanded Frémont's order.

Frémont still could have retained his command had he delivered any military victories in the fall of 1861. Failing to do so, he was relieved in November. A second command as head of the

Mountain Department in Virginia also ended abysmally for Frémont. He was no match for Confederate General Thomas J. "Stonewall" Jackson in the Shenandoah Valley. In June 1862, after refusing an assignment to serve under General John Pope, Frémont was relieved of command at his request. He sat out the rest of the war.

Frémont's ambitions always exceeded his talents, and his Presidential bid in 1864 petered out when Lincoln deftly isolated him from the faction of radical Republicans that had originally promoted his candidacy. His political failure in 1864 prefigured a series of financial reversals after the war that cost him his formerly wealthy holdings in California. His tenure as territorial governor of Arizona did nothing to revive his political career. In the last year of his life, the army restored him to its register as a major-general on the retirement list.

Union General John C. Frémont's public image was that of the dashing "Pathfinder" who had opened the Far West to white settlement.

SEE ALSO
Election of 1864; Emancipation

FURTHER READING
Nevins, Allan. *Frémont: Pathfinder of the West.* New York: Longmans, Green, 1955.
Rolle, Andrew F. *John Charles Frémont: Character as Destiny.* Norman: University of Oklahoma Press, 1991.

Fugitive Slave Act of 1850

Enacted as part of a sectional compromise, the Fugitive Slave Act of 1850 was a pro-Southern measure that expanded the role of the federal government in the rendition of fugitive slaves. It provoked a storm of controversy and further embittered the sectional differences over slavery.

Several Northern states passed personal-liberty laws in the 1840s that prevented state involvement in the recapturing of slaves who had fled the South. Slaveholders reacted by insisting that Congress replace the Fugitive Slave Act of 1793 with tougher legislation that would assist them in reclaiming their slave property. The result was a draconian law that gave in to all the Southern demands.

In a stunning example of how quickly states'-rights doctrine would be abandoned when the issue concerned the protection of slave property, the Southern congressmen who drafted the new Fugitive Slave Act vastly expanded the policing powers of the federal government. In addition to federal judges, specially appointed commissioners were now authorized to determine the legal status of blacks claimed as fugitives. The commissioners would receive a fee of $10 in each case where they ruled in favor of the slaveowner, but only $5 if they ruled that the accused was a free person—thereby stacking the deck somewhat against the accused. Denied all legal protections, the accused were not even allowed to testify at their hearings. The act also empowered federal marshals to deputize bystanders into a local posse for assistance in arresting an accused fugitive and provided stiff penalties for anyone who refused to help.

Abolitionists denounced the act as a moral abomination. Joined by free blacks and whites concerned over the coercive nature of the law, they mounted daring rescues of accused

Escaped slave Anthony Burns fled to Boston in 1854. His arrest, trial, and return to slavery that same year outraged many Northerners and intensified the antislavery crusade.

slaves in several Northern cities. Despite this open defiance, the act was enforced. Some 300 blacks were returned to slavery under its provisions, and federal tribunals ruled in favor of the alleged slaveowner in the vast majority of cases. The South had won a legal victory, but only at the cost of increasing the hostility toward slavery in the North.

SEE ALSO

Compromise of 1850; Personal Liberty Laws

FURTHER READING

Campbell, Stanley W. *The Slave Catchers: Enforcement of the Fugitive Slave Law, 1850–1860.* Chapel Hill: University of North Carolina Press, 1968.

Fugitive slaves

SEE Contrabands; Fugitive Slave Act of 1850

Garrison, William Lloyd

ABOLITIONIST

- *Born: December 10, 1805, Newburyport, Mass.*
- *Education: some schooling in lower grades*
- *Public service: editor, Liberator, 1831–66*
- *Died: May 24, 1879, New York, N.Y.*

The most renowned of the Northern abolitionists, William Lloyd Garrison was in the forefront of the crusade against slavery for more than three decades. Although his vitriolic denunciations of slavery and of slaveholders made him a hated figure in the North,

as well as the South, he never relented in his attacks until his goal of universal emancipation was achieved through the 13th Amendment.

Garrison was only three years old when his father abandoned his family for a life at sea. After sporadic schooling, he was apprenticed out in Newburyport to learn the printer's trade. His newspaper work carried him to Boston in 1828, where he met the antislavery journalist Benjamin Lundy. Joining Lundy the following year in Baltimore, he coedited *The Genius of Universal Emancipation.* As a result of an editorial in which he accused a Newburyport merchant of engaging in the slave trade, he was imprisoned for libel. Arthur Tappan, a wealthy, antislavery New York merchant, soon paid his fine and obtained his release, but Garrison's time in jail seemed to have pushed him to a more radical position. Formerly in favor of gradual emancipation and the colonization of free blacks in Africa, he was a far more uncompromising enemy of slavery when he returned to Boston.

The first issue of Garrison's weekly antislavery journal, the *Liberator,* appeared on January 1, 1831. In it he declared his intention "to lift up the standard of emancipation...till every chain be broken, and every bondsman set free!" To charges that his language was overly severe, he replied: "I *will be* as harsh as truth, and as uncompromising as justice...AND I WILL BE HEARD." And heard he was as he continually agitated the slavery question.

After founding the New England Anti-slavery Society in 1831 and spearheading the formation of the American Anti-Slavery Society in 1833, Garrison

Unfazed by the bitter opposition that he provoked in the North, let alone the South, William Lloyd Garrison refused to soften his impassioned moral indictment of slavery. Denouncing the Constitution as a proslavery document, he publicly burned a copy of it on the Fourth of July in 1854.

had an institutional base from which to propagate his doctrine of immediatism—that is, the moral need for all white Americans to begin immediately the work of ending slavery. Condemning colonization as a moral wrong that pandered to the racial prejudices of whites, he demanded the extension of equal rights to all blacks who were then free and to those freed in the future.

The unpopularity of Garrison's views on emancipation and racial equality nearly resulted in his lynching in 1835 by an antiabolitionist Boston mob. Still, he would not be silenced. He denounced as sinful all American institutions—including its churches, political parties, and the federal government itself—that refused to break all ties with the slave system. In perhaps his most notorious utterance, he spurned the U.S. Constitution in 1843 as a "covenant with death and an agreement with hell" and called for its annulment. His fiery radicalism, including his support for women as equals in the struggle against slavery, alienated many abolitionists and led to splits within the movement after 1840. However, he retained a band of hard-core followers and continued as the most visible symbol of the abolitionist crusade.

During the secession crisis, Garrison's pacifist convictions and his belief that slavery would soon crumble without the protection of the federal Union resulted in his counseling that the slave states be allowed to depart in peace. When armed conflict erupted, he immediately backed the Union's military efforts and worked with other abolitionists in pressuring the Republicans to declare black liberation as a war aim. The Emancipation Proclamation and, more convincingly, the 13th Amendment crowned his life's work with a sense of accomplishment that for so long had seemed out of reach.

SEE ALSO
Abolitionism

FURTHER READING
Mayer, Henry. *All on Fire: William Lloyd Garrison and the Abolition of Slavery.* New York: St. Martin's Press, 1998.
Stewart, James Brewer. *William Lloyd Garrison and the Challenge of Emancipation.* Arlington Heights, Ill.: Harlan Davidson, 1992.

Gettysburg

The best known of all Civil War battles, Gettysburg was also the costliest in its human losses. On the first three days of July in 1863, 40,000 Americans were killed or wounded on the ridges and fields just south of Gettysburg, Pennsylvania. It was the greatest battle ever fought in North America. When the slaughter was over, the Army of the Potomac had turned back General Robert E. Lee's second Northern invasion and had crippled the offensive capability of his now-fabled Army of Northern Virginia.

Lee was confident, perhaps overly so, when he started moving his army north out of Virginia in early June 1863. The decision to invade the North was Lee's, and his unrivaled prestige enabled him to win approval for the plan from the rest of the Confederate high command, which initially had wanted Lee to send reinforcements from his army to shore up threatened rebel positions in the West. In addition to gaining vitally needed supplies, Lee was hoping to deliver a knockout blow to the Union forces that would win the war for the Confederacy by thoroughly demoralizing the North.

A cavalry battle at Brandy Station on June 9—the largest of the entire war—

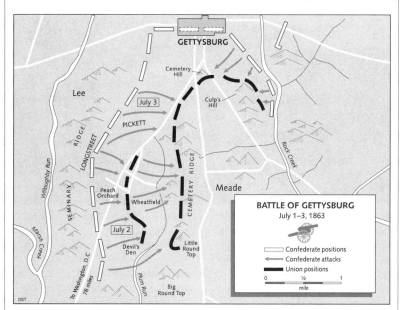

BATTLE OF GETTYSBURG
July 1–3, 1863

Confederate positions
Confederate attacks
Union positions

0   ½   1
mile

The strong defensive "hook" position of Union troops along Cemetery Ridge at Gettysburg enabled them to withstand three days of attack by Robert E. Lee's Confederate army.

confirmed the suspicions of General Joseph Hooker, commander of the Army of the Potomac, that Lee was shifting his army northward. Hooker wanted to move against the weakened Confederate position in his front and drive toward Richmond. But President Abraham Lincoln, insisting that Lee's army, and not Richmond, now had to be the primary Union objective, vetoed Hooker's proposal and ordered him to go after Lee. Soon convinced that Hooker lacked the confidence to engage Lee in battle, Lincoln replaced him on June 28 with General George Gordon Meade.

The lead columns of Lee's army crossed the Potomac River in mid-June and soon fanned across the lush farmlands of southern Pennsylvania. Although under orders not to pillage, the army liberally replenished itself, paying for supplies with Confederate paper money. Lee's veterans were lean, ragged, and cocky. In reply to a taunt from a young woman in Chambersburg, a Virginia soldier replied, "Lady, we always put on our dirty clothes when we're going to a hog-killing."

The "hog-killing" for both sides occurred somewhat accidentally at the small town of Gettysburg. On the morning of July 1, Confederates searching for shoes reported to be stored in Gettysburg clashed with Union cavalry who already occupied the town. The Confederacy was able to concentrate troops faster than the Union and easily got the best of the first day's fighting. Nonetheless, the federals did succeed in holding Cemetery Ridge, a rise just south of Gettysburg that formed the long shank of a hook-shaped line of elevated ground anchored to the northeast by the curve of Culp's Hill and Cemetery Hill and to the southwest by Round Top and Little Round Top. By controlling this elevated line, the Union forces had gained a secure defensive position.

Lee arrived at Gettysburg on the afternoon of July 1 and soon decided to renew the rebel attack the following day. He did so against the opposition of General James Longstreet, one of his corps commanders. Longstreet felt that

These soldiers were killed at Gettysburg near the peach orchard where the Confederates achieved a temporary breakthrough on the second day of the battle. This was an all too typical scene.

the Union line was too strongly defended and favored instead a move around the Union left to place Lee's army between the Army of the Potomac and Washington. Such a flanking maneuver, Longstreet reasoned, would force the Union army to abandon Gettysburg and attack Lee on open ground where it could easily be defeated. But Lee was determined to fight at Gettysburg. As he told Longstreet, "They were there in position, and I am going to whip them or they are going to whip me."

With the absence of General J. E. B. Stuart, who had left Lee's army on June 25 for a roundabout march around the Union army, Lee lacked his best "eyes and ears" for learning the size and disposition of Meade's forces. Consequently, he misjudged the speed with which Meade was able to reinforce the Union position at Gettysburg. Lee was also in the dark as to the exact location of the Union left, the target for the major Confederate attack on July 2. Led by a somewhat reluctant Longstreet, this attack never went off as planned. Longstreet was slow in deploying his troops, ran into the Union left in an unexpected position, and failed to break the federal line. In savage combat that raged through a peach orchard and wheat field, around a clump of boulders known as Devil's Den, and up the slopes of the Round Tops, the Union line buckled but held.

Having focused his attacks first on the Union right and then the left, Lee aimed at the center on July 3. Once again, he ordered an attack against the advice of a protesting Longstreet. General George Pickett's fresh division of Virginians, joined by a division led by General James Johnston Pettigrew, led a frontal assault across a mile-wide field toward an entrenched line of Union infantry backed up by formidable artillery on Cemetery Ridge. In what became a pageantry of valor and death, close to 15,000 Confederates tried to cross that field under a withering Union fire. About half of them were killed or wounded in the attempt. Lee had asked the impossible of his men, and the Union defenders easily repulsed the attack.

One third of Lee's 75,000-man army were casualties at Gettysburg. The Army of the Potomac lost 25 percent of its 88,000 men. Feeling that his army was too bloodied for an offensive, Meade refused to order a counterattack. To Lincoln's bitter disappointment, Lee's army escaped back into Virginia.

SEE ALSO

Gettysburg Address; Hooker, Joseph; Lee, Robert E.; Lincoln, Abraham; Longstreet, James; Meade, George; Stuart, James Ewell Brown.

FURTHER READING

Coddington, Edwin A. *The Gettysburg Campaign: A Study in Command.* New York: Charles Scribner's Sons, 1968.

Persico, Joseph E. *My Enemy, My Brother: Men and Days of Gettysburg.* New York: Da Capo Press, 1996.

Gettysburg Address

President Abraham Lincoln's short speech dedicating the national cemetery at Gettysburg on November 19, 1863, is probably the most famous, and certainly the most eloquent, address ever delivered by a U.S. President. In a five-minute speech of just 272 words, he succeeded in forever identifying the United States with the morally sublime purpose of demonstrating to the rest of the world that a democratic government dedicated to freedom and equality could and must survive.

The featured speaker at the Gettysburg dedication was the well-known orator Edward Everett, who, as expected, spoke for nearly two hours. Lincoln followed and, in contrast, had barely been introduced when his speech was over. Despite the brevity of his remarks, Lincoln had given them a great deal of thought. Except for the ending, he had written out his speech before leaving by train from Washington, D.C.

The poetic cadence of Lincoln's opening sentence masterfully fused themes of nationalism, equality, and liberty into a new vision of what the United States could be. "Fourscore and seven years ago, our fathers brought forth on this continent a new nation, conceived in Liberty, and dedicated to the proposition that all men are created equal." Here, unlike the First Inaugural Address, was no talk of the Union, but of the nation. Here, unlike the prewar fixation of Americans on constitutional liberties encased in the Constitution of 1787, was an emphasis on human liberty and equality

Lincoln carefully and precisely crafted this draft of the very short speech that he gave at the dedication of the national cemetery at Gettysburg. His statement that "The world will little note nor long remember what we say here, but it can not forget what they [the soldiers] did here" moved to tears a wounded Union officer in the crowd.

Four score and seven years ago our fathers brought forth, upon this continent, a new nation, conceived in Liberty, and dedicated to the proposition that all men are created equal.

Now we are engaged in a great civil war, testing whether that nation, or any nation, so conceived, and so dedicated, can long endure. We are met here on a great battle-field of that war. We have come to dedicate a portion of it, as a final resting place for those who here gave their lives, that that nation might live. It is altogether fitting and proper that we should do this.

But in a larger sense we can not dedicate— we can not consecrate— we can not hallow this ground. The brave men, living and dead, who struggled here, have consecrated it, far above our poor power to add or detract. The world will little note, nor long remember, what we say here, but can never forget what they did here. It is for us, the living, rather to be dedicated here to the unfinished work, which they have, thus far, so nobly carried on. It is rather rooted in the Declaration of Independence of 1776. Yet, as Lincoln well knew, a "proposition" is not a fixed conclusion but rather an idea to be considered and tested. For Lincoln, that testing of America's nationality defined the very essence of the war. "Now we are engaged in a great civil war, testing whether that nation, or any nation, so conceived, and so dedicated, can long endure." Those soldiers who died, and those yet to die, will have given "their lives that that nation might live...; that this nation shall have a new birth of freedom; and that this government of the people, by the people, for the people, shall not perish from the earth."

In a speech remarkable for its absence of rancor, of any reference to the hatreds of the war or even the Confederate enemy, Lincoln gave Americans a spiritual vision of their nation's potential to promote liberty and equality for all its citizens and all the world's people, slave as well as free.

Predictably, the Democratic press panned the speech as bad history couched in misleading generalities. Public reaction in the North was generally far more favorable. One of the more farsighted responses came from the Republican editor John W. Forney, who characterized the address as a "brief but immortal speech."

SEE ALSO

Lincoln, Abraham; Nationalism; Union

FURTHER READING

Gramm, Kent. *Gettysburg: A Meditation on War and Values.* Bloomington: Indiana University Press, 1994.
Greenstone, J. David. *The Lincoln Persuasion: Remaking American Liberalism.* Princeton, N.J.: Princeton University Press, 1993.
Wills, Gary. *Lincoln at Gettysburg: The Words That Remade America.* New York: Simon & Schuster, 1992.

Gold

Gold was the basis for international trade and for most national currencies in the mid-19th century. (Silver was so scarce at this time that it was rarely used in currency dealings.) Neither the Union nor the Confederacy had anywhere near enough gold to pay for their war expenses, but the Union had the decided advantage of access to a steady stream of gold from the mines in California and the payment of tariff duties. Consequently, the Union's monetary system was far more stable than the Confederacy's.

The inability of the Confederacy to finance its war effort in gold or an equivalent such as cotton ultimately doomed its economy to hyperinflation. For a brief period at the end of 1861, it appeared that the Union also might face a financial collapse. On December 31, 1861, the U.S. Treasury and Northern banks suspended specie payments—that is, they no longer pledged to redeem their debts in gold. Massive borrowings by the Treasury, in addition to hoarding by private citizens, had drained the Union's gold reserves. Unable to carry out its transactions in gold, the Treasury temporarily stopped payment to government contractors and soldiers.

Congress responded to the fiscal crisis with the passage in February 1862 of the Legal Tender Act, which authorized the Treasury to issue $150 million in paper money to pay government debts. This was the first government-controlled currency in the nation's history and a forerunner to today's paper money. These greenbacks, as they were called, enabled the Union to weather the financial storm. They injected a vitally needed currency into a monetary system starved of gold.

The creation of the greenbacks, along with the earlier suspension of specie payments, effectively took the United States off the gold standard. International trade, however, continued to be conducted in gold, and the Treasury accepted only gold for payment of tariff duties. Since the greenbacks were not redeemable at face value for gold, their value relative to gold fluctuated throughout the war. This produced the gold premium, the amount by which a dollar of gold exceeded a greenback in value. This premium was at its highest in the summer of 1864 when major Union offensives appeared to be blocked. At one point a dollar of gold commanded $2.84 in greenbacks.

One of the main priorities of the Treasury after the Civil War was to build up its gold reserves to a level at which it could redeem all the outstanding greenbacks in gold. This goal of returning to the prewar standard of specie redemption was finally achieved in 1878. Thereafter, the greenbacks were as good as gold.

SEE ALSO
Inflation; Legal Tender Acts; National Banking Acts; Taxation

FURTHER READING
Sharkey, Robert P. *Money, Class, and Party: An Economic Study of Civil War*

and Reconstruction. Baltimore: Johns Hopkins Press, 1959.
Unger, Irwin. *The Greenback Era: A Social and Political History of American Finance, 1865–1879.* Princeton, N.J.: Princeton University Press, 1964.

Government workers

The administrative and logistical demands of waging a total war caused a huge increase in the number of civilian workers employed by the Union and Confederate governments. The number in the Union jumped from 41,000 in 1861 to at least 195,000 by the end of the conflict. From a handful of workers largely inherited from the old federal government, the Confederacy was employing 70,000 at the height of the war.

Most of the increase came in the War Departments. The Union's Quartermaster Corps alone had 136,000 regularly paid workers. Under the able direction of Quartermaster General M. C. Meigs, these workers supplied the Union army with the best system of logistical support any mass army had yet enjoyed. The largest single bloc of Confederate workers—some 25,000—labored in war enterprises owned and operated by the government.

The need for labor opened up

Lined up in front of a building in Washington used to serve meals to federal employees, these government workers were among the tens of thousands of civilians who swelled the ranks of the Union bureaucracy during the war.

government employment for the first time to a significant number of women. Both governments welcomed women as clerks and copyists. Employed largely as seamstresses, women comprised about half of all the workers in the Confederate Quartermaster Department. Blacks, primarily impressed slaves, did the bulk of the hard, physical labor for the Confederate Niter and Mining Bureau.

Inflation damaged the morale of Confederate employees to a much greater extent than was true of their Northern counterparts. Southern bureaucrats were also less likely to be part of a patronage network that built administrative and political support for the war effort. Although neither government created an administrative structure to supervise activities between civil and military offices, the Union was more successful in coordinating all its resources and in streamlining bureaucratic details. This greater efficiency of its government workers was another factor in the Union victory.

SEE ALSO

Impressed laborers; Logistics; Women in the war

FURTHER READING

Van Riper, Paul P. and Harry N. Scheiber. "The Confederate Civil Service." *Journal of Southern History* 25, No. 4 (November 1959): 448–70.
———— and Keith A. Sutherland. "The Northern Civil Service, 1861–1865." *Civil War History* 11, No. 4 (December 1965): 351–69.

Grant, Ulysses S.

UNION GENERAL, 18TH PRESIDENT OF THE UNITED STATES

- *Born: April 27, 1822, Point Pleasant, Ohio*
- *Education: U.S. Military Academy, B.S., 1843*

- *Military service: U.S. Army: brevet lieutenant, 1843–45; lieutenant, 1845–47; regimental quartermaster, 1846–48; 1st lieutenant, 1848–53; captain, 1853–54; colonel, 1st Illinois Volunteers, 1861; brigadier general, volunteers, 1861; major-general, volunteers, 1862; major-general, regular army, 1863; lieutenant general, 1864–66; general, 1866–69; general-in-chief of the army, 1864–69*
- *Civilian government service: interim U.S. secretary of war, 1867–68; President of the United States, 1869–77*
- *Died: July 23, 1885, Mount McGregor, N.Y.*

Baptized Hiram Ulysses, Grant became Ulysses Simpson (his mother's maiden name) as the result of a clerical error when he was admitted to West Point. Nothing in his prewar career gave any indication that he would become the greatest general of the Civil War. Indeed, by most measures Grant was a listless failure when the war broke out. But in the next four years, he came alive, finding in the war a consistency of purpose that expressed itself in stunningly successful military leadership.

The son of a tanner, Grant had no interest in pursuing his father's trade. Nor did he aspire to a military career. West Point was his father's idea, and Grant attended out of a sense of filial duty. Very fond of horses and a superb rider since boyhood, he was disappointed that he failed to secure a cavalry command upon graduation. Assigned to the infantry, he compiled a solid

Ulysses S. Grant was described by Northern writer Richard Henry Dana as an "ordinary, scrubby-looking man with a slightly seedy look." The realistic common sense that Grant brought to warfare made him a great general.

record in the Mexican War. Bored and depressed by peacetime service, he took to drinking while stationed far from his wife on an isolated tour of duty in Oregon and northern California. He resigned from the army under something of a cloud in 1854, after a warning from his commanding officer concerning his drinking. After failing at numerous pursuits, he took a job as a clerk for his two brothers in order to support his family.

The war galvanized Grant's talents and energies in a way that peacetime never did. Very early in the war, he acquired an education in moral courage that bolstered his self-confidence. In July 1861, while leading his first field command against a rebel encampment in northeastern Missouri, he was frightened by the thought of sending men into battle. Then he discovered that the rebels had fled. "From that event to the close of the war," he related in his memoirs, "I never experienced trepidation upon confronting an enemy, though I always felt more or less anxiety. I never forgot that he had as much reason to fear my forces as I had his." Subsequently, Grant's coolness under fire became legendary. "Ulysses don't scare worth a damn," was how his soldiers put it.

After his early campaigning in Missouri, Grant commanded the Union land forces that captured Forts Henry and Donelson in February 1862. When a large Confederate force launched a counterattack at Shiloh two months later, Grant rallied his stunned army and turned a near-disaster into a Union victory. Surprised and shaken by the strength of the rebel attack, he now, in his words, "gave up all idea of saving the Union except by complete conquest."

Grant eliminated the last major Confederate stronghold on the Missis-sippi River with his daring Vicksburg campaign in the spring and summer of 1863. He then was instrumental in the lifting of the Confederate siege of Chattanooga in November and the routing of the rebel Army of Tennessee. Called east in March 1864 and given command of all the Union armies, he directed a campaign of attrition that unrelentingly wore down the rebel Army of Northern Virginia between May 1864 and April 1865, eventually forcing its surrender at Appomattox Courthouse.

Grant remained at the head of the army until 1869, and he sided with congressional Republicans in their struggle with President Andrew Johnson over Reconstruction. He served two terms as a Republican President, but his administrations were marred by indecisive leadership and massive scandals. Although honest and well meaning, he was too easily manipulated by friends and close associates. Financially as well as politically naive, he became bankrupt in the early 1880s as a result of investing in the fraudulent banking firm of Grant and Ward. He finally broke his dreary pattern of civilian failure in the writing of his *Personal Memoirs of U. S. Grant*. Finished just before his death from throat cancer in 1885, his memoirs earned $450,000 for his widow and remain one of the most lucid and powerful military narratives ever written.

SEE ALSO

Appomattox campaign; Chattanooga campaign; Forts Henry and Donelson; Grant's Virginia Campaign; Petersburg campaign; Shiloh; Vicksburg campaign

FURTHER READING

Grant, Ulysses S. *Personal Memoirs of U. S. Grant*. Ed. E. B. Long. 1985. Reprint, New York: Da Capo Press, 1982.
McFeely, William S. *Grant: A Biography*. New York: Norton, 1981.
Waugh, Joan. *U. S. Grant: American Hero, American Myth*. Chapel Hill: University of North Carolina Press, 2009.

Grant's Virginia campaign

The Virginia campaign of Union General Ulysses S. Grant against Robert E. Lee's Confederate Army of Northern Virginia in May and June 1864 produced the heaviest sustained fighting of the war. The almost-daily battles cost the Union 75,000 casualties in little more than six weeks. Confederate losses, although half the Union's in absolute numbers, were proportionately about as heavy. By mid-June, with Grant's successful crossing of the James River and the positioning of his Army of the Potomac in front of Petersburg, a vital source of rail supplies for Lee's army, the campaign settled into a military stalemate as the siege of Petersburg began.

Hailed as the savior of the Union after his victory at Chattanooga in November 1863, Grant was appointed general-in-chief of all Union armies in March 1864 and promoted to lieutenant general, a prestigious rank previously bestowed only on George Washington. His strategy for ending the war consisted of maintaining constant pressure on all rebel armies while simultaneously launching massive raids to destroy the economic resources and supply lines that sustained Confederate soldiers in the field. Grant hoped that one such raid in the East—a deployment of 60,000 federals from southeastern Virginia into North Carolina to break up the rail connection that funneled supplies to Lee's army from the South Atlantic area—would force Lee to withdraw from Richmond. But Lincoln, fearful that a weakened Army of the Potomac would be powerless to prevent Lee from striking toward Washington, rejected the North Carolina

operation and insisted that Grant make Lee's army his main objective.

In early May 1864, what was intended as a coordinated Union offensive got underway. While General William T. Sherman's western army was moving against Atlanta and the rebel Army of Tennessee, Grant accompanied the Army of the Potomac (still technically commanded by George G. Meade but in fact now supervised by Grant) when it crossed the Rapidan River on May 4 to engage Lee's army. Grant also set in motion two secondary offensives in Virginia, one in the Shenandoah Valley led by General Franz Sigel and the other up the James River toward Richmond commanded by General Benjamin F. Butler. The goals of these offensives were to divert Lee's attention from the main threat and to disrupt, if not destroy, his rail links to the west and south.

Grant had a numerical edge of almost two to one (119,000 federals to Lee's 64,000) when he crossed the Rapidan, but it was Lee who first seized the tactical offensive. Lee was anxious to savage Grant's army while it was still within the confines of the "Wilderness," a tangled, nearly impenetrable thicket of woods and underbrush that made it difficult for the Union to take advantage of its superiority in numbers and artillery. Striking at the flanks of the extended

General Ulysses S. Grant telegraphs Washington news of his Rapidan River crossing, marking the formal launch in May 1864 of his much-anticipated campaign against the Army of Northern Virginia commanded by General Robert E. Lee.

Union lines, Lee attacked on May 5. In a near repeat of his success at Chancellorsville in the same wooded area, Lee mauled both wings of Grant's army and inflicted 17,000 casualties in a two-day battle that raged along a five-mile front. Wounded soldiers trapped in woods set ablaze smothered or burned to death.

Lee seemingly had won a great victory in the Wilderness, but Grant refused to concede defeat. He was utterly determined to clamp Lee's army in a death grip and find an opening in its right flank that would enable the Army of the Potomac to get between Lee and Richmond. His goal, as he explained in a postwar report of July 1865, was to break the morale of Lee's army, and this could be accomplished only by "desperate and continuous hard fighting."

On May 7 Grant began moving his army to Spotsylvania Court House, a crossroads 10 miles southeast of the Wilderness that opened up a route to Richmond. Lee anticipated Grant's move, and Confederate troops won the race to the crossroads. For 12 days (May 9–21), the Confederates held off repeated Union attempts to gain control of Spotsylvania. The worst of the fighting occurred on May 12 at a salient (the part of a battle line that juts farthest toward the enemy) in the Confederate position originally known as the "Mule Shoe" but then renamed the "Bloody Angle." Union General Robert McAllister recalled of the fight: "It was a life or death contest. . . . The gray and blue coats with rifles in hand would spring on top of the breastworks, take deadly aim and fire, then fall dead in the trenches below. This I saw again and again."

Despite wiring Washington that "I propose to fight it out on this line if it takes all summer," Grant soon abandoned his effort to break the Confederate lines at Spotsylvania. Lee's veterans by now were probably the most skilled soldiers in the world at throwing up field fortifications that prevented their lines from being overrun. The futility of dislodging the rebels, plus information in mid-May that both Sigel and Butler had failed so miserably in their offensives that Lee was actually receiving reinforcements from the Confederate forces they were supposed to be threatening, convinced Grant to shift his army once again to the south and east in an effort to slide around Lee's right flank.

By early June the two armies were strung along a seven-mile front arcing from Totopotomoy Creek to the Chickahominy River. Grant had almost run out of room. Another shift to the southeast would plunge his army into the swamps and tidal estuary of the James River. Desperate to avoid another bloody stalemate, he ordered an all-out charge on June 3 against the Confederate position at Cold Harbor. As he admitted later, it was his most ill-advised decision of the war. His men were simply mowed down. Evander M. Law, a Confederate officer who witnessed the scene, recalled: "It was not war; it was murder." A storm of rebel fire smashed the grand Union charge within 10 minutes. Grant lost 8,000 men, or about 1,000 per minute.

Finally convinced that no series of short-range maneuvers could get him around or through Lee's army, Grant now made his boldest and most successful decision of the campaign. In mid-June he established a new base of operations on the James River and used transport vessels to carry his army to the south side of the James for an operation against Petersburg, far in Lee's rear. For once, Lee was caught off guard, and a more aggressive attack by the first federal forces to reach Petersburg most likely would have seized the city. But the opportunity was soon lost. Lee rushed down reinforcements, and by late June the armies were digging in for the elaborate trench warfare that characterized the siege of Petersburg for the next 10 months.

The horrendous casualties absorbed by the Army of the Potomac in its march from the Rapidan to Petersburg were quickly replaced, but the Confederacy had run out of troops to replace Lee's losses. Grant's Virginia campaign bled Lee's army dry and trapped it in a static form of warfare at Petersburg that it could never win.

SEE ALSO

Butler, Benjamin F.; Grant, Ulysses S.; Lee, Robert E.; Meade, George G.; Sigel, Franz

FURTHER READING

Grimsley, Mark. *And Keep Moving On: The Virginia Campaign, May–June 1864.* Lincoln: University of Nebraska Press, 2002.

Matter, William D. *"If It Takes All Summer": The Battle of Spotsylvania.* Chapel Hill: University of North Carolina Press, 1988.

Rhea, Gorton C. *The Battle of the Wilderness, May 5–6, 1864.* Chapel Hill: University of North Carolina Press, 1994.

Trudeau, Noah André. *Bloody Roads South: The Wilderness to Cold Harbor, May–June, 1864.* Boston: Little, Brown, 1989.

Great Britain

Despite widespread Confederate expectations that the British would intervene in the Civil War by recognizing Southern independence, Great Britain maintained an uneasy neutrality throughout the conflict. Contrary to the doctrine of King Cotton, both the economic and political interests of the British dictated against their intervention on the Confederate side.

Confederate hopes for British recognition rested on the fact that the slave South supplied Britain with 80 percent of the cotton needed for its textile mills. Deprived of that cotton and faced with a massive loss of jobs and profits, the British, reasoned Southerners, would naturally intervene in the war and break the Union blockade. As a South Carolinian told the British war correspondent William Howard Russell in April 1861: "[The British] are bound

This cartoon in Harper's Weekly *warns the British not to act like a baby by offering assistance to the reptilian Confederacy. John Bull is a nickname for the British, after a character in an 18th-century pamphlet by the Scottish political satirist John Arbuthnot.*

THE DANGEROUS PLAYMATE—A SINGULAR INSTANCE OF FASCINATION.
That Innocent Infant Jonny Bull *giving Aid and Comfort to the Reptile.*

to take our part; if they don't we'll just give them a hint about cotton, and that will set matters right."

When combined with the determination of nonslaveholders that planters would not unduly profit from the war, such reasoning resulted in a virtual halt of cotton exports from the South in 1861. Although the Confederate Congress did not officially impose a cotton embargo, it endorsed the public demand to cease exports. As a result, the Confederacy failed to take advantage of the very porous Union blockade in 1861 by shipping cotton abroad to support the price of its bonds and currency. The Confederate government did seize cotton and export what it could in the last half of the war, but it did so only after the failure of the earlier embargo to bring Britain into the war on its side.

The bumper Southern harvests of the late 1850s had left textile manufacturers in Britain with a large backlog of raw cotton, which they tapped while new sources of supply were being developed in Egypt and India. Meanwhile, a series of bad harvests forced the British to increase drastically their imports of wheat and other foodstuffs from the North. The Union, not the Confederacy, was able to exert the greatest economic leverage on the British, who now depended on the North for one-third to one-half of their basic food supplies.

Unemployment was rising sharply among British cotton workers by 1862, but by then it was already apparent that the U.S. Civil War was more of a stimulant than a depressant for the British economy. From 1860 to 1864 its foreign trade increased from $374 million to $509 million. As war orders poured in from both sides, the British enjoyed a boom in their munitions, iron, and shipbuilding industries. An expansion in linen and woolen production more than counterbalanced the eventual slump in cotton textiles. All the while, Confederate ships and privateers were destroying enough of the Union merchant marine to reestablish British dominance of the Atlantic trade.

Politically, as well as economically, the British had more to gain then lose by staying on the sidelines. To be sure, British diplomats recognized that their influence in the Western Hemisphere would be enhanced by a Confederate victory that weakened the growing American republic. Nonetheless, as the world's greatest imperial power, the British did not want to set a dangerous precedent of supporting a war for political independence that could serve as a model for revolts in their own empire. Moreover, by refusing to break the Union blockade, the British were allowing the Union navy to enforce the very maritime demands that the British traditionally had asserted, often against the wishes of the United States.

A final check on British recognition of the Confederacy was the forceful diplomacy of Union Secretary of State William Henry Seward and the Union minister to Britain, Charles Francis Adams. They repeatedly warned that recognition or open support of the Confederacy meant war with the Union and retaliations against British trade. Tempering their bellicosity, however, was the realization that a war against Britain would be a desperate, last-ditch measure. During the *Trent* affair in the fall of 1862, when the possibility of war with Britain loomed greatest, Seward brokered a conciliatory agreement to end the crisis.

Britain wound up granting the Confederacy no more than it had at the beginning of the war. In issuing a proclamation of neutrality on May 14, 1861, the British government granted the Confederacy the rights of a belligerent. This meant under international law a recognition of the legal right of the Confederate government to maintain agents abroad, contract for supplies, make loans, and outfit privateers to prey on Union shipping. This conferral of belligerent status, however, fell far short of recognizing the Confederacy as a nation with full powers to make treaties or enter into foreign alliances. Since the British also acknowledged the legality of the Union blockade, the North probably benefited more from Britain's neutral stance than the South.

Only a series of battlefield victories would have secured for the Confederacy British recognition of its nationhood. General Robert E. Lee hoped to win one of those decisive victories when he invaded the North in September 1862, at a time when the British were actively considering stepping into the war as a mediator. Lee's defeat at Antietam ended the Confederacy's best opportunity for foreign recognition. Working- and middle-class Britons applauded the policy of emancipation that the Union announced after Antietam, and the British government leaned ever more heavily toward the Union.

SEE ALSO

Adams, Charles Francis; *Alabama* claims; Antietam; Blockade; France; Laird rams; Seward, William Henry; *Trent* affair

FURTHER READING

Jones, Howard. *Union in Peril: The Crisis over British Intervention in the Civil War.* Chapel Hill: University of North Carolina Press, 1992.
Myers, Philip E. *Caution and Cooperation: The American Civil War in British-American Relations.* Kent, Ohio: Kent State University Press, 2008.
Owsley, Frank L. *King Cotton Diplomacy: Foreign Relations of the Confederate States of America.* 2nd ed. Chicago: University of Chicago Press, 1959.

Greenbacks

SEE Legal Tender Acts

Greenhow, Rose O'Neal

CONFEDERATE SPY

- *Born: 1817, Port Tobacco, Md.*
- *Education: some schooling in lower grades*
- *Died: September 30, 1864, at sea, off Wilmington, N.C.*

A society matron in Washington recruited to head a Confederate espionage operation, Rose Greenhow was one of the Confederacy's most celebrated spies. Before her arrest and imprisonment by federal authorities, she passed on information that is widely credited with alerting rebel generals to the plans for the Union offensive in the First Bull Run Campaign.

The daughter of a wealthy planter, Greenhow was still an infant when a household slave killed her father in 1817. As a teenager she was initiated into the world of political intrigue when she and

Confederate spy Rose O'Neal Greenhow and her daughter in the courtyard of the Old Capitol Prison. Greenhow remained outspoken in her support of the Confederacy even after her imprisonment.

her sisters moved to Washington to live with their aunt, the proprietress of a fashionable boardinghouse frequented by congressmen. John C. Calhoun of South Carolina was her personal favorite, and his states'-rights philosophy became her political Bible. Following her marriage in 1835 to Robert Greenhow, a Virginia lawyer and linguist employed by the State Department, she emerged as a charming social hostess whose party invitations were among the most prized in Washington. After her husband died in 1854 while on an assignment for the State Department in California, she was one of the most sought-after widows in the city. Renowned for her beauty and wit, she became the confidant of many politicians, most notably President James Buchanan.

Greenhow's openly pro-Southern sympathies and her ready access to the gossipy Washington elite made her an attractive candidate for the Confederate secret service. In all likelihood, Thomas Jordan, a Virginian and West Point graduate who resigned his commission to serve as a staff officer in the Confederate army, recruited her as an agent during the winter of 1860–61.

Supplied with a cipher code and a network of agents and couriers, Greenhow passed on a steady flow of useful material to Richmond. Trusting her instincts, she was quite skillful at deducing Union intentions from sketchy information. "I was, of course, a close observer of the smallest indications," she noted in her wartime memoirs, "and often drew accurate conclusions without having any precise knowledge on the subject." Her greatest coup came in July 1861, when she relayed a warning that General Irvin McDowell's army was about to leave Washington for an advance on Manassas Junction. The information likely contributed to the Confederate victory at First Bull Run,

and rebel soldiers, as Mary Chesnut recorded in her diary, were soon hailing Greenhow as "our good angel."

As part of a general tightening of security after McDowell's stunning defeat, federal authorities placed Greenhow under house arrest on August 23, 1861. Exasperated over her continued ability to send messages to the South, they transferred her to the Old Capital Prison in January 1862. Her remarkable flair for publicizing herself as the innocent victim of a despotic government, however, soon made her continued imprisonment a political liability to the Union cause. In May 1862, she was sent into Confederate lines, where she was greeted as a heroine.

Greenhow traveled to Europe in the summer of 1863 on a tour during which she tried to enlist support for the Confederacy. While in England, she published her memoirs under the title of *My Imprisonment and the First Year of Abolitionist Rule at Washington*. On her return voyage a storm forced her ship aground off Wilmington, North Carolina, and she drowned when the boat taking her ashore capsized. Confederate officials honored her with a military funeral.

SEE ALSO
Secret services

FURTHER READING
Ross, Ishbel. *Rebel Rose: Life of Rose O'Neal Greenhow.* New York: Harper, 1954.

Guerilla warfare

Irregular or guerrilla warfare, touched off by partisan bands of both Unionists and Confederates, resulted in some of the most

Guerilla warfare caused serious concern, meriting a cover story on Harper's Weekly *in the Christmas Eve 1864 issue. The caption to this illustration reads, "Your money or your life!"*

savage, pitiless fighting of the Civil War. Although the small-scale raids and pillaging expeditions that comprised most guerrilla activities rarely affected the campaigns of the regular armies, they spawned an ongoing brutalization of the war by provoking increasingly savage reprisals that in turn spawned further bursts of vicious resistance.

Guerrilla warfare characterized the fighting in at least three major areas: Missouri, West Virginia, and eastern Tennessee. Although the Unionists were in the majority in those areas, a hard core of pro-Confederates led by the younger sons

of slaveholding families contested their leadership. Both the Union and Confederacy tried to convert the undecided and win back those who had gone over to the other side.

The guerrilla, whether a Confederate sympathizer in Missouri or West Virginia or a Unionist in eastern Tennessee, relied on harassment by means of ambushes and attacks against supply and communications lines. These tactics, plus the responses they provoked, resulted in a type of warfare that set neighbor against neighbor and knew no rules save those of survival. In addition to ordering summary executions of suspected guerrillas, frustrated authorities on both sides resorted to the forced depopulation of regions believed to be harboring the enemy's sympathizers.

Outside of the Appalachian Mountains and the contested border regions of the Confederacy, Unionists were usually too few in numbers to mount any organized opposition. Guerrilla resistance in the Confederate heartland was nonetheless pervasive. It was directed at slowing the federal advance and undermining the new system of free labor that Union authorities were trying to establish in occupied areas. Although this resistance was often organized by the Confederate Partisan Ranger Act of 1862, much of it was a spontaneous civilian reaction to the presence of federal troops.

In either case, the enraged federal response intensified the destructiveness of the war. Villages were burned in retaliation for raids on Union supply depots and property was seized to indemnify Unionists for guerrilla-inflicted losses. By 1864 in the lower Mississippi Valley, a fine of $10,000 was levied for every lessee of a federally leased plantation who was killed by partisans. The fine was collected by confiscating property within a thirty-mile radius of the killing.

As ongoing losses of territory by the Confederacy resulted in a breakdown of the ability of public authorities to maintain law and order, local communities struggled to create some semblance of security. Guerrilla bands emerged as defenders of lives and property. Depending on the political complexion of the immediate neighborhood, their targets could be Unionists, Confederates, or roving bands of deserters and draft evaders. In October 1862, after a summary trial by the so-called Citizens' Court, Gainesville, Texas, witnessed the hanging of 44 suspected Unionist sympathizers. Citizens took the law into their own hands as they sought to cleanse their neighborhoods of those considered to be enemies, whether political or personal. They gave little if any quarter as they settled old scores.

By the late stages of the war vast swaths of the Confederacy were a no man's land as irregular warfare degenerated into sheer banditry devoid of any political purpose. War weariness settled over the home front, shaped as much by the lawless conditions at home as by Confederate military reverses. The will to go on had largely evaporated and the Confederate and state government took the brunt of the blame. Guerrilla warfare had surely disrupted Union supply lines and proved to be a thorn in the side to Union military operations, but Southern civilians had paid a terrible price for such limited successes. Just before he surrendered his army at Appomattox, General Robert E. Lee rejected the option of continuing the war by guerrilla tactics. To do so, he concluded, not only offered no prospect of success but also would prove to be far more damaging to Southerners than to their Unionist enemy.

SEE ALSO

Dissenters; Lee, Robert E.

FURTHER READING

Mountcastle, Clay. *Punitive War: Confederate Guerrillas and Union Reprisals.* Lawrence: University Press of Kansas, 2009.

Sutherland, Donald E. *A Savage Conflict: The Decisive Role of Guerrillas in the American Civil War.* Chapel Hill: University of North Carolina Press, 2009.

Habeas corpus, suspension of

Habeas corpus is a basic legal right that protects individuals from being detained without the presentation of formal charges against them. Under a writ of habeas corpus, a prisoner must be released so that a civil court can determine the legality of the charges. Both the Union and Confederate governments suspended the writ of habeas corpus during the war. The Union was the first to do so and its suspensions were more thorough and held more individuals under military arrest than the more limited curtailment of civil liberties in the Confederacy.

In April 1861, when Washington was in danger of being cut off from the North, President Abraham Lincoln suspended the writ of habeas corpus on the military line of railroads from Philadelphia to Washington. By so doing, he gave the Union military the power to arrest suspected rebel sympathizers and detain them indefinitely. One of those arrested, John Merryman, secured a writ for his release from the presiding judge of the federal circuit court of Maryland. That judge happened to be an old Republican nemesis, Roger Taney, the Chief Justice of the United States when he was not serving on the federal circuit in Maryland. Taney ordered Merryman released on the grounds that only Congress, not the President, had the constitutional authority to suspend the writ of habeas corpus. Citing the outbreak of rebellion and his powers as commander-in-chief, Lincoln rejected Taney's argument and ignored his order.

Throughout 1861 and 1862 Lincoln continued to suspend the writ of habeas corpus without any congressional authorization. In announcing a fresh round of suspensions in September 1862, he declared that persons who discouraged enlistments or aided and abetted the Confederacy in any way were subject to military arrest. During the war, some 15,000 such arrests were made, most of them in the border states

of the Upper South or in occupied areas of the Confederacy.

In March 1862, Congress passed the Habeas Corpus Act. In effect, the act confirmed what Lincoln had been doing all along. Although most Republicans intended the act to set up judicial guidelines for the suspension of the writ, they also made it clear that civil liberties in the North would be curbed under the wartime emergency. Measured against the far more draconian suppression of civil liberties during World War I, however, those curbs were relatively mild. Most of those arrested were detained only briefly, and taking an oath of loyalty to the Union usually returned those arrested to civilian life.

On three separate occasions, the Confederate Congress authorized President Jefferson Davis to suspend the writ of habeas corpus for a limited period of time. The first authorization came in February 1862, in the wake of the Confederacy's stunning defeats at Forts Henry and Donelson. Aimed against spies, saboteurs, and Unionists in areas under danger of a federal attack, the act was renewed in October 1862. The second suspension triggered a furious protest led by Alexander H. Stephens, the Confederate vice president. "Our liberties, once lost, may be lost forever," he warned, and several state legislatures supported his position by passing resolutions condemning the suspension.

In response to the charges that it was stripping Southern whites of their constitutional liberties, the Confederate Congress did not extend Davis's authorization to suspend the writ past February 1863. It was renewed for six months beginning in February 1864. At this stage of the war, suspension of the writ offered about the only hope of enforcing obedience to Confederate conscription. Despite the evermore desperate condition of Confederate armies, opponents of the legislation continued their criticisms. Few measures of the Confederate government ever aroused such bitter opposition.

SEE ALSO
Confederate politics

FURTHER READING
Neely, Mark E., Jr. *The Fate of Liberty: Abraham Lincoln and Civil Liberties.* New York: Oxford University Press, 1991.
———. *Southern Rights: Political Prisoners and the Myth of Confederate Constitutionalism.* Charlottesville: University Press of Virginia, 1999.
Robbins, John B. "The Confederacy and the Writ of Habeas Corpus." *Georgia Historical Quarterly* 55, No. 2 (Summer 1971): 83–101.

Halleck, Henry W.

UNION GENERAL

- *Born: January 16, 1815, Westernville, N.Y.*
- *Education: Union College, A.B., 1837; U.S. Military Academy, B.S., 1839*
- *Military service: lieutenant, engineers, 1839–45; 1st lieutenant, 1845–53; captain, 1853–54; major-general, 1861–72; general-in-chief of the army, 1862–64; chief of staff, 1864–65*
- *Died: January 9, 1872, Louisville, Ky.*

A superb administrator but a timid strategist, Henry W. Halleck was President Abraham Lincoln's chief military advisor and overall commander of Union armies for much of the war. Although reluctant to exercise decisive leadership, his insistence on order and discipline in the management of the war was a key factor in Union victory.

While growing up in western New York, Halleck came to despise the tedium of farmwork, and at the age of 16 he ran away from home. Adopted by his maternal grandfather, who provided him with an excellent education, he proved to be a brilliant student. Upon graduating from West Point near the top of his class, he earned the nickname "Old Brains" for his scholarly work as a military engineer and theorist. His major publications included *Elements of Military Art and Science* (1846), *International Law* (1861), and a translation from the French of Henri Jomini's *Political and Military Life of Napoleon* (1864). After holding a number of administrative positions in California during the Mexican War, he studied law before resigning from the army in 1854. His California law practice and business investments soon enabled him to amass a fortune.

Recommended by General Winfield Scott for a top post at the outbreak of the Civil War, Halleck brought a dazzling prewar reputation to his assignment as a major-general. Replacing General John C. Frémont in charge of the Department of Missouri in November 1861, he restored order to the administrative muddle left by his predecessor. After General Ulysses S. Grant, one of his subordinates, broke through Confederate defenses at Forts Henry and Donelson, Halleck gained command of all Union operations in the West.

Once Halleck assumed field command of the combined western armies after the Union victory at Shiloh in April 1862, his lack of combat experience soon revealed his shortcomings as a general. He amassed twice as many troops as the Confederates in the western theater were able to muster, but his advance on Corinth, Mississippi, was so slow and ponderous that the Confederate army was able to escape intact in late May 1862. Still, unlike his Union counterpart in the East, General George B. McClellan, Halleck had gained his strategic objective. As a reward, he was brought east in July 1862, and elevated to general-in-chief of all Union land forces.

When he arrived in Washington, Halleck fully intended to direct the strategic deployment of Union armies. However, fearful that he would be blamed for the federal rout at Second Bull Run in August 1862, he soon shrank from assuming strategic responsibilities or giving decisive orders and became, in President Lincoln's biting phrase, "little more than a first-rate clerk." Moreover, his abrasive personality and penchant for blaming others for his mistakes made him so unpopular in Washington that Lincoln once remarked that "he was Halleck's friend because nobody else was." In fact, Lincoln valued the technical advice that Halleck gave him, and he appreciated Halleck's talent in translating Presidential directives on waging the war into the military language that generals could understand. His greatest contribution, however, was in streamlining and coordinating the endless details involved in raising men and material for the Union armies.

Demoted to chief of staff after Grant replaced him in the spring of 1864, Halleck served as a liaison between Lincoln and Grant in the last year of the war. By so doing, he relieved Grant of burdensome administrative chores and provided a clear line of communication between the commander-in-chief and general-in-chief. Continuing to hold administrative assignments in the postwar army, Halleck died while in command of the Division of the South.

SEE ALSO
Command structure

FURTHER READING
Ambrose, Stephen E. *Halleck: Lincoln's Chief of Staff*. Baton Rouge: Louisiana State University Press, 1962.
Marszalek, John F. *Commander of All Lincoln's Armies: A Life of General Henry W. Hallek*. Cambridge: Belknap Press of Harvard University Press, 2004.

Hampton Roads conference

The closest that Union and Confederate authorities ever came to holding a peace conference during the Civil War was a meeting at Hampton Roads, Virginia, on February 3, 1865. Representing the Union were President Abraham Lincoln and his secretary of state, William H. Seward. The Confederate emissaries were Vice President Alexander H. Stephens, Senator Robert M. T. Hunter of Virginia, and Assistant Secretary of War John A. Campbell. The conference, in Lincoln's words, "ended without result," because the Confederates would accept nothing less than Union recognition of Southern independence.

Lincoln repeatedly had opposed any negotiations with the Confederacy out of fear that peace talks would dampen army morale or, and worse yet, result in an armistice that put emancipation on hold and in effect recognized Confederate independence. By the beginning of 1865, however, these fears had subsided. Union arms were finally smashing the Confederacy into submission and the legal end of slavery seemed assured when Congress passed the 13th amendment on January 31 and sent it to the states for ratification. Now in a position of great strength, and anxious to end the bloodshed, Lincoln was willing to explore the possibility that lenient terms might hasten the collapse of the Confederacy.

By mutual agreement, no notes or written records of any kind were kept of the four-hour meeting. The fullest account of what was said comes from Stephens's postwar recollections published in his *A Constitutional View of the Late War Between the States.* Scraps of contemporary evidence and the sketchier accounts of others at the meeting corroborate the main thrust of what Stephens related.

Lincoln made it clear at the onset that there could be no armistice or any formal agreement until the Confederates, "those who were resisting the laws of the Union," agreed to return to the Union. Once reunion was achieved, Lincoln hastened to add, former Confederates could expect the same restoration of personal and political rights he had already included in his program of reconstruction. As to property rights in slavery, he pledged to seek congressional approval of up to $400 million in appropriations as monetary compensation to slaveholders. Half would be distributed by April 1 to the Southern states (including the border states) if all military resistance to the Union had ceased. The other half would be paid by July 1 if the 13th amendment was ratified.

No agreement was reached at Hampton Roads, but Lincoln did submit a plan of compensated emancipation to his cabinet on February 5. The cabinet unanimously disapproved of the proposal, and Lincoln never did send it on to Congress. Even while his fellow Repub-

licans were criticizing Lincoln's peace terms as overly generous, Confederate President Jefferson Davis was denouncing those same terms as the humiliating demands of "His Majesty Abraham the First." Contrary to Lincoln's wishes, the war would drag on a bit longer.

SEE ALSO
Stephens, Alexander H.

FURTHER READING
Donald, David Herbert. *Lincoln.* New York: Simon & Schuster, 1995.
Stephens, Alexander H. *A Constitutional View of the Late War Between the States.* Vol. 2. Philadelphia: National Publishing Co., 1870, 599–610.

Harpers Ferry

SEE Brown, John

Homestead Act

Probably the best known of the domestic legislation passed by the Republicans during the Civil War, the Homestead Act

These Nebraska homesteaders dug their house out of a hillside. A cow grazes on the grassy sod roof.

of 1862 granted 160 acres of public land to citizens who would live on the land for five years and pay a modest registration fee. During the war years alone, Americans registered some 27,000 homestead entries. Eventually, homestead land amounted to more than 80 million acres.

The Northern public had long favored a homestead measure, but Southerners fought against passing such a bill. Southerners feared that "free land" would speed up the development of a free-labor West and strengthen the cause of the abolitionists. According to Senator James Mason of Virginia, the homestead bill of 1860 was part of a Northern design for "command and control of the destinies of the continent." This bill did pass Congress, but it was vetoed by President James Buchanan.

The Republicans had put a homestead plank in their 1860 platform, and they moved quickly in the 37th Congress (1861–63) to enact legislation. Passed in May 1862, the Homestead Act fulfilled their pledge to offer a fresh start in the West for farmers and workers. Although a half-million families farmed homesteads, including many from the Border South seeking a safe refuge from the ravages of the Civil War, the Homestead Act never lived up to its promise. Speculators and railroad companies acquired control of most of the best land in the West, and a 160-acre homestead was too small to be economically viable on the dry, treeless plains. The agricultural future belonged to the large, commercial farmer, not the small, independent one whom the Homestead Act tried to promote.

FURTHER READING

Robbins, Roy M. *Our Landed Heritage: The Public Domain, 1776–1936.* Lincoln: University of Nebraska Press, 1962.

Hood, John Bell
CONFEDERATE GENERAL

- *Born: June 1, 1831, Owingsville, Ky.*
- *Education: U.S. Military Academy, B.S., 1853*
- *Military service: U.S. Army: brevet lieutenant, infantry, 1853–55; lieutenant, cavalry, 1855–58; 1st lieutenant, 1858–61; Confederate army: 1st lieutenant, 1861; major, 1861–62; brigadier general, 1862; major-general, 1862–64; lieutenant general, 1864–65; general (temporary), 1864–65*
- *Died: August 30, 1879, New Orleans, La.*

Known as the "Gallant Hood" for his superb record as a brigade and division commander, John Bell Hood was one of the fiercest fighters in the Confederate army. Temperamentally ill-suited to command an entire army, however, he virtually hurled the Army of Tennessee to its death during his disastrous invasion of Tennessee in the fall of 1864.

An unruly youth with a reputation for enjoying fistfights, Hood decided on a military career and with the intervention of his uncle, Congressman Richard French, secured an appointment to West Point. A poorly prepared and indifferent student, he ranked in the bottom fifth of his graduating class. After two years with the infantry in California, he again called on his uncle's political influence to gain a transfer to the more prestigious cavalry. He gained his first combat experience in 1857 while leading a column of cavalry against Native Americans on the Texas frontier. When his native state of Kentucky refused to secede, Hood entered Confederate service from Texas, the state he henceforth referred to as "my adopted land."

Hood performed well in his first assignment as a cavalry lieutenant on the Yorktown Peninsula, and in the fall of 1861 was given command of a Texas regiment raised to serve with the main Confederate army in Virginia. Hood made it clear that he expected his troops to be fighters. As he later wrote, he strove "to impress upon them that no regiment in that Army should ever be allowed to go forth upon the battle-field and return with more trophies of war than the Fourth Texas." Hood did know how to instill pride in his men and inspire them to fight, and as the commander of what was soon called "Hood's Texas Brigade," he emerged as one of Lee's best combat generals in the Virginia battles of 1862.

In 1863, Hood paid a heavy physical price for his reckless bravery on the battlefield. While leading the main rebel attack on the second day at Gettysburg, he was hit by a fragment of a Union shell that permanently crippled his left arm. He had barely recovered from this wound when, while rallying his troops at Chickamauga, he was hit in the right thigh, a wound that necessitated the amputation of his leg. If anything, his injuries enhanced his popularity, and he was promoted to lieutenant general. Assigned to lead a corps in General Joseph E. Johnston's Army of Tennessee in February 1864, he criticized Johnston's defensive strategy from the very start of the Atlanta campaign. With the Union army on the outskirts of Atlanta, Hood replaced Johnston in July 1864. He was now the youngest full general in the Confederate army.

Upon hearing of Hood's appointment, William H. T. Walker, one of his division commanders, remarked: "Hood has 'gone up like a rocket.' It is to be hoped…that he will not come down like the stick." Walker's hope was not realized. Hood never learned how to control an army and coordinate its movements. The series of attacks he ordered

outside of Atlanta cost him 20,000 men and failed to prevent the Union capture of the city. His subsequent move into Tennessee was badly conceived and poorly planned. After his shattering defeat at Nashville, Hood was relieved of command at his own request.

Hood raised a large family and engaged in a variety of business pursuits in New Orleans after the war. He, as well as his wife and eldest daughter, died in the yellow fever epidemic of 1879.

SEE ALSO

Atlanta campaign; Hood's Tennessee campaign

FURTHER READING

McMurry, Richard M. *John Bell Hood and the War for Southern Independence.* Lexington: University Press of Kentucky, 1982.

Confederates charge the troops under Union general George Thomas at Chickamauga, where a shell made a massive wound in John Bell Hood's leg, requiring its amputation.

Hood's Tennessee campaign

In November 1864, General John Bell Hood invaded Union-occupied Tennessee in a desperate attempt to regain the initiative for the Confederacy in the western theater. Hood hoped that his Army of Tennessee could capture Nashville, move north into Kentucky, and then swing east to link up with General Robert E. Lee's forces in Virginia. At the very least, he expected to bolster flagging Confederate morale and force the

Union army under General William T. Sherman to abandon its Georgia campaign and rush north to the defense of Tennessee and Kentucky. None of these objectives were realized. Instead, Hood succeeded only in shattering the fighting strength of his Army of Tennessee.

After being forced to abandon Atlanta on September 1 and spending a month harassing Sherman's supply line north of Atlanta, Hood moved his army into northern Alabama in mid-October. Lacking the troop strength to engage Sherman's much larger army in a pitched battle, Hood now decided to strike north into Tennessee. Although any chance of success depended upon speed, he delayed for three weeks while reprovisioning his army and waiting for his cavalry to return from raiding operations. This delay gave Union forces in Tennessee under General George H.

Thomas time to prepare for Hood's invasion.

Hood's army crossed into Tennessee on November 19. After missing an opportunity at Spring Hill to circle behind and trap 30,000 federals commanded by General John M. Schofield, Hood caught up with the Union army at Franklin. He then ordered on November 30 one of the most senseless charges of the war. Without any artillery support, he sent close to 20,000 men in a frontal assault across an open, two-mile-long field against a well-entrenched Union position. "On came the enemy, as steady and resistless as a tidal wave," recalled Colonel Henry Stone, one of the Union defenders. "It is impossible to exaggerate the fierce energy with which the Confederate soldiers, that short November afternoon, threw themselves against the

Supported by a massive supply line that stretched back to these railroad yards at Nashville, the Union army was far too strong for Hood's Tennessee campaign to succeed.

works, fighting with what seemed the very madness of despair." More heroic and suicidal than even Confederate General George Pickett's charge at Gettsyburg, the assault resulted in 6,000 rebel casualties, including the death of six generals. Union losses were less than one-third as heavy.

Despite having depleted his offensive firepower at Franklin, Hood followed Schofield's army to the outskirts of Nashville and virtually invited a Union force that now totaled 70,000 troops to attack his weakened and dispirited army of 24,000 men. General Thomas, the Union commander at Nashville, waited two weeks before accepting Hood's invitation. Thomas wanted to be thoroughly prepared both to attack and to pursue Hood's army. Then, when he was ready, an ice storm forced a postponement of the offensive. As Thomas patiently waited for his opportunity, the authorities in Washington grew increasingly impatient and on two separate occasions almost relieved Thomas of his command. Finally, the weather cleared, and on December 15 Thomas unleashed a devastating offensive that silenced his doubters.

Thomas's battle plan pinned down Hood's right flank while hurling the bulk of the federal army against Hood's left. The Confederate position simply crumbled. On the Confederate left, in the words of Stone, "an army was changed into a mob, and the whole structure of the rebellion in the Southwest, with all its possibilities, was utterly overthrown. . . . Everywhere the [Union] success was complete." Although Confederate killed and wounded were only about 1,500 men, some 4,500 rebels surrendered.

For the next two weeks, federal cavalry pursued what was left of Hood's army as it fled southward. The retreat ended in Tupelo, Mississippi, where 18,000 rebels straggled into winter quarters. Hood had lost half of the 35,000 troops that he had taken into Tennessee just a month earlier. For all practical purposes, the Confederate Army of Tennessee no longer existed as a fighting force.

SEE ALSO

Hood, John Bell; Sherman, William T.; Thomas, George H.

FURTHER READING

Connelly, Thomas Lawrence. *Autumn of Glory: The Army of Tennessee, 1862–1865.* Baton Rouge: Louisiana State University Press, 1971.
McDonough, James Lee and Thomas Lawrence Connelly. *Five Tragic Hours: The Battle of Franklin.* Knoxville: University of Tennessee Press, 1993.
McDonough, James Lee. *Nashville: The Western Confederacy's Final Gamble.* Knoxville: University of Tennessee Press, 2004.

Hooker, Joseph
UNION GENERAL

- *Born: November 13, 1814, Hadley, Mass.*
- *Education: U.S. Military Academy, B.S., 1837*
- *Military service: U.S. Army: lieutenant, artillery, 1837; 1st lieutenant, 1838–47; major, 1847; lieutenant colonel, 1847–53; brigadier general, 1861; major-general, 1862–66*
- *Died: October 31, 1879, Garden City, N.Y.*

Once described by Noah Brooks, a war correspondent, as "the handsomest soldier I ever laid my eyes upon," Joseph Hooker compiled a solid record as a Union corps commander in both the eastern and western theaters of the war. But he failed to pass the test of leadership as the commander of the Army of the Potomac in 1863, and his loss of nerve at the battle of Chancellorsville forever tarnished his military reputation.

Joseph Hooker cut a proud figure on a horse and looked every bit like a confident general, but his loss of confidence at Chancellorsville handed Lee one of his greatest victories.

Hooker attended West Point and graduated in the middle of his class in 1837. He saw service in the Seminole War in Florida and on the frontier before fighting with distinction in the Mexican War. In 1853 he resigned his commission and took up farming in California, but with marginal success. Even before the Civil War broke out, he was anxious to return to the army.

Back in the army by the summer of 1861, Hooker rose rapidly in the command structure of the Army of the Potomac. Leading first a division and then a corps, he handled his troops well in the Peninsular, Second Bull Run, and Antietam campaigns. He was tagged as Fighting Joe Hooker when a typesetter left out the dash in a battle dispatch headed "Fighting—Joe Hooker." Even though he disliked the nickname—he said, "people will think I am a highwayman or bandit"—it enhanced his reputation as an aggressive, successful general.

After the federal disaster at Fredericksburg in December 1862, President Abraham Lincoln needed a winning general with Hooker's apparent leadership abilities. In January 1863, Lincoln chose Hooker to replace Ambrose E.

Burnside as commander of the Army of the Potomac. In his letter of appointment, Lincoln gently but pointedly admonished Hooker for his intriguing against Burnside and his loose talk about the country's need for a dictator. "Only those generals who gain success can set up dictators," he pointed out. "What I now ask of you is military success, and I will risk the dictatorship."

Hooker exuded supreme confidence upon taking over the Army of the Potomac. Indeed, Lincoln remarked: "That is the most depressing thing about Hooker. It seems to me that he is over-confident." Lincoln was right. After devising a brilliant strategy, Hooker panicked at a critical point in the battle of Chancellorsville when the Confederates unexpectedly slammed into the exposed right wing of his army. He pulled back his larger army and gave the rebels a victory almost by default.

Relieved as head of the Army of the Potomac just before the battle of Gettysburg, Hooker was sent to the West, where he again performed well as a corps commander in the Chattanooga and Atlanta campaigns. Disappointed when passed over for command of the Army of the Tennessee, Hooker asked to be relieved in June 1864. His field service was over, and he spent the rest of his army career as a department commander. He resigned from the army in 1868 after suffering a paralytic stroke.

SEE ALSO

Chancellorsville; Lincoln, Abraham

FURTHER READING

Catton, Bruce. *Glory Road: The Bloody Route from Fredericksburg to Gettysburg.* Garden City, N.Y.: Doubleday, 1952.
Hassler, Warren W., Jr. *Commanders of the Army of the Potomac.* Baton Rouge: Louisiana State University Press, 1962.
Herbert, Walter H. *Fighting Joe Hooker.* Indianapolis: Bobbs-Merrill, 1944.

Howe, Julia Ward

NORTHERN REFORMER

- Born: May 27, 1819, New York, N.Y.
- Education: private academies
- Occupation: author, philanthropist
- Died: October 17, 1910, New York, N.Y.

The author of the Union's most famous patriotic song, Julia Ward Howe beautifully captured the North's fusion of religious and nationalistic ardor when she wrote the lyrics for "The Battle Hymn of the Republic." Union soldiers quickly adopted the "Battle Hymn" as one of their favorite marching songs.

The daughter of a wealthy banker, Howe received a private education befitting a young woman about to enter the highest circles of New York City society. Before his death in 1839, her father had encouraged her to take up scholarly and literary pursuits. Her studies helped her endure the stormy early years of her marriage in 1843 to Samuel Gridley Howe, a philanthropist who pioneered improved care for the blind.

The Howes made their home in Boston, the hub of New England abolitionism, and Howe slowly overcame her earlier belief that the abolitionists were wicked fanatics. Influenced by her friendship with the abolitionist Theodore Parker and her husband's involvement in the free-soil movement, she strongly identified with the antislavery cause by the 1850s. Although still concerned by what she viewed as the intolerance of the abolitionists, she was favorably impressed by John Brown, who visited their home while raising funds for his unsuc-

cessful invasion of Harpers Ferry.

Shortly after Governor John Andrew of Massachusetts arranged for the Howes to meet President Abraham Lincoln at the White House in November 1861, Howe attended a military review on the outskirts of Washington. As members of her group began singing "John Brown's body lies a-mouldering in the grave;/His soul is marching on," a stanza from an army marching song, a friend suggested that Howe try her hand at writing new lyrics for the tune. Early the next day, as she recalled in her reminiscences, "I awoke in the gray of the morning twilight; and as I lay waiting for the dawn, the long lines of the desired poem began to twine themselves in my mind." Springing up, she hastily sketched out the lyrics in the darkness of her room and then returned to bed.

Julia Ward Howe set the lyrics of "Battle Hymn of the Republic" to the well-known melody of a hymn from around 1856. Its tempo matched the march of soldiers, who liked to make up their own words. According to some accounts, Howe decided to write a poem reflecting the tune's religious origins when she heard some troops singing obscene lyrics to it.

With imagery drawn directly from the Bible and a rolling cadence borrowed form "John Brown's Body," the "Battle Hymn" depicted a wrathful God of retribution marching with Union soldiers as they redeemed the nation from the sin of slavery.

> Mine eyes have seen the glory of the
> coming of the Lord;
> He is trampling out the vintage where
> the grapes of wrath are stored;
> He hath loosed the fateful lightning of
> His terrible swift sword:
> His truth is marching on.

Howe received $5 for the "Battle Hymn" when it was published in the *Atlantic Monthly* in February 1862. Union soldiers were soon marching to its stirring stanzas. More so than other patriotic verse, her poem seized the imagination of Northerners anxious to find a divine purpose in the carnage of the war. Howe wrote other poems and committed herself to a host of reform movements after the war, but her name remained forever linked to the stanzas that Northerners embraced as their national anthem.

SEE ALSO
Music

FURTHER READING
Clifford, Deborah Pickman. *Mine Eyes Have Seen the Glory: A Biography of Julia Ward Howe.* Boston: Little, Brown, 1979.

Impressed laborers

The Confederacy impressed African Americans, both free and slave, into war-related work. Tapping this reservoir of black labor freed up more whites for combat duty.

As early as January 1861, state officials in South Carolina and Alabama turned to slaves as workers on military fortifications. Following Florida's lead, the states passed statutes legalizing the impressment of slaves for defense-related work when they could not be obtained voluntarily from masters. After a call from the Confederate Congress on July 1, 1861, for the registration and enrollment of free blacks for military labor, six states legalized the impressment of free blacks into labor battalions.

The national Impressment Act of March 1863 specifically authorized the impressment of slaves by Confederate military authorities. Owners were to be paid $30 a month for each slave, and full value in case of death. Although care was taken to avoid conflict with state impressment laws, governors, as well as slaveowners complaining over a forced draft of their private property, balked at enforcing the act. Anxious to relieve soldiers of noncombatant military duties, the Confederate Congress responded in February 1864 with an amended act that called for the impressment of up to 20,000 slaves if military conditions warranted. In an effort to placate slaveowners, the act stipulated that slaves were to be impressed only after the supply of free blacks was exhausted.

After the passage of this 1864 legislation, Confederate free blacks were subject to periodic dragnets that forced them into government service. When Richmond was threatened by federal attack in the fall of 1864, the military indiscriminately rounded up free blacks with slaves and put them to work on fortifications. "The negroes," reported the *Richmond Examiner,* "were taken unaware on the street, at the market, from the shops, and at every point where they were found doing errands for themselves or their masters."

Even as the Confederacy crumbled,

most planters continued to oppose the impressment of their slaves, and impressment requisitions rarely produced the number of slaves demanded by the military. Still, the policy did aid the Confederacy war effort. Slave laborers, who might have escaped or otherwise been out of the military's reach, were extensively used in the building and repair of fortifications and other defense projects. At the same time, impressment siphoned off potentially rebellious slaves from the plantations and subjected them to military control. Despite their proximity to the front lines, few impressed slaves appear to have deserted. Discipline was extremely rigid, work was closely supervised, and at night a military guard herded the slaves into camps. For all the grumblings of the planters, the impressment of slave labor ultimately strengthened slavery and helped stave off Confederate defeat.

SEE ALSO

Confederate emancipation; Impressment Act of 1863

FURTHER READING

Brewer, James H. *The Confederate Negro: Virginia's Craftsmen and Military Laborers, 1861–1865.* Durham, N.C.: Duke University Press, 1969.

Wiley, Bell Irvin. *Southern Negroes, 1861–1865.* New Haven, Conn.: Yale University Press, 1938.

Impressment Act of 1863

In the Impressment Act of March 1863, the Confederate Congress legalized and attempted to regulate the seizure or impressment of private goods—including slaves—by Confederate armies. The "pressmen," as the government impress-ment agents were scornfully called, soon became the most hated of Confederate officials.

As early as the fall of 1862, Confederate armies were routinely impressing food, horses, wagons, and other supplies from civilians. Justified in terms of military necessity, these seizures provided the armies with their chief means of subsistence. Army commanders paid for what they took, but the credit certificates they offered in payment rapidly depreciated in value and rarely equaled the market value of goods seized. Public outcries against the practice finally forced the Confederate Congress to respond in the spring of 1863.

The Impressment Act replaced the haphazard army practice of seizing provisions with complicated bureaucratic procedures that combined impressment with price controls. The act stipulated that whenever the impressment agent and the producer could not agree on prices, local arbiters were to determine them, with an appeal by the Confederate officer to a state board. Nonetheless, the Confederate bureaucracy had the upper hand. Government impressment prices were generally one-third to one-half the market value of the goods seized.

Along with the Direct Tax of 1863, impressment met the immediate need of supplying the armies, but it did so at the cost of sapping civilian morale. Many farmers persisted in hoarding their goods for private use or selling them to speculators to get the full market price. This set up a vicious spiral in which government officials resorted to harsh enforcement procedures to overcome civilian resistance, which in turn intensified popular dissatisfaction. John R. Richards, a farmer in Calhoun County, Florida, wrote to his governor in 1863 asking, "if it is the law for these 'pressmen' to take the cows from the soldiers' families and leave them to starve." Even

Confederate Secretary of War James A. Seddon admitted in November 1863 that impressment had become "beyond measure offensive and repugnant to the sense of justice and prevalent sentiment of our people." Still, the War Department saw no alternative for keeping its armies supplied.

SEE ALSO
Direct tax; Impressed laborers

FURTHER READING
Goff, Richard D. *Confederate Supply.* Durham, N.C.: Duke University Press, 1969.
Ramsdell, Charles W. *Behind the Lines in the Southern Confederacy.* Baton Rouge: Louisiana State University Press, 1944.

Indians

SEE Native Americans

Industrial workers

The general economic prosperity in the North during the Civil War did not extend to most industrial workers. In the Confederacy, laborers in the new war industries suffered the most from the South's devastating inflation. Despite these economic hardships, most workers were loyal Unionists and Confederates whose contributions on the military and home fronts were vital to the war effort.

During the Civil War, workers in the North enjoyed near-full employment, but most experienced a decline in their living standards as their wages failed to keep pace with inflation. While prices almost doubled during the war, wages increased by only 50 to 60 percent. Skilled workers, the 10 to 15 per-

cent of workers whose labor was in greatest demand, were able to hold their own by resorting to work stoppages and trade unionism. Others, most notably unskilled immigrants and women, were barely able to survive.

Women, who comprised at least one-quarter of the nonagricultural workforce, received less than half of the wage increase granted to men. In the clothing industry, where women were concentrated as seamstresses, wages for piece work were actually slashed. Seamstresses in Cincinnati were not exaggerating when they wrote President Abraham Lincoln in March 1865: "We are unable to sustain life for the prices offered by contractors, who fatten on their contracts by grinding immense profits out of the labor of their operatives."

Northern workers protested their conditions, but they remained loyal patriots. By some measurements, they enlisted in the Union army at a higher rate proportionate to their numbers than any other group except professionals. The source of this loyalty lay in labor's identification with the Union as the cause of free-labor principles over the South's aristocratic system of slave labor. Even when the Lincoln government used federal troops to smash strikes in the Pennsylvania coalfields in 1863 and at the Parrott gun factory in Cold Spring, New York, in 1864, labor leaders held back from provoking a major confrontation. "In ordinary times a collision would have been inevitable," explained labor leader William Sylvis in January 1865. "Nothing, but the patient patriotism of the people, and their desire in no way to embarrass the government, prevent [sic] it."

Confederate workers faced more desperate conditions than laborers in the North. Whereas the cost of living in the South rose approximately 30 times over between 1861 and 1865, wages increased

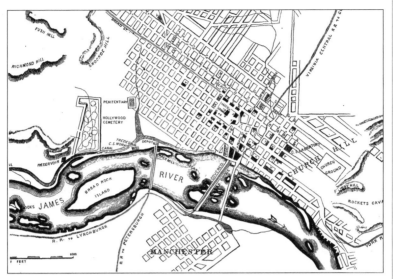

The city of Richmond was important to the Confederacy not only as its political capital, but, as home of the Tredegar Iron Works, industrially as well. The labor force at the iron works on the north bank of the James River expanded from 900 to 2,500 workers during the war.

only tenfold. Although the Confederacy always suffered a shortage of skilled labor, especially machinists and metalworkers, an ample supply of unskilled labor was available. Initially attracted by cash wages that were quite high by prewar standards, many rural families entered the industrial labor force for the first time. Once there, many became part of a nascent labor movement that struggled to raise wages to keep pace with a relentless inflationary spiral.

Touched off in the fall of 1861 by a strike for higher wages by Irish workers at the Tredegar Iron Works in Richmond, a series of work stoppages spread throughout the Confederacy. Several states considered antilabor laws to prevent strikes, but the Confederate government came up with the most effective weapon against labor when it enacted conscription in the spring of 1862. Repeatedly, the government broke strikes by either enrolling the disaffected workers in the army or threatening to do so. When women workers ineligible for the draft struck at the Confederate States Laboratory at Richmond in the fall of 1864, the govern-ment dismissed all of them and found 300 replacements.

When their work was absolutely essential to meeting a military need, Confederate workers were able to wring concessions from their employers. Even in these cases, however, skilled white workers were unable to press their advantage because of competition from impressed slave workers. However much whites protested the use of slave artisans in their crafts, the reservoir of black workers was always there to be tapped by a private or government employer.

Inflation fell after the war, and Northern workers were able to achieve gains in real wages and build on the labor organizations they founded during the conflict. Meanwhile, in the shattered postwar economy of the South, white workers were more determined than ever to drive away black competition.

SEE ALSO

Free-labor ideology; Inflation; Wartime economies; Women in the war

FURTHER READING

Dew, Charles B. *Ironmaker to the*

Confederacy: Joseph P. Anderson and the Tredegar Iron Works. New Haven, Conn.: Yale University Press, 1966.

Montgomery, David. *Beyond Equality: Labor and the Radical Republicans, 1862–1872*. New York: Knopf, 1967.

Palladino, Grace. *Another Civil War: Labor, Capital, and the State in the Anthracite Regions of Pennsylvania, 1840–68*. Urbana: University of Illinois Press, 1990.

Infantry

SEE Armies

Inflation

A minor problem for the Union, inflation proved to be disastrous for the Confederate economy. Measured by its purchasing power at the start of the war, a Confederate paper dollar was worth only 8 cents by the summer of 1863. By March 1865, it was worth less than 2 cents, and price levels in the Confederacy had ceased to have any real meaning.

The greater diversity and capital resources of the Northern economy enabled the Union to keep inflation in check. Although prices at their peak rose 80 percent during the war (about the same increase as in World Wars I and II), inflation did not seriously distort the economy. If anything, it served as a positive stimulant by lowering the cost of borrowing money to expand production and by enabling manufacturers to pay off their prewar debts in cheaper dollars.

Greenbacks, the new national paper currency authorized by the Union Congress in early 1862, accounted for most of the price increases in the North. However, contrary to the fears of fiscal conservatives, the greenbacks did not set off an unmanageable inflationary spiral. Congress had made the greenbacks legal tender at par (full face value) for all private and public debts, except for import duties and the interest on the national debt. Thus, confidence in the greenbacks remained high, and they found a ready public acceptance. The stipulation that tariff duties and interest on federal bonds would be paid only in gold bolstered the confidence of domestic and foreign investors that the U.S. Treasury would acquire enough hard currency to pay off all federal obligations in the preferred currency of gold, as it eventually did.

Two other factors helped maintain the value of the greenbacks. Most fundamentally, military victories beginning in the winter and spring of 1862 strengthened the belief in the ultimate success of Union arms and hence the permanence of the Union. Meanwhile, as the Confederacy held out for three more years, heavy new taxes dampened inflationary pressures by siphoning off more than $600 million in purchasing power from consumers and businesses.

Unlike the Union, where a combination of paper money, taxation, and borrowing provided a sound approach to financing the war, the Confederacy excessively relied on paper money to pay its bills. The almost inevitable result was a monstrous inflationary spiral that ate away confidence in the Confederate government.

The prewar South held only 20 percent of the nation's banking assets and just 30 percent of the nation's wealth. Specie (hard assets in gold) was in short supply; during the entire war, the Confederate government never acquired more than $27 million in specie. This was totally inadequate to pay for a war

This blockade runner ran aground near Sullivan's Island, South Carolina. By depriving Southern consumers of bulky shipments of goods from abroad, the Union blockade was a major factor in Confederate inflation.

money, in 1861 and 1862. By the winter of 1862, these notes were covering three-fourths of all Confederate expenses. They fell in value almost as fast as they were printed. Throughout the war, Confederate paper money depreciated in value by an average of 10 percent per month.

By January 1863, the Southern price index stood eight times above the level in early 1861. Prices skyrocketed not only because of a redundant money supply but also due to a Union blockade that created shortages in imported consumer goods. Prices rose as Southerners competed for the fewer available goods and tried to get rid of their money before its value fell even further.

The Confederate Congress finally turned to a comprehensive program of taxation in April 1863. The new excise and income taxes came far too late to reverse inflationary pressures that worsened with every report of another Union victory. Efforts in 1864 to force an exchange of the old notes for a smaller amount of new notes simply destroyed what little confidence remained in Confederate paper money.

Civilians, especially urban dwellers, the poor, and those dependent on a cash wage, bore the brunt of the devastating inflation. Most of them had turned against the Confederacy even while Southern armies were still struggling in the field.

whose cost came to more than $500 million in equivalent gold value. Thus, the fiscal problems facing the Confederacy were staggering. What made them even worse was the common assumption in the spring of 1861 that no extraordinary measures were needed because the war was expected to be very short.

The Confederacy began digging its fiscal grave when it failed to levy any high taxes at the start of the war. Secretary of the Treasury Christopher G. Memminger tried to plug the revenue gap through loans. Early bond sales went well, but within a year they had drawn in most of the available cash in the Confederacy. Produce loans—that is, a pledge by planters to pay for a Confederate bond through the proceeds from the sale of their crops—also fizzled after a promising beginning. As the price of cotton kept climbing, planters increasingly withheld it from Confederate authorities. In all, bonds provided only about 35 percent of the Confederacy's wartime costs.

Unable to borrow enough money, and unwilling to impose meaningful taxes, the Confederate government took another tack. It printed more than $500 million in treasury notes, or paper

SEE ALSO

Cost of the war; Gold; Legal Tender Acts; Memminger, Christopher G.; National Banking Acts; Taxation; Wartime economies

FURTHER READING

Ball, Douglas B. *Financial Failure and Confederate Defeat.* Urbana: University of Illinois Press, 1991.

Hammond, Bray. *Sovereignty and an Empty Purse: Banks and Politics in the Civil War.* Princeton, N.J.: Princeton University Press, 1970.

Ironclad Oath

Passed by Congress on July 2, 1862, this was a federal test oath subsequently required of all federal officeholders. The oath consisted of a statement of allegiance to the Constitution and a declaration of never having voluntarily borne arms against the Union or aided a rebellion in any way. Radical Republicans attempted to use the oath as a means of assuring that only bona fide Unionists held power in the South after the Civil War.

SEE ALSO
Wade-Davis bill

FURTHER READING
Hyman, Harold M. *The Era of the Oath: Northern Loyalty Tests During the Civil War and Reconstruction.* Philadelphia: University of Pennsylvania Press, 1954.

Jackson, Thomas J. ("Stonewall")

CONFEDERATE GENERAL

- *Born: January 21, 1824, Clarksburg, (West) Va.*
- *Education: U.S. Military Academy, B.S. 1846*
- *Military service: U.S. Army: lieutenant, 1847; 1st lieutenant, 1847–52; Confederate army: colonel, 1861; brigadier general, 1861; major-general, 1861–62; lieutenant general, 1862–63*
- *Died: May 10, 1863, Guiney Station, Va.*

A daring and resourceful general, Thomas J. "Stonewall" Jackson was a legend in his own lifetime. He became a military celebrity as a result of his bril-liant Shenandoah Valley campaign in the spring of 1862, and his death moved General Robert E. Lee to remark: "I know not how to replace him." Many feel that his absence cost the Confederacy a victory at Gettysburg.

Raised by his uncle after the death of his parents, Jackson entered West Point as an ungainly, ill-educated youth. His academic performance steadily improved, and he graduated in the top third of his class. After serving with distinction in the Mexican War and briefly holding post assignments, he resigned from the army to teach at the Virginia Military Institute. He commanded a company of V.M.I. cadets at John Brown's hanging in 1859.

At Harpers Ferry in the early months of the war, Jackson organized the brigade that shortly shared with him the nickname "Stonewall" for its defensive stand at First Bull Run in July 1861. Until the spring of 1862, Jackson's reputation, as recalled by Confederate General Edward Porter Alexander, "had simply been that of a desperate & stubborn fighter." But then, Alexander continued, Jackson "suddenly broke loose in the Valley of Virginia & ... dazzled the eyes of military men all over the world by an aggressive campaign which I believe to be unsurpassed in all military history for brilliancy & daring." Although outnumbered three-to-one, Jackson used rapid marches and unorthodox tactics to pin down 60,000 Union troops. He defeated the federals in five of six battles before slipping away to reinforce Lee's army during the

"Stonewall" Jackson was the Confederacy's first great war hero. His death after Chancellorsville moved the editor of the Richmond Daily Enquirer to write: "The hero of the war, the great genius, that noble patriot, the support and hope of this country, is no more."

Seven Days battles in front of Richmond.

After an uneven performance during the Seven Days, Jackson confused and soundly defeated General John Pope's Army of Virginia at Second Bull Run. During Lee's Maryland invasion in September 1862, Jackson captured the Union garrison at Harpers Ferry and then wheeled his men north just in time to stave off the likely defeat of Lee's army at Antietam. Following his promotion to a corps commander, he headed the right wing of the Army of Northern Virginia at Fredericksburg.

Jackson's most spectacular exploit occurred within days of his death. On May 2, 1863, his flanking march at Chancellorsville completely surprised the right wing of the Union Army of the Potomac and was the key to the audacious rebel victory. While returning to camp in the twilight, Jackson was accidentally wounded by some of his own men. Pneumonia set in after the amputation of his left arm, and he died on May 10. The last words of this devout Presbyterian were, "Let us cross over the river and rest under the shade of the trees."

SEE ALSO

Antietam; First Bull Run; Chancellorsville; Peninsula Ccampaign; Second Bull Run

FURTHER READING

Cozzens, Peter. *Shenandoah 1862: Stonewall Jackson's Valley Campaign.* Chapel Hill: University of North Carolina Press, 2008.

Henderson, G. F. R. *Stonewall Jackson and the American Civil War.* 1898. Reprint, New York: Da Capo, 1988.

Robertson, James I. *Stonewall Jackson: The Man, the Soldier, the Legend.* New York: Macmillan, 1997.

Jackson's Valley campaign

SEE Peninsula campaign

Johnson, Andrew

17TH PRESIDENT OF THE UNITED STATES

- *Born: December 29, 1808, Raleigh, N.C.*
- *Political party: Democrat; Unionist*
- *Education: no formal education*
- *Military service: military governor of Tennessee, 1862–64*
- *Government service: alderman, Greenville, Tenn., 1829–30; mayor of Greenville, 1831–35; Tennessee House of Representatives, 1835–37, 1839–41; Tennessee Senate, 1841–43; U.S. House of Representatives, 1843–53; governor of Tennessee, 1853–57; U.S. Senate, 1857–62, 1875; Vice President of the United States, 1865; President of the United States, 1865–69*
- *Died: July 31, 1875, Carter Station, Tenn.*

A lifelong Jacksonian Democrat from Tennessee elected Vice President on the coalition Unionist ticket of 1864, Andrew Johnson had a stormy Presidency after assuming office upon Abraham Lincoln's assassination. His repeated clashes with the Republican Congress over the nature and limits of Reconstruction culminated in his trial for impeachment in 1868.

Johnson rose from plebeian origins of poverty and illiteracy to become a successful politician and slaveholder. Following the death of his father, his widowed mother struggled to make ends meet and apprenticed the young Johnson out to a tailor. He moved as a teenager to East Tennessee, where he opened his own tailoring shop and learned to read and write from his wife, Eliza. After joining a debating society in Greenville and gaining confidence as a public speaker, he entered local politics. By continually reminding the voters that he was a "plebian mechanic, and not

Flanked on his left by fellow Republican John A. Bigham, Thaddeus Stevens announces to the Senate the passage in the House of impeachment charges against President Andrew Johnson.

ashamed nor afraid to own it" and denouncing wealthy planters as an "upstart, swelled-headed, iron-heeled, bobtailed aristocracy," he attracted a loyal following that pushed him into the top ranks of the Tennessee Democratic party. Despite his attacks on the rich, he defended slavery as an institution that offered common whites a chance to escape a life of drudgery.

Johnson was an unwavering Unionist who blamed secession on the same slaveholding aristocrats whom he had battled throughout his political career. As the only senator from a seceded state who remained in Washington, he became quite valuable to the Republicans. Appointed military governor of Tennessee in 1862, he established a reputation for being tough on rebels, especially when he declared that "treason must be made odious, and traitors punished and impoverished." When the Republicans chose a Unionist party label in 1864 in an effort to broaden their support, Johnson was seemingly

the perfect running mate for Lincoln.

Once thrust into the Presidency in April 1865, Johnson soon revealed that he differed fundamentally with the Republicans over how Reconstruction should be approached and defined. Union victory for Johnson meant a return of the Southern white masses to their prior loyalty. All he asked as proof of this loyalty was an oath of future allegiance to the Union, a formal renunciation of secession, an acceptance of emancipation by ratifying the 13th amendment, and an acknowledgment that the Confederate war debt would not be repaid. Once these terms were met under his direction, Reconstruction, or restoration as he called it, would be over. Contrary to Johnson, nearly all Republicans believed that Congress should have a say in a Reconstruction policy that included political penalties for leading Confederates and some federal protection of the civil and political rights of the former slaves. Given Johnson's refusal to compromise, a clash was inevitable.

When Congress convened in December 1865, the Republicans rejected the Southern delegations elected under the President's guidelines. After initial disagreements in the winter of 1865–66 over a civil rights bill and legislation to extend the life of the Freedmen's Bureau, Johnson openly broke with Congress in the spring when he opposed the 14th amendment, in effect the terms of Union victory as set down by Congress. Faced with the refusal of the former rebel states (Johnson's home state of Tennessee, ironically, was the lone exception) to ratify the 14th amendment, Congress responded in March 1867, with legislation that placed these states under military rule and required voting rights for the freedmen as a precondition for readmission to the Union.

As Congress formulated a Reconstruction policy, Johnson opposed it every step of the way. In 1866 he tried to defeat the Republicans at the polls by backing a National Union Movement of Democrats and conservative Republicans. The movement succeeded only in arousing Northern fears that Johnson was about to squander the hard-won Union victory, and the voters returned even larger Republican majorities to Congress.

The enmity between Johnson and Congress climaxed in his impeachment trial. Anxious to prevent Johnson from interfering further with Reconstruction, Congress passed the Tenure of Office Act in 1867, which barred the President from removing cabinet members or other high-ranking officials without the consent of the Senate. When Johnson defied the act by removing Secretary of War Edwin M. Stanton, the Republican House brought impeachment charges— the first time in history a President had been impeached. The Senate trial on the charges in May 1868 fell one vote short of the two-thirds majority necessary for conviction.

Johnson and his successor, Ulysses S. Grant, refused to speak with one another on Inauguration Day in March 1869. An angry and resentful Johnson believed that he had been treated unfairly and that the Republicans had been guilty of imposing despotic governments on the Southern states that he had already restored to the Union. He exacted a measure of political redemption when he was returned to the U.S. Senate in 1875. Shortly thereafter, he died from a stroke.

SEE ALSO

14th amendment; Freedmen's Bureau; Military Reconstruction Act; Reconstruction; 13th amendment

FURTHER READING

Castel, Albert. *The Presidency of Andrew Johnson.* Lawrence: Regents Press of Kansas, 1979.

McKitrick, Eric L. *Andrew Johnson and Reconstruction.* New York: Oxford University Press, 1988.
Sefton, James. *Andrew Johnson and the Uses of Constitutional Power.* Boston: Little, Brown, 1980.

Johnson's program of Reconstruction

President Andrew Johnson implemented a program of Reconstruction in the spring and summer of 1865 when Congress was not in session. After initially giving Johnson's approach cautious support, the Republican party turned against it by the fall of 1865 and called upon the President to cooperate with Congress in formulating a more comprehensive program designed to safeguard the rights of the freedmen and to assure that Northern expectations of victory were met.

For Johnson, Reconstruction was an executive responsibility whose sole purpose was the speedy restoration to the Union of former rebel states once new state governments were organized under the control of a white majority that had sworn future loyalty to the Union. Believing that the states legally never could have left the Union and hence retained their constitutional rights, he made but minimal demands of the defeated Southerners as they set up new governments. All he asked was that they ratify the 13th amendment freeing the slaves and declare void the secession ordinances and the public debts incurred to support secession.

Johnson's program began with two proclamations issued on May 29, 1865. The first offered a general pardon and full restoration of political rights to nearly all Confederates who would take an oath of future allegiance. Exempted from this pardon were high-ranking officials and those with taxable property worth more than $20,000. These exempted individuals, however, could personally appeal to Johnson for a pardon. The other proclamation, which applied originally to North Carolina, appointed a provisional governor with the responsibility of registering voters (based on the white voting list of 1860) for the election of a state constitutional convention. Following this convention, elections could then be held for state and federal officers. Upon completion of these elections and the ratification of the 13th Amendment, Reconstruction, according to Johnson's thinking, was complete. All that remained was the formality of Congress readmitting the Southern states by seating their congressional delegations.

When Congress met in December 1865, the Republican majority refused to seat the Southern congressmen elected under Johnson's guidelines. The Republicans were not acting out of vindictiveness. Rather, they were concerned that Johnson's program was throwing away the fruits of Union victory. Johnson had been so lenient in dispensing pardons that a host of former Confederate generals and politicians swelled the ranks of the men sent to Congress. Far from offering some limited form of black suffrage, the new state governments in the South passed legislation, known collectively as the Black Codes, that denied African Americans even the pretense of equality before the law. The codes treated blacks as a separate and inferior legal caste. Reports also reached the North of attacks and reprisals against white Unionists.

By the fall of 1865, many Northerners, and nearly all Republicans, felt that Southern whites were forgetting who had won the war. Blacks, it seemed, had been returned to a condition little better than slavery, and unrepentant rebels were back in power. Thus, the Republicans, the majority party in the North, were reflecting public sentiment when they rejected Johnson's contention that Reconstruction was over. They insisted that Congress now needed to move beyond Johnson's program by offering protection of black rights and prescribing penalties for those who had led the rebellion. When Johnson refused to cooperate with Congress, Reconstruction entered a new and more radical phase.

SEE ALSO
Congressional Reconstruction

FURTHER READING
Carter, Dan T. *When the War Was Over: The Failure of Self-Reconstruction in the South, 1865–1867.* Baton Rouge: Louisiana State University Press, 1985.

Johnston, Albert Sidney
CONFEDERATE GENERAL

- *Born: February 2, 1803, Washington, Ky.*
- *Education: U.S. Military Academy, B.S. 1826*
- *Military service: 1st Texas Rifle Volunteers: colonel, 1846–47; Army of the Republic of Texas: private, 1835; adjutant-general, 1836; senior brigadier general, 1837; U.S. Army: lieutenant, 1826–34; paymaster, 1849–55; colonel, cavalry, 1855–61; brevet brigadier general, 1858–60; Confederate army: general, 1861–62*
- *Government service: secretary of war, Republic of Texas, 1838–40*
- *Died: April 6, 1862, battle of Shiloh*

A large, erect man with broad shoulders, Albert Sidney Johnston had a commanding physical presence that added to his stature as one of the finest soldiers produced in the prewar U.S. Army. His reputation in 1861 was such that Confederate President Jefferson Davis later called him "the greatest soldier, the ablest man, civil or military, Confederate or Federal, then living." Whether Johnston would have proven to be a great Civil War general has been debated ever since he was mortally wounded at Shiloh, his first major battle.

After attending Transylvania University in Kentucky, Johnston received an appointment to West Point and graduated second in his class. He fought in the Black Hawk War before resigning from the army in 1834 to care for his sick wife. After her death in 1835, he enlisted in the Texas army and rose to the rank of brigadier general during the Texas War for Independence. He served as secretary of war in the Republic of Texas and then commanded Texas volunteers in the Mexican War. Following his reappointment to the U.S. Army in 1849, he held departmental commands in the West and led the Utah expedition against the Mormons in 1857.

Upon learning that his adopted state of Texas had seceded, Johnston declined an offer of a top rank in the Union army, resigned his commission, and headed east to accept command of the Confederacy's Western Department, a huge area that sprawled west of the Allegheny Mountains. The most vulnerable area in his command was the Confederacy's long border stretching across Kentucky and Tennessee. Johnston occupied Bowling Green in September 17, 1861, and positioned his 40,000 troops in a defensive arc across Kentucky. But this line, as Johnston was well aware, was very thin, and the much-larger Union forces could penetrate it at virtually any point they chose. When they seized Forts Henry and Donelson in February 1862, Johnston had no choice but to retreat and redeploy his army for a surprise counterattack.

After his army was reinforced at the rail town of Corinth, Mississippi, Johnston counterattacked at Shiloh on April 6. It was the first great battle of the war and one that Johnston believed would determine Confederate fortunes in the West. "My son," he told Colonel John S. Marmaduke before the battle, "we must this day conquer or perish." His bold counterstroke almost succeeded, but the rebel attack lost momentum once Johnston fell while leading his men in battle. He bled to death in the afternoon, minutes after a sniper's bullet severed his femoral artery. Jefferson Davis always believed that Johnston's death cost the Confederacy "our strongest pillar."

SEE ALSO

Forts Henry and Donelson; Shiloh

FURTHER READING

Roland, Charles P. *Albert Sidney Johnston: Soldier of Three Republics.* Austin: University of Texas Press, 1964.

Albert Sidney Johnston was the favorite general of Confederate President Jefferson Davis. "I hoped and expected that I had others who would prove generals," Davis recalled, "but I knew I had one, and that was Sidney Johnston."

Johnston, Joseph E.
CONFEDERATE GENERAL

- *Born: February 3, 1807, Farmville, Va.*
- *Education: U.S. Military Academy, B.S. 1829*
- *Military service: U.S. Army: lieutenant, 1829–36; 1st lieutenant, 1836–37; 1st lieutenant, topographical engineers, 1838–46; captain, 1846–55; lieutenant colonel, cavalry, 1855–60; quartermaster general, 1860–61; Confederate army: brigadier general, 1861; major-general, 1861; general, 1861–65*
- *Died: March 21, 1891, Washington, D.C.*

Despite his sound grasp of strategy and mastery of defensive warfare, Joseph E.

Johnston was an enigmatic general who never led a Confederate army to victory. As a result of a running feud with Confederate President Jefferson Davis, he was inactive for much of the war and never fulfilled his prewar promise as a great field commander.

After graduating from West Point, Johnston had a long and active career in the army. He fought in the Black Hawk War and in Florida against the Seminoles. After leaving the army briefly to take up civil engineering, he served with distinction in the Mexican War. He held commands in the West before his appointment as quartermaster general of the army in 1860. He resigned in April 1861, once his native state of Virginia seceded.

In the spring of 1861, Johnston was commanding all Confederate forces in northern Virginia. Slipping away from federal forces in the Shenandoah Valley, he arrived at Manassas in time to give the rebels their first victory of the war. His promotion to full general after that victory ignited his feud with Davis. Johnston's appointment placed him fourth in seniority among Confederate generals, a ranking that wounded his pride since his staff commission in the U.S. Army had put him above the other three (including Robert E. Lee). In an indignant letter to Davis, Johnston staked his claim to "rightfully hold the rank of first general of the Armies of the Southern Confederacy." Davis peevishly replied that Johnston's "insinuations [were] as unfair as they are unbecoming." Their feuding poisoned their relations throughout the war.

Johnston molded the Army of Northern Virginia into a fighting force during the autumn and winter of 1861–62 and led it at the start of the Peninsula campaign. Wounded at Fair Oaks, he relinquished command of the army to Robert E. Lee on June 1, 1862. Returning to duty in November 1862,

Johnston went to Tennessee to head the Department of the West. Against his advice, the Confederacy failed to concentrate its western armies and suffered a series of defeats in 1863. Put in charge of the Army of Tennessee in December 1863, Johnston directed a skillful defense that slowed to a crawl the Union advance toward Atlanta in the spring of 1864. His defensive strategy, however, was too passive for Davis, and he replaced Johnston with John Bell Hood in July 1864. Johnston did not receive another field command until February 1865, when he was given the hopeless task of trying to stop William T. Sherman's army from pushing north through the Carolinas. Johnston made one stand at Bentonville and then signed an armistice with Sherman on April 18.

A successful insurance and railroad executive after the war, Johnston served in Congress from 1879–81 as a representative from Virginia. He died of pneumonia that many say he contracted while standing bareheaded in a cold rain at the funeral of Sherman, his old wartime adversary.

SEE ALSO

Atlanta campaign; Bentonville; First Bull Run; Davis, Jefferson; Vicksburg campaign

FURTHER READING

Govan, Gilbert E. *A Different Valor: The Story of General Joseph E. Johnston, C.S.A.* Indianapolis: Bobbs-Merrill, 1956.
Symonds, Craig L. *Joseph E. Johnston, A Civil War Biography.* New York: Norton, 1992.

Kansas-Nebraska Act

Soon after its passage in May 1854, the Kansas-Nebraska Act dramatically altered the politics of the United States.

HO! FOR KANSAS!

ELDRIDGE BROTHERS'
Express & Daily
POST COACH LINE

Fare to Lawrence $3.50

THROUGH FROM KANSAS CITY TO LECOMPTON IN ONE DAY

One Daily Line from LAWRENCE to OSAWATOMIE, and Two Daily
Lines from LAWRENCE to LEAVENWORTH CITY.

Passengers by this Line have an opportunity of traveling over the most attractive and
cultivated portion of the Territory in Splendid Four Horse Concord built Coaches, and will save
at least ten miles of tedious travel, making it the Shortest, as well as the Cheapest and most
agreeable Route to the

INTERIOR OF KANSAS.

Passengers leaving Kansas City by the Morning Line, breakfast at Wyandott, dine at Wolf
Creek, and arrive at Lecompton in time for supper, making five changes of horses between
Kansas City and Lecompton.

Express Freights taken at the Lowest Rates & delivered with Promptness & Despatch.

OFFICE, 109 LEVEE, Opposite the Steamboat Landing, KANSAS CITY.

AGENTS.—Kansas City, M. F. Caswell; Wyandott & Lawrence, Eldridge Bros.; Leavenworth, Buckley.

S. W. ELDRIDGE,   J. M. ELDRIDGE,
T. B. ELDRIDGE,   E. S. ELDRIDGE, Prop's.

The reaction to the act triggered the formation of a new, sectionalized Republican party, accelerated the collapse of the national Whig party, and solidified the dominance of the states'-rights Democrats in the Lower South.

The act had such an explosive impact because it reopened the entire question of slavery in the territories. Kansas and Nebraska were part of the northern portion of the Louisiana Purchase territory of 1803. Both lay north of the 36° 30' line above which Congress had banned slavery in the Missouri Compromise of 1820. For this reason, proslavery Southerners had no interest in organizing these territories. In order to gain their support, Senator Stephen A. Douglas of Illinois authored a bill that declared the Missouri Compromise prohibition on slavery "null and void." Borrowing language from the Compromise of 1850 when it organized the territories of New Mexico and Utah, Douglas turned to the principle of popular sovereignty, which conferred

upon the settlers in the territories the right to determine the status of slavery for themselves. His strategy succeeded in gaining the Southern votes he needed for the passage of his bill, which became known as the Kansas-Nebraska Act.

Perhaps because he had no strong feelings for or against slavery, Douglas was genuinely surprised when the Kansas-Nebraska Act unleashed a storm of protest in the North. Antislavery Northerners viewed the act as a moral outrage, a shameful betrayal of a national pledge to the cause of freedom north of 36° 30'. Joined by other Northerners who feared that they now would have to compete against slave labor in the territories, they organized a new Republican party dedicated to stopping the expansion of slavery. The Whig party, unable to reconcile the divisions between its sectional wings, collapsed, and the Lower South became a virtual stronghold for a single party: the Democrats. The party system had now become dangerously sectionalized, and clashes over slavery soon spilled over into the violence that produced "Bleeding Kansas."

SEE ALSO
Bleeding Kansas; Compromise of 1850; Douglas, Stephen A.; Republican party; Whig party

FURTHER READING
Johannsen, Robert W. *Stephen A. Douglas.* New York: Oxford University Press, 1973.

Kenner mission

In a last attempt to gain foreign recognition for the Confederacy, President Jefferson Davis sent Duncan Kenner of Louisiana on a secret mission to Europe

Following the passage of the Kansas-Nebraska Act, businessmen quickly opened up the interior of the Kansas Territory to settlement by offering regularly scheduled stagecoach service.

in January 1865. He authorized this wealthy planter to state that the Confederacy would emancipate its slaves in return for the immediate recognition of its existence as a legal government.

Slipping through the Union blockade in disguise, Kenner made contact with Confederate diplomats James Mason in London and John Slidell in Paris. Although shocked by Kenner's instructions, the envoys relayed to the British and French governments the offer of emancipation in return for recognition. Consistent with his stand throughout the war, Napoleon III said he would willingly recognize the Confederacy if England did so first. However, the British flatly rejected the offer, and the mission was a failure.

Some Confederates were surprised that this offer of emancipation had not attracted a European suitor. In arguing against resorting to the use of black soldiers, Howell Cobb of Georgia had instead proposed to the Davis administration that it "yield to the demands of England and France and abolish slavery, and thereby purchase their aid." But emancipation was never an issue with Napoleon III, and the Confederate offer of it came far too late to affect British diplomacy.

When he learned of Kenner's failure, Davis felt he had no choice but to push for a Confederate program of arming and freeing the slaves. Like Kenner's mission itself, such a program revealed how desperate Davis's commitment to Southern independence had become.

SEE ALSO

Confederate emancipation; France; Great Britain

FURTHER READING

Durden, Robert F. *The Gray and the Black: The Confederate Debate on Emancipation.* Baton Rouge: Louisiana State University Press, 1972.

Ku Klux Klan

From its origins in the spring of 1866 as a fraternal club of rebel veterans, the Ku Klux Klan soon became the best known of a host of paramilitary organizations that sprang up in the South to overthrow Radical Reconstruction. Its tactics of organized terrorism were so successful that Congress finally responded with legislation designed to suppress the Klan.

The new Republican parties formed after the passage of the Military Reconstruction Act of 1867 provided the Klan's political target. Its broader goal, however, was the reversal of the remarkable steps toward political and social equality taken by African Americans in the aftermath of emancipation. In favor of what it called a "white man's government," the Klan beat, whipped, and killed blacks who were "uppity"; that is, acquired or leased land, voted

Under Reconstruction, the KKK and similar paramilitary societies such as the White League terrorized and intimidated any black who tried to advance in politics, business, or, as shown here, education.

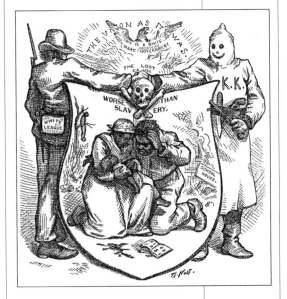

Republican, educated themselves or their children, or in any way acted as free and equal citizens. White teachers, ministers, and politicians who supported black advancement were also singled out for retribution.

The Klan's appeal cut across class lines. Although yeoman farmers impoverished by the Civil War filled its ranks, planters, businessmen, and even ministers commonly comprised its leadership and directed its strategic aim of restoring political control to conservative white elites. At its height between 1867 and 1871, the Klan likely operated in as many as one-quarter of all Southern counties. It tended to be most active in racially mixed hill counties politically balanced between Democrats and Republicans.

Klan violence peaked during the 1868 Presidential election campaign. The Republican editor of the *Huntsville Advocate* reported from northern Alabama that bands of Klansmen had inspired "a *nameless terror* among negroes, poor whites, and even others." Systematic terrorism carried Georgia and Louisiana for the Democrats and cut into the Republican vote across the South. In Louisiana alone, riots and assassinations claimed the lives of some 1,000 persons, mostly blacks.

The Republican governors in Tennessee, Arkansas, and Texas were able to mobilize a largely Unionist white base of party supporters to suppress the Klan. Elsewhere, the Republicans were reduced to pleading for military assistance from Washington. Congress responded in 1870 and 1871 with a series of laws based on the enforcement clauses of the Fourteenth and 15th Amendments. These enforcement acts prohibited state officials from interfering with a citizen's right to vote on the grounds of race, outlawed the Klan and other conspiratorial organizations that sought to deprive citizens of their civil and political rights, and authorized the President to call upon the military to restore law and order in areas he declared to be in a state of insurrection. Armed with these powers, the Grant administration broke the back of the Klan but failed to destroy it. Democrats continued to rely on organized violence in their campaigns to overturn the last of the Republican parties in the South.

SEE ALSO

Military Reconstruction Act of 1867; Radical Reconstruction in the South

FURTHER READING

Trelease, Allen W. *White Terror: The Ku Klux Klan Conspiracy and Southern Reconstruction*. New York: Harper & Row, 1971.

Laird rams

Rams were steam-powered, armor-plated warships equipped with a battering ram mounted on a massive prow. The Confederacy contracted for 14 of these rams, the most famous of which was the CSS *Alabama*. The two most powerful rams built during the war were commissioned by the Confederacy from the Laird shipyards in Liverpool, England. Had the Confederacy been able to take possession of the Laird rams, it would have had the weapons to disrupt the Union blockade and possibly retake New Orleans and the lower Mississippi Valley.

Loopholes in British law gave James D. Bullock, the purchasing agent for the Confederate navy in England, an opening to sign contracts for the construction of warships. As long as these ships were not actually armed in British territory, the authorities allowed them

In June 1863, the Union navy captured the Confederate ram Atlanta, *when it had trouble maneuvering in a shallow sound south of Savannah. Built in Savannah shipyards from the iron hull of a purchased British steamer, the ram required 600 tons of iron for its armoring.*

to be passed off as merchant vessels. The *Florida*, the first cruiser commissioned by Bullock, sailed on March 22, 1862, and the *Alabama* followed on July 22. Bullock's highest hopes, however, rested on the Laird rams, the construction of which began in the summer of 1862.

The Laird rams promised to be the finest warships in the world. Ingeniously designed, they were seagoing vessels also capable of operating in shallow coastal waters. Equipped with rifled guns protected in armored turrets and powered by 350-horsepower engines that generated speeds in excess of 15 knots, these ironclads were more than a match for any ship in the Union navy. Understandably, Confederate Secretary of the Navy Stephen R. Mallory pressed Bullock for a rapid delivery of the rams. "Not a day, not an hour must be lost in getting these ships over," he wrote in August 1862, "and money is of no consequence in comparison to the speedy accomplishment of this work."

Despite efforts at secrecy, including a subterfuge by which formal ownership of the Laird rams was transferred to a French firm for ostensible sale to the viceroy of Egypt, the Confederate intentions regarding the rams could hardly escape the attention of the Union. The success of the *Florida* and *Alabama* in ravaging Union shipping had aroused a storm of protest in the North and

increased the diplomatic pressure on the British government to rein in the Confederate shipbuilding program. Charles Francis Adams, the U.S. minister to Great Britain, inundated the Foreign Office with protests and provided evidence that the Laird rams were to be sold to the Confederacy for deployment against the Union blockade.

On September 5, 1863, Adams informed Lord John Russell, the British Foreign Minister: "One of the ironclads is about to leave.... It would be superfluous in me to point out to your Lordship that this means war." Unknown to Adams, Russell had taken action against the ironclads a day earlier. On September 4, he had issued an order forbidding delivery of the rams, and on October 26 the British government took possession of them.

Influenced by the Confederate defeats at Vicksburg and Gettysburg in July 1863, but even more so by the desire to avoid an open break—perhaps even war—with the North, the British government finally clamped down on the Confederate program of building a battle fleet in Great Britain. In failing to acquire the Laird rams, the Confederacy lost its best chance of shattering the blockade and taking the offensive against the Union navy.

SEE ALSO

Adams, Charles Francis; Blockade; Great Britain; Mallory, Stephen R.; Naval warfare

FURTHER READING

Jones, Wilbur D. *The Confederate Rams at Birkenhead: A Chapter in Anglo-American Relations.* Tuscaloosa, Ala.: Confederate Publishing Co., 1961.

Merli, Frank J. *Great Britain and the Confederate Navy, 1861–1865.* Bloomington: Indiana University Press, 1970.

Spencer, Warren F. *The Confederate Navy in Europe.* University, Ala.: University of Alabama Press, 1983.

Lee, Robert E.

CONFEDERATE GENERAL

- *Born: January 19, 1807, Westmoreland County, Va.*
- *Education: U.S. Military Academy, B.S., 1829*
- *Military service: U.S. Army: lieutenant, engineers, 1829–36; lst lieutenant, 1836–38; captain, 1838–55; lieutenant colonel, cavalry, 1855–61; colonel, cavalry, 1861; Confederate army: brigadier general, 1861; general, 1861–65; general-in-chief of the army, 1865*
- *Died: October 12, 1870, Lexington, Va.*

A legend in his own lifetime, Robert E. Lee remains the most revered of all Confederate generals. He had no equal as a battlefield tactician. A master of defensive warfare, he frustrated for nearly three years the efforts of larger federal forces to capture Richmond. He was less successful in his two invasions of the North, and his defeat at Gettyburg forced him back on the defensive for the remainder of the war.

Lee's family had distinguished roots in Virginia's past, and his father, "Light-Horse Harry," was a famed cavalry commander in the Revolutionary War. Lee graduated second in his class at West Point and served in the Engineering Corps, including a brilliant stint in the Mexican War, before he was appointed superintendent at West Point

from 1851 to 1855. He was in the cavalry when he commanded a detachment of marines that crushed John Brown's raid at Harpers Ferry in 1859.

Widely considered to be the best officer in the U.S. Army, Lee was offered command of that army in April 18, 1861. He declined because, as he wrote his sister, "I have not been able to make up my mind to raise my hand against my relatives, my children, my home." He resigned his army commission on April 20 and accepted command of Virginia's troops. In May he entered Confederate service.

Lee's first field command was in western Virginia, where the Unionist sympathies of the populace and problems of supply prevented him from checking the federal advance. After a transfer to the South Atlantic seaboard to organize Confederate defenses, he was called back to Richmond in March 1862 to

Flanked by his son General Custis Lee (left) and by Colonel Walter Taylor, one of his former staff officers, General Robert E. Lee posed at his home in Richmond for the photographer Matthew Brady shortly after the war. The defeated Confederates hailed Lee as their supreme war hero, and his stature reached near mythic proportions.

act as military adviser to President Jefferson Davis. Although frustrated by his lack of any real power, Lee did achieve one notable success in his advisory role. He formulated the rebel counteroffensive in the Shenandoah Valley—General "Stonewall" Jackson's Valley campaign—that pinned down federal forces in middle Virginia and kept them from joining the Union's invasionary army on the peninsula.

Lee assumed command of the army that he renamed the Army of Northern Virginia on June 1, 1862, after the wounding of its previous commander, Joseph E. Johnston. He immediately went on the offensive and beat back the Union army from the outskirts of Richmond during the Seven Days Battles. His stunning victory at Second Bull Run two months later highlighted his skills as a general: he seized the initiative from a numerically superior enemy and daringly deployed his army to achieve a surprise concentration of his forces at a weak point in the enemy's dispositions.

Stymied in his first Northern invasion at Antietam, Lee returned to Virginia and threw up an impregnable defense at Fredericksburg. His breathless audacity at Chancellorsville resulted in a military masterpiece and the apogee of his success. Lee's repulse at Gettysburg, a battle he probably never should have fought, cost his army its offensive firepower and forced it into a defensive role for the rest of the war. Although hampered by dwindling supplies of men and material, Lee fought the huge Army of the Potomac under General Ulysses S. Grant to a virtual standstill in the long, grinding Virginia campaign that began in May 1864 and lasted for the next 11 months. Lee's army inflicted three casualties for every one that it absorbed, but Grant's relentless pounding inevitably wore it down to a nub and stretched its thin lines to the breaking point. Seven

days after the fall of Petersburg, Lee reluctantly surrendered the remnants of his once-magnificent army. "I have done the best I could for you," he told his soldiers after the surrender.

Lee applied for but was denied a pardon after the war. He spent his last years as president of Washington College (now Washington and Lee University). His dying words, according to Southern tradition, were "Strike the tents."

SEE ALSO

Antietam; Appomattox campaign; Chancellorsville; Fredericksburg; Gettysburg; Grant's Virginia campaign; Peninsula campaign; Petersburg campaign; Second Bull Run

FURTHER READING

Connelly, Thomas L. *The Marble Man: Robert E. Lee and His Image in American Society.* New York: Knopf, 1977.

Freeman, Douglas S. *R. E. Lee.* 4 vols. New York: Scribners, 1934–35.

Pryor, Elizabeth Brown. *Reading the Man: A Portrait of Robert E. Lee Through His Private Letters.* New York: Penguin, 2007.

Thomas, Emory M. *Robert E. Lee.* New York: Norton, 1995.

Legal Tender Acts

Passed by the Union Congress in 1862, 1863, and 1864, these acts created the paper money that played a vital role in financing the Northern war effort. Eventually, $447 million in non–interest-bearing Treasury notes, or greenbacks as they were commonly known, were issued, and they accounted for 13 percent of the war's cost in the North.

At the beginning of the Civil War, the federal government was obligated to pay all its bills in specie—that is, gold or silver. The amount of available specie, however, was not nearly enough to meet the monetary needs of the government

Imprinted with an image of Secretary of the Treasury Salmon P. Chase, the first dollar note authorized under the Legal Tender Act was issued on August 1, 1862.

and private bankers, and as early as December 30, 1861, the Treasury and Northern banks suspended specie payments. In the ensuing fiscal crisis, the government temporarily stopped paying its soldiers and other creditors.

The first Legal Tender Act, passed in February 1862, resolved this crisis by authorizing the issuing of $150 million in greenbacks. Except for import duties and the interest on the national debt, the greenbacks were legal tender for all public and private debts. They furnished the Treasury with the money needed to pay its bills and allowed the banks to resume specie payments. By providing a national currency that raised mass purchasing power, they also made it possible for the government to sell its war bonds directly to the Northern public.

The Legal Tender Acts marked a revolutionary departure in the nation's fiscal history. For the first time, the federal government issued a currency that was not backed by an explicit promise of redemption in gold or silver. The Republican-controlled Congress passed the legislation only out of a sense of necessity when faced with the unprecedented costs of the war.

SEE ALSO
Gold; Inflation; National Banking Acts

FURTHER READING
Hammond, Bray. "The North's Empty Purse, 1861–1862." In *American Historical Review* (October 1961): 1–18.
Sharkey, Robert P. *Money, Class, and Party: An Economic Study of Civil War and Reconstruction.* Baltimore: Johns Hopkins Press, 1959.

Liberal Republicans

The Liberal Republicans were a dissident faction of Republicans that formed during the first administration of President Ulysses S. Grant. They attacked the Grant Republicans for persisting in an overly harsh Reconstruction policy and for allowing the party to be converted into the corrupt tool of special interests. Merging with the Democrats, they unsuccessfully ran Horace Greeley for the Presidency in 1872.

The intellectual leadership of the Liberal Republicans came from the country's self-styled "best men": wealthy, highly educated members of prominent old families in the Northeast. They blamed the excesses of political democracy for the incompetence and corruption they believed characterized public life. The root of the problem, according to E. L. Godkin, the editor of the *Nation,* was that too many voters were "unendowed with the self-restraint and discrimination of men bred to the responsibilities of citizenship." Thus, they criticized their party for having pushed suffrage on a black race in the South that presumably lacked the education, property, and moral fitness necessary for exercising the privilege of the vote. They called for a return to "honest" government in the South by allowing former Southern leaders to return to power.

For the Liberal Republicans, Reconstruction symbolized all the excesses that had destroyed efficient, good government under the Grant Republicans. They called for an end to protective tariffs to restore the "natural" flow of international trade and eliminate special favors to business groups. They pushed for civil service reform in an effort to assure that only educated men of merit were appointed to government office.

The "best men" provided the Liberal Republicans with an intellectual foundation, but professional politicians soon came to dominate the movement. Republicans pushed aside by the so-called Stalwarts (pro-business Republicans most loyal to Grant) and Democrats anxious to exploit the split in Republican ranks took over the party. Their nomination of Horace Greeley for the Presidency turned out to be a major blunder.

Greeley's major qualification, apart from the fact that his newspaper career as editor of the *New York Tribune* had made him a household name, was his recent break with the Grant administration for its alleged subversion of white self-government in the South. This made him potentially attractive to a Democratic party hoping to establish a new image as a party of moderation working for sectional reconciliation. However, Greeley had a strong anti-slavery record and consistently had been anti-Democratic in his politics. He turned out to be quite unappealing to Southern Democrats. Meanwhile, Northern Republicans shunned him as a party renegade. Grant easily defeated Greeley with the largest share of the popular vote gained by any Presidential winner between 1828 and 1904.

In the wake of their resounding defeat, the Liberal Republicans disintegrated as an organized political party. Nonetheless, their indictment of Reconstruction became party orthodoxy within a few years and foreshadowed the Republican abandonment of Reconstruction in 1877.

SEE ALSO

Congressional Reconstruction; Democratic party; Election of 1876; Republican party

FURTHER READING

Sproat, John G. *"The Best Men": Liberal Reformers in the Gilded Age.* New York: Oxford University Press, 1968.

Lincoln, Abraham
16TH PRESIDENT OF THE UNITED STATES

- *Born: February 12, 1809, near Hodgenville, Ky.*
- *Political parties: Whig, Republican*
- *Education: sporadic schooling in lower grades*
- *Military service: captain, Illinois volunteer regiment, 1832*
- *Government service: postmaster, New Salem, Ill., 1833–36; Illinois General Assembly, 1834–41; U.S. House of Representatives, 1847–49; President of the United States, 1861–65*
- *Died: April 15, 1865, Washington, D.C.*

An extraordinary wartime President whose commitment to preserving the Union never wavered, Abraham Lincoln changed the nature of the Civil War and the very meaning of the American experiment in democratic government when he issued his Emancipation Proclamation on January 1, 1863. His wartime messages revealed an unparalleled ability to express the nation's highest ideals in prose that was both lucid and poetic. The first U.S. President to be assassinated, Lincoln died before he had an opportunity to advance those ideals in the postwar nation.

The son of a restless, struggling farmer, Lincoln moved with his family from Kentucky to Indiana when he was seven. Following the death of his mother two years later, he was raised by his stepmother, Sarah Bush Johnston. Anxious to escape from the rural poverty of his youth, he borrowed books whenever he could and largely educated himself in his spare time from work as a manual laborer. In 1831, he moved to New Salem, Illinois, where he worked at a variety of jobs and studied law. While serving as a Whig in the state legislature, he gained admission to the bar in 1836 and settled in Springfield, the state capital, to begin his practice. Six years later, he married Mary Todd, the daughter of a prominent Kentucky slaveholding family.

By the mid-1850s, Lincoln had established himself as a successful lawyer whose clients included prominent Illinois corporations, but his political career appeared to be at a dead end. His single term of service in Congress had been undistinguished, and his Whig party collapsed in the uproar over the Kansas-Nebraska Act. By potentially opening up the territories to slavery, however, the Kansas-Nebraska legislation gave birth to the Republican party and offered Lincoln a political vehicle to express his hatred of slavery and his opposition to its spread. He helped organize the Illinois Republican party, and in his debates with Stephen A. Douglas in the senatorial campaign of 1858 continually denounced "the monstrous injustice of slavery itself" and emphasized the need to bring slavery to an eventual end by first restricting it to those states where it then existed. Although Lincoln lost the senate race in 1858, he gained the national reputation that helped him secure the Republican nomination for the Presidency in 1860.

By carrying nearly all of the electoral votes in the free states, Lincoln won the Presidency. When states from the Lower South began to secede in opposition to his election, he held firm and refused to placate the seceders by compromising on the Republican pledge not to allow the spread of slavery into the western territories. After categorically rejecting secession as a legal right, he made his first critical decision as President when he decided to resupply the federal garrison at Fort Sumter with provisions, but not reinforcements unless the fort were attacked. When rebel guns opened fire on the fort, the Confederacy could then be blamed for starting the war. A unified North now rallied behind Lincoln's call for 75,000 volunteers to reassert federal authority and save the Union.

Despite a lack of any administrative or military experience, Lincoln from the very beginning proved to be a

The tall, somewhat awkward President Abraham Lincoln towers over his generals, including General George B. McClellan with the mustache on the left, on his visit to the headquarters of the Army of the Potomac after the battle of Antietam.

resourceful and decisive war leader. Rather than calling Congress into special session during the initial stages of the war, he relied on his constitutional powers as commander-in-chief to shape Union policy. On April 19, 1861, he proclaimed a blockade of Confederate ports; on April 27, he suspended the writ of habeas corpus (thus allowing military authorities to arrest and hold suspected rebel sympathizers without a judicial hearing) along the corridor between Washington and Philadelphia; and on May 3, he enlarged the size of the regular army and navy. Lincoln's actions were of dubious legality, but when Congress met in July, it ratified what he had done.

Sooner than most of his generals, Lincoln realized that a winning Union strategy had to be keyed to applying simultaneous pressure along all Confederate military fronts. In explaining his "general idea of the war" in early 1862, he noted that since "we have the greater numbers, and the enemy has the greater facility of concentrating forces upon the point of collision," the Union could best exploit the manpower edge by "menacing [the enemy] with superior forces at different points, at the same time." Finally, with the emergence of Ulysses S. Grant, he found the general he needed to implement his strategic design.

Lincoln made no move against slavery until he was assured that the border states were under firm Union control. The very success of Confederate resistance slowly swung the Northern public and the army around to a position that favored as a war measure the freeing of slaves in Confederate areas, a policy that Lincoln announced in his Emancipation Proclamation on January 1, 1863. By linking emancipation with the arming of the freed slaves, Lincoln dealt the Confederacy a double blow.

As Union armies overran portions of the Confederacy, Lincoln found himself in a running battle with Congress over who should control the restoration of rebel states to the Union and what the terms of readmission should be. Although Lincoln and Congress never agreed on a fixed policy for Reconstruction, their differences narrowed as the war progressed. The support of both was essential to the passage of the 13th Amendment, freeing all of the slaves, and both moved toward a policy of expanding and protecting the rights of the freed blacks.

In beating back the challenge of radical Republicans to his leadership, as well as in handling the strong-willed personalities that he appointed to his cabinet, Lincoln was a masterful politician whose support was always strongest among the soldiers in the Union armies. His reelection in 1864 clinched the Union victory. Although he did not live to oversee a postwar political settlement, having been assassinated by John Wilkes Booth only a few months after his reelection, his legacy of greatness was secure. He was instrumental both in preserving the Union and in infusing it with a higher moral purpose.

SEE ALSO

Booth, John Wilkes; Election of 1860; Election of 1864; Emancipation Proclamation; Gettysburg Address; Kansas-Nebraska Act; Lincoln-Douglas debates; Reconstruction; Secession; 13th Amendment

FURTHER READING

Carwardine, Richard J. *Lincoln.* London: Pearson Longman, 2003.

Donald, David Herbert. *Lincoln.* New York: Simon & Schuster, 1995.

McPherson, James M., ed. *"We Cannot Escape History": Lincoln and the Last Best Hope of Earth.* Urbana: University of Illinois Press, 1995.

Neely, Mark E. *The Abraham Lincoln Encyclopedia.* New York: McGraw-Hill, 1982.

Paludan, Phillip Shaw. *The Presidency of Abraham Lincoln.* Lawrence: University Press of Kansas, 1994.

Lincoln-Douglas debates

These debates during the Illinois senatorial race of 1858 brought into sharp relief the moral and philosophical differences over slavery that divided white Americans in the late antebellum period. By establishing Abraham Lincoln's national reputation, the debates also made it possible for Lincoln to claim the Republican Presidential nomination in 1860.

In the summer of 1858, Lincoln was still a little-known Republican politician from the prairie state of Illinois. That would soon change after he accepted his party's nomination for the U.S. Senate, a contest to be decided by the balloting of the Illinois legislature when it met in the fall. He was running for the Senate seat then held by Stephen A. Douglas, the most powerful Northern Democrat. What made Douglas all the more formidable was the praise he was receiving from eastern Republicans for his recent stand against admitting Kansas as a slave state under the Lecompton Constitution.

From the very beginning of the campaign, Lincoln stressed the moral differences between himself and Douglas over the issue of slavery. In accepting the Republican nomination, he declared in his now-famous "House Divided" speech that "I believe this government cannot endure permanently half *slave* and half *free.*" He repeatedly returned to this theme of a fundamental conflict between slavery and freedom in his seven public debates with Douglas that attracted large crowds up and down the length of Illinois.

The key to Lincoln's strategy was Douglas's indifferent attitude regarding slavery. "When he invites any people willing to have slavery to establish it," Lincoln charged in the debate at Jonesboro, "he is blowing out the moral lights around us. When he says he 'cares not whether slavery is voted down or voted up,'—that it is a sacred right of self-government—he is in my judgment penetrating the human soul and eradicating the light of reason and the love of liberty in this American people." Contrary to Douglas, who insisted on the right of local (white) majorities to determine the question of slavery, Lincoln believed that American democracy embodied a moral sense of national purpose enshrined in the egalitarian principles of the Declaration of Independence. For Lincoln, Douglas's denial of those national principles sapped the will of Northerners to resist the spread of slavery and reduced the moral evil of slavery to just another political issue susceptible to the will of local majorities.

Douglas countered by rejecting Lincoln's belief in a core set of moral values that stood at the center of American democracy. In his most effective tactic, he accused Lincoln and the Republicans

This 1858 photograph shows Abraham Lincoln as he appeared to the crowds in the debates with Senator Stephen A. Douglas (Democrat–Illinois) that garnered him a national reputation.

of endangering the Union by trying to force black equality on reluctant whites. Lincoln responded to these attacks by denying that he had ever favored social and political equality between the races. Still, he never backed down from his contention that black men and women were fully equal with whites in their inalienable right to better their condition by enjoying the fruits of their own labor.

The fall election in Illinois for the state legislature resulted in Republican gains, but as a result of their holdover strength the Democrats still controlled the legislature. Douglas narrowly retained his Senate seat. In defeat, however, Lincoln had gained a national political reputation when the eastern press covered his debates with Douglas. He had guaranteed that slavery would remain the pivot of national politics and had positioned himself to emerge as the moral voice of the Republican party.

SEE ALSO

Douglas, Stephen A.; Lincoln, Abraham; Republican party

FURTHER READING

Jaffa, Henry V. *Crisis of the House Divided: An Interpretation of the Issues in the Lincoln-Douglas Debates.* Chicago: University of Chicago Press, 1982.

Lincoln's assassination

SEE Booth, John Wilkes

Lincoln's plan of Reconstruction

SEE Proclamation of Amnesty and Reconstruction

Literature

The Civil War produced some fine literature but no great national epic. Perhaps the war was too huge in its canvas, too numbing in its casualties, or too minutely recorded in the writings of the soldiers themselves for writers of fiction to dramatize the struggles effectively. Or, most likely, perhaps the issues over which it was fought were too conflicted to ever permit a satisfactory resolution in literary form.

Critics generally praise Stephen Crane's *The Red Badge of Courage* (1895) as the finest novel of the war. A masterpiece in its depiction of the coming of age of a raw recruit who overcomes his fears in battle to become a hardened veteran unthinkingly obeying orders, the novel is nonetheless noteworthy for what it leaves out. Missing in Crane's psychological study are African Americans, politicians, and the whole constellation of hatreds and ideologies that drove Americans to slaughter one another for four bitter years.

The same shortcomings characterize the work of Ambrose Bierce, a Union veteran whose *Tales of Soldiers* (1891) is a collection of some of the best short stories to come out of the war. Bierce was a master at dramatizing the absurdity of war and the macabre horrors that befell soldiers caught up in its wake. Battles became, as he later wrote, a form of "criminal insanity" and the fate of soldiers was to accept "meekly to be blown out of life by level gusts of grape—to clench our teeth and shrink helpless before big shot pushing noisily through the consenting air." So complete was his disillusionment that the issues that had brought on the war found no place in his writings. He could find no grand meaning in the atrocities unleashed by the war.

Henry Timrod's "Ode" of 1866 to slain Confederate soldiers buried in Charleston stands out as one of the most hauntingly beautiful poems inspired by the war. Among Civil War poets, however, only Walt Whitman succeeded in capturing something of the war's reality for the common soldiers. Unlike nearly all the formulaic and highly romanticized poetry produced during the war on both sides, the verse in his *Drum-Taps* (1865) and *Sequel to Drum-Taps* (1865–66) has endured because, as Whitman wrote a friend in January 1865, it expressed "the pending action of this *Time & Land we swim in*, with all their large conflicting fluctuations of despair & hope." Whitman neither glorified the war nor retreated into Bierce's black pessimism.

Much of the best Civil War literature remains the nonfiction written by participants in the conflict. President Abraham Lincoln's wartime speeches and addresses express with a matchless grace and power the ideals for which the Union was fighting. The wartime diaries and letters of Billy Yanks and Johnny Rebs are a priceless collection of literary documents that can still yield fresh insights on how Americans experienced their Civil War. Many of the wartime memoirs, especially those of Union Generals Ulysses S. Grant and William T. Sherman, set standards for clean, hard prose that became a hallmark of a distinctively American writing style. For its cast of characters and dramatic reenactment of life in the Confederacy, Mary Chesnut's wartime journal has no peers among any fictional treatments of the war. Perhaps the closest competition is the best-known Civil War novel, Margaret Mitchell's *Gone with the Wind* (1936).

The Civil War still awaits its literary masterpiece, a work that does justice to all the issues over which the war was fought, and most notably the still-unresolved issue of the place of African Americans in American life. If such a

Walt Whitman's "O Captain! My Captain!," a somber tribute to the martyred President Lincoln, was one of the most popular poems to come out of the war.

work is ever penned, it might finally put to rest the lament of the writer William Dean Howells when he noted in 1867: "Our war has not only left us a burden of a tremendous national debt, but has laid upon our literature a charge under which it has hitherto staggered very lamely."

SEE ALSO

Chesnut, Mary; Evans, Augusta Jane; Gettysburg Address; Howe, Julia Ward; Whitman, Walt

FURTHER READING

Aaron, Daniel. *The Unwritten War: American Writers and the Civil War.* New York: Knopf, 1973.
Fahs, Alice. *The Imagined Civil War: Popular Literature of the North & South, 1861–1865.* Chapel Hill: University of North Carolina Press, 2001.
Masur, Louis P., ed. *"The Real War Will Never Get in the Books": Selections from Writers during the Civil War.* New York: Oxford University Press, 1993.
Wilson, Edmund. *Patriotic Gore: Studies in the Literature of the American Civil War.* New York: Oxford University Press, 1962.

Logistics

In a military sense, logistics refers to the moving, supplying, and quartering of troops. Without a functioning logistical system, armies simply cannot fight.

As was true in nearly all areas, the economic superiority of the Union also covered logistical support. Compared to the Confederacy, the Union began the war with twice the rail mileage and nearly double the horses and mules needed to transport troops and supplies. In addition, more than a third of the draft livestock in the South was in Kentucky, Tennessee, and Texas, states beyond the effective reach of the Con-

federacy for much of the war.

Once mobilized, Civil War armies were a huge, cumbersome amalgam of men, horses, and equipment, weighted down by columns of supply wagons in the ratio of 25 wagons per 1,000 troops. Because they had to operate in enemy territory and could rely on a more efficient and productive economic base in their rear, Union armies were more unwieldy than their leaner Confederate counterparts. A Union army of 100,000 men consumed 600 tons of supplies on a daily basis. It needed 35,000 horses and mules for its cavalry mounts, artillery batteries, and supply wagons.

Factory production in both sections expanded to meet the military demand not just for armaments but also for such consumer staples as bread, meat, shoes, and clothes. Animal-drawn wagons, riverboats, and railroads provided the logistical support for the massive problem of supply and resupply. This support

This Union supply depot at Yorktown, Virginia, provided logistical support for General George B. McClellan's Peninsula campaign in the spring of 1862. Parked in the middle of the photograph in front of the white tents are huge mortars used to pound the enemy.

reached a field army after snaking over country roads back to a supply depot located on a river or at a railway junction. Railroads were indispensable, for they alone could move the tons of goods and thousands of troops needed for military operations not tied to navigable bodies of water. As long as the railroads funneled provisions and reinforcements to the military theaters, the armies could fight almost indefinitely.

A shrinking base from which to draw agricultural and industrial goods, destructive Union raids, and a deteriorating rail system all confronted the Confederacy with nearly insurmountable problems in supplying its troops. Both military and civilian morale fell as the Confederacy scrambled to collect and transport the essential items needed to sustain its armies. Starvation rations were commonplace for many rebel soldiers in the last half of the war. Meanwhile, the Union army had the distinction of being the best fed and equipped in the history of warfare.

SEE ALSO
Railroads

FURTHER READING
Goff, Richard D. *Confederate Supply.* Durham, N.C.: Duke University Press, 1969.
Weigley, Russell F. *Quartermaster General of the Union Army: A Biography of M. C. Meigs.* New York: Columbia University Press, 1959.

Longstreet, James
CONFEDERATE GENERAL

- *Born: January 8, 1821, Edgefield District, S.C.*
- *Education: U.S. Military Academy, B.S., 1842*
- *Military service: U.S. Army: brevet lieutenant, infantry, 1842–45; lieutenant, 1845–47; 1st lieutenant, 1847–52; captain, 1852–61; major paymaster, 1858–61; Confederate army: brigadier general, 1861; major-general, 1861–62; lieutenant general, 1862–65*
- *Died: January 2, 1904, Gainesville, Ga.*

Solid and unpretentious in his physical appearance as well as in his battlefield leadership, James Longstreet was one of Robert E. Lee's most trusted generals. Nicknamed "Old Pete" by his troops and "Old War Horse" by Lee, Longstreet was an excellent corps commander. He was less successful when he was in charge of an independent command, and his popularity plunged in the postwar South when he joined the Republican party and was blamed for the Confederate defeat at Gettysburg.

The son of a planter, Longstreet was raised by an uncle in Alabama and Georgia. After compiling an undistinguished record at West Point, where he graduated 54th in a class of 62, he served with the infantry in Florida, the Mexican War, and on the western frontier. He resigned his commission in June 1861, when he volunteered his services to the Confederacy. A month later he was leading a brigade at First Bull Run.

Longstreet first gained Lee's confidence while serving as a division commander during the Seven Days Battles in June 1862. When Lee reorganized his unwieldy command structure in the summer of 1862, he initially placed Longstreet in charge of three-quarters of his infantry. Longstreet's corps became known for its solid reliability, and it provided a perfect counterpoint to the more free-spirited command of General Thomas J. "Stonewall" Jackson in Lee's army.

Longstreet worked in tandem with Jackson to defeat the overmatched Union army at the battle of Second Bull

Known for his steadiness in battle, General James Longstreet rarely made a mistake when maneuvering his troops. Had he revealed more daring and imagination, he would have ranked as one of the war's great generals.

Run, and his defensive stand at Antietam was critical in preventing the center and right of the Confederate line from breaking. At Fredericksburg, Longstreet's corps occupied Marye's Heights, the anchor of an impregnable rebel defense. Detached to a separate command along the Carolina coast, Longstreet returned to Virginia too late to take part in the battle of Chancellorsville.

After the rebel victory at Chancellorsville, Longstreet urged Lee to send massive reinforcements to the west for a surprise counteroffensive to be launched out of middle Tennessee. Instead, Lee embarked on his second invasion of the North. Doubting the wisdom of the campaign into Pennsylvania, Longstreet particularly opposed Lee's decision to take the offensive at Gettysburg on July 2 and 3. "If he is there," Longstreet told Lee in reference to the Union position on Cemetery Hill, "it will be because he is anxious that we should attack him: a good reason, in my judgment, for not doing so." Lee went ahead with his plan, and postwar critics insisted that Longstreet's reluctance to carry out those attacks cost the Confederacy a priceless victory.

In September 1863, Longstreet took his corps to Tennessee and played a key role in the Confederate victory at Chickamauga. Returning to Lee's army after an ineffective campaign against Knoxville, he was seriously wounded during the Battle of the Wilderness in May 1864. He recovered in time to lead his corps in all the major battles in Virginia from the fall of 1864 through Lee's surrender at Appomattox in April 1865.

Settling in New Orleans after the war, Longstreet entered the insurance business. He was an active Republican and a supporter of Reconstruction, political stands that further embittered Southern whites led by Jubal A. Early, who now made him the scapegoat for the Confederate defeat at Gettysburg. In his memoirs, published in 1896, Longstreet responded to his critics in an effort to salvage his military reputation.

SEE ALSO
Early, Jubal A.; Gettysburg

FURTHER READING
Piston, William G. *Lee's Tarnished Lieutenant: James Longstreet and His Place in Southern History.* Athens: University of Georgia Press, 1987.
Wert, Jeffrey D. *James Longstreet: The Confederacy's Most Controversial Soldier.* New York: Simon & Schuster, 1993.

Mallory, Stephen R.
CONFEDERATE POLITICIAN

- *Born: c.1813, Trinidad, West Indies*
- *Political party: Democrat*
- *Education: private academies*
- *Government service: customs inspector, Key West, Fla., 1833–40; county judge, Fla., 1840–45; collector of port of Key West, 1845–49; U.S. Senate, 1851–61; Confederacy: secretary of the navy, 1861–1865*
- *Died: November 9, 1873, Pensacola, Fla.*

One of only two members to serve continuously in the cabinet of President Jefferson Davis, Stephen R. Mallory was a bold innovator as Confederate secretary of the navy. By taking advantage of revolutionary changes that were transforming naval warfare, he was able to build a fleet from scratch that counterbalanced much of the Union's overwhelming naval superiority.

The son of a civil engineer whose

work took him to the West Indies, Mallory spent most of his youth in Key West, a setting that nurtured his love of the sea. Both his father and older brother died before he was 15, and his widowed mother sent him to a Moravian school in Pennsylvania. Called home when the tuition money ran out, he studied law under a local judge. He entered politics as a Democrat, became a county judge, and, following a patronage appointment in Key West, entered the U.S. Senate in 1851. Although a defender of Southern rights, he inclined toward moderate Unionism. As chairman of the Committee on Naval Affairs, he became thoroughly conversant with the latest naval technology and pushed for the modernization of the U.S. Navy. A reluctant convert to secession, he resigned from the Senate when Florida seceded in January 1861.

Alone among Davis's initial cabinet appointees, Mallory aroused some opposition in the Confederate Congress. He had been slow to endorse secession, and his critics charged that he had prevented Florida authorities from occupying Fort Pickens in Pensacola Harbor. He weathered the storm and proved to be not only a steadfast Confederate but also a very resourceful head of the Confederate navy.

Mallory understood that the Confederacy would have to resort to ingenuity when faced with the vastly greater size and resources of the Union navy. In a major report to Davis in late April 1861, he outlined the ideas that would shape his naval strategy. Above all, he insisted on the need to embrace technological change. "Rifled cannon are unknown to naval warfare," he pointed out, "but those guns having attained a range and accuracy beyond any other form of ordnance, both with shot and shell, I propose to introduce them into the Navy." The navy that he envisioned

would be built around commerce-destroying cruisers and armored warships. A month later, in calling for a crash program to develop an ironclad, he shrewdly argued that "inequality of numbers may be compensated by invulnerability" and that "naval success dictate[d] the wisdom and expediency of fighting with iron against wood, without regard to first cost." In addition, he pushed for such new weapons as torpedoes (underwater mines) and submarines.

The Confederacy lacked the skilled labor and manufacturing facilities to implement most of Mallory's blueprint for a modern navy. Still, he did a remarkable job in keeping the Union navy off balance with his limited resources. By making the defense of rivers and harbors, and not the breaking of the Union blockade, the major responsibility of his small navy, he succeeded for most of the war in protecting the rear of Confederate armies from waterborne invasions and in defending vital coastal ports.

Mallory remained loyal to Davis until the very end. Captured along with Davis in Georgia in May 1865, he was imprisoned for nearly a year. Upon receiving his parole, he returned to his home in Pensacola and practiced maritime law until his death.

SEE ALSO
Naval warfare; Submarines

FURTHER READING
Durkin, Joseph T. *Stephen R. Mallory: Confederate Navy Chief.* Chapel Hill: University of North Carolina Press, 1954.

McClellan, George B.
UNION GENERAL

- *Born: December 3, 1826, Philadelphia, Pa.*
- *Education: U.S. Military Academy, B.S., 1846*
- *Military service: U.S. Army: lieutenant,*

1847–53; 1st lieutenant, 1853–55; captain, cavalry, 1855–57; major-general, Ohio Volunteers, 1861; major-general, 1861–64; general-in-chief of the army, November 1861–March 1862
- *Died: October 28, 1885, Orange, N.J.*

The most controversial of all Union generals, George B. McClellan was a superb strategist and administrator who was revered by his troops. But he lacked the killer instinct as a field commander and never won the smashing victory that his superiors in Washington expected of him. Relieved of command in November 1862, he sat out the rest of the war and unsuccessfully ran for the Presidency on the Democratic ticket in 1864.

McClellan attended the University of Pennsylvania before his appointment to West Point, where he graduated second in the famous class of 1846 that produced 20 Civil War generals. He served as a military engineer in the Mexican War and then taught for three years at West Point. After a tour of surveying duty in the West, he was sent abroad to study European military installations during the Crimean War. He resigned from the army in 1857 and was a successful railroad president in Cincinnati when the Civil War broke out.

In May 1861, just three weeks after his appointment as commander of Ohio's volunteer forces, McClellan was placed in charge of the Union Department of the Ohio. His command included the western counties of Virginia, a Unionist area through which ran the strategically vital Baltimore and Ohio Railroad. McClellan led an expedition into the region and secured what became West Virginia for the Union cause. This otherwise-minor campaign thrust McClellan into the public limelight and into command of the Army of

the Potomac in August.

For the remainder of 1861, McClellan built the Army of the Potomac into what many observers felt was the finest army ever assembled on the North American continent. Something of a perfectionist, he was reluctant to commit that army to action until he was convinced that it was absolutely ready. As pressure mounted on him to go on the offensive, antislavery Republicans pointed to his politics as a conservative Democrat and his opposition to emancipation and charged that he was "soft" on the rebels and wanted to prolong the war into a stalemate that would return the Democrats to power.

McClellan never did have the full confidence of the Lincoln administration when his long-awaited offensive got underway in March 1862. Convinced that McClellan had left Washington underdefended, Lincoln held back General Irvin McDowell's corps during the entire Peninsula campaign. McClellan won most of the battles in that campaign, but his inability to take Richmond was deemed a major failure. Ordered on August 3, 1862, to bring his army back to Washington, McClellan argued in vain:

"Here, directly in front of this army, is the heart of the rebellion. . . . Here is the true defense of Washington; it is here, on the banks of the James, that the fate of the Union should be decided."

Following the Union defeat under General John Pope at Second Bull Run, Lincoln turned again to McClellan and restored him to full command of the Army of the Potomac. At Antietam, McClellan gained the victory that Lincoln had been waiting for to issue his Preliminary Emancipation Proclamation. An acrimonious dispute over McClellan's failure to pursue the defeated rebels, however, soon resulted in his removal. He never received another command.

McClellan remained active in politics after his Presidential defeat in 1864, and he served as Democratic governor of New Jersey from 1878 until 1881. And, in the last analysis, it was his open partisanship and unwillingness to sanction a war of emancipation that made him expendable as a Union general.

SEE ALSO

Antietam; Election of 1864; Peninsula campaign

FURTHER READING

Hassler, Warren W., Jr. *General George B. McClellan: Shield of the Union.* Baton Rouge: Louisiana State University Press, 1957.
Rowland, Thomas J. *George B. McClellan and Civil War History: In the Shadow of Grant and Sherman.* Kent, Ohio: Kent State University Press, 1998.
Sears, Stephen W. *George B. McClellan: The Young Napoleon.* New York: Ticknor & Fields, 1988.

McDowell, Irvin

UNION GENERAL

- *Born: October 15, 1818, Columbus, Ohio*
- *Education: U.S. Military Academy,*

B.S., 1838
- *Military service: U.S. Army: brevet lieutenant, artillery, 1838; lieutenant, 1838–42; 1st lieutenant, 1842–61; brigadier general, 1861–72; major-general, volunteers, 1862–66; major-general, 1872–82*
- *Died: May 4, 1885, San Francisco, Calif.*

Despite an imposing physical presence that seemed to promise decisive leadership, Irvin McDowell was more pompous than effective as a field general. Given command of the first Union army raised in the East, his name has forever been linked with the ignominious federal defeat at First Bull Run.

Raised in a Scotch-Irish family on the Ohio frontier, McDowell attended the Collège de Troyes in France before his appointment to West Point. After gaining a brevet promotion to captain for his service in the Mexican War, he spent most of his pre–Civil War military career in Washington on the staff of the adjutant general of the army. Although he had little experience in leading troops, McDowell did have powerful political friends. With the support of General Winfield Scott and Secretary of the Treasury Salmon P. Chase, he was placed in command of the volunteers streaming into Washington in the spring of 1861.

McDowell was the first American general ever to command an army as large as 30,000 men, and he was fully aware of the difficulties he faced in trying to whip a mob of raw recruits into a disciplined fighting force. Indeed, he dwelled on his problems and failed to project the confidence necessary to inspire his fellow officers or troops. Henry Villard, a war reporter, perceptively noted: "With his evident want of confidence in himself, he appeared to be

The stout figure leaning on his sword in the middle of this photograph is General Irvin McDowell, surrounded by his staff of officers on the steps of the Arlington Mansion, Robert E. Lee's ancestral home. McDowell loved to eat, and his soldiers remembered him more for his prodigious appetite than his leadership.

full of misgivings from the start. This self-distrust showed itself in his constant talk of the difficulties surrounding him and of the doubts he felt of the possibility of overcoming them."

Referring to what then was called "The Grand Army of the United States," McDowell confided to a friend in June, "This is not an army; it will take a long time to make an army." But McDowell did not have the luxury of time. He was ordered in late June to make a major advance against the rebel army at Manassas Junction. Thus, it was a poorly trained army commanded by a doubting general that carried the hopes of the Union into the first major battle of the war. The result was even worse than McDowell had feared. His troops panicked at Bull Run when rebel reinforcements reached the battlefield, and neither he nor his officers could restore order.

Four days after the Union defeat at Bull Run, George B. McClellan replaced McDowell as the top federal general in the East. By the spring of 1862, McDowell was a corps commander in the Army of the Potomac. At Second Bull Run, his military reputation suffered another setback when his poor performance came under heavy criticism. He demanded a court of inquiry, and although he was exonerated of any

dereliction of duty, he did not receive another field command.

McDowell became commander of the Department of the Pacific late in the war, and he continued to hold departmental commands until he retired from the army in 1882. He was later park commissioner of San Francisco, the city in which he is buried.

SEE ALSO
First Bull Run

FURTHER READING
Hassler, Warren W., Jr. *Commanders of the Army of the Potomac.* Baton Rouge: Louisiana State University Press, 1962.

Meade, George G.
UNION GENERAL

- *Born: December 31, 1815, Cadiz, Spain*
- *Education: U.S. Military Academy, B.S., 1835*
- *Military service: U.S. Army: lieutenant, 1835; lieutenant, topographical engineers, 1842–51; 1st lieutenant, 1851–56; captain, 1856–62; brigadier general, volunteers, 1861; major, 1862; major-general, volunteers, 1862; brigadier general, regular army, 1863; major-general, regular army, 1864–65*
- *Died: November 6, 1872, Philadelphia, Pa.*

A solid, unspectacular general nicknamed "the old snapping turtle" by his soldiers, George G. Meade assumed command of the Army of the Potomac just two days before it fought Robert E. Lee's Army of Northern Virginia at Gettysburg, the war's most celebrated battle. Upon hearing that Meade had replaced Joseph Hooker, Lee remarked: "General Meade will commit no blunder on my front, and if I make one he will make haste to take advantage of it." Meade's performance at Gettysburg justified that assessment.

Although born in Spain, where his father was pursuing mercantile interests, Meade spent most of his youth in Pennsylvania. Soon after graduating from West Point, he resigned his commission to become a civil engineer. By 1842 he was back in the army as a topographical engineer. With the exception of brief service in the Mexican War, his army assignments consisted largely of surveying work in coastal areas.

Despite his lack of combat experience, Meade proved to be a very competent handler of troops during the Civil War. He had a superb eye for topography and an excellent feel for detecting troop movements. After his first command in charge of a brigade of Pennsylvania volunteers during the Peninsula and Second Bull Run campaigns, he headed a division at Antietam and Fredericksburg. By the spring of 1863 he was a corps commander, and as Lee's army swung north into Pennsylvania in late June, Meade received the overall command of the Army of the Potomac.

Meade concentrated his army faster and in a stronger defensive position at Gettysburg than Lee had expected, and he correctly reasoned that Lee would go on the offensive if faced with a large Union army. Meade's tactical skill at Gettysburg in deploying his troops and reinforcing threatened points in the federal lines was a major factor in the Union's victory over the Confederacy's best army. Still, he had fought a purely defensive battle, and he refused to order a counterattack. Deluged with pleas from Washington to attack before the rebels recrossed the Potomac River, Meade responded: "I expect to find the enemy in a strong position well covered with artillery, and I do not desire to imitate his example at Gettysburg and

assault a position where the chances were so greatly against success." Lee had prepared a strong defensive line north of the Potomac, and whether or not Meade should have attacked remains one of the great controversies of the war.

Although Meade retained the command of the Army of the Potomac for the remainder of the war, he was placed in an awkward position after March 1864, when Ulysses S. Grant, the top-ranking Union general, decided to accompany Meade's army and direct its strategic movements. Grant issued most of the orders, and Meade did his best to see that they were executed.

After the war Meade commanded the Division of the Atlantic and Military District No. 3 in the reconstructed South. An old war wound flared up in 1872 and contributed to his death from pneumonia.

SEE ALSO
Gettysburg

FURTHER READING
Cleaves, Freeman. *Meade of Gettysburg.* Norman: University of Oklahoma Press, 1960.

Medicine

Although crude and even barbaric by modern standards, medical care during the Civil War compares favorably with that received by soldiers in other wars of the 19th century, either in the United States or abroad. Mortality rates from disease and wounds were most likely the lowest yet recorded in a major war.

In medicine, as in all other facets of the war, both sides had to improvise as they went along. Unprecedented numbers of battle casualties and disease-ridden soldiers swamped government

Medical staff at Gettysburg prepare to amputate a man's leg in a hospital tent, in July 1863

medical bureaus that had no concept of the problems they would face. For example, no one had considered how to recover the wounded from the battlefield. In the first year of the war, they either had to make their own way to the rear or be carried by a comrade. Especially early in the war, churches, public buildings, homes, and barns functioned as makeshift hospitals.

With neither any knowledge of bacteriology nor the bulldozers and gasoline used by 20th-century armies to bury and destroy their organic wastes, army doctors were as much in the dark as to the prevention and treatment of disease as any civilian. Overworked and frustrated, they often struck the soldiers as being callously indifferent to providing proper care. "When a person is sick in camp they might as well dig a hole and put him in as to take him to one of thee infernal hells called hospitals," complained the federal cavalryman Albinus R. Fell

The crude medical instruments of the Civil War era did not allow for very sophisticated surgical techniques.

to his wife. When doctors did attempt a cure, they most often prescribed alcoholic stimulants or opium-based painkillers. As a result, addiction was widespread in both armies.

Surgeons had anesthetics in the form of chloroform and morphine, but no awareness of the need for sterilization to prevent infection. In addition to operating with unsterilized knives and saws, they routinely applied moist, reusable cotton bandages to postsurgical wounds. Unsurprisingly, gangrene and blood poisoning were rampant in army hospitals. In order to avoid the almost-certain onset of lethal infections, surgeons treated gunshot wounds to joints and extremities by amputation. An army surgeon had a ghastly task. "My hands are constantly steeped in blood," wrote Union surgeon Claiborne Walton of his work in an army hospital. "I have amputated limbs until it almost makes my heart ache to see a poor fellow coming in the Ambulance to the Hospital.... The horror of this war can never be half told."

Appalling as they were, medical conditions did improve by the midpoint of the war. William A. Hammond, appointed surgeon general of the Union army in 1862, introduced reforms in the Medical Bureau that were pushed even further by his successor in 1864, Joseph K. Barnes. These surgeon generals increased appropriations for the Medical Bureau more than tenfold; attracted talented young surgeons to government service; and supervised the development of a general system of hospitals that by 1865 had the capacity to provide a bed for one in eight soldiers in the army. These new hospitals were larger and airier then those they replaced and provided much better care. Battlefield treatment also improved with the creation of trained ambulance corps, a reform that originated with General George M. McClellan in the Army of the Potomac. In addition, the War Department sanctioned the use of volunteers from the civilian-run U.S. Sanitary Commission and the Christian Sanitary Commission. These agencies provided supplies and personnel for nursing and hospital work.

Although limited in what it could do by far fewer resources, the Confederacy instituted similar reforms in its system of medical care. Under the innovative leadership of Dr. Samuel Preston Moore, the Confederate Medical Department centralized medical care for its soldiers in general hospitals that were better equipped than the former field hospitals operated by each of the states. The largest complex of military hospitals— 34 in all—was in and around Richmond. It included Chimborazo, the largest hospital in North America. Moore worked tirelessly to bring in medical supplies through the blockade, and he exhorted Southerners to improvise medicines from herbal sources. His efforts enabled the Confederacy to provide a reasonably adequate level of care for its sick and wounded soldiers.

SEE ALSO
Casualties; Disease

FURTHER READING

Adams, George Washington. *Doctors in Blue: The Medical History of the Union Army in the Civil War.* New York: Henry Schuman, 1952.

Cunningham, H. H. *Doctors in Gray: The Confederate Medical Service.* Baton Rouge: Louisiana State University Press, 1958.

Denney, Robert E. *Civil War Medicine: Care & Comfort of the Wounded.* New York: Sterling, 1995.

Rutkow, Ira M. *Bleeding Blue and Gray: Civil War Surgery and the Evolution of American Surgery.* New York: Random House, 2005.

Memminger, Christopher G.

CONFEDERATE POLITICIAN

- *Born: January 9, 1803, Nayhingen, Wurttenberg, Germany*
- *Political party: Democrat*
- *Education: South Carolina College, A.B., 1819*
- *Government service: South Carolina House of Representatives, 1836–52, 1854–60, 1877–78; Confederacy: secretary of the treasury, 1861–64*
- *Died: March 7, 1888, Charleston, S.C.*

As Confederate secretary of the treasury for most of the war, Christopher G. Memminger faced the hopelessly difficult task of bringing some order to Southern finances. In part because he expected a short war, he moved too slowly in implementing measures to raise revenue and was unable to arrest the spiraling inflation that eroded the value of Confederate paper money.

Brought to South Carolina as an infant by his widowed mother, Memminger was only four when his mother died. He spent seven years in the Charleston Orphan House before his adoption by Thomas Bennett, later a governor of South Carolina. An excellent student, he studied law upon graduating from college and was admitted to the South Carolina bar in 1824. After opposing Nullification in 1831–32, he entered the South Carolina legislature in 1836, where he specialized in banking and monetary issues.

Memminger opposed any separate move by South Carolina toward secession until January 1860, when he was sent by the governor as a special commissioner to Virginia. Unable to enlist Virginia's support for a united front of Southern states opposed to the antislavery stand of the North, he concluded that "we farther South will be compelled to act and drag after us these divided states." He actively backed South Carolina's secession in December 1860, and two months later at Montgomery, Alabama, chaired the committee that drafted the provisional Confederate Constitution.

Despite his financial background as a state legislator, Memminger received the post of secretary of the treasury primarily because of the political need to have a representative from South Carolina in the Confederate cabinet. Characterized by Robert Kean, a clerk in the War Department, as "a man of smartness, finesse but tricky, shifty, and narrow," Memminger lacked the flexibility and boldness needed for successful planning and administration of Confederate finances. To be sure, the problems confronting him were immense, and perhaps insurmountable. Military reverses, the Union blockade, and a popular aversion to taxation all undermined much of what he tried to accomplish. Still, Memminger compounded his problems by refusing to push immediately and hard for a meaningful program of taxation and by failing to grasp the imperative need for the Confederate government to secure cotton early in the war and send it to Europe as collateral for loans.

After the first Confederate bond issue in the spring of 1861 raised $15 million in specie (hard assets in gold), Southerners had little hard currency left to invest in the Confederate government. Produce loans enabled the government to acquire some cotton, but little effort was made to export it to Europe in exchange for specie until 1864. Meanwhile, as early as February 1862, treasury notes (that is, paper money) accounted for 76 percent of the government's income. Inflation skyrocketed, and efforts in 1864 to force an exchange of the paper money for long-term bonds simply drained what little public confidence remained in Confederate currency.

Forced out in June 1864, Memminger retired to his country home in Flat Rock, North Carolina, and withdrew from the Confederate war effort. After receiving a Presidential pardon in 1867, he resumed his law practice in Charleston and became a successful business investor. Until his death, he continued his prewar work on behalf of the public schools in Charleston.

SEE ALSO
Inflation

FURTHER READING
Ball, Douglas B. *Financial Failure and Confederate Defeat.* Urbana: University of Illinois Press, 1991.
Capers, Henry D. *The Life and Times of C. G. Memminger.* Richmond, Va.: Everett Waddy Co., 1893.

Mexican War

The Mexican War (1846–48) had the paradoxical result of enhancing the national power of the United States while simultaneously poisoning its

domestic politics. The war also served as a training ground for many of the officers who fought in the Civil War.

The openly aggressive designs of the United States on the Mexican province of Upper California, combined with the smoldering resentment of Mexico over its loss when Texas fought a successful war for independence in 1836, touched off the Mexican War in the spring of 1846. The United States easily achieved its territorial objectives. The Mexicans fought bravely, but they lacked the leadership, modern artillery, and naval strength to check the U.S. advances. By the terms of the Treaty of Guadalupe Hidalgo, signed in February 1848, Mexico surrendered any claim on Texas and ceded Upper California and most of what today is the American Southwest.

Although a brilliant military success for the United States, the war became a political nightmare. As became apparent with the introduction of the Wilmot Proviso in August 1846, the war pitted Northerners against Southerners in an endless debate over the status of slavery in any newly acquired territories. The failure to resolve that debate was the single most direct cause of the sectionalization of U.S. politics that led to secession and, ultimately, the Civil War.

Robert E. Lee, Ulysses S. Grant, George H. Thomas, and a host of other future generals received their first combat experience in the Mexican War. In most instances, the lessons they learned contributed to the high casualties on Civil War battlefields. The basic lesson they took from the Mexican War was that massed, frontal assaults by infantry could carry the enemy's position. Such assaults had succeeded for the Americans against the Mexicans because that war was fought with smoothbore muskets and cannon whose range and firepower harkened back to the weapons of the 18th century. In the era of rifled firearms, introduced for the first time on a mass scale in the Civil War, frontal assaults almost invariably failed. Rifles and improved cannons tore huge gaps out of the ranks of advancing infantry. The result was casualty lists that were unimaginable by the standards of earlier wars.

A final lesson of the Mexican War for some Americans was a political one. Many Northerners shared the belief expressed by Grant in his memoirs when he wrote, "The Southern rebellion was largely the outgrowth of the Mexican War." Particularly for those Northerners who joined the Republican party, the Mexican War unleashed Southern ambitions for additional slave territory that soon led to a breakup of the Union. Unified against permitting the South any room to expand slavery, the Republicans swept to a victory in 1860 that precipitated secession.

SEE ALSO
Casualties; Rifles; Wilmot Proviso

FURTHER READING
Morrison, Michael A. *Slavery and the American West: The Eclipse of Manifest Destiny and the Coming of the Civil War.* Chapel Hill: University of North Carolina Press, 1997.
Weigley, Russell F. *The American Way of War: A History of United States Military Strategy and Policy.* New York: Macmillan, 1973.

Mexico

SEE France; Mexican War

Military Reconstruction Act of 1867

The first of four Reconstruction acts passed by Congress in 1867 and 1868, this complex measure mandated black suffrage in the 10 former Confederate

states still out of the Union in the spring of 1867. This extension of suffrage to the freedmen created a loyal majority in the South that would ratify the 14th amendment and form the basis of new Southern Republican parties.

Confronted with the Southern rejection of the 14th amendment and the continued defiance of President Andrew Johnson, congressional Republicans were at a crossroads in the winter of 1866–67. They either had to accede to Johnson's program of Reconstruction, which returned former rebels to power and offered no protection for black rights, or else formulate an enforceable plan that would embody what the Republicans believed were the just demands of the North. Knuckling under to Johnson and rewarding Southern intransigence were out of the question, but the party debated just how far to go to force Southern compliance with the North's terms. The result was an act that was a cumbersome, almost desperate, compromise between party moderates and radicals.

The Reconstruction Act divided the 10 excluded Southern states into five military districts. Under the ultimate authority of the commanding general in each district, voters were to be enrolled and elections held for constitutional conventions in which all male citizens,

Harper's Weekly featured the generals assigned to duty as district commanders in the first phase of military Reconstruction. From left to right they are Daniel Sickles, John Pope, George H. Thomas, Ulysses S. Grant, John M. Schofield, Philip H. Sheridan, and E.O.C. Ord.

except those politically disqualified by the 14th amendment, were eligible to vote. New state constitutions had to be drafted and ratified that provided for black suffrage. Finally, state legislatures elected under the new constitutions had to ratify the 14th amendment. Once these conditions were met, the state would be readmitted to the Union.

The mandatory features of the act, most notably its imposition of black suffrage, were fully in accord with the demands of Republican radicals. But contrary to their wishes, Congress pulled back from stripping former rebels of the right to vote for any extended period, confiscating and redistributing the land of planters, or abolishing the Johnsonian governments before the new state governments were established. For George Julian, a Republican radical from Indiana favoring indefinite territorial status for the former Confederate states, these areas were "not ready for reconstruction as independent States, on any terms or conditions which Congress might impose." Most Republicans, however, wanted to bring Reconstruction to an end as soon as possible, and they backed the act as the best they could get.

Passed over Johnson's predictable veto in March 1867, the Reconstruction Act needed to be supplemented by three additional measures in order to overcome obstructionist tactics in the South. Indeed, the enforcement of the act bred a counterrevolution that within a decade restored conservative white rule in the South.

SEE ALSO

Congressional Reconstruction; 14th amendment; Johnson's program of Reconstruction; Radical Reconstruction in the South

FURTHER READING

Benedict, Michael Les. *The Fruits of Victory: Alternatives in Restoring the Union,* *1865–1877.* Philadelphia: Lippincott, 1975.
Donald, David. *The Politics of Reconstruction, 1863–1867.* Baton Rouge: Louisiana State University Press, 1965.
Sefton, James E. *The United States Army and Reconstruction, 1865–1877.* Baton Rouge: Louisiana State University Press, 1967.

Missionary Ridge

SEE Chattanooga campaign

Monitor-Merrimack duel

SEE Naval warfare

Morrill Land-Grant Act

Named after its sponsor, Republican Congressman Justin Morrill of Vermont, the Land-Grant Act of 1862 marked the first major effort of the federal government to underwrite higher education. The act stimulated a significant diffusion of public education, especially in the Middle West and the Far West.

Morrill's bill granted public land to those (loyal) states that would establish public colleges "for the benefit of agriculture and the mechanical arts." Based upon proportional representation, it allotted these states 30,000 acres for each of their senators and representatives then in Congress. In monetary terms, this amounted to an endowment equivalent to $10 million in the free states alone. Proceeds from the sale of the land were to be invested in interest-bearing bonds, and colleges had to be established within five years of receiving the federal grant.

The bill embodied the belief of the Republican party that the federal government had a positive responsibility to make a practical education more widely available to Americans. Democrats and, before the Civil War, Southerners had opposed and blocked federal subsidies to education, but with the absence of Southern congressmen and the support of President Abraham Lincoln, the Republicans were able to pass the bill and have it signed into law. Under its provisions, the states established 69 land-grant colleges, and agricultural research received a tremendous boost.

FURTHER READING

Parker, William Belmont. *The Life and Public Services of Justin Smith Morrill.* 1924. Reprint, New York: Da Capo Press, 1971.

Music

Singing songs came easily to Civil War soldiers. Music provided a cadence for marching and a break from its tedium. Played by brass bands, it helped inspire men as they went into battle. Tunes accompanied by a banjo or fiddle offered an emotional release from the ache and loneliness of being away from home. The Civil War easily produced the most enduring music of any major U.S. war.

The most popular camp music blended sentimental and patriotic themes. "Home, Sweet Home" was a favorite in both armies. As Union and Confederate armies gathered on a still night before the battle of Fredericksburg, a Union bugler played its notes. Leander W. Cogswell, a New Hampshire soldier, recalled that "all listened

intently, and I don't believe there was a dry eye in all the assembled thousands." "When This Cruel War Is Over," another sad melody, sold a million copies during the war. George F. Root, a prolific Northern songwriter, catered to the soldiers' tastes with such favorites as "Just Before the Battle, Mother," "Tramp, Tramp, Tramp," and "The Battle Cry of Freedom," a marching song originally written to help spur Union enlistments.

"John Brown's Body," which seemed to gain more stanzas with every federal conquest, remains the best known of the Union marching songs. Its tune came from a slave melody sung in the Carolina low country. When Julia Ward Howe wrote new lyrics for the melody, the result was "The Battle Hymn of the Republic," a powerful expression in music of the North's

Written by a Northerner for the minstrel stage, "Dixie's Land" was the song that came to represent the South during and after the Civil War. Many believe that its origins derive from a work tune sung by the slaves.

growing commitment to emancipation.

"The Girl I Left Behind Me," for Union soldiers, and "The Yellow Rose of Texas," for Confederates, were among the most popular ballads to sweethearts at home. "Loreena" and "Aura Lee" ("Love Me Tender" in its modern form) were the most hauntingly beautiful of these songs.

The short existence of the Confederacy saw an explosion in the publishing of songbooks and sheet music by Southerners. Music was easily the most popular medium by which Confederates celebrated their victories and mourned their losses. Yet, ironically, outsiders wrote the Confederacy's two most popular songs. Daniel Emmett of Ohio wrote "Dixie's Land" or "Dixie," a prewar minstrel song that became the Confederacy's unofficial national anthem after it was played at Jefferson Davis's inauguration. Harry McCarthy, a prewar comedian who had emigrated to the South from Ireland, transformed the lilting tune of an old Irish song into "The Bonnie Blue Flag," a patriotic marching song second only to "Dixie" in popularity.

Music helped sustain soldiers and civilians alike during the war. President Abraham Lincoln paid tribute to its importance when, while touring Richmond in the last days of the war, he asked a Union band to play "Dixie" as a symbol of reconciliation.

SEE ALSO
Howe, Julia Ward

FURTHER READING
Abel, E. Lawrence. *Singing the New Nation: How Music Shaped the Confederacy, 1861–1865.* Mechanicsville, Pa.: Stackpole Books, 1999.
Harwell, Richard B. *Confederate Music.* Chapel Hill: University of North Carolina Press, 1950.
Kelley, Bruce C. and Mark A. Snell, eds. *Bugles Resounding: Music and Musicians of the Civil War Era.* Columbia: University of Missouri Press, 2004.

Nast, Thomas
UNION CARTOONIST

- *Born: September 27, 1840, Landau, Germany*
- *Political party: Republican*
- *Education: lower grades*
- *Occupation: artist/cartoonist, primarily for* Harper's Weekly, *1862–86*
- *Died: December 7, 1902, Guayaquil, Ecuador*

As staff artist of *Harper's Weekly* during the Civil War, Thomas Nast was a satirical cartoonist for the Union cause. His politically charged illustrations were so effective in mobilizing public opinion that President Abraham Lincoln praised him as one of the best recruiters for the Union army.

The son of a German musician, Nast came to the United States with his mother in 1846. His father joined them four years later in New York City. As a youngster, Nast became fascinated with drawing. After briefly attending the Academy of Design in New York, he was hired at the age of 15 by *Frank Leslie's Illustrated Newspaper.* He soon developed the biting style that enabled him to convey political messages through pictures. Work at other illustrated newspapers followed, and upon returning from a European assignment in early 1861, he devoted his talent and wit to the Union war effort.

In 1862 Nast became the chief illustrator for *Harper's Weekly,* an influential journal with a large middle-class following in the North. His war drawings circulated widely, and they fixed in the popular imagination graphic images of the moral righteousness of the Union cause while heaping scorn on the Confederacy and all those who would

In this detail from Thomas Nast's 1864 Presidential campaign drawing "Compromise with the South," Liberty mourns the Union dead who might have lost their lives in vain if Democrat George B. McClellan defeated Republican incumbent Abraham Lincoln. The Union Republican party distributed hundreds of thousands of copies of the picture.

compromise with the enemies of the Union. Among his most powerful pieces was an 1863 illustration entitled "Southern Women Gloating Over Dead Union Soldiers." It captured perfectly the hostility of federal soldiers toward Southern women who devoted themselves selflessly to Confederate victory. "Attack on Fort Wagner," another 1863 work, depicted the heroism under fire of Union black troops and is one of the best indicators of how the racial attitudes of Northern whites began to change as the result of black combat service in the Union armies.

A committed Republican and the originator of the elephant as the symbol for the Republican party, Nast contributed to Lincoln's reelection in 1864 with a sarcastic cartoon that came out soon after the Democrats nominated George B. McClellan for the Presidency. Entitled "Compromise with the South," it centered on the figure of a gloating Confederate shaking hands over the grave of Union heroes with a maimed

Northern soldier.

Nast gained his greatest fame after the war when he turned his scornful wit on Boss William M. Tweed's notoriously corrupt political machine in New York City. The publicity that his cartoons aroused was instrumental in bringing Tweed down. Unable to escape Nast's ridicule, a frustrated Tweed complained to the reformers in 1875: "I don't care a straw for your newspaper articles, my constituents don't know how to read, but they can't help seeing those damned pictures."

After leaving *Harper's Weekly* in 1886, Nast briefly managed his own paper, but his best work was behind him, and he had lost most of his money in bad investments. He died within months of accepting a patronage position as U.S. consul in Ecuador.

FURTHER READING
Keller, Morton. *The Art and Politics of Thomas Nast.* New York: Oxford University Press, 1968.

National Banking Acts

A new banking system emerged from the Civil War with the passage of groundbreaking legislation in 1863. As amended in 1864, the National Banking Act of 1863 replaced a hodgepodge of state banks with a centralized system of nationally chartered banks.

A national banking system arose out of the Union's need for a stable, uniform currency, what Secretary of the Treasury Salmon P. Chase referred to as the "circulation of notes bearing a common impression and authenticated by a common authority." Prior to 1863, states chartered and regulated banks. Some 1,600 banks issued more than 12,000 different kinds of banknotes, most of which fluctuated widely in their value. Although these banknotes supplied the bulk of the circulatory currency, none of them could be used as payment for federal taxes or bonds. This was of little account before the Civil War, when the federal government played only a minor role in the economy, but it became a critical problem when the Treasury confronted the urgent need to borrow huge sums of money to finance the war. The marketing of government bonds, the source of 60 percent of the Union's funds during the war, required that the currency be both enlarged and standardized. Greenbacks, paper money first issued in 1863, helped alleviate the problem, but they were widely viewed as a stopgap, emergency measure.

The National Banking Act met the Union's financial requirements. At its core was a provision that allowed nationally chartered banks the right to issue banknotes for up to 90 percent of the value of the federal bonds they deposited with the Treasury. By joining the national system, bankers would profit both from the interest on their government bonds and from the lending of their national banknotes. Despite this enticement, most state banks stayed out of the system until a prohibitive tax on state banknotes in 1865 forced them into it. The new banking structure remained in place until the coming of the Federal Reserve system in 1913.

SEE ALSO

Gold; Legal Tender Acts

FURTHER READING

Hammond, Bray. *Sovereignty and an Empty Purse: Banks and Politics in the Civil War.* Princeton, N.J.: Princeton University Press, 1970.

Nationalism

American nationalism—the sense of the United States as the political expression of a national people with common values—was slow to develop before the Civil War. American identity was a product primarily of local and regional allegiances that formed in physical isolation from the nation as a whole. Then, just as revolutionary changes in transportation and communications forged by steamboats, railroads, and the telegraph shrank distances and brought Americans closer together, the intensification of sectional differences over slavery undermined any sense of a common national purpose.

Americans had always taken immense, even boastful, pride in their country as the world's greatest republic of free men, and the Puritans had bequeathed a sense of national mission with their belief in America as the new Israel of God's chosen people. Nationalism

This was one of many patriotic prints produced soon after the assassination of President Lincoln. Now linked with George Washington as the nation's greatest statesman, the martyred Lincoln holds his Emancipation Proclamation while Washington grasps the Constitution.

existed in the early republic, but it grew primarily out of attachments to particular localities or states. What brought Americans together as Americans were shared memories of the Revolutionary War against Britain and a common allegiance to the Constitution as the enshrinement of their individual liberties. But once the sectional controversy focused on the constitutional status of slavery in the territories, the Constitution itself became another source of division, for each section interpreted it according to its own needs and interests.

By the mid-19th century, Northerners were espousing an economic and moral nationalism that Southerners saw as a dangerous invasion of their rights. An alliance of farmers, manufacturers, and workers that came together in the Republican party was calling for a national program of economic development funded by subsidies and benefits from the federal government. Southerners responded that such a program violated states' rights and enriched the North at the expense of the agrarian South. Even more threatening to the South was the moral nationalism of the abolitionists and other Northern reformers. This nationalism was implicit in the abolitionists' demand for a common labor system based upon freedom for all workers. Also flowing into this nationalism was the Northern evangelical vision of the United States as a redeemer nation destined to take the lead in God's plan for universal freedom and progress. The ultimate goal of this nationalism was a morally uniform country with a single standard of freedom and legal equality for all its citizens.

Most Southern whites drew back in horror from such a nationalist vision of the United States. They found the very talk of freedom and rights for blacks to be morally offensive and a virtual call for slave uprisings. Their America pre-supposed the acceptance of divergent moral principles and the unqualified right of local white majorities to enforce those principles. Thus, in the Southern mind, abolitionism and the North's moralistic nationalism were two sides of the same coin. For Senator Jefferson Davis, the very source of abolitionism was the "political heresy that ours is a union of the people, the formation of a nation, and a supreme government charged with providing for the general welfare."

When it appeared after the election of Abraham Lincoln that the Republicans were on the verge of implementing the North's nationalist principles, the states of the Lower South seceded from the Union. In crushing Southern nationalism during the Civil War, the victorious Union armies laid the foundation for the vastly expanded national powers enacted into law by the Republicans during Reconstruction.

SEE ALSO

Abolitionism; Federalism; Religion; Republican party; Union

FURTHER READING

Arieli, Yehoshua. *Individualism and Nationalism in American Ideology.* Cambridge: Harvard University Press, 1964.
Lawson, Melinda. *Patriot Fires: Forging a New American Nationalism in the Civil War North.* Lawrence: University Press of Kansas.

Native Americans

Native Americans tried to maintain neutrality during the Civil War, but small numbers of them did fight. As they had during the Revolutionary War, Indians chose sides based on their own political objectives.

By 1861, the federal government had herded onto reservations or forcibly relocated west of the Mississippi River nearly all the Indian peoples whose ancestral homelands had been east of the Mississippi. The Iroquois of western New York, a confederation of tribes that had resisted for decades efforts to move them to the West, sent nearly 2,000 men into the Union army in the hope that such a show of support would gain them postwar friends in Washington. Eli S. Parker, a leader of the Iroquois Confederacy, rose to the rank of assistant adjutant general on General Ulysses S. Grant's staff. Despite this military contribution, which the federal government interpreted as a desire for greater assimilation into white culture, the Iroquois faced renewed pressure after the war to leave New York.

The bulk of the Indian troops raised by each side came out of the Indian Territory (present-day Oklahoma), the home of the so-called civilized tribes: the Cherokee, Chickasaw, Choctaw, Creek, and Seminole. The Confederacy took the initiative in securing Indian

allies. On May 17, 1861, the Confederate Congress annexed the Indian Territory to the Confederacy and sent Albert Pike to negotiate treaties spelling out a political and military alliance. The ultimate Confederate goal was to incorporate enough of the trans-Mississippi region to serve as a corridor through the Southwest to the Pacific Ocean.

The success of Confederate diplomacy touched off a civil war of its own among the tribes in the Indian Territory. Most of the slaveholding Indians, who tended to be racially mixed, backed the Confederacy in the hope not only of having their slave property permanently recognized but also of protecting their lands from the grasping federal government. The nonslaveholding, full-blooded Indians were generally loyal to the Union. As raids and counterraids swept over the Indian Territory, each of the rival factions raised several regiments of troops for Union or Confederate service.

The Union victory at Pea Ridge, Arkansas, in March 1862, ended any Confederate hope of establishing effec-

By fighting on the Union side, many Native Americans hoped to gain favor in Washington. Members of Company K of the 1st Michigan Sharpshooters are shown here recovering from injuries received in the Battle of the Wilderness in May of 1864.

tive control over the Indian Territory. Confederate Indian regiments continued to fight valiantly under Cherokee Brigadier General Stand Watie—indeed, Watie's was the last Confederate force to surrender on June 23, 1865—but Indian enthusiasm for the Confederacy dropped markedly after Pea Ridge. During and after the war, however, the federal government cited the Indian defections to the Confederacy as justification for further limiting the rights of tribal governments in the Indian Territory.

Even where Native Americans were not involved directly in the Civil War, tensions between Indians and whites escalated into violence. A Sioux uprising in Minnesota, provoked in part by the government's failure to deliver goods promised under its treaty obligations, led to massive reprisals and ended in the mass execution of 38 Indians at Mankato, Minnesota, on December 26, 1862. When sporadic guerrilla warfare erupted on the Plains, volunteer regiments of local whites exacted a terrible vengeance. The worst episode occurred on November 28, 1864, when white volunteers slaughtered and mutilated a peaceful band of Cheyenne and Arapaho at Sand Creek, Colorado.

The Civil War had tragic results for Native Americans. By reaffirming and enhancing national power, Union victory paved the way for the accelerated white settlement of the trans-Mississippi West and the rapid defeat of the remaining independent tribes. Regardless of what side they favored, Indians were among the chief losers of the war.

SEE ALSO
Pea Ridge

FURTHER READING
Hauptman, Laurence M. *Between Two Fires: American Indians in the Civil War.* New York: Free Press, 1995.

Naval warfare

Although predominately a war fought on land, the Civil War also had a naval component that made a vital contribution to Union victory. Nowhere was the material disparity between the two sides greater than in the industrial advantage enjoyed by the Union in building and deploying naval vessels. The Union navy blockaded Confederate ports, assisted in the transporting and supplying of federal invasionary forces, and cooperated with the army in establishing enclaves on the Confederate coast and gaining control of inland waterways. Despite a remarkably innovative naval program of its own, the Confederacy was never able to counter Union seapower effectively.

The first task of the Union navy, and the one that drew on most of its strength throughout the war, was the blockade of the Confederacy. In his first major strategic decision of the war, President Abraham Lincoln proclaimed the blockade on April 19, 1861. Designed both to strangle the overseas trade of the rebels and to isolate them diplomatically from outside powers, the blockade initially existed only on paper. The Union began the war with only 90 warships, less than half of which were ready for active duty. Such a small force had little hope of sealing off ports on a Confederate coastline that stretched for more than 3,000 miles and offered numerous entry points for ships to dart in and out.

The blockade began to take effect in late 1861. Union army and naval forces seized Cape Hatteras Inlet, North Carolina, in August 1861. Three months later, a Union squadron

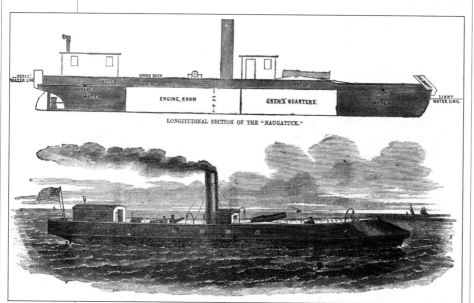

LONGITUDINAL SECTION OF THE "NAUGATUCK."

Stationed at Fort Monroe at the tip of Virginia's Yorktown peninsula, the Naugatuck was a Union gunboat whose iron plating and steam engines typified advances in naval technology ushered in by the Civil War.

commanded by Flag Officer Samuel F. Du Pont captured the prize of Port Royal Sound, South Carolina, the site of a deep harbor that served as the federal base for the South Atlantic Blockading Squadron. The keys to Du Pont's success were the maneuverability of his steam-powered warships and the explosive power of their new shell-firing guns—the Columbiads and Dahlgrens—that reduced the hastily erected forts of the rebel defenders.

Port Royal was the first in a series of Union naval victories that gained control of key strategic points along the South Atlantic coast and in the Gulf of Mexico. In the most crippling Confederate loss, a Union fleet led by Flag Officer David G. Farragut captured New Orleans, the largest city in the Confederacy and the gateway to the lower Mississippi Valley, in April 1862.

By December 1864, the size of the Union navy was up to 671 vessels, one-third of which were steam-powered ships specially constructed for the war. Of the Confederacy's major ports, only

Charleston, South Carolina, and Wilmington, North Carolina, were still open to blockade runners. And by now, running the blockade was no longer a sure thing. Whereas 90 percent of Confederate ships had evaded the blockade in 1861, the odds of being captured had now increased to one in three.

For one brief moment, it appeared that the Confederacy had a weapon that could break the tightening Union blockade. Stephen G. Mallory, the Confederate secretary of the navy, had argued in a report of May 10, 1861, that the "possession of an iron-armed ship [was] a matter of the first necessity." Earlier than his Union counterparts, Mallory had grasped that ironclad ships—the first prototypes of which were being built by the French and British—were on the verge of revolutionizing naval warfare. Once operational, such ships would render wooden navies obsolete. As a result of Mallory's initiative, the Confederacy converted the *Merrimack*, a captured and partially scuttled Union steam frigate, into the

In the turret of this Union warship, the USS Passaic, *are mounted two powerful guns: a 15-inch Dahlgren smoothbore on the left and an 8-inch rifled cannon, called a Parrott gun.*

first armor-plated warship to appear in U.S. waters. Rechristened the CSS *Virginia,* the ironclad steamed out of Norfolk into Hampton Roads on March 8, 1862, and wrecked havoc among the wooden ships of the federal squadron. Only the fortuitous arrival of the USS *Monitor,* a Union ironclad hastily built in response to news of the *Virginia* project, saved the Union fleet from a disaster. On March 9, in the world's first naval battle between ironclads, the *Monitor* fought the *Virginia* to a draw and sent it back into Norfolk. Forced to evacuate Norfolk two months later, the Confederates scuttled the unseaworthy *Virginia.*

Despite the loss of major shipyards with the fall of Memphis and New Orleans in the spring of 1862, the Confederacy managed to build 21 ironclads. However, this was less than half the number of ironclads that the Union launched, and the Confederate ironclads were unable to prevent determined Union offensives from capturing port cities throughout the war. Moreover, the Confederacy was never able to seriously contest Union naval control of navigable rivers in the West. By providing naval support and riverine lines of communication for invading federal forces, and simultaneously impeding the flow

of Confederate troops and supplies, such control was a major factor in Union victories in the western theater.

The upstart Confederate navy achieved its greatest success in disrupting Union commerce. Sleek and powerful raiders, the best of which were built in Britain, preyed upon the U.S. merchant marine throughout the war. Since it was difficult to bring captured ships back to Southern ports or to find a neutral port willing to admit them, rebel raiders aimed at destroying Union merchant ships on the high seas rather than just capturing them. They sank hundreds (after first removing the crews), drove countless others into the refuge of foreign registry, cut the volume of U.S. shipping by 60 percent, and dealt the U.S. shipping industry a crippling blow from which it never fully recovered.

For the Union, the most notorious of the rebel raiders was the *Alabama,* commanded by Captain Raphael Semmes. Built at the Laird Shipyards in England, the *Alabama,* noted executive officer John McIntosh Kell, was designed "for speed rather than battle. Her lines were symmetrical and fine; her material of the best." Mounting eight guns and powered by steam and sail, the *Alabama* roamed the Atlantic and Indian Oceans with impunity and terrorized Union shipping. Under the daring leadership of Semmes, it destroyed or captured 68 Union ships. Its 22-month voyage ended in June 1864 off the coast of France. Alerted that the *Alabama* was in Cherbourg Harbor for repairs, Captain John Winslow of the USS *Kearsarge* was waiting when Semmes came forth to give battle on June 19. After a one-hour engagement, the fearsome Confederate raider was sunk.

Few in the Union ever expected that a Confederate navy that had to be built from scratch would be as resourceful and troublesome as it became under

Mallory's command. Still, there were limits to what Mallory could accomplish with his limited resources, and the Confederacy simply could not match the size and growing strength of the Union navy. By maintaining an increasingly effective blockade, controlling western rivers, and supporting federal armies, the Union navy was instrumental in defeating the Confederacy.

SEE ALSO

Alabama claims; Blockade; Blockade runners; Du Pont, Samuel F.; Farragut, David C.; Fort Fisher; Laird rams; Lincoln, Abraham; Mallory, Stephen G.; Semmes, Raphael; Submarines; Torpedoes

FURTHER READING

Anderson, Bern. *By Sea and by River: The Naval History of the Civil War.* New York: Knopf, 1962.
Jones, Virgil C. *The Civil War at Sea.* 3 vols. New York: Holt, Rinehart & Winston, 1961–62.
Luraghi, Raimondo. *A History of the Confederate Navy.* Annapolis: Naval Institute Press, 1996.
Musicant, Ivan. *Divided Waters: The Naval History of the Civil War.* New York: HarperCollins, 1995.
Roberts, William H. *Now for the Contest: Coastal and Oceanic Naval Operations in the Civil War.* Lincoln: University of Nebraska Press, 2004.
Symonds, Craig L. *Lincoln and His Admirals: Abraham Lincoln, the U. S. Navy, and the Civil War.* New York: Oxford University Press, 2008.

Navies

SEE Naval warfare

New Mexico-Arizona operations

Although the number of troops involved was paltry compared to the campaigns east of the Mississippi River, the military operations in the Southwest had the potential to disrupt the entire Union war effort. Early in the war, the Confederacy tried to send a column of Texas troops across the Southwest to rally prosecessionist elements. The ultimate goal was the possession of California, with its gold and Pacific ports. Had the Confederacy succeeded, it could have broken the federal blockade, solidified its finances, and crippled the Union economy.

In June 1861, Henry H. Sibley, a former major in the U.S. Army, gained the backing of Confederate President Jefferson Davis to raise an army in Texas for a campaign into New Mexico. Sibley dazzled Davis with a vision of a Confederate empire in the Southwest stretching to the shores of the Pacific. Once the conquest of New Mexico was completed, Sibley predicted that pro-Confederate volunteers would rally to his army as it marched westward under the slogan "On to San Francisco." Having secured California, the Confederacy could then annex or conquer the northern states of Mexico and build a base for further expansion to the south. Davis was convinced, but he made it clear that he had neither men nor arms to spare. Sibley's expedition would have to sustain itself by attracting volunteers and capturing enemy supplies.

Even before Sibley set out from Texas in late 1861 with three mounted regiments, the Confederacy had established a beachhead of support in the Southwest. In the early summer of 1861, John R. Baylor, a captain in the Texas militia before receiving a commission as a lieutenant colonel in the Confederate army, led the Texas Mounted Rifles to El Paso and captured Fort Bliss. Baylor and his 300 men then moved up the Rio Grande Valley to Mesilla, where, on July 27, a timid

This frontal attack by the charging Texans was the key to the Confederate victory at Valverde in the New Mexico Territory.

Union commander surrendered Fort Fillmore and its supplies. A triumphant Baylor issued a proclamation on August 1, 1861, declaring that the territory south of the 34th parallel now constituted the Confederate Territory of Arizona, with himself as its military governor.

Sibley and Baylor joined forces at Fort Bliss in December 1861. Led by Sibley, a rebel force of 2,600 men started up the Rio Grande in early January. Determined not to surrender the initiative seized by Baylor, Sibley aimed at sweeping New Mexico clear of its federal defenders. His opponent was Colonel Edward R. S. Canby, commander of the Federal Department of New Mexico. Canby had spent the summer and fall organizing an army of 4,000 men from volunteers, militia, and regular U.S. troops.

On February 21, 1862, outside of Fort Craig, Sibley's Texans defeated Canby's larger force at the battle of Valverde. But Sibley chose not to fight to gain possession of the fort. Instead he pushed ahead to Albuquerque, where he

expected to find badly needed supplies for his troops. He reached Albuquerque on March 1, only to discover that the federal depot had been burned. The same fate awaited him when his force took Santa Fe on March 23. Under Canby's orders, the federal garrisons were pursuing a "scorched-earth" policy of destroying provisions. Canby's strategy, as recalled by Union General Latham Anderson, was to harass Sibley's columns from the rear and "burn or remove all supplies in his front, but avoid a general engagement, except where the position was strongly in our favor."

Sibley's supply problem was now becoming critical. This was parched and barren desert country, and the lack of food and water was as deadly a foe as any enemy army. Sibley's only hope for bringing his campaign to a quick and successful conclusion rested on capturing Fort Union, the last major federal position in the territory. He headed east to take the fort. On March 28, rebel and federal forces approaching from opposite directions clashed at Glorietta Pass in the narrow confines of Apache Canyon, 20 miles southeast of Santa Fe. By a slim margin, the federals got the best of the fight. The real Union victory, however, occurred in the rebel rear. A force of 300 Colorado volunteers fell upon Sibley's supply train and destroyed it.

Unable to resupply his troops, and outnumbered two to one once Canby moved north from Fort Craig, Sibley now could think only of the survival of his men. Detouring around the federals, who, under Canby's orders, were shadowing more than pursuing them, Sibley's men embarked on a nightmarish march across the desert to reach the safety of Fort Bliss. Once there, they learned that additional federal troops were approaching from California.

In mid-May, Sibley continued the retreat back to San Antonio. Of the 3,700 men he had brought into New Mexico, only 2,000 made it back to Texas. Thirst and starvation accounted for most of these losses. A disgusted Sibley informed Richmond that New Mexico was not worth any more Confederate "blood and treasure. I cannot speak encouragingly for the future," he added, "my troops having manifested a dogged, irreconcilable detestation of the country and the people." On that sour note ended the Confederate dream of an empire in the Southwest.

SEE ALSO
Mexico

FURTHER READING
Alberts, Don E. *The Battle of Glorietta: Union Victory in the West.* College Station: Texas A & M University Press, 1998.
Colton, Ray C. *The Civil War in the Western Territories.* Norman: University of Oklahoma Press, 1959.
Frazier, Donald S. *Blood & Treasure: Confederate Empire in the Southwest.* College Station: Texas A&M University Press, 1995.
Thompson, Jerry. *Henry Hopkins Sibley: Confederate General of the West.* Natchitoches, La.: Northwestern State University Press, 1987.

New York City draft riot

In July 1863, New York City experienced the wartime Union's worst explosion of civil unrest—four days of rioting that resulted in a death toll of nearly 150 lives. The trigger for the riot was the Union's new draft law.

Although the draft provoked sporadic resistance throughout the North, especially in the lower Midwest and Democratic districts with large numbers of immigrants, nothing came close to matching the murderous fury of the anti-draft mobs in the North's largest city. Long a hotbed of opposition to the war policies of the Republicans, New York City harbored a powerful Democratic machine that continually appealed to white working-class fears over an invasion of Northern labor markets by freed slaves. The Emancipation Proclamation enflamed those tensions, and the provisions of the draft law permitting a commutation fee of $300 or the hiring of a substitute (the going rate was about $1,000) struck the city's large class of poor, immigrant workers as a club that would force them to fight in a war that would benefit only the Republican rich. Barely surviving on annual wages of less than $500, few Irish workers could afford to buy their way out of the draft, while the rich easily could.

As the first names were being drawn by lottery for the draft, a predominately Irish working-class mob of men and women poured out of the city's slums on July 13 and terrorized draft officials and blacks for the next four days. The rioters ransacked draft offices, attacked federal buildings, looted stores, and destroyed homes of

In addition to terrorizing African Americans, the rampaging mobs in New York City's draft riot pillaged the homes of Republican businessmen believed to support emancipation and the Union draft.

the Republican elite. Most of their rage, however, focused on blacks. After burning the Colored Orphan Asylum, they hunted down and killed any unfortunate black they could get their hands on. Mattie Griffith, a white abolitionist looking on from the safety of her home, described some of the horrors inflicted on the city's black population: "A child of three years of age was thrown from a fourth-story window and instantly killed. A woman one hour after her confinement was set upon and beaten with her tender babe in her arms.... Men were burnt by slow fires."

Only the arrival of combat-hardened federal troops from Gettysburg stopped the hideous carnage. Brute force, including the killing of some 100 rioters, restored order to the city. What ensured future peace was the willingness of the city's badly shaken elite to subscribe to a $2.5-million bond issue that provided funds for the municipal government to purchase commutation fees for poor working men. Money, as well as guns, put an end to one of the worst riots in the nation's history.

SEE ALSO
Conscription; Industrial workers

FURTHER READING
Bernstein, Iver. *The New York City Draft Riots: Their Significance for American Society and Politics in the Age of the Civil War.* New York: Oxford University Press, 1990.
Cook, Adrian. *The Armies of the Streets: The New York City Draft Riots of 1863.* Lexington: University of Kentucky Press, 1974.

Nullification

The nullification crisis of 1832–33 was the most serious challenge to federal authority in the antebellum period until the outbreak of secession in the winter of 1860–61. Although the nullifiers eventually backed down, their grievances and states'-rights doctrines continued to feed a growing sense of Southern separatism.

The nullification movement

centered in South Carolina, an old cotton state mired in a prolonged economic slump in the 1820s as cotton prices fell and whites left for cheaper, more fertile lands to the west. The States Rights and Free Trade party, or nullifiers as they were popularly called, blamed these economic problems on a series of ever-higher protective tariffs passed in the 1820s by a Northern majority in Congress. According to the nullifiers, these tariffs were both unconstitutional, in that the Constitution did not specifically authorize tariffs to protect manufacturing, and grossly inequitable, in that the agrarian South bore most of the burden of the tariffs in the form of the higher prices they had to pay for manufactured goods produced in Europe and the North. In their most telling argument, the nullifiers rallied public support by proclaiming that the expanded national power embodied in protective tariffs was but a prelude to a direct Northern attack against slavery.

John C. Calhoun provided a constitutional justification for nullification in *The South Carolina Exposition and Protest* of 1828. The individual states, he reasoned, retained their ultimate sovereign power within the Union. Acting through a popularly elected convention, a state could nullify or declare unenforceable a federal law. Once nullified, such a law was to remain inoperative within that state's borders unless three-fourths of all the states approved a constitutional amendment delegating the challenged power to the national government. If such an amendment passed, the nullifying state as a last resort had the right to leave the Union.

In November 1832, a South Carolina convention nullified the tariff and declared that customs duties would not be collected in South Carolina after February 1, 1833. President Andrew Jackson denounced nullification as a constitutional travesty that would paralyze any expression of the national will. In January 1833, he asked for and received from Congress the Force Act, legislation authorizing him to use military force if necessary to put nullification down. Since the nullifiers had vowed to meet force with force, an armed conflict was a distinct possibility. Based on alarming reports sent him by Charleston Unionists, Jackson expected that "a civil war of extermination" would soon break out.

Violence was averted when Congress passed a compromise tariff acceptable to Calhoun and most of the nullifiers. In a last gesture of defiance, the nullifiers then passed an ordinance nullifying the Force Act. The immediate crisis was over, but the fears over slavery that had fueled it both persisted and intensified. When those fears led to calls for secession a generation later, South Carolina was no longer isolated among the slave states.

SEE ALSO

Calhoun, John C.; States' rights; Union

FURTHER READING

Ellis, Richard E. *The Union at Risk: Jacksonian Democracy, States' Rights, and the Nullification Crisis.* New York: Oxford University Press, 1987.
Freehling, William W. *Prelude to Civil War: The Nullification Controversy in South Carolina, 1816–1836.* New York: Harper & Row, 1965.

Nurses

Army medical services on both sides were totally unprepared for the unprecedented carnage of the Civil War. The shortage of personnel in the traditionally male-dominated medical

The two women sitting by one of the cots in Carver Hospital in Washington were probably volunteers in the Union nursing corps, which helped to alleviate the suffering of the wounded soldiers.

profession was so great that women were able to carve out new roles for themselves as nurses.

At least 3,200 women, including enslaved and free blacks, served as nurses. Nearly all of them experienced what Union nurse Sophronia Bucklin characterized as a "systematic course of ill treatment [designed] to drive women from the service." Surgeons and military officers believed that respectable, well-bred women had no place in a hospital and that no female should be exposed to unclad male bodies. Professional pride was also at stake. Doctors resented the criticisms of many female nurses that they were cold and indifferent and hopelessly ensnared in bureaucratic red tape that prevented proper care for the wounded in their charge. The boldest of the nurses bypassed their male superiors in the military chain of command and encouraged government investigators to visit the hospitals in an effort to improve conditions.

The work of the nurses was physically and emotionally draining, and their pay, especially in the Confederacy, failed to keep pace with the rate of inflation. Old prejudices against women in medicine never disappeared. When Dr. Mary Walker, one of a handful of women physicians in the Union army (the Confederate service had none), was captured on the Chattanooga front in 1864, she was a source of amusement to the Confederates assigned to guard her. Concerning this "female doctor," Confederate Captain Benedict Joseph Semmes wrote his wife that he and his men "were all amused and disgusted... at the sight of a *thing* that nothing but the debased and depraved Yankee nation could produce."

Given the entrenched values of the United States in the mid-19th century, perhaps what is most remarkable about the record of the women nurses was the genuine praise they occasionally garnered from erstwhile male critics. Frederick Law Olmstead, the executive secretary of the U.S. Sanitary Commission, commented in 1863: "God knows what we should have done without them; they have worked like heroes night and day, and though the duty is frequently most disagreeable . . . I have never seen one of them flinch for a moment." Such praise was rare, but, as indicated by the opening of nursing schools for women in Northern cities during the war, the pioneering work of Civil War nurses speeded up the entry of women into nursing as a profession.

SEE ALSO

Barton, Clara; Dix, Dorothea L.; Medicine; Military hospitals; Women in the war

FURTHER READING

Brumgardt, John R., ed. *Civil War Nurse: The Diary and Letters of Hannah Ropes.* Knoxville: University of Tennessee Press, 1980.
Schultz, Jane E. *Women at the Front: Hospital Workers in Civil War America.* Chapel Hill: University of North Carolina Press, 2004.

Officers

The vast majority of Civil War officers had been civilians when the war broke out. Nevertheless, men trained at West Point provided a solid core of leadership that was instrumental in molding the raw recruits on both sides into effective soldiers.

The number of officers in the professional U.S. Army stood at just over 1,000 men at the start of the war, and most of them were West Point graduates. Added to this number were men trained at private military academies and those who had experience as volunteer troop leaders in the Mexican or Indian wars. In all, only about 3,000 trained officers were available to command the 3 million soldiers who eventually fought in the Civil War. The war itself provided the training for nearly all the officers on both sides.

The upper echelons of command absorbed most of the officers with prior military training or experience. Just under half of all the generals in both armies were graduates of West Point and other military schools or had been civilian appointees in the regular army before the war. The Confederacy built its military leadership around the 313 officers, most of whom were Southern-born, who resigned from the U.S. Army in 1861. The nonprofessional generals fell into two categories: "political" generals, who owed their appointments to their political connections, and "civilian" generals, who worked their way up through the ranks.

Regardless of the leadership at the top, the performance of a Civil War army rested primarily on the quality of its field commanders at the company and regimental levels. Following the precedent set by the militias and

The officers of the Army of the Potomac meet with Generals Ulysses S. Grant and George Meade for a council of war at Massaponax Church, Virginia, on May 21, 1864. Grant is second from the left on the pew directly beneath the trees, and Meade is at the far end looking at a map.

volunteers, the soldiers initially elected their company officers, the captain and lieutenants. These junior officers in turn selected the regimental leaders—the colonel, lieutenant colonel, and major—subject to formal confirmation by the state governor. This system of choosing officers was in keeping with the values of a democratic society, but it often undercut the military discipline essential in a combat situation. Many soldiers soon realized how a popular, but incompetent, officer could put them at risk. As Ira S. Jeffers, a New York soldier, wrote of his captain early in the war: "he is full of fun and makes a good deal of noise but if we was a going into battle I should rather he would stay behind for he is no military man at all."

Following its woeful performance at the battle of First Bull Run in July 1861, the Union army modified the election of officers. A military board now instituted examinations to screen out incompetent officers and lay down minimal professional standards. The Confederacy followed suit a year later with a less rigorous screening system for its officers.

Thanks in large measure to an infusion of trained officers from the Virginia Military Institute, the Confederacy probably had an edge over the Union in the quality of its officer corps early in the war. The Union, however, had a deeper pool of military talent to draw on, and its generals were less likely to be killed or wounded in battle. The experienced cadre of officers that emerged in the Union armies by 1863 provided field leadership that was now equal or superior to anything that the depleted rebel armies could muster.

SEE ALSO
Armies

FURTHER READING
Buell, Thomas B. *The Warrior Generals:*

Combat Leadership in the Civil War. New York: Crown, 1997.
Warner, Ezra J. *Generals in Gray: Lives of the Confederate Commanders.* Baton Rouge: Louisiana State University Press, 1959.
————. *Generals in Blue: Lives of the Union Commanders.* Baton Rouge: Louisiana State University Press, 1964.

Pacific Railroad Acts

The Pacific Railroad Acts were at the center of the Republican program to promote economic development through governmental aid. Passed in 1862 and 1864, these acts chartered the Union Pacific, Central Pacific, and Northern Pacific Railroads. These were huge transportation projects that accelerated the transformation of the postwar economy into an integrated national market.

The growing conflict between Northern and Southern interests had prevented any Pacific railroad bill from passing Congress in the 1850s. Secession removed the obstacle posed by Southern congressmen and heightened the appeal of legislation that promised to augment the Union's wealth and strength in its war against the Confederacy.

Promoted as a military measure, the Pacific Railroad Bill passed Congress in July 1862. In chartering the Union Pacific and Central Pacific, it authorized a central transcontinental railroad running from an eastern terminus at Omaha, Nebraska, to a western terminus at San Francisco. The bill provided the railroads military protection from Indian attacks, granted alternate plots of public land on either side of the right-of-way, and pledged national credit through the loan of federal bonds. Another bill with similar provisions in 1864 chartered the Northern

This Currier and Ives print idealizes the white settlement of the West as a civilizing process of progress and prosperity spearheaded by the building of the transcontinental railroads.

Pacific Railroad running from St. Paul, Minnesota, to Seattle, Washington.

Additional transcontinental railroads chartered by Congress soon after the Civil War resulted in government subsidies that totaled 158 million acres in public lands and $64 million in federal bonds to underwrite construction. This lavish aid certainly resulted in waste and corruption, but it also speeded up the development of a newly nationalized economy knit together by rails. As consumers of heavy industrial products and as marketing outlets for the commercial agriculture they had made feasible in the trans-Mississippi West, the transcontinental railroads proved to be a sound venture in government-supported capitalism. Not only did the entire economy benefit, but the federal government also profited from the railroad charters. The railroads paid back their loans with interest, and as they opened up new areas to settlement, they increased the value of the alternate strips of land retained by the government along their rights-of-way.

SEE ALSO
Republican party

FURTHER READING
Curry, Leonard P. *Blueprint for Modern America: Nonmilitary Legislation of the First Civil War Congress.* Nashville: Vanderbilt University Press, 1968.

Paroles and prisoner exchanges

In military parlance, a parole refers to the practice of releasing prisoners of war from captivity in return for a pledge or oath not to take up arms again until formally exchanged. Paroles and exchanges were commonplace early in the war, but these arrangements broke down in 1863 when both sides accused the other of violating the exchange cartel.

When the fighting in the winter and spring of 1862 produced large numbers of prisoners, the rival armies (the Lincoln administration was always careful to avoid officially recognizing the Confederate "government") agreed to a formal exchange cartel on July 22, 1862. City Point, Virginia, in the East and Vicksburg, Mississippi, in the West were the official points of exchange. Men of the same rank were to be swapped on a one-for-one basis. A weighted system based on rank set up a series of ratios for prisoners of different ranks: a general for 60 enlisted men, a colonel for 15, and so forth. Any surplus prisoners were to be paroled.

The cartel arrangement held up for about 10 months, and it kept the population of Civil War prisons to a minimum. However, when the Union began to employ black troops, the exchanges ground to a halt. Reacting against Confederate threats to reenslave or execute captured black prisoners, the Union suspended all exchanges on May 25, 1863. President Abraham Lincoln announced he would retaliate prisoner for prisoner if any of the Union's black prisoners were murdered. In effect, the Union now held Confederate prisoners as hostages to ensure the decent treatment of its captured black soldiers in the South.

The suspension of prisoner exchanges in 1863 became a permanent Union policy. Citing the continuing refusal of Confederate authorities to exchange black prisoners on an equal basis with whites, as well as reports that released Confederates had violated the terms of their paroles, the Union rejected all Confederate efforts to resume exchanges. As a result, the prison populations soared, and controversies over the treatment of prisoners became one of the most bitter legacies of the war.

SEE ALSO
Prisons

FURTHER READING
Hesseltine, William B. *Civil War Prisons: A Study in War Psychology.* Columbus: Ohio State University Press, 1930.

Pea Ridge

Fought on March 7–8, 1862, the battle of Pea Ridge (or Elkhorn Tavern, as the Confederates named it) in the northwestern corner of Arkansas secured Union control of the key border state of Missouri. Although savage guerrilla warfare would continue to rage across the state, this Union victory broke the back of organized rebel resistance in Missouri.

The fighting at Pea Ridge climaxed a yearlong struggle for control of Missouri. In the spring of 1861, the secessionist minority in Missouri rallied behind Claiborne Jackson, the

When the war ended in the spring of 1865, the last Union soldiers released from Vicksburg returned North by the U.S. riverboat Sultana. The boat's boilers exploded en route, and it sank almost immediately. Roughly 1,900 homebound soldiers died.

pro-Confederate governor. Jackson's success in organizing a prosecessionist militia provoked a Unionist response on May 10 when Captain Nathaniel Lyon marched a group of home guards and regular troops into the rebel camp and disarmed the militiamen. Lyon then brazenly paraded the captured militiamen through the streets of St. Louis, an act that infuriated rebel sympathizers and touched off a riot that left 28 civilians dead. Moderation was now impossible, and Missouri was plunged into a civil war within the Civil War.

An overconfident Lyon was killed at Wilson's Creek on August 10 when he tried to dislodge a larger rebel force of secessionist militia under General Sterling Price and regular Confederate troops under General Benjamin McCulloch. The Confederates followed up this victory with another at Lexington in mid-September. For a brief period, the rebels controlled the southern half of Missouri. Supply difficulties and superior Union numbers, however, soon forced Price to retreat to the southwest corner of the state.

During the winter of 1861–62, each side appointed a new commander for its forces in Missouri. Samuel R. Curtis, a solid and somewhat methodical general headed the Union Army of the Southwest. His opponent was Earl Van Dorn, a bold, dashing general who was in charge of the Confederacy's sprawling Trans-Mississippi Department. Upon receiving his command in mid-January 1862, Van Dorn exuberantly wrote his wife: "I must have St. Louis—then huzza!" He confidently expected to clear Missouri of the federals and then swing his rebel forces into Illinois by the spring of 1862.

All that stood in Van Dorn's path was Curtis's army of 11,000 men. By late February 1862, that army had forced Price's Missourians to retreat into

northwestern Arkansas. Rushing west to Arkansas from his former command in Virginia, Van Dorn ordered Price to link up with McCulloch's division and a force of 2,000 Indians, mostly Cherokees, who had been recruited into Confederate service by Albert Pike. With this combined force of about 17,000 men, Van Dorn headed north on March 4, hoping to catch Curtis off guard. However, Union scouts, including one better known for his postwar exploits in the West, "Wild Bill" Hickok, alerted Curtis to the rebel advance. The cautious Curtis ordered a Union pullback to a strong defensive position backed up by Pea Ridge, just south of the Missouri border.

Rather than frontally assaulting the federal breastworks, Van Dorn sent half of his forces under Price on a night march around the Union lines for a dawn attack against the left rear of Curtis's army. Once this attack was underway, Pike's Indian troops and McCulloch's men were to slam into the federal right rear from the west end of Pea Ridge. It was a daring plan, and it might well have succeeded had Price's men not been impeded by road obstructions that delayed them from being in position to attack until 10:30 on the morning of March 7. That delay gave Curtis time to turn his army around and hastily erect a new defensive line. While one end of that line contained the main rebel attack in the vicinity of Elkhorn Tavern, the other recovered from an initial setback to throw back McCulloch's troops and their Indian allies.

General Albert Pike led the Indian allies of the Confederacy at the battle of Pea Ridge. Dressed here in Masonic regalia, Pike was a colorful character whose uneven battlefield performance led Douglas Cooper, another Confederate general, to remark that he was "either insane or untrue to the South."

Van Dorn resumed the battle on March 8. Unwilling to admit defeat, and aware that the federals now stood between him and his supply train of ammunition, he ordered a perfunctory artillery action in an effort to gauge Curtis's intentions. Curtis had correctly reasoned that the rebels were nearly spent, and he concentrated his forces at Elkhorn Tavern. After a devastating artillery barrage that the rebels, strapped for ammunition, could not return, a Union charge broke through Van Dorn's position. As Union General Franz Sigel later recounted, the Confederates "were now in precipitate retreat in all directions."

At a cost of about 1,300 casualties—the same as those for the larger rebel force—the federals had removed the last major Confederate threat to Missouri. Van Dorn, once he reassembled his troops, was ready for another crack at St. Louis, but he was ordered east on March 23 as the Confederacy consolidated troops for its counterattack at Shiloh. Van Dorn would not be returning to Missouri.

SEE ALSO

Border South; Van Dorn, Earl

FURTHER READING

Hartje, Robert G. *Van Dorn: The Life and Times of a Confederate General*. Nashville: Vanderbilt University Press, 1967.

Shea, William L. *Pea Ridge: Civil War Campaign in the West*. Chapel Hill: University of North Carolina Press, 1992.

Pemberton, John C.

CONFEDERATE GENERAL

- *Born: August 10, 1814, Philadelphia, Pa.*
- *Education: U.S. Military Academy, B.S., 1837*
- *Military service: U.S. Army: lieutenant, artillery, 1837–42; 1st*

lieutenant, 1842–50; captain, 1850–61; Confederate army: lieutenant colonel, 1861; brigadier general, 1861; major-general, 1862; lieutenant general, 1862–64
- *Died: July 13, 1881, Penllyn, Pa.*

Although a thoroughly loyal Confederate who broke with his mother and brothers in casting his lot with the South, John C. Pemberton was always suspect in the minds of his fellow Confederates because of his Northern birth. Vilified for having surrendered Vicksburg in July 1863, he never received another major command.

Despite his Quaker ancestry, Pemberton entered West Point and pursued a military career. While on an early assignment in South Carolina, he embraced the Southern position on states' rights and remained pro-Southern for the rest of his life. He fought with distinction in the Mexican War and then served at frontier outposts in the 1850s. In April 1861, he rejected a colonelcy in the U.S. Army and followed the wishes of his wife, the daughter of a Virginia shipowner, in joining the Confederate cause.

Pemberton's first major command was in Charleston, where he was responsible for the defense of the South Atlantic seaboard. Abrupt, autocratic, and quick to resort to martial law, he was unpopular from the start with Charlestonians. He then completely fell out of favor when he suggested that Fort Sumter be abandoned and replaced with Fort Wagner as the anchor of coastal fortifications. An irate Francis Pickens, the South Carolina governor, complained to President Jefferson Davis that Pemberton was "confused and uncertain about everything." Nonetheless, Davis had great confidence in the unbending Pennsylvanian, and he eased him out of Charleston in the fall of 1862 only to give him command of the Department of Mississippi and Eastern Mississippi, an area that included Vicksburg and Port Hudson, the last rebel strongholds on the Mississippi River.

Davis instructed Pemberton to consider a successful defensive stand "as the first and chief object of your command." Yet, in carrying out the assignment, Pemberton was at a serious disadvantage. However committed he may have been to defensive warfare, he had had no combat experience since the Mexican War. He was also caught in the middle of a confusing command structure in the West that subjected him to often-conflicting orders from Davis and General Joseph E. Johnston. As a result, when General Ulysses S. Grant launched his daring Vicksburg campaign in the spring of 1863, a hesitant Pemberton simply did not know what to do. In the caustic assessment of Confederate General Richard Taylor, he "then illustrated the art of war by committing every possible blunder. He fought a series of actions with fractions against the enemy's masses, and finished by taking his defeated fragments into the Vicksburg trap."

Pemberton immediately became the scapegoat for the Confederate loss of Vicksburg. Never given another army to command, he resigned his commission as a lieutenant general in 1864 and ended the war as a lieutenant colonel of artillery. After spending most of his postwar years on a farm near Warrenton, Virginia, he returned to Pennsylvania before his death.

SEE ALSO
Vicksburg campaign

FURTHER READING
Ballard, Michael B. *Pemberton: A Biography.* Jackson: University Press of Mississippi, 1991.

Peninsula campaign

Named after a peninsula formed by the York and James Rivers to the southeast of Richmond, the Peninsula campaign was the first great Union offensive of the war. Following a series of Union victories in the winter of 1861–62, this campaign in the spring of 1862 aimed at capturing Richmond and bringing the war to a quick end. Although General George B. McClellan, the Union commander, was victorious in most of the battles, his failure to seize Richmond stamped the campaign as a Union failure and provided a tremendous boost to Confederate morale.

In late July 1861, McClellan replaced Irwin McDowell as the top Union commander in the eastern theater. McClellan spent the rest of the year strengthening the fortifications around Washington and organizing and drilling a huge force that he named the Army of the Potomac. While McClellan busied himself with administrative details, a Confederate army of 35,000 men under General Joseph E. Johnston remained encamped at Centerville, Virginia, close to the Bull Run battlefield. In response to anxious proddings from President Abraham Lincoln, McClellan came up with a plan of operations in December. He proposed moving most of his army by sea to Urbanna, a small city on the Rappahannock River. Such a move, by threatening to cut Johnston's line of supplies, would force the Confederates to abandon Centerville and retreat to the south.

McClellan scrapped the Urbanna expedition when Johnston pulled out of Centerville on March 9 and took up a more defensible line along the Rappa-

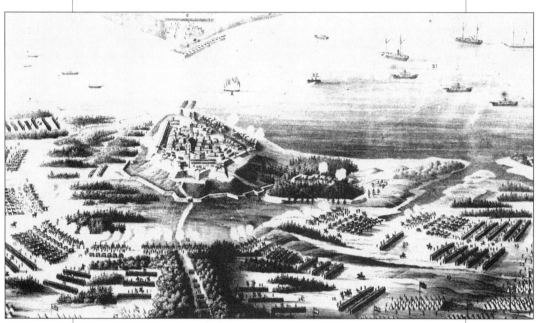

A New York soldier drew an early version of this map, which depicts federal troops besieging the Confederate stronghold at Yorktown. The Confederates are firing on the Union warships in the York River from Yorktown and from Gloucester Point, just across the river.

hannock. Still committed to moving by sea, McClellan shifted the landing site to Fortress Monroe, a Union-held position at the tip of the Yorktown peninsula, some 70 miles from Richmond. On March 17 the expedition got under way. In the next three weeks, a flotilla of Union ships transported some 120,000 men, 14,000 animals, 1,200 wagons, and more than 200 artillery pieces to Fortress Monroe. On April 4 McClellan's seemingly irrepressible juggernaut started toward Richmond.

A swift push by McClellan up the peninsula most likely would have rendered hopeless any Confederate defense of Richmond. But McClellan was a cautious general, prone to exaggerate the size of the enemy forces opposing him. He wasted a month in laying siege to Yorktown, a position initially held by a pathetically small number of rebel troops. He committed himself to the siege only after learning that the naval support he was relying upon to reduce the rebel batteries at Yorktown and at

Gloucester Point across the York River would not be forthcoming. Moreover, McClellan had counted on the 40,000 men in General McDowell's First Corps to land upriver from Yorktown and force the Confederates to retreat up the peninsula. But Lincoln, convinced that McClellan had left an inadequate force for the defense of Washington, retained McDowell's corps at the last minute and kept it out of McClellan's reach.

The Confederate line at Yorktown, one reinforced to 56,000 men by the arrival of Johnston's army, gave way on May 3. After a skirmish the next day at Williamsburg, Johnston pulled back to Richmond. The Army of the Potomac was finally on the move, and optimism ran high. "God seems to be fighting our battles and giving us victory after victory," wrote Union General Robert McAllister to his wife on May 4. "Unless the enemy turns this into a gurillar [sic] war, it will soon be over."

McAllister was wrong. By playing upon Lincoln's fears for the safety of

Washington and exploiting the faulty placement of Union troops on the peninsula, the Confederate high command kept McClellan at bay.

In late April General Robert E. Lee, now acting as chief military adviser to the Confederacy, urged General Thomas J. "Stonewall" Jackson to create a major diversion in the Shenandoah Valley and thereby prevent reinforcements from being sent to McClellan. Jackson brilliantly achieved his strategic objective. Although outnumbered three to one by the scattered Union forces in the valley, he used speed, deception, and unexpected offensive thrusts to win five battles and pin down 60,000 federal troops. Worried that Washington itself was now threatened by Jackson, Lincoln continued to hold back McDowell's First Corps.

As he approached to within five miles of Richmond in late May, McClellan kept his army divided north and south of the now rain-swollen Chickahomin River. Three of his five corps were north of the river to shield the Union supply base on the York River and to cover the still-hoped-for arrival of McDowell's corps. Johnston tried to exploit this division by sending the bulk of his army on May 31 against McClellan's southern wing. Plagued by faulty execution, the Confederate attack at the

Battle of Fair Oaks (also known as Seven Pines) bogged down and the Union position held. Severely wounded in the battle, Johnston was now replaced by Lee as commander of the Confederate army.

By mid-June McClellan had redeployed all but one of his army corps south of the Chickahominy. It was this isolated corps under General Fitz John Porter that Lee targeted in what became the first of the Seven Days Battles between June 26 and July 1. Lee battered Porter's corps at Mechanicsville and Gaines' Mill but did not soundly defeat it. Then, as McClellan began withdrawing his entire army southward to a new base of operations along the James River, Lee attacked at Savage Station and Frayser's Farm. Still, the Union army was making good its escape. Lee's last chance to smash part of it came at Malvern Hill, a ridge just north of the James that was well defended by Union artillery. Here, on July 1, the Confederates suffered 5,000 casualties in suicidal attacks. As Confederate General Daniel H. Hill recalled the scene: "Most of [the rebel brigades] had an open field half a mile to cross, under the fire of field-artillery in front, and the fire of the heavy ordnance of gun-boats in their rear. It was not war—it was murder."

The slaughter at Malvern Hill

General Philip Kearny leads his division against the Confederate rear guard at Williamsburg, on the Yorktown Peninsula. Kearny, known for his bravery in battle, told his corps commander, "I can make men follow me to hell!"

concluded the Peninsula campaign. Lee's offensive strategy had been costly. His army had casualties of more than 20,000 during the Seven Days, about one-fourth of its troop strength. Union losses, on the other hand, were about 15 percent. McClellan had executed a masterly retreat, and his repositioned army, entrenched at Harrison Landing on the James, still threatened Richmond. But Lee was the strategic victor. Richmond had been saved, and Confederate morale restored. A disappointed Lincoln, unwilling to send McClellan the massive reinforcements he demanded, soon ordered the Army of the Potomac to withdraw.

SEE ALSO

Jackson, Thomas J. ("Stonewall"); Johnston, Joseph E.; Lee, Robert E.; Lincoln, Abraham; McClellan, George B.; McDowell, Irwin

FURTHER READING

Burton, Brian K. *Extraordinary Circumstances: The Seven Days Battles.* Bloomington: Indiana University Press, 2001.
Dowdey, Clifford. *The Seven Days: The Emergence of Lee.* Boston: Little, Brown, 1964.
Gallagher, Gary W., ed. *The Richmond Campaign of 1862: The Peninsula and the Seven Days.* Chapel Hill: University of North Carolina Press, 2000.

Sears, Stephen W. *To the Gates of Richmond: The Peninsula Campaign.* New York: Ticknor & Fields, 1992.

Perryville

SEE Bragg's Kentucky invasion

Personal liberty laws

State statutes passed in the North, the personal liberty laws offered legal protection to blacks claimed as slaves in other states. Originally designed to prevent free blacks from being kidnapped and sold as slaves, the laws evolved after the passage of the Fugitive Slave Act of 1850 into measures intended to block the recovery of fugitive slaves.

The federal government first created a legal mechanism for the recapture of slaves who had crossed state lines in the Fugitive Slave Act of 1793. The act failed to provide accused fugitives with such basic legal safeguards as habeas corpus, a jury trial, or even the right to testify on one's own behalf. In response, Northern states passed laws granting these safeguards and punishing the kidnapping of free blacks as a

A reporter in the 1820s takes down the testimony of free blacks seized in the North and sold as slaves. Although it is unlikely that many kidnapped free blacks were ever able to talk to a reporter, reports of kidnappings were instrumental in the passage of the personal liberty laws.

criminal offense. Pennsylvania's antikid-napping act of 1826 provoked a challenge to the Supreme Court, and in ruling the statute unconstitutional in *Prigg* v. *Pennsylvania* (1842), a divided Court declared that the federal government alone was responsible for the recapture of fugitives. As a result, nine states enacted laws in the 1840s forbidding their officers from assisting claimants in fugitive-slave cases.

Congress responded to Southern demands for assistance with the Fugitive Slave Act of 1850. Since the act was so biased in favor of slaveowners or their agents, 10 states passed a new round of personal liberty laws aimed at impeding its enforcement within their boundaries. The strongest protest came from Wisconsin, where the highest state court declared the 1850 law unconstitutional. In *Ableman* v. *Booth* (1859), the Supreme Court overturned the Wisconsin ruling and explicitly denied the right of a state to interfere with the enforcement of a federal law. Angry Southerners demanded the unconditional repeal of all the personal liberty laws and cited them as one of the reasons why they were justified in leaving the Union.

SEE ALSO
Fugitive Slave Act of 1850

FURTHER READING
Morris, Thomas D. *Free Men All: The Personal Liberty Laws of the North, 1780–1861.* Baltimore: Johns Hopkins University Press, 1974.

Petersburg campaign

The Union campaign against Petersburg, Virginia, lasted from June 1864 through April 1865. Situated 20 miles

south of Richmond at the junction of rail lines from the south and west that provided Richmond and Robert E. Lee's Army of Northern Virginia with the bulk of their supplies, Petersburg absolutely had to be held by the Confederacy. Following a missed opportunity by the Union to seize the city in mid-June, the campaign settled into a siege during which the Union army gradually encircled the city. Finally, on April 2, 1865, federal forces broke through the Confederate lines, and Lee's army desperately tried to escape to the west.

Lee was caught by surprise in early June when General Ulysses S. Grant withdrew the Army of the Potomac from Cold Harbor and redeployed it across the James River for a strike against Petersburg. The lead elements of Grant's army under General William F. "Baldy" Smith reached Petersburg on June 15, and the city was virtually theirs for the taking. As General Pierre G. T. Beauregard, the Confederate commander in Petersburg put it after the war, "Petersburg at that hour was clearly at the mercy of the Federal

This Union signal tower was built on a high point along the Petersburg line. The soldiers of the Signal Corps stationed on the tower to relay messages in cipher by waving flags were constant targets of Confederate sharpshooters.

Once Petersburg fell, Union soldiers could safely stand on the parapets of the Confederate forts and pose like tourists for the camera.

commander." But Smith was hesitant, as were most of his troops. The futile horror of the Cold Harbor assault still haunted the federals, and they failed to press their advantage. Rebel reinforcements rushed into the city and turned back the Union's cautious attacks on June 16 and 17. Despite having massed 70,000 federals against the 14,000 defenders of the city, Grant called off the Union offensive the following day. Lee's Army of Northern Virginia was now arriving in the city, and Grant resigned himself to conducting a siege.

Even though Grant had failed to take Petersburg quickly by a direct assault, he had achieved his objective of preventing Lee from sending any troops to aid in defending Atlanta against the main Union army in the West under General William T. Sherman. Moreover, by pinning Lee in the Petersburg trenches, Grant had robbed Lee of his mobility and forced him into the siege warfare that he most wanted to avoid.

Before the siege was over, both sides constructed trenches and massive earthworks that ran continuously for about 30 miles. "We almost came to suspect," recalled Major Abner R. Small of the 16th Maine, "that the war was degenerating into a digging match." This was a war that Lee's outnumbered and nearly famished army could not win. Union troops, amply supplied from a base on the James River at City Point and a specially constructed military railroad, extended their siege line first to the east and then the west and south, stretching the thin Confederate line of defenders ever thinner.

The Union's best chance to smash the rebel defense came on July 30 with the explosion of four tons of gunpowder placed at the end of a 500-foot-long tunnel that had been dug beneath a portion of the Confederate line. The explosion produced an awesome sight. Major Charles H. Houghton, waiting to take part in the planned Union assault, recalled that "the earth along the enemy's line opened, and fire and smoke shot upward 75 or 100 feet. The air was filled with earth, cannon, caissons, sandbags and living men, and with everything else within the exploded fort."

The Union, however, failed to exploit the gap ripped open by the explosion. A black division specially trained to lead the assault was pulled back at the last minute and replaced by unprepared white troops. The Union generals not only doubted the combat-worthiness of their black troops; they also wanted to protect themselves from charges of squandering black lives in case the assault failed. As it turned out, the assault was a fiasco. After wasting precious minutes gawking at falling earth and bodies, the white federals rushed into the crater formed by the explosion rather than moving around it to rout the fleeing rebels. Milling around in the crater, these troops were an easy target for Confederate artillery. Black troops were finally committed to the battle, but by then the Confederates had organized a counterattack that caught the blacks in a withering cross-fire. The ineptitude of the assault resulted in nearly 4,000 Union casualties.

Grant relied on more conventional tactics for the remainder of the campaign. Taking advantage of his huge superiority in manpower, he kept probing for a weakness in the rebel right flank that protected Lee's rail communications. In August the Union closed off a portion of the Weldon Railroad coming up from North Carolina. As the Union net grew tighter, Lee eventually had no choice but to attack in a desperate bid to break loose from Grant's army and join the rebel forces of General Joseph E. Johnston in North Carolina. Lee's attempt to break out was turned back at Fort Stedman on March 25 in an attack that cost Lee 3,500 men, about 10 percent of his entire troop strength.

In heavy fighting around Dinwiddie Court House and Five Forks on March 31 and April 1, the federals gained control of the Southside Railroad, Lee's lifeline to the west. On April 2, a Union corps broke through the Confederate line near Poplar Spring, and that evening Lee ordered the evacuation of both Petersburg and Richmond. The campaign was over, and Lee's only hope now was to keep ahead of the pursuing federals in a last-ditch effort to find a way to link up with Johnston's army.

SEE ALSO

Appomattox campaign; Beauregard, Pierre G. T.; Grant, Ulysses S.; Grant's Virginia campaign; Lee, Robert E.

FURTHER READING

Catton, Bruce. *A Stillness at Appomattox.* New York: Doubleday, 1952.
Sommers, Richard J. *Richmond Redeemed: The Siege at Petersburg.* Garden City, N.Y.: Doubleday, 1981.
Trudeau, Noah Andre. *The Last Citadel: Petersburg, Virginia, June 1864–April 1865.* Boston: Little, Brown, 1991.

Photography

One of the most modern features of the Civil War was the use of photographs to capture the horror of battles and the

Like so many soldiers, Private Edwin Jennison of Georgia posed for a photograph before he went off to war. Barely able to shave when he enlisted, he was killed at Malvern Hill, Virginia, in June 1862.

This is the field darkroom of Samuel A. Cooley, a Union photographer accompanying Sherman's army when Savannah fell in December 1864. The wagons carried his chemicals, glass plates, and finished negatives.

grisly wounds inflicted on the combatants. The infant art of photography found a mass audience during the war, and hundreds of thousands of visual images recorded the war with a shocking sense of reality for civilians on the home front.

The earliest photographs to come out of the war were predominately of young soldiers posing stiffly for a *carte de visite*, a portrait mounted on a small card that could be sent home as a memento. The first photographic image of the war itself was a scene of Fort Sumter shortly after the Confederate bombardment. In this early stage of the war, the public relied primarily upon the drawings of artists commissioned by newspapers and magazines for actual scenes of the fighting and its aftermath.

The battle of Antietam in September 1862 marked a turning point in the visual depiction of the war. For the first time, photographers accompanying the armies recorded scenes of battlefield carnage. Within a month of the battle, Matthew Brady, the most famous Civil War photographer, mounted an exhibit of these Antietam scenes at his studio in New York City. These shocking images of the war both fascinated and appalled the viewing public. As the *New York Herald* commented: "Minute as are the features of the dead . . . you can by bringing a magnifying glass to bear on them, identify not merely their general outline but actual expression. This, in many instances, is perfectly horrible, and shows through what tortures the poor victims must have passed before they were relieved from their sufferings."

Along with the endless lists of military casualties printed in the newspapers, photographs of dead soldiers brought the war home to civilians with a frightening immediacy. Although Civil War photographers could record only static scenes, their images of the human cost of the war are still incredibly powerful today.

FURTHER READING

Davis, William C., ed. *Touched by Fire: A Photographic Portrait of the Civil War*, 2 vols. Boston: Little, Brown, 1985–86.

Milhollen, Hirst D. and Milton Kaplan, eds. *Divided We Fought: A Pictorial History of the War, 1861–1865.* New York: Macmillan, 1956.

Panzer, Mary. *Matthew Brady and the Image of History.* Washington, D.C.: Smithsonian Institution Press, 1997.

Pickett, George E.

CONFEDERATE GENERAL

- *Born: January 28, 1825, Richmond, Va.*
- *Education: U. S. Military Academy, B.S., 1846*
- *Military Service: U. S. Army: brevet 2nd lieutenant, 1846–47; brevet captain, 1847–48; 1st lieutenant, 1849–55; captain, 1855–61; Confederate army: major, 1861; colonel, 1861–62; brigadier general, 1862; major general, 1862–65*
- *Died: July 30, 1875, Norfolk, Va.*

Few, if any, Civil War figures acquired as much fame for accomplishing so little as George E. Pickett. Thanks in no small measure to the romantic fabrications spun after his death by his widow, LaSalle Corbell Pickett, his charge against the impregnable Union center on the third day of the battle at Gettysburg became part of Civil War lore and Pickett was elevated into a tragic hero.

Born into a prominent family of Virginia merchants and farmers, Pickett enjoyed a carefree youth on his father's Turkey Hill plantation just to the southeast of Richmond. By his adolescence, however, a prolonged agricultural depression left his father in no position to assure his first-born son an easy entry into the planter class and George entered the prestigious Richmond Acad-emy in 1837 to prepare for a career in law. Pulled out after two years, the young Pickett was then sent to Quincy, Illinois, to live with his uncle, Andrew Johnston, a successful lawyer-businessman. His uncle's political connections secured Pickett an appointment to West Point where he was a popular cadet, noted for devoting most of his energies to his social life rather than his studies. Soon after graduating last in a class of 59 students, Pickett found in the death and excitement of the Mexican War a sense of purpose and direction that previously had been missing in his life. He fought with distinction, earned two brevet promotions for his bravery, and committed himself to a career in the army. His marriage in 1851 to Sally Harrison Minge, the daughter of a local planter, soon ended when she died in childbirth. Pickett spent most of the 1850s on frontier duty in the West. He headed east from the Territory of Washington to offer his services to Virginia after his native state seceded.

Pickett cut quite a figure in the Confederate army. He dressed sharply in a somewhat dandified style and wore his perfumed hair in eye-catching ringlets that flowed over his shoulders. After serving as a colonel in command of the defenses of the Lower Rappahannock, he saw his first combat duty as a brigadier general during the Peninsula campaign. Although his foppish appearance raised questions about his self-control and ability to lead men into battle, he performed at least adequately before a wound received at Gaines's

General George E. Pickett enjoyed a privileged childhood as a member of Virginia's planter class. His carefree ways continued at West Point, where he was known as the class clown.

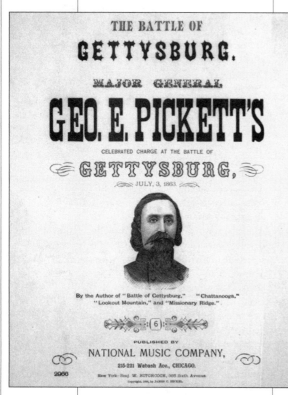

THE BATTLE OF

GETTYSBURG.

MAJOR GENERAL

GEO. E. PICKETT'S

CELEBRATED CHARGE AT THE BATTLE OF

GETTYSBURG,

JULY, 3, 1863.

By the Author of " Battle of Gettysburg," "Chattanooga,"
"Lookout Mountain," and "Missionary Ridge."

PUBLISHED BY

NATIONAL MUSIC COMPANY,

215-221 Wabash Ave., CHICAGO.

New York: Benj. W. HITCHCOCK, 385 Sixth Avenue.

In a play-by-play account, this 1888 song, published in Chicago, recalls Pickett's disastrous but glamorized assault on the Union army's center at Gettysburg.

Mill in late June 1862 required a convalescence of three months. He rejoined his command after the Antietam campaign but would see no serious combat until General Robert E. Lee ordered him into battle at Gettysburg.

Pickett's prolonged courting of LaSalle Corbell, especially the time he spent with her during the siege of Suffolk in the spring of 1863, strained Pickett's relations with his men and with Lee, his commanding general. But the third day at Gettysburg offered Pickett the opportunity for all the vindication he could ever hope for. Although three divisions, Pickett's and those of Generals J. Johnston Pettigrew and Isaac R. Trimble, were sent up the slope of Cemetery Ridge against the Union center on July 3, 1863, the attack is popularly remembered solely as Pickett's

Charge. Virginia newspapers played up the role of the state's native son and glamorized the assault into a charge. Lack of artillery support and infantry reinforcements to shore up the exposed flanks of the Confederates were among the key factors in turning the assault into a bloodbath. Exuding optimism before the assault, Pickett was inconsolable in his grief once the frightful consequences of the Confederate failure were clear.

An embittered Pickett was convinced he had unjustly lost Lee's confidence after Gettysburg. After his depleted division was placed in a defensive position in southern Virginia, Pickett lost one chance for redemption when he botched a winter expedition against the Union lines at New Bern, North Carolina. A worse humiliation followed at the battle of Five Forks on April 1, 1865. As Union troops led a successful attack against Pickett's troops, a Confederate defeat that forced Lee to order the evacuation of Richmond, Pickett was two miles away with some other officers at a shad bake.

Fearful of being indicted for war crimes related to the death of Union soldiers at Kinston, North Carolina, Pickett fled to Canada with LaSalle, whom he had married in September 1863. They returned to Virginia in late 1865 and fretfully waited for a full pardon, which finally came in 1868. Pickett failed at a number of business ventures as he struggled to support his wife and two sons. He listlessly settled down as an insurance agent in Norfolk, Virginia, where he died of "gastric fever" in 1875. Through her writings and talks on the Confederate lecture circuit, his widow succeeded where her husband had failed. She created an idealized image of Pickett as a selfless Christian warrior and a perfect Southern gentleman that blended fact and fiction into an enduring image of the man.

SEE ALSO

Gettysburg

FURTHER READING

Gordon, Lesley J. *General George E. Pickett in Life & Legend*. Chapel Hill: University of North Carolina Press, 1998.

Polk, Leonidas
CONFEDERATE GENERAL

- *Born: April 10, 1836, Raleigh, N.C.*
- *Education: U.S. Military Academy, B.S., 1827*
- *Military service: U.S. Army: brevet lieutenant, artillery, 1827; Confederate army: major-general, 1861–62; lieutenant general, 1862–64*
- *Died: June 14, 1864, Pine Mountain, Ga.*

A bishop in the Episcopal church, Leonidas Polk held a series of important Confederate commands in the western theater. His most notable military action backfired on the Confederacy. By violating the neutrality of Kentucky when he occupied Columbus in early September 1861, Polk was instrumental in committing that key border state to the Union cause.

Born into a prominent North Carolina family, Polk was intent on a career in the army until he converted to Episcopalianism in his junior year at West Point and entered the Virginia Theological Seminary after graduation. Ordained an Episcopal deacon in 1830, he quickly rose to become Missionary Bishop of the Southwest in 1838 and Bishop of Louisiana in 1841. An ardent defender of slavery, he led the movement to establish the University of the South in 1860, an institution designed to provide young Southern aristocrats with an education free from the taint of Yankee ideas.

At the start of the war, Polk lobbied President Jefferson Davis, a close friend since their days together at West Point, for a top command. His efforts were rewarded in June when he was put in charge of Department No. 2, a sprawling area that included the Mississippi Valley defenses from northern Tennessee to southern Mississippi. Despite his lack of any combat experience, he was a good choice insofar as he was a known and popular figure throughout the area of his command. However, he also had a petulant streak of insubordination that led him to overestimate his own abilities and undercut the wishes of his superior officers. As General Braxton Bragg, with whom he often clashed, later summarized his character: "Genl. Polk by education and habit is unfitted for executing the plans of others. He will convince himself his own are better and follow them without reflecting on the consequences."

Polk indeed failed to consider the consequences of his actions when he flaunted Kentucky's neutrality on his own initiative. As a district commander under General Albert Sidney Johnston in the fall of 1861, he stubbornly failed to heed warnings that Forts Henry and Donelson, the keys to the rebel inland river defense in Tennessee, needed to be fortified and strengthened. Polk did acquit himself well as a corps commander at Shiloh, but he continually feuded with Braxton Bragg once the latter took over the Army of Tennessee. Their feud culminated at the battle of Chickamauga, when Bragg accused Polk of disobeying orders. Davis refused Bragg's demand that Polk be court-martialed and transferred Polk to a new command in Alabama and Mississippi.

In May 1864, after he had misread and failed to check a devastating Union raid across Mississippi, Polk was sent back to the Army of Tennessee as the

Confederacy prepared to defend Atlanta. While surveying the federal lines outside Marietta, Georgia, he was killed by a Union shell.

SEE ALSO

Bragg's Kentucky invasion

FURTHER READING

Parks, Joseph H. *General Leonidas Polk, C.S.A.: The Fighting Bishop.* 1962. Reprint, Baton Rouge: Louisiana State University Press, 1992.

Pope, John
UNION GENERAL

- *Born: March 16, 1822, Louisville, Ky.*
- *Education: U.S. Military Academy, B.S., 1842*
- *Military service: U.S. Army: brevet lieutenant, engineers, 1842–46; lieutenant, 1846–53; 1st lieutenant, 1853–56; captain, 1856–61; brigadier general, volunteers, 1861–62; major-general, volunteers, 1862; brigadier general, regular army, 1862–82; major-general, 1882–86*
- *Died: September 23, 1892, Sandusky, Ohio*

John Pope was one of the many Union generals humbled by Robert E. Lee. Appointed in June 1862 to take command of the new Union Army of Virginia, Pope led his short-lived army for only a few months. Thoroughly outwitted by Lee at the battle of Second Bull Run in August 1862, Pope lost his command and was sent to Minnesota to deal with an uprising of the Sioux Indians.

Son of a federal judge and nephew of a U.S. senator, Pope came from a distinguished Kentucky family. He was related by marriage to the family of Mary Todd Lincoln. Following graduation from West Point and service in the Mexican War, he had an uneventful military career as a topographical engineer. On the eve of the Civil War, he was supervising the construction of lighthouses on the Great Lakes.

A tireless self-promoter, Pope used his connections to secure a commission as a brigadier general of volunteers. Based on his early war record, his relatively high appointment seemed justified. As a district commander in Missouri, he achieved some minor successes against rebel forces. Placed in charge of the Army of the Mississippi, he led a campaign in March and April 1862 that established Union control of the upper Mississippi River nearly to Memphis. These victories on the Mississippi gained Pope a reputation as an aggressive, winning general, and he was soon called to Washington and given command of all the forces in the East except those on the peninsula southeast of Richmond under General George B. McClellan.

Soon after taking over the Army of Virginia, Pope alienated his own troops by issuing a bombastic address in which he implied that the soldiers in the East had become too accustomed to retreating. "Let us understand each other," he proclaimed. "I have come to you from the West, where we have always seen the backs of our enemies." He also angered Southern whites by declaring that henceforth harsh treatment would be meted out to rebel sympathizers found within Union-occupied areas of Virginia.

An angry Lee telegraphed General Thomas J. "Stonewall" Jackson on July 27, 1862: "I want Pope to be suppressed. The course indicated in his orders if the newspapers report them correctly cannot be permitted and will lead to retaliation on our part. You had better notify him the first opportunity."

That opportunity came a month later at Second Bull Run. Completely in the dark as to Lee's strategy of sending troops into northern Virginia for a surprise offensive, Pope was caught off guard. Rashly assuming that he had the rebels on the run, he lost track of the Confederate forces closing in on him at Second Bull Run, and his army was soundly defeated. Pope retreated to Washington, where he was relieved of his command. Rather than accepting responsibility for being outmaneuvered, Pope blamed his defeat on the pro-McClellan clique within his army.

Pope remained in the army until 1886, and he held various departmental commands in the West. He died at the Ohio Soldiers' and Sailors' Home.

SEE ALSO
Second Bull Run

FURTHER READING
Cozzens, Peter. *General John Pope: A Life for the Nation.* Urbana: University of Illinois Press, 2000.
Schutz, Wallace J. *Abandoned by Lincoln: A Military Biography of General John Pope.* Urbana: University of Illinois Press, 1990.

Popular sovereignty

Associated with the Democratic party and introduced into national politics during the Presidential campaign of 1848, popular sovereignty was a doctrine holding that the settlers in a given territory should decide for themselves the status of slavery. Senator Stephen A. Douglas of Illinois popularized the doctrine in the 1850s when he wrote it into his highly controversial Kansas-Nebraska Act.

Douglas hoped that his formula of popular sovereignty would localize the problem of slavery in the territories and take the issue out of national politics.

He was wrong on both counts. Led by Abraham Lincoln, the Republicans accused him of avoiding his moral responsibility by admitting that any territory that wanted to had a right to implement slavery. On the other hand, Southerners feared that popular sovereignty would exclude slavery from the territories just as surely as would the Republicans' doctrine of congressional prohibition. Neither section was satisfied with popular sovereignty, and when applied to the Kansas Territory, the doctrine projected the slavery issue onto the very national stage that Douglas had tried to avoid.

Popular sovereignty was ambiguous as to just what point in the territorial process a decision on slavery was to be made. Southerners held that slavery was to be recognized in a territory until a state constitutional convention either legalized or prohibited the institution. To the contrary, antislavery Northerners believed that once elected, a territorial legislature could vote slavery up or down. As a result, both sections vied for political control of the Kansas Territory, and the ensuing violence produced "Bleeding Kansas."

Designed to unify the sections by eliminating national debates over the spread of slavery, popular sovereignty in practice had the opposite effect of driving them farther apart. Forces for and against the expansion of slavery were too deeply entrenched by the 1850s for popular sovereignty to offer an acceptable middle ground.

SEE ALSO
Bleeding Kansas; Kansas-Nebraska Act

FURTHER READING
Morrison, Michael A. *Slavery and the American West: The Eclipse of Manifest Destiny and the Coming of the Civil War.* Chapel Hill: University of North Carolina Press, 1997.

Porter, David Dixon

UNION ADMIRAL

- *Born: June 8, 1813, Chester, Pa.*
- *Education: sporadic schooling in lower grades*
- *Military service: U.S. Navy: midshipman, 1829–35; passed midshipman, 1835–41; lieutenant, 1841–49, 1855–57; 1st lieutenant, 1857–61; commander, 1861–62; acting rear admiral, 1862–63; rear admiral, 1863–66; vice admiral, 1866–70; admiral, 1870–91*
- *Died: February 13, 1891, Washington, D.C.*

A stocky, bearded man with a barbed tongue and a penchant for spinning tales, David Dixon Porter fit the image of a salty sea dog. A lifetime at sea taught him the tactics of naval warfare and trained him in outfitting ships for different combat situations. He was one of the most skilled Union naval officers at employing his fleet to assist the army in land operations.

Born into a distinguished naval family, Porter saw his first service at sea at the age of 10, when he accompanied his father to the West Indies to fight pirates. Following his father to Mexico, he received a commission in the Mexican Navy. After joining the U.S. Navy in 1829, he served afloat with the Mediterranean and South Atlantic squadrons and led a raiding party during the Mexican War that seized the Mexican fort at Tabasco. Frustrated at the slowness of promotions, he left the navy in 1849 for a command in the merchant marine. He returned in 1855 but was on the verge of leaving again when the Fort Sumter crisis resulted in his gaining command of the USS *Powhatan* for service in the Gulf of Mexico.

Porter's first sustained combat action came in March 1862, when he led a mortar flotilla during the Union's successful drive up the Mississippi River that led to the capture of New Orleans. He was rewarded in the fall with the command of the Mississippi Squadron, a fleet of Union gunboats that he led on the western rivers for the next 18 months. His main responsibility was to provide support for army operations, and he pursued his task with a dogged determination that emphasized results over protocol. When a young naval officer, anxious to protect his reputation after a rebel naval mine sank his ironclad on the Yazoo River, requested a court of inquiry, Porter retorted: "Court! I have no time to order courts. I can't blame an officer who puts his ship close to the enemy. Is there any other vessel you would like to have?"

Porter earned lasting fame when he slipped his fleet past the Vicksburg batteries on the night of April 16, 1863, for a downriver rendezvous with Grant's army that opened the way for the Union army to advance on Vicksburg. Of Porter's role in the campaign, Grant later wrote: "The navy under Porter was all it could be.... Without its assistance the campaign could not have been successfully made with twice the number of men engaged."

Porter attempted to play a similar coordinating role with General Nathaniel P. Banks during the Red River Campaign in the spring of 1864. But Banks was no Grant, and Porter was fortunate to escape from that campaign with his fleet intact. Following that fiasco, Porter headed the North Atlantic Blockading Squadron and participated in the joint army-navy operations that finally seized Fort Fisher in January 1865. He was in charge of the James River fleet when Richmond fell.

After serving from 1866 to 1870 as

superintendent of the Naval Academy, Porter was promoted to admiral in 1870. Although frustrated by his inability to implement what he saw as needed changes, he continued as the navy's senior officer until his death.

SEE ALSO

Red River campaign; Vicksburg campaign

FURTHER READING

Hearn, Chester G. *Admiral David Dixon Porter: The Civil War Years.* Annapolis, Md.: Naval Institute Press, 1996.

Prisons

The treatment of prisoners remains one of the most controversial features of the Civil War. Some 195,000 Union soldiers and 215,000 Confederates were detained in 150 prisons during the war. Prisoner mortality rates were high on both sides. Estimates based on surviving records indicate that 15.5 percent of federal soldiers in Southern prisons and 12 percent of rebel prisoners in the North died.

Given the expectations of a short war, no one foresaw the need for special prisons to hold captured enemy soldiers. Early in the war, when paroles and prisoner exchanges were commonplace, obsolete forts, local jails, converted warehouses, and tent camps housed a small number of prisoners on a makeshift basis for a limited amount of time. Larger, more permanent compounds became necessary only when the exchange cartel broke down in 1863 over the issue of Southern treatment of black captives and each side had to accommodate a flood of new prisoners.

After steadily rising in the summer and fall of 1863, the prison population soared in 1864. The conditions now facing prisoners, whether federals or rebels, were almost uniformly terrible. Edmund D. Patterson, a captured rebel, spoke for nearly all of them when he said of the Northern prison at Fort Delaware: "It is useless to attempt a description of the place. A respectable hog would have turned up his nose in disgust at it." Overcrowding, pathetically inadequate sanitary facilities, abominable food, filthy surroundings, and lack of medical care all combined to turn many prisons by 1864 into hellholes.

Andersonville, a Confederate stockade prison situated on a treeless, sunbaked site in south central Georgia, was the most notorious prison of all. Shortly after the war, a military tribunal convicted its commandant, the Swiss-born Henry Wirz, of war crimes. He was executed on November 10, 1865.

Opened in early 1864, Andersonville was built to accommodate 10,000 prisoners. Transfers from Virginia prisons and an influx of Union soldiers captured in the western theater soon swelled its population to a peak of 33,000 in August. Massive overcrowding (the

In the foreground of this scene from the notorious Andersonville prison is the open latrine through which ran the stream that was the camp's only source of water.

Profanity, insubordination, and theft were the most common offenses that landed soldiers in their unit's guardhouse. The more serious the offense the more humiliating the punishment, such as the barrel worn here by a petty thief or the sandwich board on the man who "tried to get a box of tobacco under false pretence."

Nº 1. *Jim how do you like the Jewelry and Uniform the Major made us a present of*

" 2. *If we hadn't been a pair of fools, we'd never got in this fix.*

" 3. *Yeah! Yeah! Barnum ought to have them fellers in his show, I think they'd pay well.*

Nº 4. *I want you what that nigger saw to laugh at; I don't think this is so very amusing.*

" 5. *If I catch any damn Reb trying to get any tobacco, I'll break his bone head for him.*

soldiers were so densely packed that each had on average only about 30 square feet of living space), shortages of even the most basic supplies, and polluted water produced nightmarish conditions that killed off more than 13,000 of the some 45,000 men imprisoned there. Its closest equivalent in the North was the Union prison at Elmira, New York, which also opened in 1864. Here, due in large measure to lack of adequate shelter from the bitter Northern winter, nearly one-quarter of the imprisoned Confederates died.

In January 1865, the Confederacy finally consented to treating blacks as equals with whites in prisoner exchanges, and the logjam in exchanges was broken. The worst of the overcrowding in the prisons eased in the final months of the war, but the resumption of exchanges came far too late for the tens of thousand soldiers who had already perished in the overpacked prisons of 1864.

Who was to blame for the horrors that the prisoners experienced? Despite mutual accusations of deliberate mis-treatment of prisoners, the real culprit was the war itself and its brutalizing impact on human sensibilities. In its defense, the Confederacy cited the collapse by 1864 of its economy and transportation system as the prime reason for the poor treatment of Union prisoners. But surely better planning could have alleviated the worst of the conditions. The Union, with its vastly greater resources, could have provided better treatment of rebel prisoners, but bureaucratic indifference and revulsion from reports of emaciated and dying federal prisoners kept that treatment from improving. Neither side can avoid responsibility for the shameful treatment of Civil War prisoners.

SEE ALSO

Paroles and prisoner exchanges

FURTHER READING

Cloyd, Benjamin G. *Haunted by Atrocity: Civil War Prisons in American Memory.* Baton Rouge: Louisiana State University Press, 2010.

Marvel, William. *Andersonville: The Last Depot.* Chapel Hill: University of North Carolina Press, 1994.

Sanders, Charles W. *While in the Hands of the Enemy: Civil War Prisons of the Civil War.* Baton Rouge: Louisiana State University Press, 2005.

Proclamation of Amnesty and Reconstruction

Announced by President Abraham Lincoln in December 1863, the Proclamation of Amnesty and Reconstruction was a wartime plan for reconstructing the Union. Lincoln hoped that implementation of his plan would weaken the Confederacy and calm the fears of Northern conservatives that emancipation would unleash violent change in the South.

Lincoln based his plan on his constitutional powers as commander-in-chief. Through the use of his pardoning powers, he set down administrative guidelines for the rapid restoration of rebel states to the Union. He required a loyalty oath pledging *future* allegiance to the Union and compliance with the wartime measures against slavery for all who wanted to participate in Reconstruction. He excluded from this offer of amnesty only high-ranking Confederate officials. For the first time, he publicly made emancipation a precondition of returning to the Union, although he did not insist that it be written into new state constitutions and said nothing about bestowing civil rights on the freed population.

In the most lenient feature of the plan, Lincoln promised executive recognition of any rebel state in which as few as 10 percent of the qualified voters of 1860 took the loyalty oath and organized a loyal state government. This was a shrewd attempt at offering Southerners a practical alternative to Confederate rule. Here, in Lincoln's words, was "a plan . . . which may be accepted by them as a rallying point, and which they are assured in advance will not be rejected here." To the surprise of few Republicans, the Confederate government scornfully dismissed the plan as another emancipation scheme and a mockery of free government. Of more concern to the Republicans were the party divisions exposed by the plan. Most Republicans felt that Lincoln was shutting Congress out of its rightful role in having a say in Reconstruction. Congressional critics blasted the plan for its failure to offer any legal protection to the freed population, and they tellingly asked what would become of the freedmen and white Unionists when unrepentant rebels regained power and overturned the 10-percent governments.

Because of these reservations, Congress refused to recognize the governments that were eventually organized in Louisiana, Arkansas, and Tennessee under Lincoln's plan. When the Republican Congress proposed its own plan for Reconstruction in the Wade-Davis bill, Lincoln pocket vetoed it in the summer of 1864. The President and Congress remained divided over Reconstruction for the remainder of the war.

SEE ALSO

Lincoln, Abraham; Wade-Davis bill; Wartime Reconstruction

FURTHER READING

Dorris, Jonathan T. *Pardon and Amnesty Under Lincoln and Johnson.* Chapel Hill: University of North Carolina Press, 1953.

Hesseltine, William B. *Lincoln's Plan of Reconstruction.* Tuscaloosa: University of Alabama Press, 1961.

Holt, Michael F. "Abraham Lincoln and the Politics of Union." In *Abraham Lincoln and the American Political Tradition,* John L. Thomas, ed. Amherst: University of Massachusetts Press, 1986.

Propaganda

In the absence of modern means of electronic communications, the Union and Confederate governments were limited in their efforts to shape public opinion in support of their respective war efforts. The Union had no official government agency to disseminate propaganda, and the Confederacy focused its propaganda ventures on Europe, where it vainly sought to gain foreign recognition. Both sides, however, were able to draw upon private and semiprivate organizations for promoting patriotic sentiments and sustaining civilian morale.

Religious sermons and the printed word were the chief means by which nationalistic sentiments were spread early in the war. Ministers, newspaper editors, and pamphleteers reached a broad audience with their calls for unity and unstinting support of the war. Colorful lithographic designs on the outside of envelopes, called patriotic covers, bombarded the public with emotionally charged symbols of the respective war efforts. The most popular designs for both the Union and the Confederacy relied on well-known symbols drawn

The rifle in this picture is a prop. Photographer Alexander Gardner and his assistants dragged this soldier's body over 70 yards from where he died and put a knapsack under his head. For publication, Gardner wrote a caption claiming that the man had been wounded and used his knapsack to rest his head before dying.

from the Revolutionary War—the flag, the eagle, and George Washington—to create a sense of nationalistic unity.

By the midpoint of the war, the governments were more consciously trying to boost civilian morale. The most effective propaganda agencies in the North were the National Union League, which was virtually an extension of the Republic Party, and the Loyal League, an organization dominated by prowar Democrats. The leagues published pamphlets calling for an energetic prosecution of the war and organized pro-Union rallies. With the financial and political assistance of the national Republican administration in Washington, they mobilized the voters in local and state elections behind prowar candidates. Meanwhile, the Committee on the Conduct of the War in Washington stepped up its attacks on generals perceived as being too lenient toward the rebels and published a series of reports on alleged Confederate atrocities.

Lacking a disciplined party organization to fall back on for disseminating domestic propaganda, the Confederacy concentrated its propaganda efforts on Europe for most of the war. Despite its use of paid agents and the successful financing of pro-Southern newspapers in England and France, the Confederacy failed to achieve its goal of European recognition. On the home front, President Jefferson Davis's government never fashioned any equivalent to the Union League in the North. Its methods of propaganda consisted chiefly of proclaiming national days of fasting and prayer, deifying fallen heroes such as General Thomas J. "Stonewall" Jackson, and warning of the horrors that awaited Southern whites if the barbaric Yankees won the war.

In 1864 the Confederacy launched its most sophisticated propaganda program. Organized by Confederate secret service agents in Canada, this clandestine operation targeted Northern civilians. By exploiting war-weariness in the North and funneling funds to Peace Democrats who were demanding a negotiated end to the war, the Confederates hoped to engineer the defeat of Abraham Lincoln in the North's Presidential election of 1864. If the Republicans lost that election, Southern independence was still a possibility. Two months before that election, however, decisive Union victories all but sealed the military collapse of the Confederacy. Those victories eliminated any chance of turning the Northern public against Lincoln and doomed the Confederacy's major propaganda offensive.

SEE ALSO
Secret services

FURTHER READING

Freidel, Frank, ed. *Union Pamphlets of the Civil War, 1861–1865,* 2 vols. Cambridge: Belknap Press of Harvard University Press, 1967.
Silver, James W. "Propaganda in the Confederacy." *Journal of Southern History* 11, No. 4 (November 1945): 487–503.

Proslavery defense

The rise of Northern abolitionism in the 1830s forced Southern whites to construct a defense of slavery. Southern ministers took the lead in combating abolitionist charges that slavery was a moral and religious abomination. These proslavery ideologues increasingly described the South as separate from and superior to the rest of the nation.

Prior to the abolitionist condemnation of the institution, Southern whites viewed slavery as a necessary evil, an unfortunate legacy from the past that was necessary to maintain racial peace. Stung by the insistence of the abolitionists that slavery was a sin, evangelical ministers in the South turned to the Bible and through a literal and selective reading found abundant evidence to proclaim that slavery was fully in accord with the moral law of God. Joined by politicians and intellectuals, they were soon portraying slavery as a positive good, an institution ordained by God as the foundation of Southern prosperity, white democracy, and Christian instruction for heathen Africans.

More common than the biblical defense of slavery was the openly racist argument that blacks were unfit to live as a free people among whites. Drawing in part on the scientific thinking of the day, proponents of slavery alleged that blacks were a lazy, inherently inferior race that would work only under white direction. If ever emancipated, according to this argument, they would rob, pillage, and rape. Without slavery to control the blacks, the South would become a wasteland.

The defenders of slavery gained few converts outside the South. To be sure, most Northern churches did not endorse abolitionism, but they did express moral concerns over slavery. Moreover, the schisms that slavery sparked in the major denominations in the 1830s and 1840s continued to divide Protestants along sectional lines. By the 1850s, international religious conventions were barring slaveholders. As for the racial defense of slavery, nothing in the internal logic of racist doctrines mandated slavery. Racial prejudice in the North shunted aside African Americans as second-class citizens without resorting to slavery.

The publication in 1857 of Hinton Rowan Helper's *The Impending Crisis of the South* revealed the limits of the proslavery message even within the

South. Helper, a white native of North Carolina, indicted slavery for stunting economic opportunities for nonslaveholding whites. His book undercut the argument that slavery fostered harmonious class relations among all whites. Once the South struck for independence, the class tensions revealed by Helper would worsen under wartime conditions.

SEE ALSO

Abolitionism; Churches; Religion

FURTHER READING

Genovese, Eugene D. *The Slaveholders' Dilemma: Freedom and Progress in Southern Conservative Thought, 1820–1860.* Columbia: University of South Carolina Press, 1992.
Jenkins, William S. *Pro-Slavery Thought in the Old South.* Chapel Hill: University of North Carolina Press, 1935.

Radical Reconstruction in the South

The Military Reconstruction Act of 1867 spawned the creation of new Republican parties in the South that, for a brief period known as Radical Reconstruction, controlled politics in the postwar South. What made Reconstruction radical was the conferral of the vote on black males. They in turn provided the bulk of the voting support for Republican state organizations that a Southern white majority always viewed as an alien presence that had to be expelled at all costs.

Three groups came together in these new parties. Northern-born whites, or "carpetbaggers" as they were pejoratively labeled, supplied most of the lead-

ership. Their voting strength was inconsequential—about 2 percent of the party total—but they held more than half of the Republican governorships, half of the party seats in Congress, and one-third of the elected Republican offices in the South. Contrary to their stigmatization as footloose adventurers bent on looting the prostrate South, most of these Republicans were former Union army officers who brought badly needed capital into a region they now viewed as their permanent home. Combined with Northern missionaries and teachers, these entrepreneurial Republicans hoped that they could usher in a new age of prosperity for the South based upon legal equality for blacks and state-sponsored support for schools, railroads, and industry.

About 20 percent of Southern whites became Republicans in the late 1860s. Branded in contemporary jargon as "scalawags"—sleazy scoundrels from the dregs of white society—these

TO THE
Freedmen.
WENDELL PHILLIPS
ON LEARNING TO READ AND WRITE.

BOSTON, July 16, 1865.

My Dear Friend:

You ask me what the North thinks about letting the Negro vote. My answer is, *two-thirds* of the North are willing he should vote, and *one* of these *thirds* is determined he *shall* vote, and will not rest till he does. But the opposition is very strong, and I fear we may see it put off for many a year.

Possibly there may be an agreement made, that those who can read and write shall vote, and no others.

Urge, therefore, every colored man *at once* to learn to read and write. His right to vote may very likely depend on that. Let him lose no time, but learn to read and write *at once.*

Yours truly,

Mr. JAMES REDPATH.   WENDELL PHILLIPS.

During Radical Reconstruction some Southern states tried to prevent African Americans from voting by making literacy a requirement. A close associate of abolitionist William Lloyd Garrison, Wendell Phillips replaced him as president of the American Anti-Slavery Society in 1865, and urged the freedmen to learn to read and write.

In the minds of most Southern whites, Radical Reconstruction unleashed untold horrors on the South and violated the sanctity of not only states' rights but white womanhood as well.

Republicans in fact came predominantly from the small farming class in the hill country and mountainous interior of the South. Most of them had been Unionists or had turned against the Confederacy, and they had long resented the rule of Democratic planters. Heavily in debt at the end of the Civil War, they turned to the Republicans for economic relief and political protection from reprisals by their rebel neighbors. Joining them as Southern-born Republicans were planters and businessmen attracted to the party's program of economic development.

The freedmen accounted for about 80 percent of the vote for the Southern Republican parties, but they held only 15 to 20 percent of the political offices. At the upper echelon of leadership, federal offices, black politicians were well-educated men drawn primarily from a Northern-born professional class of ministers, lawyers, and teachers. Out of this group came most of the 16 African Americans who served in Congress during Reconstruction. State and local offices were filled primarily by former slave ministers and artisans, those who had acquired some literacy while holding positions of leadership and trust in the slave community. At all levels of political activism, blacks eagerly embraced the Republicans as the party of freedom and equality. Public support for education and legal recognition of black equality topped the list of their political demands.

The Republicans attempted to push through significant—even revolutionary—changes in Southern life. The new state constitutions they wrote opened up politics and government through universal male suffrage and the lowering of property qualifications for a host of elected offices that had formerly been filled by appointments. The constitutions expanded the responsibilities of the states in the areas of social welfare and public services. Most important, they provided for the first state-supported systems of public education in Southern history.

Even as these changes were just being introduced, the fragile Republican coalition began to break apart. The first to leave the party were the Southern-born whites. Scorned by their fellow Southerners as race traitors, and resenting the heavy tax increases needed to pay for social programs such as public schools that now served both races, they bolted within a few years. By 1871, those states in which the Republicans had depended most on the support of native whites—Virginia, Tennessee, North Carolina, and Georgia—were either back under Democratic control or ruled by a coalition of conservative Republicans and Democrats. Three years later, the Republicans retained power only in South Carolina, Mississippi, Louisiana, and Florida, the states with the largest black populations.

The onset of a nationwide economic depression in 1873 and a continued slump in cotton prices doomed any lingering hope that the surviving Republican parties in the Lower South would be able to deliver on their promise of restoring prosperity. In toppling these governments, the Democrats effectively relied on charges of fiscal mismanagement, but their most telling tactic was the use of physical intimidation. After mobilizing white voters with appeals to racial pride and Southern patriotism, the Democrats organized paramilitary groups that broke up Republican meetings, threatened Republican voters, and, when deemed necessary, assassinated Republican activists. As part of a sectional compromise in 1877 that settled the disputed Presidential election of 1876, the Republicans in Washington abandoned what remained of their party organiza-

tions in the South. Radical Reconstruction was over.

SEE ALSO

Congressional Reconstruction; Election of 1876; Ku Klux Klan; Military Reconstruction Act of 1867

FURTHER READING

Du Bois, W. E. B. *Black Reconstruction in America, 1860–1880.* Cleveland: World Publishing Co., 1964.
Foner, Eric. *Reconstruction: America's Unfinished Revolution, 1863–1877.* New York: Harper & Row, 1988.
Perman, Michael. *The Road to Redemption: Southern Politics, 1869–1879.* Chapel Hill: University of North Carolina Press, 1984.

Radicals

The label attached to the most committed antislavery Republicans and those party members who pushed for a thorough restructuring of Southern society, the Radicals were an aggressive minority within the Republican party. Led by Thaddeus Stevens of Pennsylvania in the House and by Charles Sumner of Massachusetts in the Senate, they played an influential role during the Civil War and Reconstruction.

From the very beginning of the war, the Radicals, like the abolitionists and Northern free blacks, demanded an immediate end to slavery through the war powers of the federal government. The Radicals also led congressional efforts to enlist blacks as soldiers, expand civil rights for blacks, and force new state governments based on egalitarian principles on defeated portions of the Confederacy. Although differing sharply with President Abraham Lincoln on issues of timing and political tactics, they were Lincoln's most loyal supporters on the sweeping war measures that enhanced national powers in a successful prosecution of the war.

The heartland of Republican radicalism was in the rapidly growing rural areas and small towns of the upper North settled by reform-minded New Englanders and their descendants. Like many of the Radicals themselves, these Republicans were upwardly mobile entrepreneurs and farmers who embraced the free-labor ideal of a country in which individual merit was the only mark of social distinction. Senator Sumner spoke to that ideal when he proclaimed, "For the sake of the whole country [and] for the sake of reconciliation, which can be complete only when justice prevails, we must insist upon Equal Rights as the condition of the new order of things."

The Radicals represented a significant segment of public opinion in the North, but their ability to set much of the agenda for Reconstruction after the war resulted primarily from the intransigence of President Andrew Johnson. Once it was clear by the spring of 1866 that Johnson wanted to shut Congress out of any say in Reconstruction and was prepared to permit Confederate leaders to return to power and ignore the rights of former slaves and white Unionists in the South, momentum shifted to the Radicals.

The most unified of all the Republican factions, the Radicals were also the most persistent in their demands that the North not forfeit the fruits of its victory. Their call for subjecting the defeated South to the full weight of federal authority and for underwriting a national commitment to equal rights soon provided the basis of the Republicans' program for Reconstruction. Although Congress rejected Stevens's plan for revolutionizing Southern society by distributing the confiscated land of planters to the freedmen, it eventually endorsed the Radicals' call for black suffrage.

Republican radicalism had spent itself as a political force by the early 1870s. As the former rebel states returned to the Union, the North quickly lost interest in Reconstruction. The Republican party was now more concerned in forging alliances with businessmen than in enforcing the egalitarian principles championed by the Radicals.

SEE ALSO

Congressional Reconstruction; Committee on the Conduct of the War; Republican party; Stevens, Thaddeus; Sumner, Charles; Wartime Reconstruction

FURTHER READING

Trefousse, Hans L. *The Radical Republicans: Lincoln's Vanguard for Racial Justice.* New York: Knopf, 1969.

When the Republicans came to power in South Carolina after the passage of the Military Reconstruction Act in 1867, African Americans dominated the radical faction of the party.

Raids

Temporary incursions into enemy territory by rapidly moving forces, raids accounted for a majority of the military encounters in the Civil War. Confederate raids in the West prolonged the war by forcing a dispersal of federal forces to defend territory and communications. By 1863, the Union was countering with its own raids aimed at the economic resources and civilian morale of the Confederacy.

Confederate cavalry raiders such as Generals John Hunt Morgan and Nathan Bedford Forrest continually bedeviled the Union war effort in the western theater. Their slashing raids in Kentucky, Tennessee, and northern Mississippi pinned down large numbers of federal forces and kept them off bal-

This rebel guerrilla raid illustrates the savagery of the marauding bands of federals and rebels who terrorized civilians in the western settlements along the Missouri-Kansas border.

ance. Exasperated by their success in the winter of 1862–63, President Abraham Lincoln remarked: "In no other way does the enemy give us so much trouble, at so little expense to himself, as by the raids of rapidly moving small bodies of troops... harassing, and discouraging loyal residents, supplying themselves with provisions, clothing, horses, and the like, surprising and capturing small detachments of our forces, and breaking our communications."

By the spring of 1863, Lincoln was shrewdly encouraging his commanders to launch raids in retaliation. Most of these raids consisted of small detachments of cavalry swarming over rebel countryside in quick-striking, ravaging expeditions. Their purpose, as noted by Union Quartermaster General Montgomery C. Meigs, was "never to pass a bridge without burning it, a telegraph wire without cutting it, a horse without stealing or shooting it, a guerrilla without capturing him, or a negro without explaining the President's proclamation [on emancipation] to him."

In 1864 the Union high command incorporated massive, army-sized raids into its grand strategy for winning the war. Recognizing the futility of trying to destroy Confederate armies in the field, this strategy made Confederate supply lines, economic resources, and morale more of a target than the rebel armies themselves. The raids sent large infantry units, supported by cavalry, against railroads, telegraph lines, factories, crops, and indeed any resource that might be used to support or move Confederate armies. Their purpose was to deprive rebel armies of their mobility and sustenance while simultaneously relieving Union armies of the need to detach troops to protect occupied areas and the supply lines leading into them.

General William T. Sherman's march across Georgia in the fall of

1864 remains as the best-known of these large-scale raids. No other Union operation was so successful in undermining the confidence of Southern civilians in the Confederacy. In terms of sheer economic damage, however, it could not match the Union raid in the early spring of 1865 directed by General James Wilson. Wilson's raid demolished the remaining industrial base of the Confederacy by razing the ordnance and foundry centers of Selma, Alabama, and Columbus, Georgia. Such raids left much of the defeated South in shambles at the war's end.

SEE ALSO

Logistics; Sherman's March to the Sea; Strategy

FURTHER READING

Jones, James P. *Yankee Blitzkrieg: Wilson's Raid through Alabama and Georgia.* Athens: University of Georgia Press, 1976.

Ramage, James A. *Rebel Raider: The Life of General John Hunt Morgan.* Lexington: University of Kentucky Press, 1986.

Railroads

The Civil War marked the first use in warfare of railroads to move and supply large armies in the field. Roadbeds, rolling stock, and rail junctions thus became vital strategic assets. The Union always had rail superiority, and this advantage became overwhelming as the war progressed.

A Civil War army required tons of supplies a day. Without secure access to a navigable river or a railroad, it would have withered and died in the field. The Union began the war with 22,000 miles of railroads, more than twice as much as the 9,000 miles in the Confederacy. This disparity widened as the North

continually improved the operating efficiency of its rail network and, under the government-operated U.S. Military Rail Roads, acquired or built more than 2,000 miles of track in occupied areas of the South. On the other hand, the rebel rail system all but disintegrated. The Confederacy lacked the industrial capacity to maintain or replace its railroads and, in the one undeniable success of the Union blockade, was unable to import track and rolling stock. As Southern railroads broke down or were captured, the Confederacy found it increasingly difficult to furnish its soldiers and factories with the supplies necessary to carry on the war.

In the West, where the Confederacy lost the war, Union control of rivers and railroads was critical to federal victories. The only east-west rail lines that connected Richmond to the Mississippi River—the Memphis and Charleston, and, via a circuitous route in Kentucky, the Memphis and Ohio—were unavailable to the Confederacy for most of the war. Meanwhile, the early success of a federal campaign in what became West Virginia secured Union control of the

Union General William Tecumseh Sherman declared that "railroads are the weakest thing in war." Retreating Confederates destroyed this section of the Orange and Alexandria Railroad in central Virginia by pulling up light rails and placing them across piles of ties. When lit, the ties heated the rails, which then sank of their own weight into a useless heap.

Baltimore and Ohio Railroad, the main line that connected Washington to the Midwest.

For all their importance, there was still much truth in Union General William T. Sherman's observation early in the war that "railroads are the weakest thing in war; a single man with a match can destroy and cut off communications." An army, especially an invading one, that depended upon a railroad was highly vulnerable to sabotage and guerrilla attacks on its line of communications. Offensive operations for that army had to wait while its commander built up a string of rail depots to accumulate supplies and forward them to advancing troops. To overcome these limitations, the Union turned to massive raids late in the war as a way to restore speed and maneuverability to its offensive operations. The raiders moved from one secure base to another while temporarily living off the land. Sherman's devastating march across Georgia was the most famous of these raids.

SEE ALSO

Logistics; Raids

FURTHER READING

Black, Robert C. *The Railroads of the Confederacy.* Chapel Hill: University of North Carolina Press, 1952.
Clark, John E., Jr. *Railroads in the Civil War.* Baton Rouge: Louisiana State University Press, 2001.
Turner, George E. *Victory Rode the Rails: The Strategic Place of Railroads in the Civil War.* Indianapolis: Bobbs-Merrill, 1953.
Weber, Thomas. *The Northern Railroads in the Civil War, 1861–1865.* New York: King's Crown Press, 1953.

Reconstruction

SEE Congressional Reconstruction; Johnson's program of Reconstruction; Military Reconstruction Act of 1867; Proclamation of Amnesty and Reconstruction; Radical Reconstruction in the South; Wartime Reconstruction

Recruiting bounties

As the brutality of the war sank in and enlistments began to dry up by the summer of 1862, the Union increasingly resorted to cash bounties as a means of spurring volunteer enlistments. (The cash-starved Confederacy also offered bounties, but the sums involved were paltry compared to Northern expenditures.) The cost of the bounties was considerable. Governments at all levels in the North paid more than $500 million in bounties.

In calling upon the states to supply 300,000 additional men in the summer of 1862, the War Department assigned each state a quota. Desperate to avoid federal conscription, state and local governments competed for recruits by offering enlistment bounties. The competition heated up a year later when Congress instituted a national draft with the provision that it would be inoperative in congressional districts that met their quota of volunteers.

By parlaying a federal bounty of $300 authorized in October 1863 with bounties offered by cities and counties, a clever recruit could receive a total of about $1,000. At a time when a workingman's annual wages ranged between $300 and $600, such a cash sum was a sizable inducement to join up. Indeed, the monetary reward was so great that a class of bounty jumpers emerged. These men would take the money, leave their unit before fighting, collect more bounties under a different name in another location, desert again, and continue

The playful banter in this scene belies the seriousness with which many draft-eligible Northerners sought out substitutes for their military service.

SCENE, FIFTH AVENUE.

HE. "Ah! Dearest Addie! I've succeeded. I've got a Substitute!"
SHE. "Have you? What a curious coincidence! And *I* have found one FOR YOU!"

the process as long as they could.

The bounty system was inherently unfair in that it rewarded volunteers in the last two years of the war with higher cash payments than the pre-bounty volunteers of 1861–62 who chose to re-enlist. As Union Private Wilbur Fisk of New Hampshire put it in writing home in January 1864: "Having been engaged in our country's service so long, and proved our ability to endure its toils and privations, it never occurred to us that our services brought a lower price in the market than those of new recruits." And, without a doubt, these recruits were more likely to desert or shirk their duties than the veterans. Union General Ulysses S. Grant estimated that no more than one in eight of the high-bounty recruits was a good combat soldier. The best that can be said of the bounty system is that it offered a noncoercive means of bringing new volunteers into the Union army.

SEE ALSO

Conscription; Desertion

FURTHER READING

Murdock, Eugene C. *Patriotism Limited, 1862–1865: The Civil War Draft and the Bounty System.* Kent, Ohio: Kent State University Press, 1967.

Red River campaign

Motivated more by political and economic considerations than any specific strategic objective, the Red River campaign in the spring of 1864 was an abysmal Union failure. This federal drive up the Red River in northwestern Louisiana aimed to bring out immense stores of rebel cotton and shore up political support for the Unionist government that President Abraham Lincoln was trying to organize in Louisiana. Henry W. Halleck, Lincoln's chief of staff, also envisioned the campaign as the springboard for a federal invasion of east Texas. None of these objectives were achieved.

The Lincoln administration committed itself to the Red River campaign before the appointment of General Ulysses S. Grant in March 1864, as overall commander of Union armies. Grant reluctantly went along with an operation that he felt squandered Union military strength in the West. He believed that the best use for the army and naval units assigned to the campaign would have been a move against Mobile to open up a corridor into Alabama from the Gulf of Mexico and to pin down rebel troops that otherwise would be sent east to defend Atlanta. General William T. Sherman, Grant's top commander in the West, also had little enthusiasm for the Louisiana operation. Like Grant, he supported it on the understanding that it would be conducted as a quick raid that would soon free the troops for more important Union offensives in Alabama and Georgia.

Unfortunately for Grant and Sherman, the commander in charge of the

This loading chute sent cotton bales down the steep slope to the waiting steamboat for shipment to market. When normal trading channels were blocked during the war, the Confederacy stockpiled cotton along river-banks; the seizure of the stockpile on the Red River was a prime objective of the Union's Red River campaign.

Red River campaign, General Nathaniel P. Banks, was neither a forceful leader nor a keen strategist. Appointed to a top command because of his political strength in Massachusetts, he mismanaged the entire operation. The plan called for Banks to move up the Red River with 17,000 troops and link up with 10,000 federals led by General A. J. Smith on loan from Sherman's army. Additional support was to come from 15,000 troops under General Frederick Steele advancing into northern Louisiana from Arkansas. Accompanying the ground forces was the most powerful Union flotilla yet assembled on western waters: 13 ironclads and 7 gunboats under Admiral David D. Porter.

Escorted into the Red River by Porter's flotilla, Smith's force reached Alexandria on March 18, where it was joined a week later by Bank's expedition. Despite assurances to Sherman that he would be in Alexandria before Smith, Banks had delayed his departure from New Orleans to oversee the inauguration of a Union governor. Once in Alexandria, Banks continued to dawdle. He supervised elections for Union candidates and tried to sort out the scram-

bling for cotton by military personnel and private speculators. He was also concerned with the abnormally low level of the Red River, which made it difficult for the navy to travel upriver. When he did leave Alexandria on April 2, he was confused and hesitant. Baffled by the terrain, he failed to find a road that ran up the west bank of the river and instead allowed his army to become strung out on an interior road that took it away from the river and naval support. It was along this road that the Confederates counterattacked.

General Richard Taylor, the son of former President Zachary Taylor, commanded a Confederate force of about 14,000 men in Louisiana. On April 8, he struck Banks's army at Sabine Crossroads near Mansfield. Taken by surprise and outflanked on both sides, the federals soon panicked and fell back in a rout. John Russell Young, a Northern reporter in the rear, wrote that "suddenly there was a rush, a shout, the crashing of trees, the breaking down of rails, the rush and scamper of men.... [W]e found ourselves swallowed up, as it were, in a hissing, seething, bubbling whirlpool of agitated men." The federals regrouped at Pleasant Grove, 10 miles to the south, where they turned back another attack by Taylor's troops on April 9.

Despite his victory at Pleasant Grove and the superiority in numbers that he still held, Banks now decided to retreat and give up the campaign. The Union fleet was in danger of being marooned at Alexandria by the low level of the Red River, and Steele's force from Arkansas was nowhere to be seen. Held up by rebel cavalry and guerrillas, it was eventually forced to turn back.

Banks was fortunate to get back to the safety of southern Louisiana. Only the ingenuity of Lieutenant Colonel Joseph Bailey, an engineer and former lumberman from Wisconsin, in rigging up a dam and jetties to raise the Red River enabled Porter's fleet to pass the rapids above Alexandria. And only the decision of General Edmund Kirby Smith, Taylor's commanding officer in the Confederate Trans-Mississippi Department, to send rebel reserves north into Arkansas saved Banks's army from having to fight its way through a large rebel force blocking its retreat. As it was, Banks lost five Union boats and tons of supplies on the retreat, and his army had to beat off harassing attacks along the way.

Banks's disastrous campaign had brought out little cotton, failed to extend Union political control in Louisiana, and forced Grant's planned move against Mobile to be postponed for several months. Without the need to defend against a Union thrust into Alabama in the spring of 1864, the Confederacy was able to shift an additional 15,000 troops to the defense of Atlanta. It is no wonder that Banks never received another field command.

SEE ALSO

Banks, Nathaniel P.; Grant, Ulysses S.; Porter, David Dixon; Sherman, William T.; Smith, Edmund Kirby

FURTHER READING

Johnson, Ludwell H. *Red River Campaign: Politics and Cotton in the Civil War.* Baltimore: Johns Hopkins University Press, 1958.
Joiner, Gary D. *Through the Howling Wilderness: The 1864 Red River Campaign and Union Failure in the West.* Knoxville: University of Tennessee Press, 2006.

Reform

One of the features that differentiated the antebellum North and South was the greater willingness of Northerners to embrace a host of reform movements that emerged after the War of 1812. The impetus for reform was strongest in those areas of the North where traditional social and economic relations were undergoing wrenching changes associated with the spread of cities, factories, and commercialized farms. In relative terms, the South experienced far fewer of these changes, and the overriding need to protect slavery always acted as a brake on reform activities.

The religious revivals of the 1820s and early 1830s spread the message that all Christians, not just those predestined by God to be saved, could aspire to and attain salvation. All individuals, preached the revivalists, were accountable for their own actions. By seeking God's grace and committing themselves to lives of Christian perfectionism, the converted could cleanse themselves and society of sin. Here was the religious message that triggered Northern reform movements aimed at social improvement.

The reformers began by establishing Sunday schools, Bible-tract societies, and missionary endeavors. By the 1830s, they helped lobby for institutional changes that resulted in state-supported

Charles Finney, the North's most successful evangelist, used this revival tent for his religious crusade in upstate New York in 1824. Evangelical fervor fueled many of the North's reform movements.

FURTHER READING

Abzug, Robert. *Cosmos Crumbling: American Reform and the Religious Imagination*. New York: Oxford University Press, 1994.

Mintz, Steven. *Moralists and Modernizers: America's Pre–Civil War Reformers*. Baltimore: Johns Hopkins University Press, 1995.

Refugees

systems of public education and new asylums for orphans and the mentally ill. Their greatest success came in the temperance crusade, a mass-based movement aimed at prohibiting the production and consumption of alcohol. The per capita consumption of alcoholic beverages fell four times over between 1820 and 1850. Women, notably those in the evangelical middle class, provided the bulk of the grassroots support for all these reforms.

Abolitionism and the drive for women's rights were the most radical extensions of the reform impulse. Both causes struck directly at the religiously sanctioned male-dominated and slave-based society of the South. Southerners recoiled in anger from what they increasingly viewed as an endless spiral of fanatical reforms that threatened social chaos. As a Louisiana editor put it in 1860, Northern reformers, especially those who had joined the antislavery Republican party, were unreasoning extremists who would stop at nothing in "promulgating the teachings of their accursed fanaticism." Northern notions of reform and progress became one more factor in driving the South to secede.

SEE ALSO

Abolitionism; Women's rights movement

Upwards of 250,000 Southern whites became refugees during the Civil War. Most often, they chose to flee from the advance of Union armies, but as the war progressed, Union commanders increasingly expelled them from occupied areas. As the refugees crowded into the shrinking boundaries of the Confederacy, they placed an additional burden on the already beleaguered Southern home front.

From a trickle of Southern sympathizers who evacuated the area around Washington in the early months of the war, the flow of uprooted civilians picked up considerably in 1862. Federal invasions of northern Virginia, Tennessee, and Southern coastal regions sent tens of thousands of civilians deeper into the Confederacy. At the same time, large numbers of whites from the border states of Maryland, Kentucky, and Missouri, which had remained loyal to the Union, voluntarily left to cast their lot with the Confederacy.

Most of these refugees now became homeless wanderers, and they remained so for the rest of the war as Union raids and invasions continually swelled the refugee population. Women made up a disproportionate number of this displaced class. Fearing for the safety of themselves and their families in the absence of menfolk off in the Confederate army, and unwilling to accept Yankee rule, they packed what belongings they could onto a wagon and braced themselves for the uncertainties of refugee life. Most often, they left behind most of their possessions as well as their homes.

Whenever possible, wealthier refugees forced their slaves to accompany them. In directly threatened regions, Confederate authorities urged and then ordered them to do so as a way of keeping as many slaves as possible out of Union hands. These unwilling black refugees traced a path of migration that carried them in the lower Mississippi Valley from the Gulf states to Texas, and in the East from exposed coastal areas to the uplands.

Refugees accompanied by their slaves were in the best position to support themselves. Hiring out their slaves in a new locale gave these refugees a badly needed source of cash income and relieved them of the cost of feeding their slaves. It also aroused the envy and resentment of local nonslaveholders who were being impoverished by the war. Nothing angered townspeople so much as wealthy refugees whose slaves enabled them to lord it over the local population. In turn, planter refugees snubbed their poorer neighbors as their social inferiors. As Meta Morris Grimball, a wealthy Charlestonian refugeeing in the upcountry village of Spartanburg, South Carolina, said of the local citizens, they were "of low character in morals."

Hostility toward refugees was widespread and grew worse as their numbers multiplied during the last half of the war. In the absence of a national Confederate relief program, poorer refugees were unwelcome because their new communities would have to support them in some way. The flood of refugees intensified shortages of food and housing. Both prices and the crime rate soared as refugees gathered in Southern cities, many of which doubled in population in the course of the war. Well aware of the additional strain that refugees placed on overtaxed Confederate resources, Union General William T. Sherman ordered the mass evacuation of Atlanta, Georgia, after he captured the city in September 1864.

"There is no doubt…that there is suffering, and the refugees are the principal sufferers," noted the *Athens Southern Banner,* a Georgia newspaper, in April 1864. Despite their plight, the refugees received no government aid during the war except for the sporadic efforts of the Union or Confederate

This refugee family is trying to get behind Union lines. By depriving the Confederacy of their labor services, the fugitives strengthened the Union war effort.

army. In March 1865, the Union Congress chartered the Freedmen's Bureau to provide emergency supplies and to assist the displaced in returning to their homes. For most of the Southerners who had lost everything in the war, however, this aid was too little, too late.

SEE ALSO
Freedmen's Bureau; Women in the war

FURTHER READING
Grimsley, Mark. *The Hard Hand of War: Union Military Policy Toward Southern Civilians, 1861–1865.* New York: Cambridge University Press, 1995.
Massey, Mary Elizabeth. *Refugee Life in the Confederacy.* Baton Rouge: Louisiana State University Press, 1964.

Religion

Despite a massive influx of Catholic immigrants between 1845 and 1855, Protestantism was the dominant religion in the United States on the eve of the Civil War. As a result of a wave of revivals in the first third of the 19th century known as the Second Great Awakening, most Protestants in both the North and the South subscribed to the tenets of evangelical Christianity. Nonetheless, once the slavery issue split the major Protestant denominations— Methodists, Baptists, and Presbyterians—into separate sectional camps by 1845, religion became another factor driving Americans apart along sectional lines.

Revivalist ministers won converts by preaching that the individual alone was accountable to God for his or her salvation. By renouncing sin, the individual could will an infusion of God's forgiving grace in the conversion experience. Once converted, evangelicals could aspire—indeed were expected— to lead lives of active Christian benevolence in which they rooted out sin. In the North, this religious impulse triggered a host of reform movements aimed at social betterment in the antebellum period. The most radical of these reform efforts was abolitionism. For many Northern evangelicals, slavery was the greatest sin because it denied its victims their God-given right to determine their own moral destiny.

Most Northern evangelicals never did become abolitionists. But once some Northern evangelicals began to turn to abolitionism in the 1830s, a sharp

Members of the 31st Ohio Volunteers gather to hear their chaplain preach at Camp Dick Robinson, Kentucky, in November 1861. Army chaplains were always in short supply, but they played a key role in the religious revivals that swept through both armies.

reaction in the South was inevitable. Southern evangelical ministers took the lead in rejecting the abolitionist view that slaveholding was a sin per se, and they pulled their churches out of the national denominations rather than accept the position of abolitionist evangelicals that Christian fellowship demanded a renunciation of slavery. Certain that holy Scripture sustained the holding of slaves, Southern theologians branded their Northern counterparts as infidels for violating God's word. They also turned to the Bible in renouncing any notions of universal rights and social perfection. They pointed to the biblically sanctioned patriarchal authority of the husband over his wife, his children, and his slaves as the model of subordination upon which all Christian societies should rest.

Religion played a central role in forging a sense of separate sectional identities in the generation that fought the Civil War. Depending on the section in which they lived, Protestant Americans increasingly worshiped either a pro- or antislavery God, and they were certain that God was on their side when the war began. Mass revivals swept the armies on both sides in 1863 and 1864. Converted Union soldiers gained confidence that God was willing them on to victory, and Confederates found solace from the war's horrors as they steeled themselves to fight on. The same religious convictions that helped bring on the war also sustained it to the end.

SEE ALSO

Abolitionism; Churches; Reform; Proslavery defense

FURTHER READING

Carwardine, Richard J. *Evangelicals and Politics in Antebellum America.* New Haven, Conn.: Yale University Press, 1993.
Miller, Randall M., Harry S. Stout, and Charles Reagan Wilson, eds. *Religion and the American Civil War.* New York: Oxford University Press, 1998.
Shattuck, Gardiner H., Jr. *A Shield and a Hiding Place: The Religious Life of the Civil War Armies.* Macon, Ga.: Mercer University Press, 1987.
Snay, Mitchell. *Gospel of Disunion: Religion and Separatism in the Antebellum South.* New York: Cambridge University Press, 1993.
Scott, Sean A. *A Visitation of God: Northern Civilians Interpret the Civil War.* New York: Oxford University Press, 2011.

Republican party

The most successful third party in U.S. history, the Republicans captured the Presidency in 1860, just six years after their party's founding. For the next 14 years, as they first shaped Union war policy and then implemented a program of Reconstruction for the defeated South, the Republicans remained the dominant party in national life.

Although the origins of the Republicans dated back to the Liberty and Free-Soil parties of the 1840s, both of which pushed antislavery into national politics and opposed the spread of slavery, the party did not come together until 1854, when Northerners abandoned former party ties and joined a new antislavery coalition. Northern anger over the Kansas-Nebraska Act was the catalyst that drove antislavery or "Conscience" Whigs, anti-Nebraska Northern Democrats, Free-Soilers, and former Liberty party members into the Republican ranks. What united these diverse groups was their determination to prevent the expansion of slavery.

For the first two years of their existence, the Republicans competed with the nativist and anti-Catholic Know-Nothing party to replace the Whigs as the major opposition party to the

Democrats in the North. The turning point in the party's fortunes came in May 1856, when the caning of Senator Charles Sumner (Republican–Massachusetts) by Representative Preston Brooks of South Carolina, combined with the sacking of Lawrence, Kansas, by a proslavery mob, dramatically highlighted the Republican charge that a "Slave Power" conspiracy of Southerners threatened the liberties of Northern whites. Antislavery Know-Nothings and conservative Whigs now joined the Republicans, and the party pushed the Know-Nothings into the background. Running behind John C. Frémont on a platform denouncing slavery as a "relic of barbarism" and opposing its spread into the territories, the Republicans carried 11 of the 16 free states in the 1856 Presidential election. Had Frémont also won Pennsylvania and Indiana or Illinois, he would have gained the Presidency.

The key to the Republican strategy in 1860 was increasing its vote throughout the lower North, the belt of states running westward from New Jersey through Illinois. Victory here, combined with holding onto the states that had voted Republican in 1856, would deliver the Presidency. Abraham Lincoln, a former Whig from the critical state of Illinois, met the party's need for a candidate who combined a moderate image with undeniable antislavery credentials. The party's 1860 platform also toned down the antislavery rhetoric of 1856 and adopted economic planks calling for a protective tariff, free homesteads, internal improvement, and a Pacific railroad.

Much to the surprise—indeed shock—of the Republicans, Lincoln's victory in 1860 was so unacceptable to so many Southern whites that 11 slave states had seceded from the Union by the spring of 1861. The cause of the Union, of majority rule itself, now supplanted opposition to slavery as the major political force in Northern public life. In pledging to preserve the Union, however, the Republicans did not lose sight of the antislavery principles that had given birth to the party. In a step-by-step process, Lincoln moved the Union toward a policy of emancipation that culminated in the passage of the 13th Amendment in 1865.

In their confrontation over Reconstruction with President Andrew Johnson after the war, the Republicans continued the process of nation-building they had begun during the Civil War. Their program of Reconstruction for the South entailed a vast expansion of federal power, especially in the constitutional sphere, and at least momentarily held out the promise of using national authority to secure equal rights for all American men. With the passage of the 15th Amendment in 1870, the Republicans reached the limits of their reforming efforts, and no unifying principles, except those of winning and holding office, emerged to set the party on a new course.

Massive scandals in the administration of President Ulysses S. Grant and the onset of an economic depression in 1873 cost the Republicans dearly, as the Democrats made huge gains in the congressional elections of 1874. The long era of Republican dominance was over. As Reconstruction came to an end, the

Democrats were now fully competitive with the Republicans in national politics.

SEE ALSO

Bleeding Kansas; Congressional Reconstruction; Democratic party; Election of 1860; 15th Amendment; Free-labor ideology; Kansas-Nebraska Act; Liberal Republicans; Radicals; Sumner, Charles; 13th Amendment; Union politics; Whig party

FURTHER READING

Foner, Eric. *Reconstruction: America's Unfinished Revolution, 1863–1877.* New York: Harper & Row, 1988.
Gienapp, William E. *The Origins of the Republican Party, 1852–1856.* New York: Oxford University Press, 1987.

Rhett, Robert Barnwell

CONFEDERATE POLITICIAN

- *Born: December 24, 1800, Beaufort, S.C.*
- *Political party: Democrat*
- *Education: sporadic schooling in lower grades*
- *Government service: South Carolina House of Representatives, 1826–32; attorney general of South Carolina, 1832–35; U.S. House of Representatives, 1837–49; U.S. Senate, 1850–52; Confederacy: Provisional Congress, 1861–62*
- *Died: September 14, 1876, St. James Parish, La.*

Known as the "Father of Secession," Robert Barnwell Rhett was the consummate Southern radical. Virtually his entire political career before 1861 was devoted to achieving political independence for the slave South. Ever fearful of encroaching federal power, he warned his fellow Southerners as early as 1833, "A people, owning slaves, are mad, or worse than mad, who do not hold their destinies in their own hands."

Rhett's father was a struggling rice planter, and the young Rhett was reared and taught to read and write by his grandmother. After studying law under Thomas Grimké, Rhett was admitted to the South Carolina bar in 1821, and he soon developed a lucrative practice that solidified his position in the planter class. Building upon his reputation as a skilled orator, he won election to the South Carolina House in 1826.

Rhett first stamped himself as a firebrand in the late 1820s when he championed nullification, the constitutional argument that a state had the right to declare null and inoperative any federal legislation deemed to violate its co-equal rights in the Union. He attacked the protective tariffs of 1828 and 1832 as tyrannical legislation, the opening wedge in a Northern campaign to deprive the South of its honor, rights, and property. The greatest danger was a move against slavery, and Rhett repeatedly warned that the South's ultimate salvation could be found only outside the Union. After briefly trying to work through the national Democratic party upon entering Congress, he emerged as a committed secessionist by the mid-1840s.

The election of the antislavery Republican Abraham Lincoln as President in 1860 provided Rhett with the opportunity that he had despaired would never come. Fears that a Republican administration would threaten slave property and white racial control suddenly generated popular support for the secessionist doctrines that Rhett had long preached. And, just as he had first predicted in 1844, secession was accomplished only *"after the proper issue [was] made by the conduct of a single State."* South Carolina seceded first on December 20, 1860, and the other states of the Lower South soon followed.

When delegates from the seceding states met at a convention at Montgomery, Alabama, in February 1861, Rhett tried to mold the Confederacy into a unified slaveholding republic. His key proposals called for reopening the African slave trade, the full counting of slaves for purposes of apportioning political representation, and a stipulation that only slave states could ever be admitted to the Confederacy. Not only were these proposals rejected, but he also failed in his bid for the Presidency of the Confederacy or indeed any high office. His leadership had been spurned, and in his mind the Confederate revolution had been stillborn.

Frustrated and disappointed, Rhett soon lashed out at President Jefferson Davis as a despot seizing power in "an unchecked career of mischief." He denounced Davis's military strategy and his policy of conscription. Defeated in an election for the Confederate Senate in the fall of 1862, Rhett returned to Charleston, where he continued to blame Davis for all that went wrong in the Confederacy.

Impoverished by the war, Rhett retired to a lonely, private life on an isolated plantation. Though ravaged by the cancer that claimed his life in 1876, he remained defiantly self-righteous until the very end. In his autobiography, he claimed that secession had failed primarily because the South had waited too long in its effort to free itself from Northern tyranny.

SEE ALSO

Fire-eaters; Nullification; Secession

FURTHER READING

Davis, William C., ed. *A Fire-Eater Remembers: The Confederate Memoir of Robert Barnwell Rhett*. Columbia: University of South Carolina Press, 2000.
White, Laura A. *Robert Barnwell Rhett: Father of Secession*. New York: Appleton-Century-Crofts, 1931.

Richmond bread riot

High prices, shortages of supplies, and war weariness spawned a series of food riots throughout Confederate cities and towns in the spring of 1863. The most notable of these breakdowns in public order occurred in the capital city of Richmond.

The population of Richmond, like that of other Southern cities, ballooned in the first two years of the war as refugees poured in from the countryside and jobs opened up in new government bureaus and factories engaged in military production. Currency inflation was a devastating problem for these workers when their wages failed to keep pace with the sharp rise in the cost of goods, especially basic foodstuffs. Following the passage of the Confederate Impressment Act in early March 1863, government commissary agents compounded the food problem by aggressively seizing supplies of food in and around Richmond for Robert E. Lee's Army of Northern Virginia. A snowstorm and subsequent muddy thaw in late March then turned a threatening situation into a full-blown crisis by temporarily disrupting the flow of meat and grains into the city.

On the morning of April 2, women workers organized a protest meeting and marched on the governor's mansion demanding access to food supplies at prices they could afford. When asked by a male bystander what they wanted, a young woman replied: "We celebrate our right to live. We are starving. As soon as enough of us get together we are going to the bakeries and each of us will take a loaf of bread. This is little enough for the government to give us

At Capitol Square in Richmond, a crowd of working-class women presented their demands to Virginia Governor John Letcher before the rioting over bread began.

after it has taken all our men."

Governor John Letcher offered sympathy but no promises of relief. The crowd, now swelling into an angry, armed mob, then ransacked stores and shops, seizing bread and other items that otherwise were available only at unconscionably high prices. Soldier reserves, joined by President Jefferson Davis, rushed to the scene and dispersed the mob with a show of military force.

Despite government efforts to suppress news of the riot, reports filtered out, and conditions comparable to those in Richmond sparked riots throughout the spring and summer of 1863 in such urban centers as Raleigh, Augusta, Columbus, Savannah, Atlanta, and Mobile. As in Richmond, impoverished working-class women made up the majority of the rioters. Their violent protests and seizures of private property soon produced a series of locally run welfare programs that diverted public funds toward feeding some of the hungry and providing relief for soldiers' families.

Apart from indicating the corrosive impact of inflation on Confederate unity and exposing severe strains in the system of producing and distributing agricultural supplies, the riots revealed how the war was increasingly pushing Southern women into the previously unthinkable roles of forceful, active agents in public affairs. By 1864, when more and more of these women had turned against the war, morale correspondingly fell in the Confederate armies filled with their husbands and sons.

SEE ALSO

Industrial workers; Inflation; Wartime economies

FURTHER READING

Bynum, Victoria E. *The Long Shadow of the Civil War: Southern Dissent and its Legacies.* Chapel Hill: University of North Carolina Press, 2010.
Chesson, Michael. "Harlots or Heroines? A New Look at the Richmond Bread Riot." *Virginia Magazine of History and Biography* 92, No. 1 (April 1984): 131–75.

Rifles

The Civil War was the first large-scale conflict fought with modern weapons of mass destruction. In particular, the new rifled firearms revolutionized land warfare, a revolution that commanders on both sides were slow to recognize.

Shock tactics—the massing of infantry to overrun an enemy's position—could succeed before the Civil War because of the inaccuracy of smoothbore muskets, the standard arm of the infantry. Smoothbores had an effective range of only about 80 yards, but they were preferred over rifles (so named because of the grooves cut into the bore) because they could be reloaded faster and much more easily. Civil War armies, however, were equipped with rifled muzzleloaders fitted with a percussion cap, a metal cover that exploded a powder charge with greater reliability than the old flintlock system. The standard arm for Union soldiers was the .58-caliber Springfield, and for most Confederates it was the .577-caliber Enfield rifle, a British weapon imported in large quantities despite the Union blockade.

What made rifles both practical and devastating by the time of the Civil War was the introduction in the 1850s of the minié ball (called the "minnie ball" by Civil War soldiers), an elongated bullet

By splitting into four sections when fired, this musket ball inflicted greater damage on impact than earlier versions.

The Henry repeating rifle was equipped with a novel magazine that held 15 rounds. Issued to some federal cavalry units late in the war, the rifle had so much firepower that Confederates quipped it could be "loaded on Sunday and fired all week."

with a soft, hollow base that expanded upon firing to fit into the rifle's grooved barrel, thereby greatly increasing range and accuracy. This new bullet solved problems of loading and reliability that hitherto had limited rifles to a specialized role in warfare. Rifles had an effective range up to some 400 yards, five times the killing field of smoothbores. To be sure, the wooded terrain in which most battles occurred meant that the opposing armies were typically able to close within 100 yards of each other before the firing began, and most soldiers were not trained to adjust for the parabolic flight of the minnie ball when aiming at distant targets. Nonetheless, the impact of the new rifles was enormous. Such a withering fire could be laid down that artillery gunners could no longer close in to offer much support for advancing infantry and cavalry charges now bordered on the suicidal. Infantry on the defensive had a huge advantage over attacking forces.

The Civil War also speeded the development of breechloading rifles (the breech is the part of a gun behind the barrel). Breechloaders could be fired more rapidly than muzzleloaders. For that reason, as well as concerns over retooling production facilities, the U.S. Ordnance Bureau opposed introducing them into the infantry. The bureau worried that inexperienced soldiers would waste too much ammunition. The Union cavalry, however, adopted breechloading carbines, smaller, lighter

versions of rifles, as soon as they were available. The best of these new carbines was the seven-shot repeating Spencer, one of the keys to the improved performance of the federal cavalry late in the war.

The new rifles gave the defense an inherent advantage of three to one over attackers, and five to one if the defense were entrenched behind breastworks or supported by artillery. As a result, most battles produced mass slaughter, with casualty rates of 20 percent and higher. Only one of eight frontal assaults succeeded in the Civil War. Still, most generals persisted in their outmoded tactics, formations, and battle plans.

SEE ALSO
Artillery; Casualties; Tactics

FURTHER READING
Davis, Carl L. *Arming the Union: Small Arms in the Civil War.* Port Washington, N.Y.: Kennikat Press, 1973.
Hess, Earl J. *The Rifle Musket in Civil War Combat: Reality and Myth.* Lawrence: University Press of Kansas, 2008.

Rosecrans, William Starke

UNION GENERAL

- *Born: September 6, 1819, Little Taylor Run, Ohio*
- *Education: U.S. Military Academy, B.S., 1842*

- *Military service: U.S. Army: lieutenant, 1843–53; 1st lieutenant, 1853–54; colonel, 1861; brigadier general, 1861; major-general, 1862–67*
- *Died: March 11, 1898, Redondo Beach, California*

Called "Old Rosy" by his troops, William S. Rosecrans held several important Union commands in the West. A superb strategist who tended to get overly excited during a battle, he was a successful general until his military career effectively came to an end when he made a command error that contributed to the Union defeat at Chickamauga in September 1863.

Largely self-taught as a youth, Rosecrans secured an appointment to West Point and graduated fifth in the class of 1842. After spending 10 years in the Engineering Corps, he resigned from the army in 1854. He saw his first service in the war as commander of a brigade in the western Virginia campaign of 1861. After George B. McClellan left to assume leadership of the Union army, Rosecrans directed the campaign that gave the Union control of what became the new state of West Virginia.

Transferred to the West after his success in the Virginia mountains, Rosecrans led the Army of the Mississippi in the indecisive battles of Iuka and Corinth, Mississippi, in October 1862. Ordered to relieve Don Carlos Buell, he took over the Army of the Cumberland on October 27, 1862. Unlike Buell, Rosecrans had an open, engaging personality, and he soon gained the confidence of his new troops. After much prodding from Washington, he moved against General Braxton Bragg's Army of Tennessee in late December 1862. He personally rallied his army at Stones River in a battle that forced the rebels to withdraw to Tullahoma.

Rosecrans defeated Bragg at Stones River, but he had neither destroyed Bragg's army nor gained much territory. For the next several months, Rosecrans parried repeated requests for him to go on the offensive. Digging in his heels, he insisted that "the most fatal errors of this war have begun in an impatient desire of success," and he informed his superiors that he would not be bullied into moving before he was ready. True to his word, he waited until late June 1863 before launching a campaign in which he skillfully and almost bloodlessly maneuvered Bragg out of middle Tennessee and then out of Chattanooga.

After his flawless Tullahoma campaign, Rosecrans failed to heed his own warning against "an impatient desire of success." He rashly pursued the rebels into a trap sprung by the counterattacking Bragg at Chickamauga in north Georgia. Rosecrans's faulty handling of his troops opened up a huge gap in the Union lines and nearly resulted in destruction of his army. His beaten army barely escaped back to Chattanooga. With his confidence apparently shattered, Rosecrans allowed Bragg to bring up the rebel army and lay siege to Chattanooga. Ulysses S. Grant replaced Rosecrans on October 19 and lifted the siege.

After completing his war service as commander of the Department of Missouri, Rosecrans resigned from the army in 1867. He served as U.S. minister to Mexico in 1868–69 and was a Republican congressman from California from 1881 to 1885.

William Starke Rosecrans had been a steady, effective general before he lost his confidence at Chickamauga. After that near-disaster for his army, he appeared, in President Lincoln's words, "confused and stunned, like a duck hit on the head."

He spent most of his postwar years as a rancher in California.

SEE ALSO
Bragg, Braxton; Chattanooga campaign; Chickamauga; Stones River

FURTHER READING
Lamers, William M. *The Edge of Glory: A Biography of General William S. Rosecrans, U.S.A.* New York: Harcourt, Brace, 1961.

Ruffin, Edmund
SOUTHERN SECESSIONIST

- *Born: January 5, 1794, Prince George County, Va.*
- *Political parties: Whig, Democrat*
- *Education: College of William and Mary, 1810*
- *Occupation: gentleman farmer*
- *Government service: Virginia Senate, 1823–26*
- *Died: June 17, 1865, Amelia County, Va.*

At the age of 67, Edmund Ruffin gained notoriety for firing the first shot of the Civil War over Fort Sumter in 1861. It was a fitting capstone to the career of perhaps the South's most dedicated secessionist.

Born into a gentry family whose roots in Virginia stretched back to the 17th century, Ruffin inherited a worn-out plantation on Virginia's northern neck. Suspended after a year of lackadaisical study at the College of William and Mary, he enlisted as a private in a militia company but saw no service in the War of 1812. Settling down to the life of a planter after his marriage in 1813, he soon revealed a genius for agricultural reform. His experiments in rotating crops and using marl (shell deposits) as a fertilizer to neutralize

overly acidic soils were a great success in restoring the productivity of his plantation. As editor of the *Farmers' Register* from 1833 to 1842, he spread the gospel of agricultural reform throughout the Upper South.

Eminently successful as an agricultural entrepreneur, Ruffin failed miserably as a politician. Frustrated with his ineffectiveness as a public speaker and disdainful of the need for political compromise, he resigned from the Virginia Senate in 1826. Too dogmatic and elitist in his views to ever again hold public office, he channeled his thwarted ambitions first into agricultural reform and then into the cause of Southern independence.

Ruffin responded to the abolitionist attacks of the 1830s by becoming a fervid defender of slavery. Rising Northern hostility to slavery in the 1840s converted him into a Southern nationalist. As a prophet biding his time, he urged Southerners to cast off corrupting party allegiances and join with him in securing the salvation of slavery and Southern honor outside the Union.

After retiring from farming in 1856, Ruffin devoted his time to writing pro-secessionist articles and traveling throughout the South preaching his secessionist message. All his efforts, including the formation of a League of United Southerners in 1858, failed to fire the Southern heart. In despair, he contemplated suicide in the fall of 1859. Then came the election of Abraham Lincoln to the Presidency in 1860, the catalyst for the secession movement Ruffin feared he would never see. "It is good news for me," he recorded in his diary upon hearing of Lincoln's victory.

South Carolina was in the forefront of secession, and Ruffin immediately went to Columbia, the state capital, to experience firsthand the realization of his dream. "The time since I have been

here has been the happiest of my life," he wrote to his sons in mid-November. From Columbia, Ruffin traveled to Milledgeville to encourage the Georgia secessionists, and in early January he addressed the secession convention in Florida. Refusing to return to Virginia until his native state seceded, he was in Charleston when the crisis over Fort Sumter climaxed. The Palmetto Guard welcomed him as an honorary member and permitted him to fire the first shot that arched over the fort on April 12, 1861. As he noted in his diary, he was "delighted to perform the service."

The exaltation that Ruffin felt with the triumph of secession turned into anguished disappointment as the Confederacy was slowly hammered into submission. Although he fired an artillery shot at the battle of First Bull Run, he was clearly too old to fight. He spent much of the war trying to keep one step ahead of the Union soldiers who invaded his Virginia countryside and burned Marlbourne, his beloved estate. Unwilling to live in a postwar world dominated by the victorious Northerners, he rigged up a shotgun and took his own life on June 17, 1865.

SEE ALSO
Fire-eaters; Secession

FURTHER READING
Craven, Avery O. *Edmund Ruffin, Southerner: A Study in Secession.* New York: Appleton, 1932.
Mitchell, Betty L. *Edmund Ruffin: A Biography.* Bloomington: Indiana University Press, 1981.

Russia

Russia was the most consistently pro-Union of the European powers during the Civil War. Still smarting from their defeat at the hands of the British and the French in the Crimean War (1854–56), the Russians favored the Union as a check on British aggression.

The Russian minister in Washington, Edouard de Stoeckl, warned his government in April 1861 that "England will take advantage of the first opportunity to recognize the seceded States and that France will follow her." Tsar Alexander II shared his minister's

These Russian peasants are gathered on an estate near Moscow to listen to a reading of the czar's proclamation freeing the serfs of obligatory service to aristocratic landlords. In that same year began the Civil War in America, which would strip another great landowning class of its unfree labor.

concerns. Fearing that British intervention would escalate the U.S. Civil War into a full-scale global conflict, the tsar was anxious to remain on friendly terms with the Union. If a European war did break out, the Russians would need access to Union ports and Union assistance against the British.

In the fall of 1862, when the British and French threatened to intervene and mediate an end to the Civil War, the Russians held firm against any European meddling. Convinced that a united European front was essential if mediation were to succeed, the British foreign office backed off and refused to issue a call for an armistice. As Lord John Russell, the British foreign secretary, explained, "We ought not to move at present without Russia."

Having freed the Russian serfs in 1861, the tsar sympathized with the Union war aim of emancipating the slaves. As a show of support for the Union cause, he sent the Russian fleet on a friendly visit to Northern ports in 1863. The goodwill engendered by that visit helped prepare the way for the U.S. acquisition of Alaska from the Russians in 1867.

SEE ALSO
France; Great Britain

FURTHER READING
Saul, Norman E. *Distant Friends: The United States and Russia, 1763–1867.* Lawrence: University Press of Kansas, 1991.

Schurz, Carl
UNION GENERAL AND POLITICIAN

- Born: March 2, 1829, Liblar, near Cologne, Germany
- Political party: Republican
- Education: University of Bonn, 1847–48
- Military service: U.S. Army: brigadier general, volunteers, 1862–63; major-

general, 1863–65
- *Government service: U.S. minister to Spain, 1860–62; U.S. Senate, 1869–75; U.S. secretary of the interior, 1877–81*
- *Died: May 14, 1906, New York, N.Y.*

The most acclaimed German-American politician of the 19th century, Carl Schurz was a crusading reformer in the Republican party. Although he fought in the Civil War, his fame rested on his brilliant skills as an orator and his support for progressive causes after the war.

The son of a village schoolmaster, Schurz aspired to become a professor of history. Provided with an excellent education by his parents, he was a doctoral student at the University of Bonn when the German revolution of 1848–49 erupted. He served as an officer in the revolutionary forces before escaping to Switzerland when the Prussian army restored order. Risking his life, he briefly returned to Germany and engineered the daring rescue of one of his professors, who had been imprisoned for supporting the insurgency. After short stays in France and England, he migrated to the United States in 1852.

Schurz first settled in Philadelphia, where he soon mastered the English language. Upon moving to Wisconsin in 1856, he began a law practice and emerged as a leader in the newly formed Republican party. As chairman of the Wisconsin delegation to the Republican national convention in 1860, he backed Abraham Lincoln for the Presidency. Once elected, Lincoln rewarded Schurz with the post of U.S. minister to Spain.

Anxious to contribute to the Union cause in the Civil War, Schurz returned to the United States in January 1862 and called for the immediate abolition of slavery. Desiring not to move against slavery just yet, Lincoln sent Schurz into the army as a brigadier general, an appointment that buttressed the President's support among German Americans. Although Schurz acquitted himself well in the Second Bull Run Campaign, his Dutch units, as they were called, were badly mauled at Chancellorsville and Gettysburg. He then headed west, where he participated in the battle of Chattanooga. While assigned to administrative duties, he campaigned for Lincoln's reelection in 1864 and ended the war as a chief of staff in the Carolinas.

After reporting on conditions in the postwar South for President Andrew Johnson in the summer of 1865, Schurz supported congressional Republicans when they pushed through a more thorough program of Reconstruction than that favored by Johnson. He was an early advocate for black civil rights, including the right to vote. Nonetheless, he soon broke with Republican regulars when he became convinced that Reconstruction had spawned corrupt governments in the South that ignored the wishes of intelligent, propertied whites. He led a party revolt in 1872, known as the Liberal Republican movement, that called for a restitution of full political rights for all former rebels. As he argued in a Senate speech in January 1872: "When universal suffrage was granted to secure the equal rights of all, universal amnesty ought to have been granted to make all the resources of political intelligence and experience available for the promotion of the welfare of all."

The Liberal Republicans failed to prevent the reelection of President Ulysses S. Grant in 1872, but Schurz remained active as an editor and speaker in the cause of liberal reform, most notably in civil service. As secretary of the interior, he initiated federal efforts to preserve the public domain. He concluded his career as one of the most esteemed statesmen of the Republican party.

SEE ALSO
Liberal Republicans

FURTHER READING
Trefousse, Hans L. *Carl Schurz: A Biography.* Knoxville: University of Tennessee Press, 1982.

Scott, Winfield

UNION GENERAL

- *Born: June 13, 1786, near Petersburg, Va.*
- *Education: William and Mary College, 1805*
- *Military service: U.S. Army: captain, light artillery, 1808–12; lieutenant colonel, artillery, 1812–13; colonel adjutant general, 1813–14; brigadier general, 1814–41; general-in-chief of the army, 1841–61*
- *Died: May 29, 1866, West Point, N.Y.*

The most accomplished general in the prewar U.S. Army, Winfield Scott was general-in-chief of Union forces at the outbreak of the Civil War. Although too old and infirm to assume a field command, he outlined in his "Anaconda Plan" the core strategic ideas that eventually resulted in Union victory.

Privately educated in his native Virginia, Scott briefly attended William and Mary College before studying law in Petersburg and gaining admission to the Virginia bar in 1806. A war scare with Great Britain in 1807 prompted him to enlist in a local troop of cavalry, and he soon abandoned the law for a career in the military. Commissioned a captain in 1808, he distinguished himself during the War of 1812 in the campaigns along the Canadian border. A brigadier general at the war's end, he rose to the top command in the army by 1841. His greatest feat as a general was his Veracruz campaign during the Mexican War in which, with a minimum of casualties, he seized Mexico City and forced Mexico to surrender. In politics he was less successful. Running as the Whig candidate for the Presidency in 1852, he aroused little support.

Despite his age and spreading girth which disabled him from fighting, Scott still had a first-rate military mind when the secession crisis erupted. Although his advice was rejected by President James Buchanan, Scott quite soundly recommended the reinforcing of federal garrisons in the South during the early stages of the crisis. Then, fearful that a show of force would destroy any chance of reconciliation, he recommended the abandonment of Fort Sumter when Abraham Lincoln assumed the Presidency. He was unable to assume any active role when the war began. "If I could only mount a horse, I—" he lamented to the son of William Henry Seward, "but I am past that." Nonetheless, he provided Lincoln with daily military reports and helped coordinate the Union effort that opened Maryland for the transit of federal troops.

Scott's greatest service to Lincoln came in providing a badly needed sense of realism to the early war effort. Almost alone among the top-ranking generals, he foresaw that the war would be a long one. Hoping to contain the violence and avoid a war of conquest that would leave his native South embittered and devastated, he developed what his more impatient critics derided as the "Anaconda Plan." He called for a blockade by sea and a concentration of Union forces in northern

Meeting with his staff in July 1861, General Winfield Scott was far too old and infirm to lead an army, but he shrewdly advised President Lincoln on strategic matters in the early stages of the war.

Virginia and along the corridor of the Mississippi River. To be sure, Scott's plan relied primarily on economic and diplomatic pressure and shrank from demanding the hard fighting that would be necessary to subdue the Confederacy, but his strategic emphasis on Union naval superiority and the importance of the Mississippi Valley guided federal policy throughout the war.

By the fall of 1861, Scott's position as general-in-chief was untenable. He was heavily criticized for the Union rout at First Bull Bun, and the Union now looked to General George B. McClellan as its savior. Scott stepped down in late October. Grateful for his services, Lincoln paid him a fine tribute in his first annual message to Congress when he stated, "I cannot but think we are still his debtors."

Scott wrote his memoirs during his retirement and, appropriately enough, died at West Point.

SEE ALSO
Anaconda Plan

FURTHER READING
Eisenhower, John S. *Agent of Destiny: The Life and Times of General Winfield Scott.* New York: Free Press, 1997.
Johnson, Timothy D. *Winfield Scott: The Quest for Military Glory.* Lawrence: University Press of Kansas, 1998.

Secession

Secession occurred in two distinct waves. With South Carolina taking the lead on December 20, 1860, the seven states of the Lower South left the Union in the winter of 1860–61. Texas was the last of these, seceding on February 1, 1861. A second wave of four states from the Upper South seceded in the spring of 1861 after the Confederate firing on Fort Sumter led President Abraham Lincoln to issue a call for 75,000 militia to suppress what he now characterized as an insurrection in the South.

The mere fact of the Republican victory under Abraham Lincoln in the Presidential election of 1860 triggered secession in the Lower South. Southern radicals had preached since the formation of the Republican party that its assumption of national power would pose an immediate threat to the preservation of slavery and social peace in the South. A Republican administration, they insisted, would appoint enemies of slavery to federal jobs in the South, destroy slavery's profitability by blocking its expansion, and unleash slave uprisings. Southern honor, liberty, and safety all demanded an immediate break from a Union now headed by a sectionalized antislavery party that had not received a single electoral vote in the South.

The secessionists pushed the constitutional doctrine of states' rights to its logical extreme. They held that individual states retained ultimate sovereign power within the Union and could peacefully leave the Union the same way they had entered it through a special state convention. Anxious to move quickly before Lincoln's inauguration

This extra edition of the Charleston Mercury boldly announces the secession of South Carolina from the Union, in one of the most famous headlines in American journalism.

on March 4, 1861, they denounced all calls for delay as cowardly submission to Republican tyranny. In pursuing a strategy of separate state action, they confidently predicted that the momentum of secession would force wavering states to join those that had already gone out.

The actual mechanics of secession were fairly straightforward. State legislatures issued calls for special elections to choose delegates to conventions that would decide the question of secession. Aided by associations of "Minute Men" and other vigilante groups that silenced the opposition or frightened it away from the polls, the immediate secessionists carried most of these elections. They ran strongest in plantation counties where slaves outnumbered the whites.

South Carolina seceded first, soon to be followed by the six remaining states in the Lower South. Delegates from these states set up the provisional government of the Confederate States of America at Montgomery, Alabama, in February 1861. This original Confederacy represented those Southern states with the heaviest concentration of slaves and the highest percentage of white families owning slaves. Planters were in the forefront of secession, and what opposition they encountered came from

CHARLESTON

MERCURY

EXTRA:

Passed unanimously at 1.15 o'clock, P. M., December 20th, 1860.

AN ORDINANCE

To dissolve the Union between the State of South Carolina and other States united with her under the compact entitled "The Constitution of the United States of America."

We, the People of the State of South Carolina, in Convention assembled, do declare and ordain, and it is hereby declared and ordained,

That the Ordinance adopted by us in Convention, on the twenty-third day of May, in the year of our Lord one thousand seven hundred and eighty-eight, whereby the Constitution of the United States of America was ratified, and also, all Acts and parts of Acts of the General Assembly of this State, ratifying amendments of the said Constitution, are hereby repealed; and that the union now subsisting between South Carolina and other States, under the name of "The United States of America," is hereby dissolved.

THE

UNION

IS

DISSOLVED!

nonslaveholding farmers who had no stake in plantation slavery. Most of these farmers were not Unionists but rather cooperationists—that is, those who argued that secession should be delayed until a united bloc of Southern states agreed to secede together. After receiving about 40 percent of the vote in the secession elections, the cooperationists followed the lead of the planters and voted for secession in the state conventions. Significantly, none of these conventions (with the exception of the last one in Texas) submitted the decision on secession to a popular referendum.

While Southerners were being told that secession was a peaceful and legal remedy for the constitutional transgressions of the North, the vast majority of Northerners were rejecting the doctrine altogether. Believing that the Union was sovereign and perpetual, they viewed secession as a treasonable mockery of the Constitution. They equated secession with anarchy and feared that it would soon lead to a breakup of the United States into bickering regions and an end to the U.S. mission of serving as a beacon of free government to the rest of the world.

For all the opposition in the North to secession, no consensus existed during the secession winter on using coercion to force seceded states back into the Union. In particular, Democrats were against coercion and favored negotiations to heal the sectional rift. Along with moderates from the Upper South, they supported some variant of the Crittenden Compromise, a course of action named after Senator John J. Crittenden of Kentucky that would have recognized explicitly the right of Southerners to take slaves into all federal territories south of the 36°30' line. At the same time, Unionists in the Upper South who had turned back secession clearly hedged their unionism by proclaiming that they would resist any Republican use of military force against a seceded state.

When Abraham Lincoln assumed the Presidency on March 4, 1861, he thus faced a dilemma. If he took no action against the Confederacy, he risked demoralizing his party and shattering its still-fragile unity. He and his party would be exposed to the same derision that had pilloried the outgoing Buchanan Democrats for standing by idly while the secessionists broke up the Union. On the other hand, any forceful step against the seceded states threatened to divide the North and drive the Upper South into the Confederacy.

After a month of weighing his options, Lincoln decided to take a stand for the Union at Fort Sumter in Charleston Harbor, the most visible installation in the Confederacy that was still under federal control. Aware that the garrison at Fort Sumter would be

forced to surrender for lack of supplies sometime in early April, he ordered a relief expedition to the fort on April 6. He stressed that the fort would be supplied "with provisions only; and that, if such attempt be not resisted, no effort to throw in men, arms, or ammunition will be made without further notice, or in case of an attack upon the Fort."

This was a brilliant decision, for Lincoln in effect had placed the decision to go to war in the hands of Confederate authorities. Led to believe earlier by Lincoln's Secretary of State William H. Seward that Sumter was to be abandoned, Confederate President Jefferson Davis felt betrayed. After a perfunctory debate in his cabinet, Davis ordered General Pierre G. T. Beauregard on April 9 to demand the immediate surrender of Fort Sumter. Suspecting Union duplicity and anxious to avoid any possibility of having to fight two Union forces at the same time, Davis wanted Sumter in Confederate hands before the relief expedition arrived.

Confederate batteries opened fire on Fort Sumter in the predawn hours of April 12, 1861. The fort surrendered on April 14, and the next day Lincoln issued his call for state militia to put down what he defined as a Southern insurrection. Virginia, Arkansas, Tennessee, and North Carolina scornfully rejected Lincoln's call for troops, and all joined the Confederacy within the next five weeks. Still, Lincoln now had a North united behind the goal of preserving the Union with force. To Northerners, the Confederacy was the aggressor that had fired the first shot of the Civil War, and the North embarked on its military crusade to save the Union.

SEE ALSO

Causes of the Civil War; Fire-eaters; Slavery

FURTHER READING

Barney, William L. *The Road to Secession.* New York: Praeger, 1972.
Crofts, Daniel W. *Reluctant Confederates: Upper South Unionists in the Secession Crisis.* Chapel Hill: University of North Carolina Press, 1989.
Freehling, William W. *The Road to Disunion.* Vol II. *Secessionists Triumphant.* New York: Oxford University Press, 2007.
Wooster, Ralph A. *The Secession Conventions of the South.* Princeton, N.J.: Princeton University Press, 1962.

Second Bull Run

The battle of Second Bull Run (or Manassas) on August 29–30, 1862, culminated one of General Robert E. Lee's most clever campaigns. The origins of the campaign went back to June 26, 1862, when President Abraham Lincoln created the short-lived Union Army of Virginia under the command of General John Pope.

In mid-July Pope advanced his 50,000 troops toward Gordonsville, Virginia, a rail center that connected Richmond and Lee's army to the vital supplies of the Shenandoah Valley. In command of about 80,000 troops around Richmond, Lee now faced the threat of being crushed by the combined force of Pope's army and the 90,000 federals encamped south of Richmond under General George B. McClellan. Correctly assuming that McClellan would not order an offensive, Lee launched a new campaign by sending 12,000 men (soon reinforced to 24,000) under General Thomas J. "Stonewall" Jackson to move against Pope. Lee had seized the initiative from the federals and he was to keep them off guard and confused for the next six weeks.

Jackson first clashed with federal troops at the Battle of Cedar Mountain on August 9. By this time McClellan was under orders to withdraw his army from the James River and transport it by water to reinforce Pope. Lee's plan was now clear. He brought the bulk of his army north from Richmond and moved quickly to strike at Pope before McClellan's reinforcements could arrive.

On August 24 Lee made his most crucial decision of the campaign. Unable to maneuver effectively against the defensive line Pope had established along the Rappahannock River, Lee divided his already-outnumbered army. He sent Jackson and 23,000 troops north with orders to break up the Orange and Alexandria Railroad, the principal line of communications for Pope's army. Jackson executed the plan to perfection. His infantry—now known as Jackson's "foot cavalry"—marched 57 miles in two days under the tightest security. "No man save one in that corps," recalled General William B. Taliaferro, "whatever may have been his rank, knew our destination." By the afternoon of August 26, Jackson's men were disrupting Pope's rail communications, and in the evening they demolished a large Union supply depot at Manassas Junction.

Now alert to the danger in his rear, Pope abandoned his position on the Rappahannock River and moved north in a futile attempt to pinpoint Jackson's position and destroy his army. Pope reached Manassas on August 28 only to find that the Confederates had gone. Unknown to Pope, Jackson had slipped away a few miles to the west, where he found cover under the forward slope of Sudley Mountain. Jackson revealed his position when he attacked a Union column at the Battle of Groveton, but even then Pope mistakenly assumed that Jackson was in a full retreat to the safety of the Shenandoah Valley.

Although Pope had 60,000 men to use against Jackson's 20,000, he was so confused by Jackson's moves that he squandered his crushing advantage in numbers. Overly concerned with Jackson, Pope allowed Lee to send 30,000 troops under General James Longstreet on a circuitous march to reinforce Jackson. Longstreet's corps arrived on August 30, the day after Jackson had held off a series of piecemeal frontal assaults ordered by Pope, and Longstreet's divisions turned a possible Union success on the second day of the battle into a resounding Confederate victory. Jackson's exhausted troops had been fighting for seven hours on August 30, and many of them, noted Lieutenant Robert Healy of the 55th Virginia, "had expended their ammunition and were defending themselves with rocks." Longstreet, however, quickly turned the exposed Union left, and the demoralized federals were barely able to make a defensive stand at Henry House Hill on the old Bull Run battlefield.

The Union losses of 16,000 at Second Bull Run were almost double the 9,000 Confederate casualties. A clearly beaten Pope retreated to Washington and was soon relieved of his command. Second Bull Run was the capstone to a stunning six-week campaign in which Lee outmaneuvered both Pope and McClellan and succeeded in freeing northern Virginia of any immediate Union threat.

SEE ALSO

First Bull Run; Jackson, Thomas J. ("Stonewall"); Lee, Robert E.; Lincoln, Abraham; Longstreet, James; McClellan, George B.; Pope, John

FURTHER READING

Hennessy, John. *Return to Bull Run: The Campaign and Battle of Second Manassas.* New York: Simon & Schuster, 1993.
Krick, Robert K. *Stonewall Jackson at Cedar Mountain.* Chapel Hill: University of North Carolina Press, 1990.
Stackpole, Edward J. *From Cedar Mountain to Antietam, August–September, 1862.* Harrisburg, Pa.: Stackpole, 1959.

Secret services

Both sides created organizations to gather and sift military intelligence. The Bureau of Military Information was the Union's chief intelligence agency. The Confederate counterpart comprised a number of organizations that engaged in military sabotage and propaganda operations as well as information gathering.

Early in the war, Allan Pinkerton, the head of a private detective agency, provided the Union with its first undercover agents. Pinkerton sent spies into the seceded states and reported on Confederate troop strength during the Peninsula campaign in the spring of 1862. Far more thorough and professional, however, was the subsequent work of the Bureau of Military Information as it evolved under the leadership of Colonel George H. Sharpe.

A superb intelligence manager, Sharpe expanded and coordinated Union surveillance activities and took full advantage of the revolutionary improvements in communications made possible by field and long-distance telegraphy. In addition to pioneering the use of a mobile

Operating out of her home at Martinsburg in Virginia's Shenandoah Valley, Belle Boyd was an ardent Southern sympathizer who moved through federal lines gathering military information that she passed on to Confederate authorities.

field telegraph, the Union army laid down 15,000 miles of telegraph lines during the war. The rapid transmission of information for both tactical and strategic purposes was now possible. Special codes, which the Confederacy never cracked, ensured the secrecy of the transmitted messages. The use of this new technology enabled Sharpe's service to help the Army of the Potomac in coordinating its movements to its best advantage in countering the Confederate thrust into Pennsylvania that climaxed at the battle of Gettysburg.

The Confederate State Department, War Department, and the Signal Bureau and Signal Corps all housed espionage organizations. Funds were provided for spy networks in Washington and Canada and the maintenance of clandestine routes for couriers. President Jefferson Davis personally approved throughout the war the release of $1.5 million in gold for secret service activities.

Early in the war, the Confederacy concentrated its efforts on Europe. When hopes of foreign recognition faded, the secret service shifted attention to the Union home front. It hatched plans to free Confederate prisoners of war from Northern prison camps and to disrupt military communications. Agents based in Canada staged paramilitary raids and tried to strengthen the Northern peace movement, especially in the lower Midwest. Their most fantastic scheme involved plans to kidnap President Abraham Lincoln and hold him as a hostage. Most of these measures were too desperate ever to succeed, and none

The Signal Corps of the Union army used cipher disks such as this to encode signal-flag messages. The numbers on the outer ring and the letters on the inner correspond to standard flag movements.

of them could stave off Confederate defeat.

SEE ALSO
Booth, John Wilkes

FURTHER READING
Feis, William B. *Grant's Secret Service: The Intelligence War from Belmont to Appomattox.* Lincoln: University of Nebraska Press, 2002.
Fishel, Edwin C. *The Secret War for the Union: The Untold Story of Military Intelligence in the Civil War.* Boston: Houghton Mifflin, 1995.
Tidwell, William A. *April '65: Confederate Covert Action in the American Civil War.* Kent, Ohio: Kent State University Press, 1995.

Semmes, Raphael

CONFEDERATE ADMIRAL

- *Born: September 27, 1809, Charles County, Md.*
- *Education: sporadic schooling in lower grades*
- *Military service: U.S. Navy: midshipman, 1826–37, lieutenant, 1837–55; commander, 1855–61; Confederate navy: commander, 1861–62; captain, 1862–65; rear admiral, 1865*
- *Died: August 31, 1877, Mobile, Ala.*

The most celebrated naval hero of the Confederacy, Raphael Semmes became a legend for the devastating success of his raids on the high seas against Union shipping. The Confederate raider *Alabama,* his most renowned command, intercepted 68 Union ships, burned all but 10 of them, and alone accounted for more than 25 percent of all Union merchantmen destroyed by rebel cruisers.

Raised by an uncle in Georgetown, D.C., Semmes entered the U.S. Navy at the age of 17. He studied law during his shore leaves from frequent duty on the high seas and was admitted to the Maryland bar in 1834. From 1837 to 1846 he was on survey duty along the Southern coast and in the Gulf of Mexico. After taking part in the naval bombardment of Veracruz during the Mexican War, he accompanied General Winfield Scott's army on its march to Mexico City. He moved to Mobile, Alabama, in 1849 and served as a lighthouse inspector along the Gulf Coast in the 1850s.

On the eve of the Civil War, few naval officers could rival Semmes's detailed knowledge of the Southern coast and his hands-on experience at handling a ship on the open seas. His talents would prove invaluable to the new Confederate navy once he resigned from the U.S. Navy in February 1861 and offered his services to the Confederacy. "It had cost me pain to cross the gulf," he later wrote of his decision, "but once crossed, I never looked back."

Following a mission to the North to purchase naval war supplies and a brief stint as chief of the Confederate Lighthouse Bureau, Semmes was commissioned commander in April 1861, with orders to outfit a packet steamer, the *Havanna,* into a commerce raider. He had pushed the idea of launching economic warfare against Union shipping, and Confederate Secretary of the Navy Stephen R. Mallory shrewdly saw in Semmes the perfect sea raider.

The *Havanna,* now renamed the *Sumter,* slipped through the blockaders at the mouth of the Mississippi River on the evening of June 30, 1861. It snared its first Union ship three days later off the coast of Cuba and set it ablaze in an inferno that Semmes recorded as "like the fires of a hundred furnaces, in full blast." Another 17 prizes (with a value 10 times what it had cost the Confederacy to outfit the *Sumter*) were caught in

When Raphael Semmes wrote about the sinking of the Alabama, his fabled raiding ship, by the U.S.S. Kearsage, he defiantly proclaimed that he and his chief officer "had buried her as we had christened her, and she was safe from the polluting touch of the hated Yankee!"

the next six months before Semmes abandoned the *Sumter* at Gibraltar, where three Union ships blocked its exit.

Before Semmes could return to the Confederacy, he was given command of an English-built ship that soon became famous as the *Alabama*, the most fearsome of all Confederate commerce raiders. He took command in the Azores in August 1862. For the next 22 months, he kept the *Alabama* on the move, shifting from the Caribbean south along the coast to Brazil and then into the Indian Ocean before returning to the Atlantic and putting in for repairs. The USS *Kearsarge* sunk the *Alabama* off Cherbourg, France, in June 1864, but not before Semmes had destroyed more than $6 million of Union shipping.

Rescued by an English yacht as the *Alabama* was sinking, Semmes made it back to the Confederacy and was commanding the James River Squadron when Richmond fell. After surrendering in North Carolina and signing his parole, he was arrested in December 1865 and detained for four months while Union authorities sought unsuccessfully to try him on charges of treason and piracy. Upon his release, he returned to Mobile, where he practiced law until his death.

SEE ALSO
Alabama claims; Naval warfare

FURTHER READING
Spencer, Warren F. *Raphael Semmes: The Philosophical Mariner.* Tuscaloosa: University of Alabama Press, 1997.
Taylor, John M. *Confederate Raider: Raphael Semmes of the Alabama.* Washington, D.C.: Brassey, 1994.

Seven Days Battles

SEE Pennisula campaign

Sheridan, Philip H.

UNION GENERAL

- *Born: March 6, 1831, Albany, N.Y.*
- *Education: U.S. Military Academy, B.S., 1853*
- *Military service: U.S. Army: brevet lieutenant, 1853; lieutenant, 1854–61; 1st lieutenant, 1861; captain, 1861–62; colonel, 2nd Michigan Cavalry, 1862; brigadier general, volunteers, 1862; major-general, volunteers, 1862–64; brigadier general, regular army, 1864; major-general, 1864–69; lieutenant general, 1869–88; general, 1888; general-in-chief of the army, 1883–88*
- *Died: August 5, 1888, Nonquitt, Mass.*

An obscure officer in a staff position in 1861, Philip H. Sheridan enjoyed a meteoric rise to become the Union's premier cavalry commander. His devastating Shenandoah Valley campaign in the fall of 1864 ranks as one of the most successful cavalry operations of the war.

Raised in Ohio, Sheridan clerked in a country store before receiving an appointment to West Point. When a fellow cadet reported him for his first offense, the short but combative Sheridan chased him with a bayonet. As punishment, he was suspended for a year. He served in rank through eight years of frontier duty in the infantry and did not receive his first promotion until defections to the Confederacy opened up positions after the war started.

Sheridan served as a quartermaster and commissary until May 1862, when he was appointed commander of the 2nd Michigan Cavalry. Once in charge of a field command, he moved up rapidly. Fighting off a larger force of rebel cavalry at Booneville, Mississippi, on July 1, 1862, he won his first general's star. "He is worth his weight in gold," reported his superiors. He subsequently saw action at Perryville, Stones River, and Chickamauga. During the Chattanooga campaign in November 1863, he led the Union division that unexpectedly swept aside the Confederate position on Missionary Ridge. "To Sheridan's prompt movement," General Ulysses S. Grant later wrote in his *Memoirs,* "the Army of the Cumberland and the nation are indebted for the bulk of the capture of prisoners, artillery, and small-arms that day." Grant was so impressed by Sheridan's drive and energy that he entrusted him with the command of the Cavalry Corps in the Army of the Potomac in April 1864.

Sheridan became a favorite of the eastern press corps, and his exploits gained worldwide prominence. In May 1864, his troops killed J. E. B. Stuart, Robert E. Lee's fabled cavalry leader, at the battle of Yellow Tavern. Heading the newly established Middle Military Division, Sheridan embarked on his most famous campaign in the late summer of 1864. Under orders from Grant to turn the fertile Shenandoah Valley, a main source of food supplies for Lee's army, into "a barren waste," he led a powerful force of close to 50,000 men into the valley and cleared it of provisions and rebel troops. The campaign climaxed in October with a decisive Union victory at the battle of Cedar Creek, where Sheridan rallied his troops into mounting a furious counterattack by shouting, "There's lots of fight in you men yet! Come up, God damn you! Come up!" In his final report on the destruction he had wrought in the Valley, Sheridan noted: "A crow would have had to carry its rations if it had flown across the valley."

Attached to Grant's command at Petersburg in the final days of the war, Sheridan's cavalry smashed the right wing of Lee's retreating army at Five Forks and captured 8,000 rebel soldiers at Saylor's Creek. Moving quickly, Sheridan then sealed off Lee's last line of retreat at Appomattox.

Along with Grant and William T. Sherman, Sheridan provided the leadership for the postwar army. He served as a military governor in the Reconstructed

Philip H. Sheridan's troops advance against the Confederates near Middletown, Virginia, on October 19, 1864. They cut a path of destruction so wide during the Shenandoah Valley campaign that Robert E. Lee's Army of Northern Virginia could no longer turn to the fertile valley as a source of supplies.

South and held major commands in the West. A few years before his death, he succeeded Sherman as general-in-chief of the army.

SEE ALSO

Appomattox campaign

FURTHER READING

Morris, Roy. *Sheridan: The Life and Wars of General Phil Sheridan.* New York: Crown, 1992.

Wittenberg, Eric J. *Little Phil: A Reassessment of the Civil War Leadership of Gen. Philip H. Sheridan.* Washington, D.C.: Bracey's Inc., 2002.

Sherman, William Tecumseh

UNION GENERAL

- *Born: February 8, 1820, Lancaster, Ohio*
- *Education: U.S. Military Academy, B.S., 1840*
- *Military service: U.S. Army: lieutenant, artillery, 1840; 1st lieutenant, 1841–50; captain, 1850–53; colonel, 1861; brigadier general, volunteers, 1861; major-general, volunteers, 1862–64; brigadier general, regular army, 1863; major-general, 1864–66; lieutenant general, 1866–69; general, 1869–83; general-in-chief of the army, 1869–83.*
- *Died: February 14, 1891, New York, N.Y.*

Second only to Ulysses S. Grant for the renown that he gained as a Union general, William Tecumseh Sherman was the architect of the most celebrated campaign of the Civil War, the so-called March to the Sea in the fall of 1864. "War is cruelty and you cannot refine it," Sherman stated upon ordering the evacuation of Atlanta prior to that march. To this day, his name is associated with the concept of total war that

targets the property and morale of an enemy's civilian population.

The sudden death of his father in 1829 was the pivotal event of Sherman's childhood. Relatives and friends took in the now-impoverished Sherman children, and Thomas Ewing, a next-door neighbor who became a prominent Whig politician, raised the young Sherman. Ewing secured an appointment for Sherman to West Point, where he graduated sixth in his class. After a largely uneventful stint in the infantry, Sherman resigned from the army in 1853 to become a banker in San Francisco. When his bank failed in 1857, he tried his hand as a lawyer, with two of his brothers-in-law in Leavenworth, Kansas. Restless and not very successful as a lawyer, he accepted the superintendency of the Louisiana Military Academy in 1859. He resigned this post in January 1861 in protest of the new secessionist regime in Louisiana.

Sherman's early war record gave little hint of his future greatness. The brigade that he commanded fought well at First Bull Run, but Sherman was disgusted by the flight of the federals from the battlefield. "It was as disgraceful as words can portray," he wrote his wife, Ellen, Thomas Ewing's daughter. Sent to Kentucky in the late summer of 1861, he was soon feuding with newspaper correspondents and officials in the War Department, both of whom accused him of wildly exaggerating the number of Confederate troops in the area. "Sherman's gone in the head, he's luny,"

William Tecumseh Sherman was (and is) the devil incarnate to many Southern whites after his destructive march through Georgia and up into South Carolina. But Union officer Theodore Lyman described him as "a very homely man, with a regular nest of wrinkles on his face, which play and twist as he eagerly talks on each subject… his expression is pleasant and kindly."

reported Thomas W. Scott, the assistant secretary of war. Nearing a state of nervous exhaustion, Sherman was relieved of his Kentucky command in November.

The influence of his Ewing relatives soon resulted in another command for Sherman. At Shiloh, Sherman redeemed himself. Although his division was taken by surprise, he did not panic, and his performance in the Union victory won him a promotion to major-general. Now a trusted commander under Grant's direction, Sherman played an instrumental role in the Union campaigns to open the Mississippi Valley. He directed a corps in the campaign that captured Vicksburg and was part of the relief expedition that secured Chattanooga for the Union in the fall of 1863.

With Grant's departure to the East in March 1864, Sherman assumed command of the Union armies in the West. His Georgia campaigns—first the offensive against Atlanta that resulted in the capture of the city on September 1, 1864, and then his devastating March to the Sea and emergence at Savannah in late December—earned him his reputation as one of the top commanders of the war. From Savannah, Sherman swung northward into the Carolinas, and in April 1865, he forced the surrender of General Joseph E. Johnston's army.

Most of Sherman's postwar career was taken up with his duties as general-in-chief of the U.S. Army, a post that enabled him to apply his concept of total war against the Plains Indians. Always too fiery and outspoken to make much of a politician, he wisely rebuffed requests that he run for President in 1884 on the Republican ticket. He died at his home from a severe cold that worsened his chronic asthma.

SEE ALSO

Atlanta campaign; Bentonville; Sherman's March to the Sea; Shiloh; Vicksburg campaign

FURTHER READING

Fellman, Michael. *Citizen Sherman: A Life of William Tecumseh Sherman.* New York: Random House, 1995.
Marszalek, John F. *Sherman: A Soldier's Passion for Order.* New York: Free Press, 1993.

Sherman's March to the Sea

In November 1864, General William T. Sherman abandoned Atlanta, cut loose from his line of communications, and sent his Union army eastward across Georgia to establish a new base on the coast. The result was the March to the Sea, a campaign of physical destruction and psychological intimidation that sealed Sherman's reputation as one of the war's greatest generals and earned him the undying hatred of generations of Southern whites.

After occupying Atlanta in early September, Sherman destroyed everything of any value to the Confederate war effort. He also ordered civilians to evacuate the city. When the mayor of Atlanta protested, Sherman replied: "War is cruelty, and you cannot refine it: and those who brought war into our country deserve all the curses and maledictions a people can pour out."

Sherman's actions in Atlanta reflected his belief that the Union could be victorious only by striking at the economic resources of the Confederacy and the will to resist of its civilian population. The defeat of Southern armies was still a major goal, but not the only one. Thus, when the Confederate Army of Tennessee under General John Bell Hood swung north into Tennessee in early October, Sherman refused to chase it. Sherman had spent several fruitless weeks protecting his rail line back to Chattanooga from the incursions of Hood's army, and he now decided that he could put his army to better use. He detached two corps under General George H. Thomas to check Hood's advance into Tennessee and proposed to Washington that he take the bulk of his army and "strike out with our wagons for Milledgeville, Millen, and Savannah. Until we can repopulate Georgia, it is useless for us to occupy it; but the utter destruction of its roads, houses, and people will cripple their military resources. . . . I can make this march, and make Georgia howl!"

With Lincoln's reelection safely accomplished in early November, Sherman received approval for his seemingly risky plan of plunging into enemy territory with no line of supplies. In actuality, the risk was minimal. No significant Confederate force stood in Sherman's way, and his army was able to live off the land by systematically plundering farms and plantations for needed provisions.

Against a backdrop of Atlanta in flames, Sherman's army of 62,000 men began their march on the night of November 15. Facing no threat of a major Confederate attack, the army had no need to remain concentrated. It marched across a front of 60 miles in

two broad paths, one wing sweeping through the state capital at Milledgeville and the other marching farther south through Macon. Both wings drew closer together as they approached Savannah. Apart from some cavalry skirmishes, the only "battle" during the march occurred just east of Macon on November 22 when Sherman's right wing easily brushed aside the attack of some 3,000 Georgia militia.

Sherman's men were under orders to "forage liberally on the country during the march"—that is, to seize the food, fodder, and horses needed to sustain the army. Foraging parties organized daily in each regiment performed their tasks with a vengeance. Self-appointed or especially ruthless foragers, known as "bummers," were little more than ransacking thieves as they plundered the possessions of rich and poor, of slaves as well as their masters. Dolly Lunt, a planter's wife, shuddered after her home had been vandalized: "Such a day, if I live to the age of Methuselah, may God spare me from ever seeing again."

As his army neared Savannah in early December, Sherman reopened a line of communications by seizing Fort McAllister near the Georgia coast. He was preparing to shell Savannah with siege guns when General William J. Hardee prudently decided on December

The flames in Atlanta reach to the sky as Sherman's army moves out of the city on November 15, 1864.

20 to withdraw his 15,000 rebel troops from the city and retreat into South Carolina. A jubilant Sherman wired President Abraham Lincoln: "I beg to present you as a Christmas gift the City of Savannah."

At a cost of just 2,200 casualties, Sherman's march across Georgia crippled much of the war-making potential and morale of the Confederacy. His army accounted for some $100 million in property damage as it brought the war home with a frightening reality to Confederate civilians.

SEE ALSO
Hood, John Bell; Thomas, George H.

FURTHER READING
Davis, Burke. *Sherman's March*. New York: Vintage, 1988.
Glatthaar, Joseph T. *The March to the Sea and Beyond: Sherman's Troops in the Savannah and Carolinas Campaign*. New York: New York University Press, 1985.

Shiloh

Named after a nearby backwoods church, the battle of Shiloh on April 6 and 7, 1862, marked the first major Confederate counteroffensive in the western theater. Following the Union breakthroughs at Forts Henry and Donalson in February, General Albert Sidney Johnston, the commander of the Confederacy's Western Military Department, abandoned his Kentucky-Tennessee line and withdrew his forces southward in order to secure a new base of operations. Johnston concentrated his forces in Corinth, Mississippi, at the juncture of two key Confederate railroads. President Jefferson Davis sent reinforcements, and by the end of

March, Johnston had about 40,000 men. On April 3 he moved his army out of Corinth toward Pittsburgh Landing, Tennessee. His objective was the Union army of General Ulysses S. Grant, which was encamped 25 miles away with its back on the Tennessee River. Johnston's plan was simple: In a surprise attack he hoped to destroy Grant's army before it was reinforced by another Union army under General Don Carlos Buell moving southward from Nashville.

Johnston's army was inexperienced. Few of his soldiers had seen combat, and they made so much noise as they approached the Union lines that General Pierre G. T. Beauregard, Johnston's second-in-command, wanted to call off the attack. Johnston would brook no delay. Declaring, "I would fight them if they were a million," he confidently led his troops into battle on the morning of April 6.

Fortunately for the Confederates, Grant's army was just as green. Hastily thrown-together units held the outer lines of the Union encampment. Partly because he did not want to demoralize such raw troops by ordering them to dig entrenchments, but mostly out of an overconfidence born of recent victories, Grant failed to establish an adequate defensive line. The few pickets and patrols that were ordered out were all but oblivious to the huge rebel force massing nearby. General William Tecumseh Sherman, whose fifth division took the brunt of the rebels' initial assault, was convinced that the rebel army was no closer than Corinth.

Shortly after dawn on Sunday morning, April 6, the Confederates hurled themselves out of the woods near the Shiloh church. As later recounted by General Johnston's son William Preston, they "came on in motley garb" and "waved flags and

THE BATTLE OF SHILOH, OR PITTSBURG LANDING.
APRIL 6TH & 7TH 1862

Once the initial, massive charge of the Confederates at Shiloh spent itself, Union troops were able to assume the offensive.

pennons as various as their uniforms. At each charge there went up a wild yell, heard about the roar of artillery." The surge of the onrushing rebels swept through the Union lines and sent up to one-quarter of Grant's army running toward the cover of the steep bluffs overlooking Pittsburgh Landing. As Leander Stilwell of an Illinois company recalled: "The main thing was to get out of there as quick as we could."

Johnston sent his army in waves, one corps after the other rushing into a front three miles across. The result was a tremendous initial charge that inevitably bogged down in a melee of intermingled rebel units. The momentum of the Confederate attack slackened in midmorning in a wooded area of the Union center both sides dubbed "the hornet's nest." Outnumbered federals held off repeated assaults until late in the afternoon. One of these assaults cost Johnston his life when he bled to death from an artery severed by a bullet.

The stubborn Union resistance at the hornet's nest gave Grant the time he desperately needed to rally his troops and establish a defensive perimeter around the river's edge. A total of 50 Union cannon massed above the river's edge hammered the Confederates and deafened Union soldiers huddled nearby. Beauregard, who had assumed the Confederate command, called off the rebel attacks as evening fell.

Reinforced by troops arriving from Buell's army, Grant assumed the offensive on April 7 and drove the Confederates from the field. Stragglers and casualties had reduced Beauregard's army to 20,000 fighting men, and he ordered a retreat to Corinth at 2:30 in the afternoon.

The casualties at Shiloh were unprecedented in the war up to that point. The 20,000 killed and wounded were five times the losses at First Bull Run. Grant described a field on the battle's second day that was "so covered with dead that it would have been possible to walk across the clearing, in any direction, stepping on dead bodies, without a foot touching the ground." Such scenes were part of the terrible cost of the Union victory that denied the Confederacy its best opportunity to regain the strategic initiative in the West.

SEE ALSO

Beauregard, Pierre G. T.; Buell, Don Carlos; Davis, Jefferson; First Bull Run; Forts Henry and Donelson; Grant, Ulysses S.; Johnston, Albert Sidney; Sherman, William Tecumseh

FURTHER READING

Frank, Joseph Allan. *"Seeing the Elephant": Raw Recruits at the Battle of Shiloh.* Westport, Conn.: Greenwood Press, 1989.

McDonough, James L. *Shiloh—in Hell before Night.* Knoxville: University of Tennessee Press, 1977.

Sigel, Franz

UNION GENERAL AND POLITICIAN

- *Born: November 18, 1824, Sinsheim, duchy of Baden, Germany*
- *Political parties: Republican, Democrat*
- *Education: Karlsruhe military academy, 1840–43; University of Heidelberg, 1848*
- *Military service: U.S. Army: colonel, 3rd Missouri Infantry, 1861; brigadier general, volunteers, 1861–62; major general, volunteers, 1862–65*
- *Government service: Internal Revenue collector, 1870; registrar of New York City, 1871–74; equity clerk, New York City, 1885–86; pension agent for the New York District, 1886–89*
- *Died: August 21, 1902, New York, N.Y.*

Far more successful in attracting a loyal following from his fellow German Americans in the North than in leading federal troops, Franz Sigel was a major disappointment as a Union general. He never did fulfil his early military promise and failed badly in the Shenandoah Valley in the spring of 1864.

The son of a judge, Sigel received an excellent education in his native Germany. Upon graduating from the military academy of Karlsruhe, he entered the German army as a lieutenant. His liberal political views, however, repeatedly clashed with the authoritarian traditions of the army, and he resigned his commission in 1847 to begin a new career in law. Just after enrolling in the University of Heidelberg, he was swept up in a revolutionary movement that sought to reform the German political and cultural order. He joined the revolutionary forces as a military commander and served as their secretary of war in Baden, but the German army soon crushed the movement. Along with other revolutionary leaders, known as the Forty-Eighters, Sigel was forced into exile. After living in Switzerland and then England, he emigrated to New York in 1852.

Fluent in five languages, including English, Sigel established himself as a popular teacher in the German American community of New York City. In 1854 he married Elise Dulon, the daughter of a fellow Forty-Eighter, and three years later moved to St. Louis to accept a teaching position at the German American Institute. He joined the Republican party and campaigned for Lincoln's election in 1860.

Sigel immediately committed himself to the Union cause when the war broke out. After organizing the 3rd Missouri Infantry and performing well in the early federal efforts to keep Missouri within the Union, he was commissioned in August 1861, as a brigadier general of volunteers. His rapid promotion from colonel to

General Franz Sigel's popularity among his fellow German immigrants in the North inspired this comic wartime ballad. His handling of Federal operations in the Shenandoah Valley, however, was so inept that some of his soldiers added a new refrain: "I fights no more mit Sigel."

general indicated how valuable he was to the Lincoln administration as an ethnic leader around whom German Americans could rally behind the Union. He led a successful charge during the Union victory at Pea Ridge in March 1862, and this earned him a promotion to major general.

Declining health forced Sigel to take a leave of absence from active duty in April 1862. There was some doubt as to whether he would ever again be healthy enough to resume his command. As he ruefully noted years later, had he then retired from the army or passed away, his name forever would have been associated with "gallantry, chivalry and victory."

Unfortunately for his reputation, he did return to the army and his name became associated with military ineptitude and defeat.

Despite a very mediocre combat record in the Shenandoah Valley and Second Bull Run campaigns in the spring and summer of 1862, Sigel retained his value as a political symbol of German American support for the war. He thus continued to receive important commands. In the spring of 1864 he was ordered to pin down Confederate troops in the Shenandoah Valley and cut rebel communications to the region so that General Lee's army could no longer rely on the valley for supplies. His efforts ended with a sharp defeat at the battle of New Market on May 15, 1864, and the retreat of his army. One of his officers, Colonel David Hunter Strother, caustically noted: "We can afford to lose such a battle as New Market to get rid of such a mistake as Major General Sigel." Relieved of his command, he partially redeemed himself by rallying Union reserves when a Confederate raid threatened Washington in July 1864.

Sigel resigned from the army in

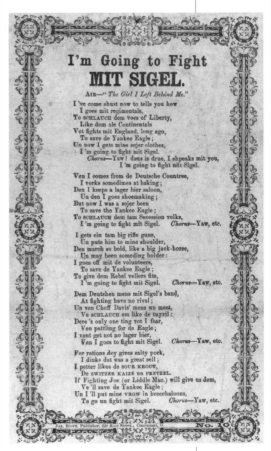

May 1865, and went into journalism in Baltimore. He moved permanently to New York City in 1867 where he remained a popular figure in the German community as a lecturer and editor. His Republican ties helped him secure a number of minor political offices. Believing that his old party had become hopelessly corrupt, he broke those ties in the 1880s and ended his life as a Democrat.

SEE ALSO
Grant's Virginia campaign

FURTHER READING
Engle, Stephen D., *Yankee Dutchman: The Life of Franz Sigel.* Fayetteville: University of Arkansas Press, 1993.

Slave resistance

Open resistance by African Americans to their enslavement was, in most instances, suicidal, and no major slave revolts erupted during the Civil War. What characterized the war years was a gradual slackening of slave discipline as the wives and daughters of Confederate soldiers struggled to exact work from the slaves. Most important, the war offered slaves the opportunity to flee to freedom as Union armies approached.

All too aware that whites had a monopoly on armed power, most slaves realized the futility of openly defying their masters or trying to stage a rebellion. Still, by drawing upon ties of family and kin, maintaining an oral culture steeped in their African heritage, and worshiping a God of deliverance in secret services, the slaves were able to retain a sense of dignity and avoid complete white domination. Since their enslavement involved, above all, hard, physical work at the command of whites, day-to-day resistance centered on efforts to reduce the imposed workloads. Slaves malingered,

feigned ignorance, broke tools, damaged crops, temporarily ran off, and, when pushed beyond endurance, destroyed plantation property or killed their masters. What resulted from these efforts was a tacit agreement over what constituted an "acceptable" workload. To be sure, whites always had the upper hand, but slaves were not totally powerless in setting some limits on their working conditions.

Once the Civil War began, slaves exploited every opportunity presented by the extraordinary wartime conditions to enlarge their personal liberties. Slave labor became critically important to the Confederate war effort. As whites grew ever more dependent on slaves for essential wartime production, slaves were able to use this dependence to gain concessions over their work conditions. This was especially the case in the countryside, where the management of slaves was now predominantly in the hands of the wives and children of male slaveowners off fighting in Confederate armies.

Largely free now of the coercive presence of able-bodied white men, the slaves refused to work as hard or as efficiently as they had before the war. Laura B. Comer of Columbus, Georgia, lodged a complaint in 1862 that was

Union troops charge the left flank of the army commanded by "Stonewall" Jackson at Cedar Mountain, Virginia. After the battle, blacks in flight from slavery followed them to the northeast.

echoed by Southern women throughout the war: "I am sure I don't know what anyone can do with [the] servants about the house; in the field where a man is with them, whom they fear all the time they will get along but I cannot, nor will not spend all these precious days of my life, following after and watching negroes. It is a terrible life!"

As a result of black initiatives and the dynamics unleashed by the war, slavery began to unravel. Slaves hastened that process when 500,000 of them made it behind Union lines and 130,000 fought in Union armies. Others were emboldened to roam off the plantations, avoid work, and in general test the limits of a new freedom that would become a reality with Union victory in the war.

SEE ALSO

Contrabands; Slavery; Underground Railroad

FURTHER READING

Mohr, Clarence L. *On the Threshold of Freedom: Masters and Slaves in Civil War Georgia.* Athens: University of Georgia Press, 1986.
Ripley, C. Peter. *Slaves and Freedmen in Civil War Louisiana.* Baton Rouge: Louisiana State University Press, 1976.
Robinson, Armstead L. *Bitter Fruits of Bondage: The Demise of Slavery and the Collapse of the Confederacy.* Charlottesville: University of Virginia Press, 2005.

Slave trade

The U.S. Constitution stipulated that Congress would have to wait 20 years before it could ban the importing of African slaves. In 1808, the first year that it could act, Congress did prohibit the African slave trade. Thereafter, and despite some intermittent smuggling, the

The slavetrading firm of Price, Birch & Company in Alexandria, Virginia, crowded slaves it purchased into pens such as this one before selling them at a profit to markets in the Lower South.

South depended on the domestic slave trade to meet the demand for slave laborers.

The internal slave trade—the organized buying, transporting, and selling of slaves—was extensive. In every decade between 1820 and 1860, more than 200,000 slaves were moved between regions in the South, and professional slave traders, as opposed to migrating planters, transported at least 60 percent of them. The dominant regional flow was from the older centers of tobacco and rice production in the Upper South and along the eastern seaboard to the newer centers of cotton production in the Lower South, where slavery was more profitable and the demand for slaves was greatest.

Market conditions dictated decisions on whether to buy or sell slaves. Contrary to the myth of planter paternalism, most slaveowners had no compunction about breaking up slave families if they stood to profit from the sale. As a result, the slave trade ended one of every five marriages of slave couples in the Upper South, and about half of all slave sales separated family members.

Slave children born in the Upper South after 1820 faced a one-in-three chance of being sold during their lifetime. No feature of slavery brought more anguish to the enslaved than this forcible breakup of their families.

The Confederacy, like the U.S. government earlier in the century, banned the African slave trade. The internal slave trade, however, continued to flourish in the early years of the Civil War. A permanent decline in the volume of sales did not set in until the Confederate military reversals in the summer of 1863. Still, even in the dying days of the Confederacy, speculators were betting that they could turn a profit in the trade. J. B. Jones, a Confederate clerk in Richmond, noted in his diary on March 22, 1865, that "although the insecurity of slave property is so manifest yet a negro man will bring $10,000 at auction." Only the imposition of Union authority put an end to the trade.

SEE ALSO
Slavery

FURTHER READING
Tadman, Michael. *Speculators and Slaves: Masters, Traders, and Slaves in the Old South.* Madison: University of Wisconsin Press, 1989.

Slavery

Slavery was a thriving, seemingly permanent institution in the South on the eve of the Civil War. Virtually all studies indicate a profit rate to slaveholders of 8 to 10 percent a year. These profits fueled the growth of the Southern economy, and planters, who usually owned 20 or more slaves, had immense social prestige as the leaders of Southern society.

In 1860, 15 slave states made up the South, and one-fourth of Southern white families owned slaves. The vast majority of these slaveholders, some 75 percent, owned fewer than 10 slaves, and half held fewer than 5. Planters, though constituting less than 3 percent of all Southern whites, owned more than half of the slaves.

Although used throughout the Southern economy, most slaves labored on plantations and medium-sized farms, where they produced the cash staples of cotton, sugar, rice, and tobacco. Cotton was the mainstay of the Southern economy, and slavery assumed its greatest importance in the seven states of the Lower South, where the soil and climate were most favorable for the production of cotton. In these states, slaves comprised half of the total population in 1860, and more than 40 percent of white families owned slaves. These states—South Carolina, Georgia, Florida, Alabama, Mississippi, Louisiana, and Texas—took the lead in secession and comprised the original Confederate States of America.

The harvest was the busiest time on a cotton plantation, and slaves would spend weeks picking cotton. Slave labor accounted for more than 90 percent of cotton production in the pre–Civil War South.

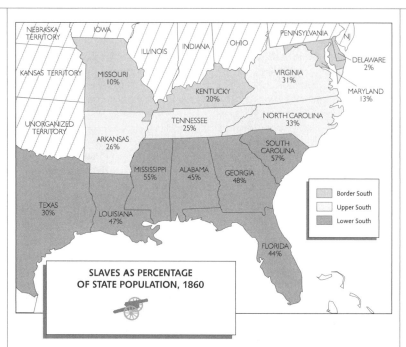

SLAVES AS PERCENTAGE OF STATE POPULATION, 1860

Border South
Upper South
Lower South

NEBRASKA TERRITORY
IOWA
KANSAS TERRITORY
UNORGANIZED TERRITORY
MISSOURI 10%
ILLINOIS
INDIANA
OHIO
PENNSYLVANIA
NJ
DELAWARE 2%
VIRGINIA 31%
MARYLAND 13%
KENTUCKY 20%
TENNESSEE 25%
NORTH CAROLINA 33%
ARKANSAS 26%
SOUTH CAROLINA 57%
MISSISSIPPI 55%
ALABAMA 45%
GEORGIA 48%
TEXAS 30%
LOUISIANA 47%
FLORIDA 44%

The eight slave states of the Upper South hung back from immediate secession. In these states, slavery lacked the overwhelming importance that it had in the Cotton South as both an economic investment and a means of racial control. Rates of slave ownership and concentrations of slaves were roughly half those of the Lower South. Four of these states—Virginia, North Carolina, Tennessee, and Arkansas—eventually joined the Confederacy in the spring of 1861 in the wake of the Fort Sumter crisis. The states of the Border South abutting the North—Delaware, Maryland, Kentucky, and Missouri—remained in the Union. Slavery in the border states had been declining gradually since 1800, and economic ties to the Union overrode any attachment to the Confederacy.

The relative strength or weakness of slavery had been an accurate barometer of Southern political loyalties during the secession crisis. That crisis mobilized the major slaveholding interests, and Con-federate leaders pledged to defend the institution of slavery at all costs. Slavery, as Confederate Vice President Alexander H. Stephens proclaimed on March 22, 1861, was the "cornerstone" of the new Southern republic.

The Confederacy entered the Civil War confident that slavery would enable it to emerge victorious. The *Montgomery Advertiser*, an Alabama newspaper, argued in the fall of 1861 that the institution was a "tower of strength" and "really one of the most effective weapons employed against the Union by the South." With slave labor to fall back on, the Confederacy could place in its armies a higher percentage of its white manpower than the free-labor North. After the war, Union General Ulysses S. Grant conceded, "The 4,000,000 colored noncombatants were equal to more than three times their number in the North, age for age, sex for sex."

Until 1863 slavery was an undoubted asset to the Confederacy, as black labor proved indispensable in the war economy. Slaves produced foodstuffs to feed the armies, dug out coal and other raw materials, built and repaired fortifications and railroads, manufactured the implements of war, and nursed the wounded. Slaves performed not only the bulk of the physical labor but also a surprising amount of the skilled tasks. For example, railroad brakemen and firemen were typically slaves, and many of the skilled technicians at the Tredegar Iron Works in Richmond, one of the Confederacy's most important war factories, were slaves.

Slave discipline was always grounded in fear, and Confederate authorities stepped up security measures in order to keep the slaves in line. The primary responsibility for maintaining internal surveillance rested on home guard units of all white males not in the army. The slightest rumor of a slave revolt triggered reprisals in the form of executions, beatings, and imprisonment.

The slaves could not revolt, but they could flee to advancing Union armies and contribute their labor to hasten Confederate defeat. Their growing presence behind federal lines pushed forward a debate that culminated in the Union's decision in 1863 to liberate and arm the former slaves of the Confederacy. Slavery now was a source of weakness for the Confederacy, and it remained so for the rest of the war as the Union drew on more and more black laborers and soldiers.

SEE ALSO

Causes of the Civil War; Contrabands; Secession; Slave resistance; Wartime economies

FURTHER READING

Berlin, Ira. *Generations of Captivity: A History of African-American Slavery.* Cambridge: Harvard University Press, 2003.

Roark, James L. *Masters Without Slaves:*
Southern Planters in the Civil War and Reconstruction. New York: Norton, 1977.

Stampp, Kenneth M. *The Peculiar Institution: Slavery in the Ante-Bellum South.* New York: Vintage, 1956.

Smalls, Robert

AFRICAN-AMERICAN POLITICIAN

- *Born: April 5, 1839, Beaufort, S.C.*
- *Political party: Republican*
- *Education: no formal schooling*
- *Military service: U.S. Navy, captain, 1863–66*
- *Government service: South Carolina House of Representatives, 1868–69; South Carolina Senate, 1870–72; U.S. House of Representatives, 1875–79; 1882–87; collector of the port of Charleston, 1889–93; 1897–1913*
- *Died: February 22, 1915, Beaufort, S.C.*

A slave at the start of the Civil War, Robert Smalls became a black war hero in May 1862, when he gained his freedom by commandeering the *Planter*, a Confederate steamer docked in Charleston, South Carolina, and piloting the boat to the offshore Union blockading fleet. Commissioned as a pilot and then a captain in the U.S. Navy, he brought in supplies for black refugees along the coast of Georgia and South Carolina. After the war, he was an influential Republican politician in South Carolina.

Born a slave to John McKee of Beaufort, South Carolina, Smalls acquired a new master in 1848 when McKee died and willed his slaves to his son Henry. When Henry McKee moved to Charleston in 1851, he hired out Smalls at a variety of urban jobs. Working as a boatman, Smalls learned piloting skills and gained a sailor's

Robert Smalls became a hero in the North when he ran the Confederate steamer Planter out of Charleston harbor and delivered it to the Union navy. Harper's Weekly featured the man and the boat.

knowledge of the waters in and around Charleston. Impressed into Confederate service after the fall of Fort Sumter, he and a dozen other slaves were assigned to the *Planter,* a transport steamer supplying the Confederate installations in the Charleston area.

Taking advantage of the absence of the captain and his white crew, Smalls smuggled his wife and children aboard the *Planter* on the morning of May 13, 1862, eased the steamer past the unsuspecting sentries in Charleston Harbor, and delivered it to offshore U.S. naval forces. His daring exploit made him an instant celebrity in the North and earned him a modest fortune when he was awarded part of the prize money for the *Planter.* After serving as a Union pilot and taking part in the assault on Charleston in April 1863, he became the first African American to command a ship in the U.S. Navy when he was appointed captain of the *Planter,* now refitted as a Union gunboat, in December 1863.

When interviewed by the American Freedman's Inquiry Commission in 1863, Smalls declared that South Carolina slaves were anxious to fight for their freedom. "If they had a chance," he noted, "there would be no difficulty in raising a military force." Making the same argument to President Abraham

Lincoln and Secretary of War Edwin M. Stanton at a meeting in Washington, he helped convince the War Department to accept 5,000 South Carolina contrabands as Union soldiers.

After his ship was decommissioned in 1866, Smalls returned to the South Carolina low-country and emerged as the region's leading black politician. As a delegate to the South Carolina constitutional convention in 1868, a member of the state legislature, and a U.S. congressman, he championed the civil rights of blacks, especially in the area of equal access to transportation facilities. He might well have had in mind his own experience in Philadelphia in January 1865, when he was ejected from a streetcar and forced to walk several miles to the navy yard.

The overthrow of Republican rule in South Carolina at the end of Reconstruction and the disfranchisement of black voters undercut most of Smalls's political influence. He, like many other black politicians, survived on the party jobs distributed by national Republican administrations. After 1889, he served nearly continuously as customs collector of the port of Charleston until shortly before his death.

SEE ALSO

Contrabands

FURTHER READING

Miller, Edward A. *Gullah Statesman: Robert Smalls from Slavery to Congress, 1839–1915.* Columbia: University of South Carolina Press, 1995.

Uya, Okon Edet. *From Slavery to Public Service: Robert Smalls, 1839–1915.* New York: Oxford University Press, 1971.

Smith, Edmund Kirby

CONFEDERATE GENERAL

- *Born: May 16, 1824, St. Augustine, Fla.*
- *Education: U.S. Military Academy, B.S., 1845*
- *Military service: U.S. Army: lieutenant, infantry, 1845–51; 1st lieutenant, 1851–55; captain, cavalry, 1855–61; major, 1861; Confederate army: lieutenant colonel, 1861; brigadier general, 1861; major-general, 1861–62; lieutenant general, 1862–64; general, 1864–65*
- *Died: March 28, 1893, Sewanee, Tenn.*

The last major Confederate general to surrender his forces, Edmund Kirby Smith spent most of the war as commander of the Trans-Mississippi Department. He assumed such extraordinary powers in this isolated region of the Confederacy that it became known as "Kirby Smithdom."

Urged by his family to pursue a military career, Smith attended a preparatory school in Virginia before his appointment to West Point. Poor eyesight almost prevented him from receiving a commission, but he established a fine combat record in the Mexican War. After teaching mathematics at West Point, he transferred to the cavalry and fought in Indian campaigns on the Texas frontier. Despite refusing to surrender his command at Fort Colorado in Texas to secessionist forces, he resigned his commission on April 6, 1861, and followed his native state of Florida out of the Union.

Assigned initially to the Shenandoah Valley, Smith was severely wounded while leading a brigade at First Bull Run in July 1861. His timely arrival at the battle made him an early war hero, and upon recuperating, he was placed in charge of the department of East Tennessee. Ordered to link up with General Braxton Bragg's army in the Kentucky invasion of the late summer of 1862, Smith scored an impressive victory at Richmond, Kentucky, on August 30, 1862, that opened a rebel path to Lexington. But he was too headstrong and independent-minded to cooperate effectively with Bragg, and, contrary to Smith's expectations, white Kentuckians failed to rally behind the Confederate cause.

Shortly after his appointment as head of the Trans-Mississippi Department in early 1863, Smith complained to his former commander, General Joseph E. Johnston: "I have a herculanian task before me on this side of the Miss—no army—no means—an empire in extent, no system, no order, all to be done from the beginning." He commanded a huge area that had been stripped of military manpower and neglected by the authorities in Richmond. Already tenuous communications across the Mississippi River were virtually cut off when Vicksburg fell in July 1863.

With the tacit approval of Jefferson Davis's administration, Smith assumed civil as well as military powers. Necessity forced him to replicate the administrative bureaus for the furnishing and equipping of arms that had been established by the Richmond government east of the Mississippi. His authority also extended to such areas as collecting taxes, conscripting troops, exchanging prisoners of war, maintaining diplomatic relations with Mexico, and purchasing or impressing cotton and exporting it through Mexican ports for arms and supplies.

On the military front, Smith stymied the Union's Red River campaign in the spring of 1864 and then divested rebel troops to block a federal column advancing south from Arkansas. After unsuccessful efforts to send reinforcements into Mississippi, he directed General Sterling Price to launch a raid into Missouri in the fall of 1864. This raid was the last organized military operation of the Confederacy west of the Mississippi.

Largely because of his administrative abilities, Smith succeeded in maintaining a structure of Confederate authority in the Trans-Mississippi region, and his department was never overrun by federal forces. After surrendering his command on May 26, 1865, he fled to Mexico and then to Cuba before returning to the United States in the fall of 1865. He briefly served as the president of a telegraph company before turning to a career in education. At the time of his death, he was a professor of mathematics at the University of the South.

SEE ALSO

Bragg's Kentucky Invasion

FURTHER READING

Kerby, Robert L. *Kirby Smith's Confederacy: The Trans-Mississippi South, 1863–1865.* New York: Columbia University Press, 1972.
Parks, Joseph H. *General Edmund Kirby Smith, C.S.A.* Baton Rouge: Louisiana State University Press, 1954.

Soldier aid societies

SEE United States Sanitary Commission; Women in the war

Soldiers, profile of

Ample written records, especially for the Union army, make it possible to draw a profile of Civil War soldiers. What stands out from the records is the raw youth of many of the soldiers and their common agricultural background.

The most typical Civil War soldier was a young citizen-soldier from a farm or plantation who volunteered to serve. Half of all soldiers were 24 or younger at the date of their enlistment, and nearly 40 percent were 21 or younger. They were motivated to fight out of a patriotic sense of duty and a desire to prove to their families and communities that they were good sons and worthy husbands. Whether they wore Union blue or Confederate gray, they saw themselves as defending the notions of freedom and liberty embedded in their respective societies.

Although poorly disciplined by the standards of European armies, Civil

These Union soldiers are on guard duty in an area of tangled underbrush like the choked woods of the Wilderness where the armies of Lee and Grant clashed in May 1864.

In the brief lull between the fighting at Spotsylvania and Cold Harbor during Grant's Virginia campaign, some soldiers in the Army of the Potomac enjoyed the luxury of a bath in the North Anna River.

War soldiers compiled a remarkable combat record. Regiments repeatedly demonstrated the ability to absorb battlefield casualties of 20 percent or higher and still be effective fighting units. This record reflected not only the self-motivation of the soldiers but also the bonds of local communities that were reproduced at the company level within individual regiments. Especially in the first half of the war, the soldiers fought alongside friends and neighbors and followed the leadership of officers they knew and trusted. Anxious not to dishonor themselves in the eyes of friends or loved ones, they stressed in their letters home that they had measured up and had not turned and run in battle. "All I need say about the 14th," wrote James Newton to his parents about his Wisconsin regiment at the battle of Shiloh, "is that they *didn't run.*"

Occupational data on the soldiers reveals that in the aggregate, Civil War armies were quite representative of the home fronts that had sent them off to war. As can be seen in the bar graph, the occupational breakdown of the men in both armies corresponds closely with that of civilian societies of 1860 in the North and South. Data from wealth categories would depict the same pattern.

The graph also reveals that, contrary to Southern charges that the North recruited foreigners to fill up its armies, the foreign-born were proportionately underrepresented in the Union army and overrepresented in the Confederacy army. Not shown in the graph is the racial makeup of a Union army that eventually recruited African Americans for 10 percent of its soldiers. It is likely that the refusal of the Confederacy

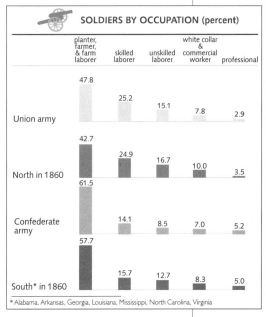

SOLDIERS BY OCCUPATION (percent)

	planter, farmer, & farm laborer	skilled laborer	unskilled laborer	white collar & commercial worker	professional
Union army	47.8	25.2	15.1	7.8	2.9
North in 1860	42.7	24.9	16.7	10.0	3.5
Confederate army	61.5	14.1	8.5	7.0	5.2
South* in 1860	57.7	15.7	12.7	8.3	5.0

* Alabama, Arkansas, Georgia, Louisiana, Mississippi, North Carolina, Virginia

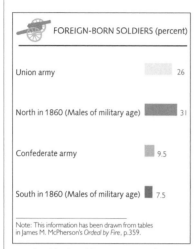

FOREIGN-BORN SOLDIERS (percent)

Union army — 26

North in 1860 (Males of military age) — 31

Confederate army — 9.5

South in 1860 (Males of military age) — 7.5

Note: This information has been drawn from tables in James M. McPherson's *Ordeal by Fire*, p.359.

to enlist black soldiers accounts for its proportionately greater reliance on its white immigrant population.

SEE ALSO

Armies

FURTHER READING

Lonn, Ella. *Foreigners in the Confederacy.* Chapel Hill: University of North Carolina Press, 1940.

———. *Foreigners in the Union Army and Navy.* Baton Rouge: Louisiana State University Press, 1951.

Robertson, James I., Jr. *Soldiers Blue and Gray.* Columbia: University of South Carolina Press, 1988.

Wiley, Bell Irvin. *The Life of Billy Yank: The Common Soldiers of the Union.* Indianapolis: Bobbs-Merrill, 1952.

———. *The Life of Johny Reb: The Common Soldier of the Confederacy.* Indianapolis: Bobbs-Merrill, 1943.

Southern Union soldiers

About 275,000 Southern whites fought in Union armies. Their allegiance to the Union was a major factor in Confederate defeat.

The largest bloc of Southern white soldiers in the Union army came out of the Border South—the slave states of Delaware, Kentucky, Maryland, Missouri, and those counties in northwestern Virginia that joined the Union as the state of West Virginia in 1863. These areas in the Upper South supplied the Union with nearly 200,000 white troops, twice what they furnished the Confederacy.

With the exception of South Carolina, the Union also raised at least a battalion of white troops in each of the 11 slave states that comprised the Confederacy. The likeliest candidates to join the Union army were nonslaveholding farmers in upland or mountainous regions where slavery was of marginal economic importance. East Tennessee, where the Confederacy never established effective control, alone supplied more than half of the 70,000 Confederate whites who fought for the Union.

Of all the Southern whites who saw military service in the Civil War, roughly one in four fought against the Confederacy. These losses to the Union cause dealt a crippling blow to a Confederate war effort that never could rest on the undivided allegiance of a united white South.

After the war, Southern white Unionists, many of whom were persecuted, often found it necessary to meet in secret. Supporters of the Confederacy controlled politics in the South under President Andrew Johnson's program of Reconstruction.

SEE ALSO
Border South

FURTHER READING
Current, Richard Nelson. *Lincoln's Loyal-
ists: Union Soldiers from the Confeder-
acy.* Boston: Northeastern University
Press, 1992.
Freehling, William W. *The South vs. the
South: How Anti-Confederate Southerners
Shaped the Course of the Civil War.* New
York: Oxford University Press, 2001.

Spotsylvania

SEE Grant's Virginia campaign

Stanton, Edwin McMasters

UNION POLITICIAN

- *Born: December 19, 1814,
  Steubenville, Ohio*
- *Political parties: Democrat,
  Republican*
- *Education: sporadic schooling in
  lower grades*
- *Government service: U.S. attorney
  general, 1860–61; U.S. secretary of
  war, 1862–68*
- *Died: December 24, 1869,
  Washington D.C.*

Opinionated, hard-driving, and energetic, Edwin M. Stanton brought order
and accountability to the Union War
Department upon taking it over in early
1862. A prewar Democrat, he quickly
earned Lincoln's respect and became
one of his most valuable allies in the
cabinet. Staying on as secretary of war
in President Andrew Johnson's administration, he protected the interests of the
army from any interference on Johnson's part and eventually broke with
Johnson over Reconstruction.

Stanton's father, a physician, died in
1827, and the financial difficulties of
his family interrupted his schooling and
forced him to withdraw from Kenyon

College. After studying law under his
guardian, David L. Collier, he was
admitted to the Ohio bar in 1836. He
moved to Pittsburgh in 1847 and soon
gained a national reputation for his
legal work. His most distinguished case
came in 1858, when he successfully represented the federal government in a
suit brought by claimants with fraudulent land patents in California.

A lifelong Democrat who accepted
the decision of the U.S. Supreme Court
in the *Dred Scott* case, Stanton was also
a staunch Unionist who personally disapproved of slavery. Appointed U.S.
attorney general in December 1860 to
help stiffen the backbone of President
James Buchanan during the secession
crisis, he was back in private life when
the Civil War began. In January 1862,
he succeeded Simon Cameron as secretary of war with a mandate to clean up
the scandal-ridden War Department and
improve its efficiency.

Upon taking over, Stanton pledged
to a future assistant that "As soon as I
can get the machinery of the office
working, the rats cleared out, and the
rat holes stopped we shall *move*. This
army has got to fight or run away."
Although often brusque and imperious,
he did bring a sense of urgency to his
department and the war effort. Workloads were systematized, funds were
secured for additional personnel, and

*Edwin McMas-
ters Stanton's
stern appear-
ance suggests
the forceful
style of his
administration
of the War
Department.
His reputation
as a martinet
was so strong
that John Hay,
Lincoln's secre-
tary, once said
that he'd rather
"make a tour
of a smallpox
hospital" than
seek any favors
from Stanton.*

fraudulent contractors were rooted out and prosecuted.

Stanton persuaded Congress to authorize the takeover of railroad and telegraph lines when military necessity dictated, and he transferred the handling of cases of suspected disloyalty from the State to the War Department. At his insistence, the War Department censored the press when military security seemed threatened. When a former personal friend and legal client, General George B. McClellan, frustrated Stanton with his cautious handling of the Army of the Potomac, the secretary of war led the drive to have him replaced. In September 1863, Stanton supervised one of the greatest logistical feats of the war: He transferred within a week a fully equipped contingent of 23,000 troops 1,200 miles overland to Chattanooga, a move that most observers thought would take a month.

A Republican by the midpoint of the war, Stanton worked closely with party leaders in Congress while he retained his post as secretary of war in Johnson's cabinet. He soon feared that Johnson would squander the fruits of Union victory by failing to maintain any meaningful national authority in the defeated South. His conflict with Johnson came to a head when the President attempted to remove him from office in 1868, an act that led to Johnson's impeachment.

Stanton finally left office on May 26, 1868. He was named to the Supreme Court in late 1869, but his death that December from the ravages of an asthmatic condition prevented him from accepting the seat.

SEE ALSO
Cameron, Simon

FURTHER READING
Thomas, Benjamin P., and Harold M. Hayman. *Stanton: The Life and Times of Lincoln's Secretary of War.* New York: Knopf, 1962.

Stanton, Elizabeth Cady

ABOLITIONIST AND FEMINIST

- *Born: November 12, 1815, Johnstown, N.Y.*
- *Education: Troy Female Seminary, 1830–32*
- *Public service: organizer, Seneca Falls Convention, 1848; president, New York's Woman's State Temperance Society, 1852–53; Women's National Loyal League, 1863–65; vice president, American Equal Rights Association, 1866–69; president, National Woman Suffrage Association, 1869–90; National American Woman Suffrage Association, 1890–92*
- *Died: October 26, 1902, New York, N.Y.*

A leader of the women's rights movement, Elizabeth Cady Stanton cofounded with Susan B. Anthony the Woman's National Loyal League in 1863. By collecting 400,000 signatures on a petition in support of a constitutional amendment ending slavery, the league was instrumental in the passage of the 13th Amendment.

Born into a wealthy upstate New York family, Stanton gained an interest in reform at an early age. Her father was a lawyer, and she soon discovered that the women who came to him had little legal recourse in the antebellum United States from the abuse they suffered from their husbands. Through her cousin Gerritt Smith, an abolitionist who ran a station on the Underground Railroad in Petersboro, New York, she met fugitive slaves and learned of the horrors of slavery. In 1856 she married the abolitionist Henry Stanton.

The refusal in 1840 of the World Antislavery Convention in London to seat the U.S. female delegates convinced Stanton of the need for an organization

Elizabeth Cady Stanton committed herself to the cause of women's rights, despite the responsibilities of raising seven children and the strong opposition of her father and her husband.

exclusively devoted to championing the legal and political rights of women. Along with Lucretia Mott, she organized the Seneca Falls Convention of 1848 that launched the feminist movement.

With an energy that belied the demands of raising seven children, she continued to be active in temperance, abolitionism, and feminism through the 1850s. Opposed to any concessions to the South on the slavery issue, she wrote in a letter to a cousin in 1856, "Our fair republic must be the victim of the monster, slavery, unless we speedily rise in our might and boldly shout freedom."

The Republican triumph in 1860 was the bold cry for freedom that Stanton demanded, but it also triggered secession and war. Unlike most female abolitionists, Stanton insisted that the cause of women's rights not be abandoned during the war. She realized her goal of linking emancipation to feminism by shaping the philosophy and assuming the leadership of the Woman's National Loyal League. Founded in April 1863, the league was committed to equal rights for all Americans, regardless of race or gender, and to the immediate and complete emancipation of all slaves, including those not freed by the Emancipation Proclamation. The league's massive petitioning campaign mobilized thousands of women in the cause of freedom and involved them more deeply than ever before in the political sphere. Their efforts resulted in signatures supporting emancipation from nearly 5 percent of all adults in

the Northern states, an astounding number in that pre-electronic age.

Stanton hoped that this wartime assertion of women's moral power in politics would pave the way for woman suffrage and equal citizenship after the war. As she proclaimed in early 1864: "By our earnestness and zeal on the exercise of this one right [to petition Congress], let us prove ourselves worthy to make larger demands in the readjustment of the new government."

Stanton was to be bitterly disappointed. Although women had played a vital role in securing complete emancipation, the postwar Republicans ignored their demands for equality. Most galling of all for Stanton was the refusal of Congress to provide for woman suffrage in the 15th Amendment that gave blacks the vote. Stanton reacted by founding the National Woman Suffrage Association in 1869. She devoted the rest of her life to winning the vote for women and denouncing what she called "an aristocracy based on sex."

SEE ALSO

Anthony, Susan B.; Emancipation; 15th Amendment; Suffrage; 13th Amendment

FURTHER READING

Griffith, Elisabeth. *In Her Own Right: The Life of Elizabeth Cady Stanton.* New York: Oxford University Press, 1984.
Venet, Wendy Hamand. *Neither Ballots nor Bullets: Women Abolitionists and the Civil War.* Charlottesville: University Press of Virginia, 1991.

States' rights

The doctrine of states' rights holds that the states retain all powers except those expressly delegated to the federal

government in the U.S. Constitution. Used throughout U.S. history whenever states feel their interests are being threatened by the federal government, states' rights before the Civil War became associated most closely with the efforts of Southern states to prevent federal interference with slavery.

The Constitution of 1787 left unclear the precise boundary between national and state powers. This ambiguity, which allowed both nationalists and states'-rights advocates to read what they wanted into the Constitution, was essential for gaining the majority support necessary for ratification. Over time, however, this lack of clarity proved fatal to the stability of the original Union. The issue of slavery, left unresolved in the gray area between federal and state sovereignty, sparked a series of escalating constitutional battles that ultimately plunged the nation into civil war.

The Virginia and Kentucky Resolutions of 1798–99, authored by James Madison and Thomas Jefferson, respectively, articulated the first significant Southern position on states' rights. The resolutions set forth a compact theory of the Union in which the states retained the sovereign power to judge the constitutionality of federal legislation. Building upon these ideas during the nullification controversy of 1832–33, John C. Calhoun of South Carolina worked out a full-blown constitutional theory by which an individual state could nullify, or declare void within its borders, a federal law. As a last resort to protect its interests, Calhoun argued that a state could legally leave the Union.

Initially, only South Carolina fully endorsed Calhoun's formulation of states' rights. The rising tide of abolitionism, however, combined with Northern efforts to block slavery from expanding into the territories, made Calhoun's ideas ever more appealing to Southerners concerned with preserving slavery. As Southern political power continued to decline in a Union dominated by a growing Northern majority, Southern radicals known as "fire-eaters" pushed the doctrine of states' rights to its logical extreme by upholding the constitutional right of a state to secede. As their ideas gained currency in the 1850s, more and more Southern whites believed that secession offered the ultimate defense against Northern transgressions. Once the North elected Abraham Lincoln President, many Southern states were prepared to act on that belief.

Even though the Confederacy these states soon joined said nothing in its constitution about the right of a state to secede, the principles of states' rights remained central to Southern political culture. Repeatedly, wartime governors resorted to them as they resisted the demands made by Confederate President Jefferson Davis during the fighting.

SEE ALSO

Calhoun; Federalism; Nationalism; Nullification; Secession

FURTHER READING

Bestor, Arthur. "The Civil War as a Constitutional Crisis." *American Historical Review* 69, No. 2 (January 1964): 327–52.

Brandon, Mark E. *Free in the World: American Slavery and Constitutional Failure*. Princeton, N.J.: Princeton University Press, 1998.

Stephens, Alexander H.

CONFEDERATE POLITICIAN

- *Born: February 11, 1812, Crawfordsville, Ga.*
- *Political parties: Whig, Democrat*
- *Education: Franklin College (now University of Georgia), A.B., 1832*

- *Government service: Georgia House of Representatives, 1836–41; Georgia Senate, 1842; U.S. House of Representatives, 1843–59, 1873–82; governor of Georgia, 1882–83; Confederacy: vice president, 1861–65*
- *Died: March 4, 1883, Atlanta, Ga.*

A leader of the prewar Georgia Whigs and a reluctant secessionist, Alexander H. Stephens served as vice president of the Confederacy. Wizened and frail in appearance—an Alabama reporter once described him in 1861 as this "little, sallow, dried-up-looking fellow"—he nonetheless was a skilled politician who emerged as the most prominent critic in the Confederacy of the centralizing war measures pushed through by the administration of Jefferson Davis.

The son of a yeoman farmer, Stephens was raised by an uncle following the death of his father in 1826. With the financial assistance of local benefactors in the Presbyterian Church, he was able to attend Franklin College. He taught school, studied law, and was admitted to the Georgia bar in 1834. He entered politics as a states'-rights Whig and soon emerged as a leader of the party. Sickly and physically weak throughout his life—he weighed less than 100 pounds—he discovered in politics a combative arena where he could excel and gain the public recognition that he craved.

Stephens once wrote a friend that principles were the "pole star of my existence." Foremost among those principles were states' rights and strict adherence to constitutional safeguards that alone, he believed, could maintain social order and protect the individual liberties of the white race. A staunch Unionist as well as a defender of slavery, he fashioned these principles into a defense of slavery that saw in the U.S.

Constitution a legal bulwark for the preservation of the institution. After directing the Unionist movement in Georgia in 1850, he finally abandoned the Whig party in 1859 when it was no longer a political force in the Lower South. He championed the Union cause during the secession crisis but relented when he realized that popular enthusiasm for secession was too strong to resist. Now himself a large slaveholder, he declared in a speech in March 1861 that the Confederacy's "corner-stone rests upon the great truth that the negro is not equal to the white man; that slavery—subordination to the superior race—is his natural and normal condition."

Stephens's election as Confederate vice president represented an effort to bury old partisan divisions in the new Confederacy. But once in office, Stephens was virtually ignored by Davis and had no active role to play. He remained in the background until 1862, when he publicly lashed out against Confederate policies regarding conscription, the suspension of the writ of habeas corpus, and the imposition of martial law in some localities. Aligning himself with Governor Joseph Brown of Georgia, he denounced Davis and his government for violating the very states' rights and white civil liberties that comprised the founding principles of the Confederacy. Although attacked as an obstructionist, if

Painfully thin, ashen in complexion, and stiffened by chronic arthritis, Confederate Vice President Alexander H. Stephens hardly looked like the forceful leader who commanded the respect of Confederates at odds with Jefferson Davis's war measures, which included conscription and martial law.

not a traitor, for his opposition to Confederate war measures, Stephens never wavered from his belief that the most loyal Confederate was one who "supports and defends the [Confederate] Constitution."

In the last year of the war, Stephens clung to the hope that Union leaders would be willing to accept Southern independence as the basis for a negotiated peace. When that hope was dashed by the Hampton Roads Conference in February 1865, he accepted the inevitability of a Confederate collapse. He was arrested by federal authorities at the end of the war and imprisoned in Boston for six months.

Stephens was an unrelenting critic of Reconstruction after the war. Following the publication of his *Constitutional View of the Late War Between the States* (1868–70), a turgid defense of the Southern position on states' rights, he was elected to Congress, where he served in the House for 10 years. He died shortly after beginning a term as governor of Georgia.

SEE ALSO
Hampton Roads Conference

FURTHER READING
Schott, Thomas E. *Alexander H. Stephens of Georgia.* Baton Rouge: Louisiana State University Press, 1988.
Von Abele, Rudolph Radama. *Alexander H. Stephens.* New York: Knopf, 1946.

Stevens, Thaddeus

UNION POLITICIAN

- *Born: April 4, 1792, Danville, Vermont*
- *Political parties: Federalist, Anti-Mason, Whig, Republican*
- *Education: Dartmouth College, A.B., 1814*
- *Government service: Pennsylvania House of Representatives, 1833–35, 1837, 1841; U.S. House of Representatives, 1849–53, 1859–68*
- *Died: August 11, 1868, Washington, D.C.*

The most prominent Radical among congressional Republicans during and after the Civil War, Thaddeus Stevens championed a stern policy toward the South, one based on an uncompromising belief in equal rights for all Americans regardless of color. He summed up his political creed when he declared in Congress: "This is not 'a white man's Government'. . . . To say so is political blasphemy, for it violates the fundamental principles of our gospel of liberty." For Stevens, that "gospel" decreed that "equal right to all the privileges of the Government is innate in every mortal being, no matter what the shape or color of the tabernacle it inhabits."

Born in rural poverty in Vermont, Stevens became moderately prosperous through a career in law, politics, and iron manufacturing. His widowed mother helped put him through Dartmouth College, and following his graduation, he moved to Pennsylvania. Admitted to the Pennsylvania bar in 1816, he soon gained a reputation for defending fugitive slaves without pay. In 1826 he invested in an iron works (part of which was burned by Confederate troops during the Gettysburg campaign). As a member of the Pennsylvania House, he led the fight for the establishment of free public schools. Elected to Congress as an antislavery Whig, he consistently opposed any expansion of slavery. In the mid-1850s, his antislavery principles carried him into the new Republican party.

Although he had supported Abraham Lincoln during the Presidential campaign of 1860, Stevens was one of the President's most caustic critics within the Republican party during the Civil War. As a leader of the party's Radical wing, Stevens charged that Lincoln was too cautious in prosecuting the war and was missing a priceless opportunity to smash forever the political and economic power of the slaveholders. Stevens's vision was that of a radically transformed United States in which all citizens, including the freed slaves, could enjoy equal civil and political rights. He insisted that the war must be treated as "a radical revolution."

Continuing after the war as chairman of the House Ways and Means Committee, Stevens was in a strategic position to push forward the Radicals' agenda for using enhanced national power to transform Southern society. He argued that the former Confederate states had forfeited their constitutional rights by seceding and were now to be ruled as conquered provinces. In order to create the conditions for an egalitarian society in the postwar South, he called for the seizure by the federal government of the landed estates of wealthy former Confederates. A portion of their confiscated land was to be redistributed to adult freemen in 40-acre plots and the remainder sold off to finance pensions for Union soldiers and to reduce the war debt.

Stevens's program of land confiscation was far too radical even for most Republicans, and it never passed Congress. Nonetheless, his mastery of parliamentary tactics and his unrivaled ability to articulate the egalitarian ideals of his party were instrumental in uniting the Republicans behind a program of Reconstruction that was far more sensitive to the needs of the recently freed slaves than the policy of President Andrew Johnson. Stevens fought every effort of Johnson's to stymie congressional Reconstruction and headed the movement for his impeachment.

Shortly after Johnson's acquittal, Stevens died. At his insistence, he was buried in an obscure cemetery that was racially integrated.

SEE ALSO
Radicals; Reconstruction

FURTHER READING
Brodie, Fawn M. *Thaddeus Stevens: Scourge of the South.* New York: Norton, 1959.
Trefousse, Hans L. *Thaddeus Stevens: Nineteenth-Century Egalitarian.* Chapel Hill: University of North Carolina Press, 1997.

Stones River

Following his withdrawal from Kentucky in October 1862, Confederate General Braxton Bragg positioned his Army of Tennessee at Murfreesboro, Tennessee, along Stones River and the railroad that ran from Nashville to Chattanooga. In Nashville, 30 miles to the northwest, General William S. Rosecrans had replaced Don Carlos Buell in charge of the reorganized Union Army of the Cumberland. Both generals were under pressure to make an aggressive move. Rosecrans was under fire for spending November and most of December gathering supplies for his army, and Bragg was still smarting from criticism that he had mishandled his Kentucky invasion. When Rosecrans moved forward in late December, Bragg was waiting, and their two armies mauled each other in the battle of Stones River (or Murfreesboro) on December 31, 1862, and January 2, 1863.

After fending off attacks from the Confederate cavalry of General Joseph Wheeler, Rosecrans's army of 43,000 troops reached the northern outskirts of Murfreesboro on December 30. Although the rebel force of 38,000 was outnumbered, Bragg decided to take the offensive. His main attack, like the one planned by Rosecrans, involved throwing the left wing of his army against the enemy's right flank. "If both [attacks] could have been carried out simultaneously," later noted G. C. Kniffin, a Union lieutenant colonel, "the spectacle would have been presented of two large armies turning upon an axis from left to right." As it was, Bragg beat Rosecrans to the punch by launching his attack at daybreak on December 31, some three hours before Rosecrans's attack was to get under way. As a result, Bragg seized the initiative, and he held it throughout the first day's battle.

The Union skirmish line on the federal right detected the rebel advance, but it made little difference, for as Kniffin recalled, "that first move was a rush as of a tornado. The skirmishers fell back steadily, fighting upon the main line, but the main line was overborne by the fury of the assault." The Union right crumbled and by late morning was pinned against the Union center. Hoping to deliver the final blow and cut off the federals from their line of supplies along the Nashville Pike, Bragg ordered General John C. Breckinridge, the commander of the Confederate right, to rush reinforcements to smash the Union center.

A thicket of cedars known as the Round Forest (but quickly dubbed "Hell's Half Acre" by the soldiers) now became the focal point of the battle. This position covered the Union approach to both the railroad and turnpike back to Nashville and had to be held at all costs by the federals. Rosecrans, his uniform splattered with blood from a Union officer whose head had been torn off by a cannonball, rode up and down the line, rallying his men. Supported by massed artillery, the federal line at Round Forest held against repeated Confederate charges. The fury of the rebel offensive was finally spent.

As a clear, bitterly cold night descended on the battlefield, Bragg wired Richmond that he had won a great victory. He assumed that Rosecrans would retreat the next day. But steeled by the resolve of his corps commanders, Rosecrans decided to stay put. On January 1 he rested his battered army and ordered the occupation of some high ground east of Stones River. Against the advice of most of his generals, Bragg ordered Breckinridge on January 2 to retake the hill from the federals. The Confederates did carry the hill, but as they descended down its forward slope, the fire from 58 pieces of Union artillery on the west side of Stones River cut them to pieces. Bragg's order had resulted in the death or wounding of more than 2,000 rebels.

Bragg evacuated Murfreesboro on the night of January 3. His army had lost almost 12,000 men, nearly one-third of its entire strength. Union casualties bordered on 13,000 (about 30 percent of its forces), but Rosecrans was now receiving reinforcements and was too powerful to be dislodged. Bragg tactically had the best of it at Stones River, the bloodiest battle of the war in terms of proportionate losses. However, a large Union army still threatened the vital rail center of Chattanooga, and the Confederacy had gained nothing strategically.

SEE ALSO

Bragg, Braxton; Bragg's Kentucky Invasion; Breckinridge, John C.; Rosecrans, William S.

FURTHER READING

Cozzens, Peter. *No Better Place to Die: The Battle of Stones River.* Urbana: University of Illinois Press, 1990.

McDonough, James Lee. *Stones River—Bloody Winter in Tennessee.* Knoxville: University of Tennessee Press, 1980.

Stowe, Harriet Beecher

NORTHERN REFORMER

- *Born: June 14, 1811, Litchfield, Conn.*
- *Education: private academies*
- *Occupation: teacher, writer*
- *Died: July 1, 1896, Hartford, Conn.*

The author of *Uncle Tom's Cabin,* an antislavery novel that became an instant best seller in the 1850s, Harriet Beecher Stowe popularized the slavery question for a vast Northern—and even international—audience. The success of her novel contributed to the antislavery sentiment that Southerners cited as a justification for secession. Upon meeting Stowe in 1862, President Abraham Lincoln reportedly remarked, "So you're the little woman who wrote the book that started this great war!"

The daughter of one of antebellum America's most prominent ministers, Lyman Beecher, Stowe was raised in a New England household that highly valued education and religion. After teaching at the Hartford Female Seminary, she accompanied her family to Cincinnati when her father assumed the presidency of Lane Theological Seminary in 1832. While in Cincinnati, she began publishing pieces of fiction and gained a firsthand knowledge of the turmoil produced by slavery. In 1836, the same year of her marriage to Calvin Ellis Stowe, a mob destroyed the printing press of an abolitionist in the city and pillaged the homes of free blacks. Three years later, a Kentuckian sought out the Stowes and demanded that a mulatto woman they were employing as a household servant be returned to him as a fugitive slave. In an escape that Stowe drew upon for *Uncle Tom's Cabin,* the Stowe family spirited the woman away to freedom on the Underground Railroad.

Shortly after the appearance of her first antislavery essay in 1845, Stowe moved with her husband and growing family to Brunswick, Maine. In the midst of the uproar in New England over the passage of the Fugitive Slave Act of 1850, she agreed to write an antislavery piece for the *National Era* in Washington. As she explained to her editor: "Up to this year I have always felt that I had no particular call to meddle with this subject. . . . But I feel now that the time is come when even a woman or a child who can speak a word for freedom and humanity is bound to speak." Appearing as weekly installments beginning in the spring of 1851, the work was published in 1852 as *Uncle Tom's Cabin; or, Life Among the Lowly.*

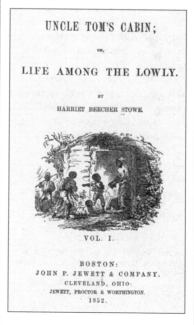

The title page of volume one of the first edition of Uncle Tom's Cabin. Before the book's publication in 1852, Harriet Beecher Stowe recalled that it had been "a general saying among conservative and sagacious people that this subject [of slavery] was a dangerous one to investigate, and that nobody could begin to read and think about it without becoming practically insane."

With sales of 300,000 copies within a year and 3 million within a decade, *Uncle Tom's Cabin* became the best-selling novel (in proportion to population) in U.S. history. Stowe's artistry in creating vivid characters and fashioning heartrending scenes of loss and redemption enabled readers to identify with slaves as fellow human beings and suffering Christians. She succeeded brilliantly in raising the moral concern of Northerners over slavery and inspired more than 500,000 British women to sign an antislavery address to their Parliament.

For the remainder of the 1850s, Stowe used her newfound fame to promote the antislavery cause. In her column in the *Independent,* a New York weekly, she described the outbreak of the Civil War as "one part of the *last* struggle for liberty—the American share of the great overturning which shall precede the coming of HIM." Her wartime writings, many of which were directed at England in an effort to combat pro-Confederate sympathies, centered on this belief in a holy Northern war against slavery. With the issuing of the Emancipation Proclamation, she saw her work as complete and retired from active involvement in the Union cause.

Before declining health curtailed her literacy production in the 1880s, Stowe continued her outpouring of novels and fictional pieces. In a marked turnabout from her earlier views, she also lent qualified support to the woman's-rights movement. Surrounded by family members, she died at her home in Hartford.

SEE ALSO

Fugitive Slave Act; Literature

FURTHER READING

Hedrick, Joan D. *Harriet Beecher Stowe: A Life.* New York: Oxford University Press, 1994.
Wilson, Forrest. *Crusader in Crinoline: The Life of Harriet Beecher Stowe.* Philadelphia: J. B. Lippincott, 1941.

Strategy

Military strategy is the art of waging a war so as to achieve one's overall political objective. More successfully than the Confederacy, the Union changed its strategic thinking in response to the total conflict of mass destruction that the Civil War became.

The Union had no choice but to go on the offensive. Its objective of restoring the seceded states to the Union amounted to an imperial task of conquest, for it involved reimposing its political authority over a vast territory controlled by a rival government. The federal rout at First Bull Run in July 1861 ended any hope that the Union high command may have had that the war would be a short affair with negligible casualties. While waiting for the Anaconda Plan to take effect and economically strangle an encircled South, President Abraham Lincoln now supervised the buildup of huge armies that would wage the war by conventional means. These armies were to retake Confederate territory and target only rebel forces. They were to avoid mass destruction and leave untouched Southern property, including slaves.

Until 1863 the North officially fought the war as a limited conflict with the objective of restoring the Union as it had existed in 1860. In this way, Lincoln sought to contain the conflict and prevent it from degenerating, in his phrase, "into a violent and remorseless revolutionary struggle." This approach, however, had failed to regain much territory or bring many Confederates back into the Union by the end of 1862. Moreover, as Union armies advanced into the Confederacy, they had to detach more and more soldiers for non-combat duties such as protecting supply lines. Without additional manpower and a new strategy for winning the war, the Union effort threatened to bog down in an endless stalemate.

Lincoln's Emancipation Proclamation embodied the core of that new strategy. The slaves were to be freed and added to the Union armies. Generals now had a free hand to punish civilians for their support of the Confederacy and destroy all property of any military value to the rebels. As General Henry W. Halleck, Lincoln's chief military advisor, expressed the new thinking in the spring of 1863: "There can be no peace but that which is forced by the sword. We must conquer the rebels or be conquered by them."

To win its war of conquest, the Union turned to a theory of war that targeted civilians as well as armies. Massive raids launched from secure Union bases in the last two years of the war cut wide bands of destruction across the Confederacy. Meanwhile, superior Union numbers pinned down General Robert E. Lee's Army of Northern Virginia in the eastern theater, and simultaneous advances of Union armies in the West delivered the victories that won the war.

The Confederacy had only to maintain itself in order to win the war. Strategically, an offensive policy was out of the question because of a lack of manpower and economic resources to sustain an invasion of the North. The inability to supply an invading army also ruled out such a policy. The Confederacy could control neither the rivers nor the railroads that it needed to maintain an army on Union soil. Lee crossed the upper Potomac on two occasions in 1862 and 1863, but his operations were more large-scale raids than prolonged offensives.

In formulating what of necessity had to be a defensive strategy, the Confederacy ruled out from the beginning small-scale resistance through guerrilla bands hiding out in mountains and swamps. Guerrilla warfare would have yielded control of the very land and slaves for which Southern whites were fighting.

The strategic choices hinged on whether Confederate generals in command of national armies would wage a passive or an aggressive defense (also known, as Confederate President Jefferson Davis put it, an "offensive-defensive"). Initially, Davis inclined toward a passive strategy that would attempt to defend all Confederate territory and sap the Northern will to continue by turning back Union forces in a war of attrition. This approach soon proved untenable. Most Confederates wanted to carry the war to the Yankees, and many, most notably Lee, felt that time was on the side of the Union, with its vastly greater material resources. For these Confederates, the only chance for success was a decisive victory over a Union army on Northern soil. In addition, by laying back and waiting for attacks, the Confederacy surrendered the initiative to Union commanders, who had the luxury of attacking the weakest points in the overextended Confederate lines.

For most of the war, therefore, the Confederacy followed the doctrine of the offensive-defensive. While assuming an overall defensive posture, Confederate commanders were to use speed and deception in concentrating their forces in surprise counterattacks against isolated Union armies. Lee was often a master of this strategy, as his brilliant victories at Second Bull Run and Chancellorsville revealed. Nonetheless, he, like most Confederate generals, overvalued the offensive over the defensive.

The Confederates were the attackers in half of the war's major battles. When they did attack, they suffered twice as many casualties as when they were on the defensive. These casualties were an irreplaceable loss for the numerically smaller rebel armies.

The Confederate high command failed to articulate or implement a consistent strategy that balanced the need for conserving manpower with the protection of critically vital positions. Once the Union seized the strategic initiative in the West with its victories at Forts Henry and Donelson in February 1862, Confederate strategy in the West wavered between a static defense and the launching of costly and futile counterattacks. Lee's successes in the East through 1863 could not compensate for the rebel defeats in the West. In the end, the Confederacy was helpless against the smashing blows of the Union's strategy of total war.

SEE ALSO

Anaconda Plan; Chancellorsville; Forts Henry and Donelson; Raids; Second Bull Run

FURTHER READING

Hattaway, Herman and Archer Jones. *How the North Won: A Military History of the Civil War.* Urbana: University of Illinois Press, 1983.
Jones, Archer. *Civil War Command and Strategy: The Process of Victory and Defeat.* New York: Free Press, 1992.
Stoker, Donald. *The Grand Design: Strategy and the U. S. Civil War.* New York: Oxford University Press, 2010.

Stuart, James Ewell Brown ("Jeb")

CONFEDERATE GENERAL

- *Born: February 6, 1833, Patrick County, Va.*
- *Education: U.S. Military Academy, B.S., 1854*
- *Military service: U.S. Army: lieutenant, mounted rifles-cavalry, 1854–55; 1st*

lieutenant, 1855–61; captain, 1861; Confederate army: colonel, 1st Virginia Cavalry, 1861; captain, cavalry, 1861; brigadier general, 1861–62; major-general, 1862–64
- *Died: May 12, 1864, Yellow Tavern, Va.*

The dashing and debonair Jeb Stuart was the most fabled of all Civil War cavalry commanders. In gathering intelligence information, screening troop movements, and leading raids, he had no equal. He aspired to be a romantic hero and took care to look every inch the part. John Esten Cooke, an officer on Stuart's staff, captured the general's chivalric image when he described him in 1862 astride his horse with "the gray coat buttoned to the chin; the light French sabre balanced by the pistol in its black holster; the cavalry boots above the knee and the hat… with its black plume floating above the bearded features, the brilliant eyes and the huge mustache."

Born into a prominent Virginia family, Stuart was raised in a deeply religious household, and he honored a boyhood pledge to his mother that he would never touch alcohol. As was true of most of the sons of the Southern gentry, his career options came down to the law or the military. The choice was an easy one. "Now tell me candidly," he wrote his cousin Bettie Hirston, "would you not rather see your cousin a bold

Jeb Stuart's first ride around the Army of the Potomac in June 1862 inspired "Riding a Raid," a song in his honor. Looking like the romantic legend that he was rapidly becoming, Stuart told his men, "a gallop is a gait unbecoming a soldier unless he is going toward the enemy."

dragoon than a petty-fogger lawyer?" Cavalry service fed his spirit of adventure, and after graduating from West Point, he was posted on the Indian frontier and in the unsettled Kansas Territory when skirmishes erupted over slavery. In October 1859, he assisted Robert E. Lee in the capture of John Brown at Harpers Ferry.

When Virginia seceded, Stuart promptly resigned from the U.S. Army. He began his Confederate military career as a colonel and was quickly promoted to major-general on the basis of his daring exploits. "I strive to inculcate in my men the spirit of the chase," he wrote early in the war, and his men did respond to his flamboyant energy. But for all his glamour and enthusiasm, he was also a highly skilled professional soldier who had a genius for deciphering the tactical flow of a battle.

Stuart first demonstrated his leadership talent at the battle of First Bull Run in July 1861. Prior to the Seven Days Battles in June 1862, he rode completely around the Union Army of the Potomac on an intelligence-gathering mission, a feat that gave Confederate morale a tremendous boost. Placed in command of the Cavalry Division of the Army of Northern Virginia in the summer of 1862, he performed superbly in the Second Bull Run campaign and at Antietam and Fredericksburg. After taking part in the famed flanking maneuver of Robert E. Lee's army at Chancellorsville, he fought a Union force to a standstill in June 1863 at Brandy Station, the biggest cavalry engagement of the war.

The Southern press uncharacteristically criticized Stuart for having been taken by surprise at Brandy Station. Perhaps in an effort to restore his tarnished luster, he then embarked on his most controversial exploit. Given rather ambiguous orders by Lee, he once again circled his cavalry around the Army of

the Potomac, but he did not return in time to give Lee vital information needed for the best disposition of rebel troops at Gettysburg.

Stuart rebounded from this flawed performance with an excellent record in fighting along the Rappahannock line and during the battles of the Wilderness and Spotsylvania. Shortly before he was mortally wounded at Yellow Tavern, he was asked by his bugler if he actually loved the prospect of facing enemy bullets. "No," Stuart responded. "I don't love 'em any more than you do. I go where they are because it's my duty. I don't expect to survive this war."

SEE ALSO

Gettysburg

FURTHER READING

Davis, Burke, *Jeb Stuart: The Last Cavalier.* New York: Rinehart, 1957.
Thomas, Emory M. *Bold Dragoon: The Life of J. E. B. Stuart.* New York: Harper & Row, 1986.

Submarines

On taking over the Confederate Navy Department in the spring of 1861, Stephen R. Mallory announced, "I propose to adopt a class of vessels hitherto unknown to naval service." He lived up to his word. The Confederate navy was an innovator in introducing armored ships, commerce-destroying raiders, and submarine weapons to naval warfare.

Although experimental underwater (semisubmersible) vessels dated to the American Revolution, the Confederacy produced the world's first combat submarine. Named the *Hunley* in honor of Horace L. Hunley, the sugar dealer who gave his money and life to the project,

This Confederate torpedo boat operating in the waters off Norfolk, Virginia, is an example of what the Northern press called that "rebel infernal machine."

this strange craft was powered by cranks turned by its eight-man crew. Shaped like a cigar, it was 30 feet long, 5 feet high, and less than 4 feet wide. Ballast tanks regulated its depth. A total of 33 men (including Hunley) died when three versions of the craft sank in trial runs. Despite these frightful accidents, Mallory pushed ahead with the project. The tests had shown that the *Hunley* could stay submerged for up to two hours. Armed with a torpedo that could be attached to the hull of an enemy ship, the quirky submarine potentially was a devastating offensive weapon against the Union blockaders.

On the evening of February 17, 1864, the *Hunley* became the first submarine in history to sink a warship. About 7 miles off the Atlantic Coast near Charleston, it pushed a torpedo against the side of the USS *Housatonic.* The 1,240-ton ship shuddered and went down stern first with a loss of five lives. The attack, however, was only a qualified success, for the *Hunley* itself went down, probably from the shock of the explosion.

The *Hunley* was the only operational submarine the Confederacy ever launched, and the only one from either side that saw service in the war (the Union navy's one submarine, the USS *Alligator,* sank off Cape Hatteras in April 1863 before engaging in any combat). Even before the *Hunley*'s last voyage, however, the rebel navy was developing torpedo boats, another class of submersible vessels. The prototype of assault boats in modern navies, these cylindrically shaped ships were steam-powered and semisubmersible. Designed to spread terror among the Union blockaders, they were armed with an explosive device attached to a spar. The first torpedo boat was the *David,* presumably so named because it was to do battle with the "Goliaths" of the Union squadron. On October 5, 1863, just off Charleston Harbor, the *David* damaged the USS *New Ironsides* to such an extent that it knocked this large Union ironclad out of the war for more than a year. On August 9, 1864, the CSS *Squib,* another torpedo boat, repeated the *David*'s success in its attack on the USS *Minnesota* off Newport News, Virginia.

Mallory committed the Confederacy to an extensive program of building torpedo boats in the last half of the war, but how many of these boats were actually launched is unknown. What is clear is that the Union navy took the threat posed by this new weapon seriously and sought to protect its blockading fleet with antitorpedo nets. Soon after the *New Ironsides* was damaged, Admiral John A. Dahlgren of the Union navy wrote: "The secrecy, rapidity of movement, control of direction, and precise explosion indicate, I think, the introduction of the torpedo element as a means of certain warfare. It can be ignored no longer." With torpedo boats, as with submarines, the Confederacy had pointed the way to future developments in naval warfare.

SEE ALSO

Mallory, Stephen R.; Naval warfare

FURTHER READING

Luraghi, Raimondo. *A History of the Confederate Navy.* Annapolis, Md.: Naval Institute Press, 1996.

Perry, Milton F. *Infernal Machines: The Story of Confederate Submarine and Mine Warfare.* Baton Rouge: Louisiana State University Press, 1965.

Sumner, Charles

UNION POLITICIAN

- *Born: January 6, 1811, Boston, Mass.*
- *Political parties: Whig, Free-Soil, Republican*
- *Education: Harvard College, A.B., 1830; Harvard Law School, L.L.B., 1833*
- *Government service: U.S. Senate, 1851–74*
- *Died: March 11, 1874, Washington, D.C.*

More than any other Republican, Charles Sumner served as the moral voice of his party. Committed throughout his political career to the principle of equality before the law, he was a champion of the antislavery cause before the Civil War and of equal treatment for the freed population after the war. Utterly opposed to the doctrine of white supremacy, he led the movement for black suffrage that culminated in the 15th Amendment of 1870.

The son of a Boston lawyer, Sumner was an ungainly youth who delighted in books and classical learning. He excelled at Harvard and had no peer as a law student. Too abstract and speculative, however, to succeed as a practicing lawyer, he found his calling in the cause of reform. Invited to deliver Boston's Fourth of July Oration in 1845, he shocked his audience by declaring that all wars were "unjust and un-Christian" and denouncing U.S. designs on Texas and Oregon. Four months later, in his first political speech, he further alienated conservative Bostonians by decrying the annexation of Texas as a great sin that implicated all who favored it in the guilt of slavery.

Sumner's oratorical skills and his insistence that moral principles should dictate political behavior put him in the forefront of the antislavery movement in Massachusetts. He and his followers, known as the "Conscience" Whigs, opposed the Mexican War and helped found the Free-Soil party in 1848. A coalition of Free-Soilers and Democrats in the Massachusetts legislature elected Sumner to the U.S. Senate in 1851.

Sumner used the Senate as a forum to propound his doctrine of universal rights, and he lashed out at every effort of Southern politicians to extend or protect slavery. His "Crime against Kansas" speech in May 1856 provoked Representative Preston Brooks of South Carolina into assaulting Sumner with a cane in the Senate chamber. The vicious attack gave the Republicans a rallying cry of "Bleeding Sumner" for the upcoming Presidential election and left

Sumner so incapacitated that he did not return to the Senate until December 1859.

From 1861 to 1871, Sumner played two important roles. As chairman of the Senate Committee on Foreign Relations, he countered the more aggressive moves of Secretary of State William Henry Seward and utilized his wide circle of European friends to promote nonintervention in the U.S. civil conflict. He also tirelessly worked for emancipation by insisting, as he put it in 1861, that "[r]ebellion is Slavery itself, incarnate, living, acting, raging, robbing, murdering, according to the essential law of its being." The self-defense of the Union demanded that slavery, "the main-spring of the Rebellion," be destroyed.

For Sumner, the end of slavery was the essential first step in committing the nation to black equality. Holding that equality was the necessary complement of liberty, he urged an end to segregated schools and all legal discrimination based upon color. Accusing Andrew Johnson of "an insensibility to right and a passion for power," he broke with the President and worked for his impeachment. After successfully leading the Republican effort to incorporate black suffrage into Reconstruction, he worked for the passage of a civil rights bill that would provide a national guarantee of equal access to public accommodations. Although the Civil Rights Act of 1875, passed a year after Sumner's death, was less sweeping than he desired, it still served as a fitting capstone to his advocacy of equal rights for all Americans.

SEE ALSO
Bleeding Kansas; 15th Amendment; Radicals; Reconstruction

FURTHER READING
Donald, David. *Charles Sumner and the Coming of the Civil War.* New York: Knopf, 1961.
———. *Charles Sumner and the Rights of Man.* New York: Knopf, 1970.

Supply and field transportation

SEE Logistics

Tactics

Tactics refers to the way in which troops are deployed to fight a battle. Most Civil War generals used the traditional assault tactics they had been taught at West Point and that had worked so well in the Mexican War. These tactics led to horrendous casualties when Civil War armies confronted each other with the new rifled firearms introduced in the war.

Once rifled muskets replaced smoothbores as standard equipment for infantry soldiers, the tactical offensive in close-order formations was murderously obsolete, for the new weapons had far greater range and power than

Sharpshooters received special training and carried rifles mounted with telescopic sights. "We are to be sent out on a scout and find where the rebels are quartered," explained Private William Greene, a Union sharpshooter, "and then we are to fall back and… go in to some place where we can get a good sight and pick off the officers."

• TACTICS •

The outmoded tactic of close-order formation failed to keep up with Civil War weapons technology. Ranks of soldiers were easily torn apart by fire from massed rifles and short-range artillery.

the inaccurate muskets they replaced. Massed rifle fire, supported by short-range artillery, blasted huge gaps in the ranks of attacking soldiers. Typically, what resulted from an infantry charge was the carnage described by Confederate General D. H. Hill at the battle of Malvern Hill during the Peninsula campaign: "As each brigade emerged from the woods, from fifty to one hundred guns opened upon it, tearing great gaps in its ranks; but the heroes reeled on and were shot down by the reserves at the guns, which a few squads reached. . . . It was not war—it was murder."

Despite the lethal potency of defensive positions, Civil War generals persisted in ordering charges intended to close quickly with defenders and break their lines. Battle after battle resulted in numbers of killed and wounded in excess of 20 percent of all the soldiers engaged. The generals were under tremendous pressure to win battles, and the massing of assault troops for a breakthrough at a supposed weak spot in the enemy's lines was the only way

they knew of doing so. The greatest concession they made to the new battlefield realities—and one often forced upon them by the common soldier—was the use of skirmishers and other loose-order formations in which small groups of men moved forward at an irregular pace. These new tactics, however, made it more difficult for generals to control the movement of their men. Lacking modern electronic means of communicating with the battlefield, most generals still relied on concentrating their troops at relatively fixed points and ordering them forward in a traditional massed charge. As a result, massive casualties continued to mount up.

SEE ALSO

Casualties; Rifles

FURTHER READING

Griffith, Paddy. *Battle Tactics of the Civil War.* New Haven: Yale University Press, 1989.

McWhiney, Grady, and Perry D. Jamieson. *Attack and Die: Civil War Military Tactics and the Southern Heritage.* Tuscaloosa: University of Alabama Press, 1982.

Taxation

Americans paid heavy taxes for the first time during the Civil War. The Union, however, was far more successful than the Confederacy in putting together a comprehensive tax package that produced significant revenues and helped dampen inflationary pressures.

Prior to the Civil War, nearly all federal revenue came from tariff duties and land sales. Most Americans paid no taxes directly to the national government. Initially, both the Union and Confederate governments were loath to anger voters by raising taxes. In August 1861, the Union Congress did approve a direct tax and an income tax, but neither produced much in the way of immediate revenue. The direct tax, one levied in proportion to the population of each state (including the seceded ones), generated only $17 million throughout the war, and the income tax, the first in U.S. history, did not take effect until 1863.

The Confederate Congress also passed its first tax legislation in the summer of 1861. However, lacking the administrative machinery to collect this light tax on real and personal property, Confederate treasury officials relied upon the states to do it for them. Nearly all the states did so by borrowing money and issuing bonds. In other words, the states avoided collecting any real taxes.

In 1862, a year earlier than in the Confederacy, Union leaders put together a comprehensive tax package. Its key feature was an excise tax on the purchase, manufacture, and distribution of nearly all the commodities produced in the national economy. This tax was the major new source of federal income, and it raised 10 times the revenue produced by the income tax. This latter tax, as revised upward in 1864, imposed a 5-percent tax on incomes over $600 and 10 percent on those over $10,000. These taxes, along with a host of minor ones on licenses, stamps, inheritances, and manufactured items, funded 21 percent of the war's cost in the North. They reduced the need to issue more greenbacks and helped prop up the value of the federal bonds that provided 60 percent of the funds for the Union's wartime expenses.

In April 1863, the Confederacy tried to follow suit with its own program of heavy taxation. A new Revenue Act slapped taxes on virtually everything but land and slaves. It imposed license taxes on occupations, profit taxes on wholesalers, ad valorem taxes on farm produce grown in 1862, flat taxes on bank deposits and commercial paper, and graduated taxes on individual incomes. Finally, there was a 10-percent tax in kind on agricultural goods.

Despite this fiscal legislation of 1863, the Confederacy succeeded in raising no more than 5 percent of its cash revenue from taxes. By the time this taxation program passed, Southerners had already lost confidence in Confederate currency and were wary of any monetary transactions with the Confederate government. Union raids also placed an additional burden on tax collections by steadily destroying Southern economic resources.

Compared to the Union, the Confederacy had a far smaller and less developed commercial economy from which to extract revenue. Moreover, the Union blockade succeeded in choking off the international channels of Southern trade and in denying the Confederate government revenue from tariff duties. As a result, the Confederacy had no choice but to turn to paper money for more than 60 percent of its wartime funds. That money steadily fell in value as Confederate finances collapsed under the pressures of a prolonged war.

SEE ALSO

Direct tax; Inflation; Legal Tender Acts; National Banking Acts

FURTHER READING

Ratner, Sidney. *Taxation and Democracy in America.* New York: Wiley, 1967.
Todd, Richard C. *Confederate Finance.* Athens: University of Georgia Press, 1954.

13th Amendment

Passed by Congress in January 1865, the 13th Amendment emancipated the slaves. When added to the Constitution in December 1865, after ratification by the states, the amendment eliminated the possibility that wartime measures against slavery might be overturned by the courts or reversed by the Southern states after the war.

The Emancipation Proclamation of January 1, 1863, and the enlistment of black troops into Union armies signaled a growing conviction in the North that emancipation should become an official war aim of the Union. When Congress met in December 1863, the Republican party committed itself to a constitutional amendment that would forever abolish slavery throughout the United States. An alliance of feminists and abolitionists working through the Woman's National Loyal League organized a grass-roots campaign that secured 400,000 signatures on a petition calling for such an amendment. Encouraged by this show of public support, the Senate approved the 13th Amendment in April 1864, but in June Democratic opposition in the House prevented the amendment from obtaining the needed two-thirds majority.

Following his reelection in the fall of 1864, President Abraham Lincoln redou-

Spectators gathered for the passage of the 13th Amendment by the U.S. House of Representatives celebrate the historic occasion.

bled his efforts on behalf of the 13th Amendment. Although most Democrats continued to hold that the federal government had no constitutional authority to interfere with slavery in the states, enough of them changed their votes to enable the 13th Amendment to pass Congress in January 1865. The necessary three-fourths of the states ratified the amendment by the end of the year.

In addition to ending slavery and all forms of "involuntary servitude," the amendment also stipulated in its second section that "Congress shall have power to enforce this article by appropriate legislation." Many Republicans interpreted this section as a mandate to eliminate all vestiges of slavery by using federal power to secure legal equality for the freed population. In this sense, the 13th Amendment was the indispensable first step in the ongoing effort to make freedom meaningful for all Americans.

SEE ALSO

Abolitionism; Emancipation; Emancipation Proclamation

FURTHER READING

Cox, LaWanda. *Lincoln and Black Freedom: A Study in Presidential Leadership.* Columbia: University of South Carolina Press, 1981.

Vorenberg, Michael. *Final Freedom: The Civil War, the Abolition of Slavery, and the Thirteenth Amendment.* New York: Cambridge University Press, 2001.

Thomas, George H.

UNION GENERAL

- *Born: July 31, 1816, Southampton County, Va.*
- *Education: U.S. Military Academy, B.S., 1840*
- *Military service: U.S. Army: lieutenant, artillery, 1840–44; 1st lieutenant, 1844–53; captain, 1853–55; major, cavalry, 1855–61; lieutenant colonel, 1861; colonel, 1861; brigadier general, volunteers, 1861; major-general, volunteers, 1862; brigadier general, regular army, 1863;*

major-general, 1864–1870
- *Died: March 28, 1870, San Francisco, Calif.*

A solid, imperturbable commander with a strong sense of duty and honor, George H. Thomas ranks just below Ulysses S. Grant and William Tecumseh Sherman in the great triumvirate of Union generals who broke the back of Confederate resistance in the western theater of the war. His gallant defensive stand at Chickamauga saved the Union Army of the Cumberland from a disastrous defeat and earned him his enduring nickname, "The Rock of Chickamauga."

As a teenager, Thomas hid in nearby woods with his widowed mother and sisters when Nat Turner's slave rebellion in 1831 threw Southampton County whites into a state of panic. Five years later, he received an appointment to West Point, and he served in the artillery for 15 years. In the Mexican War, he distinguished himself at the battles of Monterrey and Buena Vista. Following a teaching stint at the Military Academy, he entered the cavalry and saw duty on the Indian frontier in Texas. He was on a leave of absence as the result of a severe arrow wound to his face when the secession crisis broke out. Despite his Virginia roots and the Confederate allegiance of his sisters, Thomas remained loyal to the Union. He never explained why, but he hinted at his reasons when asked after a battle in 1863 if his dead soldiers should be buried according to their states." "No," he replied, "mix them up. I've had enough of states' rights."

After brief service in the Shenandoah Valley and the First Bull Run campaign, Thomas was transferred to

Kentucky. In January 1862, he commanded the Union forces at Mill Springs that crushed the right flank of the Confederate defensive line in Kentucky. He subsequently led a division at the battles of Shiloh, Corinth, and Perryville. His stoic insistence at Stones River that "[t]his army can't retreat" helped steel the resolve of the Union officer corps, and his solid defense of the Union center prevented the Army of the Cumberland from being split in two. He anchored an even more heroic defense at Chickamauga.

Thomas's stand at Chickamauga gained him the command of the Army of the Cumberland. At Missionary Ridge during the Chattanooga Campaign, his troops broke the rebel center in the most spectacularly successful frontal assault of the war. Following his participation in the Atlanta Campaign, Thomas returned to Tennessee to meet the threat of General John Bell Hood's invading rebel army. He badly mauled the Confederates at Franklin and then smashed Hood's army at Nashville in one of the best-executed offenses of the war. Despite almost losing his command because of concerns in Washington that he was too slow, Thomas had virtually destroyed the rebel Army of Tennessee.

Thomas remained in the army after the war. After refusing to allow President Andrew Johnson to pit him against Ulysses S. Grant for control of the army, Thomas secured a transfer to the Division of the Pacific. He died of a stroke while in command at San Francisco.

SEE ALSO

Chattanooga campaign; Chickamauga; Hood's Tennessee campaign

FURTHER READING

Einolf, Christopher J. *General Thomas: Virginian for the Union.* Norman, University of Oklahoma Press, 2007.

McKinney, Francis P. *Education in Violence: The Life of George H. Thomas and the History of the Army of the Cumberland.* Detroit: Wayne State University Press, 1961.

Torpedoes

The Confederacy aggressively resorted to the use of land and marine mines—which were called "torpedoes" during the Civil War—for the defense of its territory and coastal waters. The Confederate Congress in the fall of 1862 created the Confederate States Submarine Battery Service, the Torpedo Bureau, and a Secret Service Corps. These organizations developed new explosive devices that the Union decried as barbarous "infernal devices." For the Confederates, these fearsome new weapons were a legitimate tool of war necessitated by the Yankee invasion of their homeland.

The Secret Service Corps invented a deadly device known as the coal torpedo, a blackened block of cast iron filled with 10 pounds of powder. Designed to look like a piece of coal, it was planted in coal shipments destined for the Union fleet. Although there is no way of knowing how many explosions it caused, a coal torpedo was definitely responsible on November 27, 1864, for the sinking of the Union transport vessel *Greyhound* in the James River. A rebel agent smuggled the torpedo into the ship's bunker, and it was shoveled into the furnace.

The buoyant Rains keg torpedo, named after the head of the Confederate Torpedo Bureau, was the most widely used rebel mine. Wooden cones at each end stabilized small beer kegs, which contained the explosive. An anchor held the torpedo just beneath the surface of the water.

Three months earlier, another invention of the Confederate Secret Service—a time bomb concealed in a wooden chest—blew up a Union boat loaded with ordnance at City Point, Virginia, the main supply base for the Army of the Potomac during the Union siege of Petersburg. The explosion destroyed two transport ships, set warehouses afire, killed 58 men, and wounded 40 others. Union Admiral David D. Dixon was on the mark when he noted after the war: "In devices for blowing up vessels the Confederates were far ahead of us, putting Yankee ingenuity to shame."

The Submarine Battery Service took the lead in developing electrically ignited torpedoes. By January 1863, it had placed 12,000 pounds of explosives in the James River. This was the equivalent, thought Confederate Secretary of the Navy Stephen R. Mallory, of a whole naval squadron for the defense of Richmond. However, the first real success with torpedoes came on the western waters. On December 12, 1862, the USS *Cairo* struck two torpedoes on the Yazoo River above Vicksburg, Mississippi. The ironclad gunboat sank in 12 minutes.

The greatest advocate of torpedo warfare was General Gabriel J. Rains, head of the rebel Torpedo Bureau after June 1864. Credited with the first use of land mines in warfare while covering his retreat up the Yorktown Peninsula in the spring of 1862, Rains believed that torpedoes could "scatter a blockade and destroy the ships; close the Mississippi river; check the advance of an army; stop raiders; destroy cavalry; burn a city." His prodding resulted in the use of land mines to guard the approaches to Richmond, Charleston, and Mobile. He invented a sensitive fuse for contact mines and a device called the submarine marine battery, a series of marine mines strung along a wooden platform that was laid under the waterline in river defenses.

By 1863, torpedoes were an integral part of Confederate defensive strategy, especially for ports and river entrances. Technologically, these explosive devices were the most sophisticated in the world, and they were responsible for the destruction or disabling of about 50 Union warships. Although torpedoes failed to stymie the naval operations of the Union, they were a deterrent that the Union navy quickly came to dread.

SEE ALSO
Naval warfare

FURTHER READING
Luraghi, Raimondo. *A History of the Confederate Navy.* Annapolis, Md.: Naval Institute Press, 1996.
Perry, Milton F. *Infernal Machines: The Story of Confederate Submarine and Mine Warfare.* Baton Rouge: Louisiana State University Press, 1965.
Tidwell, William A. *Confederate Covert Action in the American Civil War: April '65.* Kent, Ohio: Kent State University Press, 1995.

Trent affair

Set off in November 1861 by a Union captain's seizure of two Confederate diplomats on board a British mail steamer in the Caribbean, the *Trent* affair provoked a major crisis in Anglo-American relations. The peaceful resolution of the crisis stifled Confederate hopes of having the British join them in a war against the Union.

On November 8, 1861, Captain Charles Wilkes of the USS *San Jacinto* stopped the *Trent* on its run from Havana, Cuba, to St. Thomas, searched it, and removed two Confederate envoys bound for Europe, James Mason of Virginia and John Slidell of Louisiana. He took the two men to Boston, where they were imprisoned in Fort Warren. The North hailed Wilkes as a war hero. The British, however, denounced him as a warmonger who had insulted their flag and violated international law by not bringing the *Trent* and the Confederate envoys before a prize court, a military court with authority to resolve issues of property or prizes captured at sea in wartime. Under threat of severing diplomatic relations, the British demanded an apology from the U.S. government and the release of Mason and Slidell.

The ensuing crisis carried a real risk of war. As the British waited for a response, they put their fleet on a war footing, sent reinforcements to Canada, and canceled a Union order of saltpeter, an essential component in the manufacture of gunpowder. Anti-British sentiment ran high in the North, and for more than a month President Abraham Lincoln refused to release the captured Confederates.

Despite the bellicose posturing, neither side wanted war. Both had too much to lose by it. At a Union cabinet meeting on December 26, Secretary of State William Henry Seward gained Lincoln's approval to free Mason and Slidell. In his official note to the British, Seward saved face for the Union by insisting that Wilkes had acted without the knowledge or orders of his government. He conceded that Wilkes had technically violated the law by not taking the *Trent* to a prize court, but went on to argue that the seizure of the envoys was otherwise within the legitimate rights of the U.S. government. He offered reparations for the seizure but no formal apology.

Mason and Slidell were soon in England and France, respectively. Each failed in his mission to gain foreign recognition for the Confederacy. Ironically, the very settlement of the *Trent* affair that gained their release also foreshadowed their lack of success in Europe. Notwithstanding support for a dissolution of the Union by key segments in the British and French governments, neither nation wanted to risk war with the Union by openly siding with the Confederacy. As for the British stand in favor of Mason and Slidell, the London *Times* put it in perspective when it noted: "They must not suppose, because we have gone to the very edge of a great war to rescue them, that therefore they are precious in our eyes. We should have done just as much to rescue two of their own negroes."

SEE ALSO
France; Great Britain

FURTHER READING
Ferris, Norman B. *The Trent Affair: A Diplomatic Crisis*. Knoxville: University of Tennessee Press, 1977.

Tubman, Harriet
ABOLITIONIST

- Born: c. 1820, Dorchester County, Md.
- Education: no formal schooling
- Occupation: cook, laundress, lecturer
- Died: March 10, 1913, Auburn, N.Y.

A legendary figure for her exploits in bringing slaves out of the South and into freedom, Harriet Tubman enjoyed a remarkable career after her own flight to freedom. During and after the Civil War, she continued to work on behalf of the freed African Americans.

Born to slave parents on a Maryland plantation, Tubman began earning money for her master at the age of six, when she was hired out as a nurse for

Harriet Tubman, heroine of the Underground Railroad, was always convinced that President Lincoln would do the "right thing" and free the slaves.

babies. As a teenager, she performed heavy physical labor in the fields despite suffering from bouts of unconsciousness as a result of an overseer having struck her in the head. Upon hearing in 1849 that she and her brothers were to be sold, she decided to flee to the North. Her husband, a free black whom she had been forced to marry in 1845, refused to join her, and she set out alone, guided only by the North Star. Once she safely arrived in Pennsylvania, she dropped her slave name of Araminta and called herself Harriet.

Tubman was able to support herself in the North by working as a domestic. She soon became active in the Underground Railroad, a network of agents and safe shelters that assisted fugitive slaves in their escape from bondage. With her savings and funds supplied by antislavery Quakers, she was able to finance 20 trips back into the slave South. Despite the dangers of such missions—including the risk of her own reenslavement—she returned again and again and succeeded in transporting some 300 slaves to their freedom. In 1857 she rescued her parents and brought them to Auburn, New York, where she had purchased a home and a plot of land with the assistance of local abolitionists.

Like most abolitionists, Tubman was impatient with President Abraham Lincoln's reluctance early in the Civil War to declare immediate emancipation as a Union war aim. Still, she was optimistic. "God won't let Massa Linkum beat de South till he do de right ting," the abolitionist Lydia M. Child reported her saying in late 1861. She went to the Union-occupied coastal area of South Carolina in 1862 and helped set up a school for former slaves. In addition to working as a cook, laundress, and nurse for the Union army, she also served as a scout and spy. While accompanying a

Union raiding party up the Combahee River, she supervised the removal of slaves. "One woman brought two pigs, a white one an' a black one," she recalled in her ghostwritten autobiography; "we took 'em all on board; named de white pig Beauregard, and de black pig Jeff Davis."

After the war, Tubman converted her residence in Auburn into a home for indigent and elderly blacks. Active in black reform causes until her death, she more than earned her title of "the Moses of her people."

SEE ALSO
Underground Railroad

FURTHER READING
Bradford, Sarah H. *Harriet Tubman: The Moses of Her People.* Seacaucus, N.J.: Citadel Press, 1980.
Conrad, Earl. *Harriet Tubman: Negro Soldier and Abolitionist.* New York: International Publishers, 1942.

Underground Railroad

A loosely organized network of support for fugitive slaves, the Underground Railroad assisted the hunted slaves in finding a safe refuge in the North or in Canada. Contrary to the impression often left by the post–Civil War memoirs of white abolitionists, African Americans, and not friendly whites, were the major actors in this risky business of illegally aiding and abetting fugitives on their flight to freedom.

The origins of the Underground Railroad date back to the 1780s, when Congress prohibited slavery in the territories north of the Ohio River and Northern states embarked on programs of gradual emancipation. Its colorful name (originally the "Underground Road") emerged in the 1830s when abolitionists began publicizing successful stories of escapes from slavery. According to one tale, a Kentucky slaveowner in 1831, frustrated by his failure to track down the slave Tice Davids, who had fled across the Ohio River, remarked that Davids "must have gone off an underground road." The term "Liberty Line" as a label for antislavery networks helping slaves to escape first appeared in a Chicago newspaper in 1844.

Fugitives were most at risk as they tried to get out of the slave South. Fellow slaves, free blacks, and occasionally antislavery whites helped where they could. Most successful escapes originated in the Border South, where a fortunate fugitive might locate part of the Underground Railroad and receive assistance in the form of food, temporary shelter, and, more rarely, trans-portation to the North. The free black community provided most of this aid, and its activities were usually shrouded from white view. As the white abolitionist James Birney noted in 1837 while living in Cincinnati, "such matters [of aiding fugitives] are almost uniformly managed by the colored people. I know nothing of them generally till they are past." The need for such secrecy lessened in the 1850s as many Northern whites reacted to the harsh features of the Fugitive Slave Act of 1850 by sympathizing with the plight of fugitives.

Just how many slaves the Underground Railroad assisted will never be known. Estimates based on U.S. census records indicate that about 1,000 slaves a year reached free soil in the late antebellum period. The actual number was probably higher, though still far short of the exaggerated estimates given by abolitionists and Southerners. What is clear is that the work of the Underground Railroad enflamed sectional tensions and helped sustain African Americans in their struggle against slavery.

SEE ALSO

Abolitionism; Fugitive Slave Act of 1850; Fugitive slaves; Tubman, Harriet

The Magee House in Canisteo, New York, was a station, or safe stopover, for fugitive slaves attempting to reach Canada via the Underground Railroad.

FURTHER READING

Gara, Larry. *The Liberty Line: The Legend of the Underground Railroad.* Lexington: University of Kentucky Press, 1961.

Uniforms

Regulation uniforms were virtually nonexistent early in the war. Each regiment was responsible for its own uniforms, and the variety was endless. The Union prescribed a regulation blue uniform in early 1862, and within a year it was standard issue. Confederate regulations soon called for gray uniforms, but chronic shortages of the standard uniforms and the use of different dyes resulted in a motley collection of colors throughout the war.

Gray had been a popular color for the militia, and many Northerners went off to the war in gray uniforms. Others favored the gaudy colors associated with the French Zouaves (Algerian troops in the French colonial army)— bright red for trousers and a turban, blue for a tunic, and flashy yellow for a sash around the waist. By the midpoint of the war, the Northern textile industry was easily meeting the military demand for hundreds of thousands of the standard blue woolen uniforms. What Union soldiers lost in individuality they gained in a greater ability to distinguish between friendly and enemy forces on the battlefield.

Confederate soldiers never lost their look of rough-hewn farmers out for a fight. Their trousers were typically gray or a shade of butternut, a yellowish-brown color produced by a dye of ferrous sulfate and walnut hulls. Their shirts, usually made by relatives or friends, could be any color or material. In place of regulation caps, they preferred their own hunting hats. Supply problems were so great that their clothing tended to disintegrate from excessive wear. Regarding his trousers, the South Carolinian Jesse Reid wrote in a letter to his wife, "They will soon be gone forever, but I am perfectly satisfied that

Uniforms came in various colors and styles that expressed the individuality of the soldiers, especially early in the war before either side had standardized its military clothing.

ELLSWORTH'S CAMPAIGN & BARRACK or DRESS UNIFORMS.

they will go in peace, for there is no doubt of their hol(e)iness... if you were to see me in [them] you might mistake me for a zebra, leopard, or something else equally outrageous." Against the wishes of their officers, rebel soldiers often supplied themselves with captured federal uniforms that they then dyed. Few armies that were so ragged ever fought so well.

SEE ALSO
Logistics

FURTHER READING
Lord, Francis A. *Civil War Collector's Encyclopedia: Arms, Uniforms, and Equipment of the Union and Confederacy.* New York: Castle Books, 1965.

Union

From their initial sense of the Union as an experiment in self-government, Americans developed conflicting, highly sectionalized conceptions of it by the middle of the 19th century. Northerners increasingly adopted the concept of a perpetual Union that represented the interests of the American people as a whole. To Southerners concerned with threats to slavery, such a Union violated the voluntary, consensual nature of the original federal compact and replaced it with a consolidated system of national power that placed Southern interests at the mercy of a Northern majority. The only proper Union, they insisted, was one in which limits on majority power guaranteed equal benefits to all the states.

For 40 years after the ratification of the Constitution, Americans typically thought of the Union as a voluntary means to the end of protecting liberties and promoting interregional prosperity.

In the dark days of the war this traditional feminized symbol of the American republic stood for Northerners as a beacon of strength shielding the Union from its enemies.

Joseph Lyman of Massachusetts spoke to this consensus when he reasoned in 1814 that a "Union founded upon submission is the Union of slaves." Later, however, the Northern reaction to the sectional crisis provoked by the South Carolina nullifiers produced the first sustained argument for a perpetual Union as an end in itself.

President Andrew Jackson's Proclamation on Nullification in December 10, 1832, was the most forceful statement of this position. The Declaration of Independence, insisted Jackson, gave birth to the Union when the colonists "bound themselves before God to a primitive social compact of union, freedom, and independence." The Union preceded the existence of the states, and the Constitution reaffirmed the primacy of the Union when its ratification by the people created a national authority supreme over that of the individual states. Nullification, if carried out, would dissolve "the unity of a nation," and secession was nothing less than treason.

Abraham Lincoln drew heavily on Jackson's formulation of the Union when he rejected the doctrine of secession in his First Inaugural Address on March 4, 1861. For Lincoln, and by now a majority of Northerners as well, the concept of a perpetual Union was "confirmed by the history of the Union itself," and no legal right existed to break it. Most Southern whites in the seceded states, however, embraced a profoundly different interpretation of the Constitution and the Union. They convinced themselves that secession was a constitutional right and that the Union they were leaving had been corrupted by a Northern grasp for power. Because they viewed Lincoln's Union as equivalent to a centralized tyranny that threatened their most cherished rights, a civil war was virtually inevitable.

SEE ALSO

Federalism; Nationalism; Nullification; States' rights

FURTHER READING

Nagel, Paul C. *One Nation Indivisible: The Union in American Thought, 1776–1861.* New York: Oxford University Press, 1964.
Stampp, Kenneth M. "The Concept of a Perpetual Union." *Journal of American History* 65, No. 2 (June 1978): 5–33.

Union politics

Two-party politics continued to flourish in the North during the Civil War. Although most Democrats rallied to the Union cause once the Confederacy fired on Fort Sumter, they did not abandon their traditional doctrines of states' rights and white supremacy. These War Democrats, as they were called, opposed emancipation and Republican economic legislation as a violation of constitutionally sanctioned liberties. A minority wing of the party, the Peace Democrats (or Copperheads, as the Republicans derisively labeled them) continued to hold out for a negotiated end to the war. The great fear of the Republicans was that any loss of political control would lead to an opening for the Peace Democrats to broker a settlement that recognized the independence of the Confederacy.

The lack of progress on the military front and the backlash against President Abraham Lincoln's Preliminary Emancipation Proclamation produced solid gains for the Democrats in the congressional and state elections of 1862. The party picked up 35 seats in Congress, captured the governorships of New York and New Jersey, and won control of the Indiana and Illinois legislatures. Horatio Seymour, a Peace Democrat and the newly elected governor of New York, awoke the worst Republican fears when he proclaimed: "If it be true that slavery must be abolished to save this Union, then the people of the South should be allowed to withdraw themselves from the government which cannot give them the protection guaranteed by its terms."

Despite this Democratic comeback, the Republicans still controlled Congress, thanks to their continued strength in New England and the upper Midwest. The Lincoln administration refused to back down from emancipation, and it continued to curb civil liberties by suspending the writ of habeas corpus, arresting dissenters, and using the Union army to keep secessionist sympathizers from voting in the Border South. All these policies, as well as the imposition of conscription, fed Democratic charges that the Republicans were trampling the Constitution and creating a military despotism. Still, the Democrats were unable to make additional gains at the polls, and Clement Vallandigham,

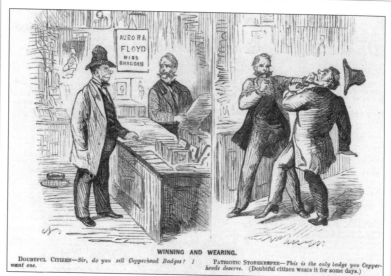

WINNING AND WEARING.

DOUBTFUL CITIZEN—*Sir, do you sell Copperhead Badges?* | PATRIOTIC STOREKEEPER—*This is the only badge you Copperheads deserve.* (Doubtful citizen wears it for some days.)

When this cartoon appeared in a Northern newspaper in the spring of 1863, the word "copperhead" had already entered the Union's political vocabulary as a term of contempt for Northern Peace Democrats who opposed the war and demanded a negotiated settlement.

the most prominent Peace Democrat, suffered a crushing defeat in his bid for the Ohio governorship in the fall of 1863.

The temporary military stalemate that had developed by the summer of 1864 provided the Democrats with their best opportunity to achieve a major political victory. General Ulysses S. Grant had suffered staggering casualties in the early stages of his Virginia campaign, and his offensive against Richmond and that of General William T. Sherman against Atlanta appeared to have ground to a halt by August. War weariness was pervasive in the North, and even Lincoln concluded that he would lose his bid for reelection in the fall.

In late August, the Democrats nominated George B. McClellan, the former Union general, for the Presidency on a platform written by the peace wing of the party. Billed as a policy for "peace and union," the platform denounced the Republican war effort as a failure and called for negotiations to restore "the basis of the Federal Union," presumably with slavery intact. McClellan fully agreed with the criticisms of the Republicans and Lincoln's

leadership, but he was too loyal to his former soldiers to risk wasting their sacrifice by placing peace before the Union. He insisted that the Confederacy had to agree to reunion as the precondition for any peace talks.

McClellan's stand split the Democratic ranks and dampened the enthusiasm of the Peace Democrats. Far more damaging to Democratic prospects, however, was a string of Union successes in the late summer and early fall. Significant victories at Atlanta and in Mobile Bay and the Shenandoah Valley lifted Northern morale and vindicated the Republicans' military strategy. After fending off an attempt of a Radical faction to cast aside Lincoln, a newly energized Republican party unified when confronted with the threat of McClellan's candidacy.

Running on a Union party label, an obvious attempt to maximize his support among War Democrats, Lincoln carried 55 percent of the popular vote and lost only New Jersey, Delaware, and Kentucky. Most impressively, he won 78 percent of the soldiers' vote. The Republicans now had a fresh mandate not only to finish the war, but also to complete the work of emancipation.

SEE ALSO

Democratic party; Emancipation; McClellan, George B.; Republican party; War governors

FURTHER READING

Long, David E. *The Jewel of Liberty: Abraham Lincoln's Re-Election and the End of Slavery.* Mechanicsburg, Pa.: Stackpole Books, 1994.

Neely, Mark E., Jr. *The Union Divided: Party Conflict in the Civil War North.* Cambridge: Harvard University Press, 2002.

Smith, Adam I. P. *No Party Now: Politics in the Civil War North.* New York: Oxford University Press, 2006.

United States Sanitary Commission

An outgrowth of various women's relief societies in the North, the U.S. Sanitary Commission was the largest private relief organization of the war. It significantly supplemented the work of government bureaus in furnishing supplies for the Union army.

In the early weeks of the war, a group of women from some of New York City's wealthiest families organized the Woman's Central Association of Relief with the goal of providing better sanitation and medical care for Union soldiers. Hoping to build on this model of voluntary assistance, Dr. Henry W. Bellows, a New York minister, traveled to Washington and, in June 1861, received official recognition from the government for an umbrella organization called the U.S. Sanitary Commission. Somewhat reluctantly, Union authorities agreed that this civilian agency could assist the Army Medical Bureau in the immense task of meeting the health needs of the soldiers.

Relying solely on private donations, the commission rendered services worth about $25 million. It coordinated relief activities throughout the North and shipped vast quantities of food, clothing, and medical supplies to the army camps. It stockpiled huge warehouses in major Northern cities and employed several hundred field agents to distribute the supplies. Its other main functions included policing sanitary arrangements in the camps and maintaining soldiers' homes and convalescent centers. All of these services rested upon a

The 1863 headquarters for the United States Sanitary Commission at Brandy Station, Virginia. Besides its active work at the front, the Sanitary Commission set up special bureaus throughout the North and Union-occupied areas of the South.

vast outpouring of voluntary support. Farmers responded to appeals for fresh vegetables; schoolchildren donated what they could; and thousands of women freely gave of their time and services.

The only parallel in size and influence to the Sanitary Commission was the U.S. Christian Commission. Launched in late 1861 by Northern evangelicals, it sent 5,000 volunteers into the army camps to conduct religious meetings and distribute Bibles and religious tracts. Through a network of local affiliates, it also funneled food and clothing to the soldiers.

No such large, centrally directed voluntary organizations ever emerged in the Confederacy, since so much of the South was itself the war front. Nor did Southern civilians have the cash reserves that enabled the U.S. Sanitary Commission to raise $4.4 million in funds through a series of huge fairs. As it was, most of the local soldiers' aid and hospital relief societies that sprang up in the Confederacy were strapped for funds and supplies by the end of 1862. On the home front, as well as the battlefield, the Confederacy lacked the resources to match the Union in fashioning an efficiently organized war effort.

SEE ALSO

Women in the war

FURTHER READING

Bremner, Robert H. *The Public Good: Philanthropy and Welfare in the Civil War Era.* New York: Knopf, 1980.
Fredrickson, George M. *The Inner Civil War: Northern Intellectuals and the Crisis of the Union.* New York: Harper & Row, 1965.
Giesberg, Judith Ann. *Civil War Sisterhood: The U. S. Sanitary Commission and Women's Politics in Transition.* Boston: Northeastern University Press, 2000.
Maxwell, William Q. *Lincoln's Fifth Wheel: The Political History of the United States Sanitary Commission.* New York: Longmans, Green, 1956.

Van Dorn, Earl

CONFEDERATE GENERAL

- *Born: September 17, 1820, Port Gibson, Miss.*
- *Education: U.S. Military Academy, B.S., 1842*
- *Military service: U.S. Army: brevet lieutenant, 1842–44; lieutenant, 1844–47; 1st lieutenant, 1847–55; captain, cavalry, 1855–60; major, 1860–61; Confederate army: colonel, 1861; brigadier general, 1861; major-general, 1861–63*
- *Died: May 8, 1863, Spring Hill, Tenn.*

A small man who cut an elegant figure, Earl Van Dorn performed his best service as a cavalry commander in his native state of Mississippi. A notorious womanizer, he was killed in the middle of the war by the husband of a woman with whom he allegedly was having an affair.

The son of a local judge in the Mississippi Delta and a distant nephew of Andrew Jackson, Van Dorn was an indifferent student at West Point and barely avoided expulsion for piling up too many demerits. However, he was a dashing officer who earned a reputation for bravery. He entered the cavalry in the 1850s and was wounded several times in Indian campaigns on the Texas frontier. After hesitating briefly, he resigned his commission on January 31, 1861, and took charge of the state forces of Mississippi, succeeding Jefferson Davis.

Van Dorn's first Confederate command was in Texas, where he organized an expedition that seized the *Star of the West,* the Union steamer that had become famous for having been fired upon back in January during an attempt to resupply Fort Sumter. This action earned him a promotion and a transfer to Virginia at the head of a division. In January 1862, he was back in the West as commander of the Trans-Mississippi Department. He had glorious plans for capturing St. Louis and moving north into Illinois. His oratory to his troops was equally flamboyant. "Soldiers! Behold your leader! He comes to show you the way to glory and immortal renown," he intoned. Instead of winning renown, however, his soldiers experienced only bitter defeat when Van Dorn's Missouri invasion was turned back at Pea Ridge in March 1862.

Transferred after this defeat to Mississippi and entrusted with its defense, Van Dorn suffered another sharp setback at the battle of Corinth in October 1862. As at Pea Ridge, he mishandled his troop movements and misread the strength of the federals. General John C. Pemberton replaced him as commander of the Army of Mississippi, and Van Dorn was put in charge of the army's cavalry.

Overly rash and too administratively inexperienced for the responsibilities of an army commander, Van Dorn now found his niche in the war. As a cavalry commander, he was resourceful and daring. His highly successful raid on a Union supply depot at Holly Springs, Mississippi, in December 1862 forced General Ulysses S. Grant to abandon his first attempt to take Vicksburg. In March 1862, while on loan to the Army of Tennessee, Van Dorn's cavalry surprised and mauled Union forces at Thompson's Station and Brentwood, Tennessee. Van Dorn was just starting to garner the fame that he craved when Dr. George B. Peters fatally shot him at his headquarters on May 7 for allegedly having an affair with the doctor's young wife.

SEE ALSO
Pea Ridge

FURTHER READING

Carter, Arthur B. *The Tarnished Cavalier: Major General Earl Van Dorn, C. S. A.* Knoxville: University of Tennessee Press, 1999.

Vance, Zebulon B.
CONFEDERATE POLITICIAN

- *Born: May 13, 1830, Buncombe County, N.C.*
- *Political parties: Whig, Democrat*
- *Education: Washington College (Tenn.), 1843–44; University of North Carolina Law School, 1851–52*
- *Military service: Confederacy: captain, North Carolina Volunteers, 1861; colonel, 26th North Carolina, 1861–62*
- *Government service: county solicitor, Buncombe County, 1852; North Carolina House of Commons, 1854; U.S. House of Representatives, 1858–61; governor of North Carolina, 1877–79; U.S. Senate, 1879–94; Confederacy: governor of North Carolina, 1862–65*
- *Died: April 14, 1894, Washington, D.C.*

One of the most popular Confederate governors, Zebulon Vance quarreled constantly with President Jefferson Davis over constitutional issues. Despite his differences with the Davis administration, he was remarkably successful in mobilizing the resources of North Carolina for the Confederate war effort.

Born and raised in the mountain country of western North Carolina, Vance left college upon the death of his father, studied law, and opened his practice in 1852. Initially a Whig in his politics, he won election to Congress in 1858 as a Democrat. He was a staunch Unionist during the secession crisis until President Abraham Lincoln's call for troops on April 15, 1861. Like other North Carolinians, he interpreted that call as a declaration of war against Southern liberties and pledged his loyalty to the Confederacy.

After raising a company of troops and seeing service at the Battle of New Bern in March 1862 and on the Virginia Peninsula during the Seven Days Battles, Vance returned to politics as the gubernatorial nominee of the Conservative Party. A coalition of former Whigs and Union Democrats dissatisfied with the leadership of the state's secessionist Democrats, the Conservatives benefited from the war-weariness that already permeated the Tar Heel state. As Vance informed Davis soon after he easily won the gubernatorial election in October 1862, "The original advocates of secession no longer hold the ear of the people."

Vance's popularity as governor rested on his ability to convince North Carolinians that he would protect them from what were widely viewed as the tyrannical policies of the Davis government, such as conscription and the suspension of the writ of habeas corpus, which seemingly threatened individual freedoms. Backed up by the North Carolina legislature, he claimed the right to exempt from the Confederate draft all officials whom he deemed necessary for the administration of state affairs. Eventually, he exempted nearly 15,000 individuals. He also upheld the right of North Carolina courts to obtain the release of civilians held under arbitrary arrest by Confederate authorities.

Because conscription, in Vance's words to Davis in March 1863, had deprived the state of "a large class whose labor was... absolutely necessary to the existence of the women and children left behind," Vance instituted a bold program of funneling relief to soldiers' families. He convinced the legislature to appropriate $6 million for poor relief and established state saltworks that distributed that essential item at one-third of its cost. A state-owned fleet of blockade runners began operating in 1863, and by war's end, it had brought in through Wilmington tons of nonmilitary supplies for civilians.

For all his condemnations of Confederate despotism, Vance remained a committed Southern nationalist. Despite his constitutional objections to conscription, North Carolina sent 7,000 more draftees into the Confederate army than any other state. Indeed, no state contributed a larger share of its manpower and resources to the Confederacy than North Carolina. When faced with a strong peace movement in 1864, Vance won a sweeping reelection in a campaign in which he declared that North Carolina would never desert the Confederacy by negotiating a separate peace with the Union.

Following his surrender at Greensboro on May 2, 1865, Vance was arrested by federal authorities and held in the Old Capital Prison in Washington until released on parole on July 6. He practiced law in Charlotte before returning to politics as North Carolina's most popular statesman. While serving as governor in 1879, he was elected to the U.S. Senate, a position he held until his death.

Although North Carolinians elected Zebulon Vance to the U.S. Senate in 1870, the Radical Republicans refused to let him take his seat. Six years later his election as governor of North Carolina marked the end of Reconstruction in that state.

SEE ALSO

Conscription

FURTHER READING

McKinney, Gordon B. *Zeb Vance: North Carolina's Civil War Governor and Gilded Age Political Leader*. Chapel Hill: University of North Carolina Press, 2004.

Mobley, Joe A. *"War Governor of the South": North Carolina's Zeb Vance in the Confederacy*. Gainesville: University Press of Florida, 2005.

Vicksburg campaign

The Vicksburg campaign elevated Ulysses S. Grant into the top ranks of Civil War generals and secured for the Union one of its primary strategic objectives: control of the Mississippi River. The campaign began with Grant's appointment as commander of the Department of the Tennessee on October 25, 1862, and culminated with the surrender of the Confederate army in Vicksburg, Mississippi, on July 4, 1863.

Grant initially planned a two-pronged assault on Vicksburg, the last major Confederate stronghold on the Mississippi, for late 1862. In November he began moving his 40,000-man army south from Tennessee down the Mississippi Central Railroad. Opposing him were 22,000 Confederates in the Army of Mississippi, commanded by General John C. Pemberton, the only Northern-born general who attained three-star rank in the Confederate army. At the same time, Union General William T. Sherman was sent down the Mississippi River from Memphis with 32,000 troops for an assault on Chickasaw Bluffs, just north of Vicksburg.

Grant's land-based offensive ground to a halt on December 20 when Confederate cavalry operating in his rear destroyed his major supply base at Holly Springs and broke up his rail and telegraph communications in southern Tennessee. Grant had no choice but to turn back. Pemberton was now free to send reinforcements to Vicksburg to assist in the repulse of Sherman's attack at Chickasaw Bluffs on December 27–29.

During the winter of 1862–63, Grant wrestled with the problem of how to crack the Vicksburg defenses. Situated on a high bluff above the eastern bank of the Mississippi, and protected from the north and south by hills

Ulysses S. Grant took the Confederate high command completely by surprise when he moved his army down the Mississippi, seized the city of Jackson, and outflanked the Confederate position at Vicksburg.

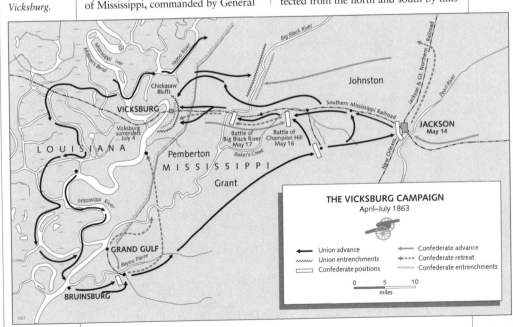

and swamps, Vicksburg was vulnerable only from the east. But the failure of the December offensive had convinced Grant that the long supply lines needed to support an approach from the east could too easily be broken by Confederate cavalry. Out of necessity, he established a new base of operations at Milliken's Landing on the west side of the Mississippi. Throughout the winter and spring he kept his soldiers and thousands of contraband black laborers busy digging canals and probing passages through a labyrinth of bayous in an effort to find a water route that could place his army on the east bank of the Mississippi close to Vicksburg.

None of these efforts succeeded, but they served Grant's purpose of maintaining pressure on the Confederates and placating the demands of his critics in the North for some sort of action. Finally, with the return of drier weather in April, Grant was in a position to launch the outflanking maneuver he had long known offered the best hope for taking Vicksburg from the east.

On the night of April 16, Admiral David Dixon Porter ran his Union fleet past the rebel batteries at Vicksburg. Of his 12 boats, 11 made it safely down the river for a rendezvous at Hard Times Landing with some 23,000 federal troops that had marched down the west bank of the Mississippi. In order to confuse the Confederates, Grant had Sherman mount a diversionary attack on Chickasaw Bluffs, and he sent Colonel Benjamin Grierson on a daring cavalry raid of 600 miles down the backbone of the state of Mississippi. Porter's fleet was unable to silence the Confederate guns at Grand Gulf across from Hard Times Landing, but Grant was still able to ferry his forces across the Mississippi at Bruinsburg, some 50 miles downriver from Vicksburg. The crossing was unopposed, and Grant

finally had the lead elements of his army on the east side of the Mississippi. "All the campaigns, labors, hardships, and exposures, from the month of December previous to this time," he recalled in his *Memoirs*, "were for the accomplishment of this one object."

Grant was now where he wanted to be, but he had no room for error. He was deep in enemy territory, and he would have to cut loose from any secure base of supplies in order to move inland against Jackson, a rail center 45 miles east of Vicksburg that was the river fortress's main lifeline for supplies. Above all, he had to strike quickly against scattered Confederate forces before they could concentrate against him.

Reinforced to a troop strength of 44,000 with the arrival of Sherman's division, Grant headed east in early May. The badly confused Confederates did not realize until too late that Grant's immediate objective was Jackson. General Joseph E. Johnston, ordered to Mississippi on May 9, found only 6,000 troops available to defend Jackson. The city fell to Grant on May 14. Meanwhile, Pemberton, believing that he had to hold Vicksburg at all costs, ignored Johnston's order to attack Grant from the rear and then link up with the army that Johnston was desperately trying to

A Southern woman prays in her makeshift cave home during the Union bombardment of Vicksburg in this drawing by German-American artist Adalbert John Volck.

throw together. A reluctant Pemberton finally did venture out of Vicksburg, but he soon returned after failing to stop Grant's advance at Champion's Hill on May 16 and at the Big Black River on May 17. Once Pemberton retreated into the Vicksburg defenses, Grant tried to take the city by assault on May 19 and 22. Turned back in heavy fighting, Grant now resorted to a siege.

Vicksburg was under siege for 48 days. Constant Union shellings forced civilians to live in underground caves dug into the sides of hills. "Our new habitation," recorded Vicksburg resident Mary Ann Loughborough in her journal, "was an excavation made in the earth, and branching six feet from the entrance, forming a cave in the shape of a T." Dwindling rations forced many to survive on a diet of mule, horse, and rat meat. Battered and nearly starved, Pemberton's army surrendered on July 4.

Grant's handling of the Vicksburg campaign was nearly flawless once he put his army in motion in April. The fall of Vicksburg (followed almost immediately by the Confederate loss of Port Hudson on July 9) reopened the Mississippi River for the Union and all but cut the Confederacy in half. In addition, the Confederacy suffered a nearly irreplaceable loss of manpower with the surrender of Pemberton's 31,000-man army.

SEE ALSO

Grant, Ulysses S.; Johnston, Joseph E.; Pemberton, John C.; Sherman, William T.

FURTHER READING

Ballard, Michael B. *Vicksburg: The Campaign that Opened the Mississippi.* Chapel Hill: University of North Carolina Press, 2004.
Catton, Bruce. *Grant Moves South.* Boston: Little, Brown, 1960.
Walker, Peter F. *Vicksburg: A People at War, 1860–1865.* Chapel Hill: University of North Carolina Press, 1960.

Wade-Davis bill

Passed by Congress in July 1864, the Wade-Davis bill proposed an alternative to President Abraham Lincoln's approach to Reconstruction as outlined in his 10-percent plan, which promised executive recognition of any rebel state in which as few as 10 percent of the qualified voters of 1860 took a loyalty oath and organized a loyal state government. Anxious to preserve the Unionist governments that he had nursed along in Louisiana and Arkansas, Lincoln pocket-vetoed the bill—that is, he failed to sign it before the congressional session came to an end.

Under the bill, Reconstruction in any state would not begin until all military resistance in that state to Union authority had been crushed and a majority of the voters of 1860 had taken an oath of future loyalty to the Union. A provisional governor, appointed by the President and confirmed by the Senate, would then oversee the calling of a state constitutional convention. Only those able to swear the "ironclad oath" that they had never voluntarily aided the Confederacy were eligible to vote for, or be members of, the required constitutional convention. Once it met, that convention had to declare slavery "forever prohibited," repudiate Confederate war debts, and disqualify leading rebels from voting and holding office. No provision was made for black suffrage, but the bill did guarantee freedom and legal equality for "all persons."

Lincoln's reservations concerning the bill centered on his belief that Congress had no constitutional authority to mandate emancipation and his insistence that nothing should upset the progress he had made in restoring Unionist governments in parts of the Confederacy. His refusal to allow the bill to become law angered congressional Republicans. On August 4, 1864, Senator Benjamin F. Wade of Ohio and Congressman Henry Winter Davis of Maryland, the cosponsors of the bill, issued a "manifesto" in which they harshly criticized Lincoln both for undercutting the role of Congress in Reconstruction and for leaving uncertain the legal status of emancipation. The two sides nearly compromised their differences during the winter of 1864–65 in a revised Wade-Davis bill, but those efforts collapsed at the last minute.

SEE ALSO

Ironclad oath; Proclamation of Amnesty and Reconstruction; Wartime Reconstruction

FURTHER READING

Benedict, Michael Les. *A Compromise of Principle: Congressional Republicans and Reconstruction, 1863–1869.* New York: Norton, 1974.

War debts

SEE Cost of the war

War governors

The war governors in both the North and the South generally supported the respective national causes of preserving the Union and establishing Southern independence. In the North, a strong Republican party organization fused this support with backing for the policies of President Abraham Lincoln's administration. In the South, on the other hand, the successful governors stayed in power by attacking President Jefferson Davis's administration for infringing on states' rights and individual liberties.

Most of the Northern war governors were Republicans, beholden for their office to the organizational efforts of the same party that had placed Lincoln in the White House. Not only did they enthusiastically endorse military measures to suppress the rebellion, but they also welcomed a greater role for the national government in raising troops. Especially after the Democratic comeback in the elections of 1862, they turned to Washington for political help. This was most evident in Indiana, where Republican Governor Oliver P. Morton faced a hostile Democratic legislature after the fall of 1862. Desperate to block Democratic attempts to recall the state's troops from the war, Morton went along with a Republican scheme to boycott the legislature and thus deny it the constitutional quorum it needed to conduct its business. For the next two years, he governed the state without a legislature. For necessary funds, he relied on loans from corporations and a subsidy of $250,000 from the War Department that Lincoln's government was only too happy to provide.

In the Confederacy, the interests of the Davis administration and those of the Southern governors often ran at cross-purposes. At the same time, Southern governors faced problems of state defense and civilian hardships that their Northern counterparts most often avoided. By the spring of 1862, Davis and his advisors concluded that only a highly centralized war effort offered the Confederacy any chance of military victory. The Confederate government had to take the lead in raising manpower and procuring needed supplies. The result was conscription and a host of economic policies that were highly unpopular among the civilian populace. What the Richmond authorities saw as necessary centralization, civilians viewed as military despotism.

The most effective Confederate governors, Zebulon B. Vance of North Carolina and Joseph E. Brown of Georgia, sold themselves to the voters as tireless defenders of Southern liberties threatened by the tyranny of the Davis government. Loudly and persistently, they railed against Confederate policies, especially conscription and periodic suspensions of the writ of habeas corpus. Vance, for example, rebuked Davis for failing to see that Confederate conscription was drawing off many men "whose labor was . . . absolutely necessary to the existence of the women and children left behind." These protests offered an outlet for civilian discontent and tended to mask the governors' very positive contributions to the Confederacy and their own programs of state centralization.

Georgia and North Carolina alone accounted for 42 percent of all Confederate conscripts east of the Mississippi River, and North Carolina gave a larger share of its manpower and resources to the Confederacy than any other state. In order to help civilians cope with the sacrifice entailed by these contributions, Vance and Brown initiated major welfare programs to provide relief for the poor. By offering economic assistance and promising to protect their citizens from Confederate despotism, these governors built up strong personal followings. This in turn gave them the political base they needed to draw heavily on the resources of their states for the support of the Confederacy.

Southern governors were frequently at odds with the Davis administration. Nonetheless, and despite frequently being characterized as locally minded politicians who undercut the Confederate cause by selfishly placing the needs of their states first, these governors played as vital a role in sustaining the war as did the Republican governors in the North.

SEE ALSO

Brown, Joseph E.; Confederate politics; Union politics; Vance, Zebulon B.

FURTHER READING

Hesseltine, William B. *Lincoln and the War Governors.* New York: Knopf, 1948.
Yearns, W. Buck, ed. *The Confederate Governors.* Athens: University of Georgia Press, 1985.

Wartime economies

The Northern economy was a growing element of Union strength as the war progressed. The reverse was true in the Confederacy. The strains and dislocations produced by the war, combined with the destructiveness of Union invasions and raids, soon crippled the Confederate economy and contributed to the defeat of rebel armies.

The early stages of the Civil War were highly disruptive for the Northern economy. The outbreak of war shut down the Mississippi River trade, which had siphoned off much of the agricultural surpluses of the Midwest. The loss of this trade outlet resulted in a sharp agricultural recession that persisted through the summer of 1862. Then the farm economy bounced back and enjoyed sustained prosperity for the remainder of the war. Agricultural prices rose sharply as farmers profited from the ever-growing military demand at home for foodstuffs and a huge increase in foreign demand for U.S. crops. Generally poor harvests in Europe between 1860 and 1862 resulted in a wartime doubling of U.S. exports of wheat, corn, pork, and beef products.

Northern farm production increased dramatically during the war despite the absence of one-third of the normal agricultural workforce, which was off fighting in the Union armies. Farmers, many of whom were now women, were able to expand output by turning to labor-saving machinery such as reapers and mowers. Sales of these agricultural implements tripled between 1860 and 1865, and the Civil War decade saw the second-highest gain in agricultural productivity of any decade in the 19th century.

A similar pattern emerged in Northern industry. After an initial slump in response to the loss of traditional markets in the South, a sustained recovery was underway by 1862 that led to an overall increase in manufacturing activity. In March 1865, the *New York Sun* noted that "business prosperity" in New York had never been greater than in the last two years of the war. Manufacturing and commercial regions in the interior likewise shared in the prosperity of New York, the mercantile and financial center of the Union.

Military demand was the key to the midwar resurgence in Northern manufacturing. Those industries most closely connected to the logistical support of the armies enjoyed the greatest production increases. The military market, for example, accelerated the growth and consolidation of the meat-packing industry. Chicago, in more than tripling its output of packed hogs, far outstripped its previous rivals in the Mississippi and Ohio valleys. Production of the pig iron essential for the booming armaments industry reached new highs in 1864, and its price had more than doubled since 1860. Coal and iron-ore producers registered similar gains in output and profits.

The most profitable industries were those engaged in supplying the military with uniforms and shoes. Clothing and shoe manufacturers were able to cope with the labor shortage, reduce costs, and standardize production by relying more heavily on labor-saving machinery. The adoption of the Howe and McKay sewing machines (the latter was a mechanical device for sewing uppers to soles in shoe production) accelerated the shift in both industries from household manufacturing to the factory system.

Railroads and canal companies benefited from a huge increase in the volume of their traffic. Built in anticipation of future demand, the railroads utilized their full carrying capacity for the first time during the Civil War. As the major trunk lines doubled their freight tonnage, passenger miles, and rolling stock, profits and stock values rose

This advertisement announces goods for sale by an enterprising Union sutler, a tradesman who followed the armies and set up shop to sell basic consumer items in the army camps.

Confederate soldiers swap their ragged clothing for U.S. Army overcoats after raiding Chambersburg, Pennsylvania, in the fall of 1862. Supply problems bedeviled the rebel armies throughout the war.

accordingly. The lines that controlled the heaviest military traffic generated enough income to begin upgrading their equipment and preparing for postwar expansion.

Whereas the Union successfully adjusted its economy to wartime demands, the Confederacy had difficulty maintaining an economy that could meet even the most basic needs of its civilians and soldiers. Agriculture was a weak spot throughout the war. Planters had no incentive to raise a cotton crop they could not market because of the Union blockade, and they responded to the increased public demand for foodstuffs by voluntarily putting more acreage into food crops. Later, as some planters eyed the immense profits to be gained by an illegal cotton trade with the advancing Yankees, these voluntary controls started to break down. In response, the states intervened by setting compulsory limits on cotton production.

Between 1860 and 1863, voluntarism and state coercion combined to double the acreage in the Confederacy devoted to corn, wheat, and potatoes. However, food production did not keep pace because yields per acre dropped throughout the war. For example, corn output in South Carolina declined from 15 bushels an acre in 1861 to 9 by 1863 and to 6 by 1865. Particularly on the farms of its nonslaveholding majority, the Confederacy lacked the manpower, tools, and livestock necessary to maintain the prewar level of agricultural efficiency.

Compounding all government efforts to come up with an effective agricultural policy were the ongoing loss of territory to the Union, the destructiveness of Union raids, and the runaway inflation that resulted in the withholding of foodstuffs as producers waited for the highest bid in the marketplace. Neither impressment legislation nor direct taxes on farmers solved these problems, and the steady shrinkage of the Confederate rail system made it ever more difficult to forward what food supplies were available to the armies.

Somewhat surprisingly, the agrarian Confederacy had more success in its economic mobilization in the industrial sphere. Starting virtually from scratch, the Confederacy organized an industrial program that supplied its armies with the means of war. By 1863 the Confederacy was largely self-sufficient in the production of basic war supplies. This program rested on centralized controls imposed by the Davis government in Richmond. Through direct ownership, subsidies, and various regulatory devices, the Confederate government intervened directly in the industrial sector and shaped it to serve military needs.

Where industrial production was most critical to the war effort, as with munitions, ordnance, and gunpowder, the government often set up its own factories. Within three years a string of government arsenals and foundries was established in the interior along a wide arc stretching from Texas to Virginia. The result, as noted after the war by Josiah Gorgas, the head of the Confederate Ordnance Department, was "a chain of arsenals, armories, and laboratories equal in their capacity and their improved appointment to the best of those in the United States."

In the procurement of essential raw materials, as well as in the management of industrial production, the Confederacy established far more centralized controls than ever prevailed in the Union. As a result, it was able to equip its armies to wage modern, industrial warfare. As Gorgas wrote in late 1863, "We are now in a condition to carry on the war for an indefinite period . . . we have war material sufficient—men, guns, powder—the real pinch is the Treasury."

Finance was indeed the weakest link in the Confederate economy. With the bulk of its capital tied up in land and slaves, the Confederacy lacked any means of financing a long war short of printing paper money that soon declined in value. Already-high rates of inflation became ruinous after the major military setbacks of the Confed-

eracy in 1863. For all the heavy-handed intervention of the Confederate government, the economy collapsed from within as Union armies hammered it from the outside.

SEE ALSO

Cost of the war; Gold; Industrial workers; Inflation; Taxation

FURTHER READING

Andreano, Ralph L., ed. *The Economic Impact of the American Civil War.* Cambridge, Mass.: Schenkman, 1962.
Gates, Paul W. *Agriculture and the Civil War.* New York: Knopf, 1965.
Gilchrist, David T. and W. David Lewis, eds. *Economic Change in the Civil War Era.* Greenville, Del.: Eleutherian Mills–Hagley Foundation, 1965.
Wilson, Harold S. *Confederate Industry: Manufacturers and Quartermasters in the Confederacy.* Jackson: University Press of Mississippi, 2002.
Wilson, Mark R. *The Business of War: Military Mobilization and the State, 1861–1865.* Baltimore, Md.: Johns Hopkins University Press, 2006.

Wartime Reconstruction

As Union armies began occupying areas of the Confederacy, the issue of readmitting rebel states to the Union acquired practical significance. The process of rebuilding the Union began during the war, but President Abraham Lincoln and the Republican-dominated Congress were unable to agree on a unified approach.

For Lincoln, and conservative Northerners in general, the rebel states theoretically had never left the Union; secession, to them, was a legal impossibility. Consequently, they viewed Reconstruction primarily as an administrative matter in which procedures would be set down for the restoration of loyal state governments. In addition,

Lincoln thought of Reconstruction as a wartime problem that fell under his control as commander-in-chief. His primary goal was always to undermine the Confederacy by giving Southern whites a workable alternative to rebel rule. In this sense his Proclamation of Amnesty and Reconstruction was a war measure designed to hasten Confederate disintegration. In order to attract the widest popular support to his "10 percent" governments, he placed no social or economic conditions on readmission apart from his highly significant insistence that emancipation had to be accepted.

Congressional Republicans contested Lincoln for control of Reconstruction. They held that the Southern states had in practical terms left the Union, and that the reality of secession and armed resistance to Union authority necessitated far-reaching changes in Southern society before the rebel states could safely be allowed back into the Union. Citing the constitutional obligation of Congress to guarantee a republican form of government to each state, they maintained that they could set terms for readmission. As outlined in the Wade-Davis bill of 1864, their program for Reconstruction was far more sweeping than Lincoln's in its guarantees for equal legal and civic treatment of blacks, political penalties for having aided the rebellion, and repudiation of the rebel war debt.

Lincoln's pocket veto of the Wade-Davis bill exposed the party rift over Reconstruction policy and perpetuated the impasse in which Congress refused to recognize the Unionist governments organized under Lincoln's direction in Arkansas, Tennessee, and Louisiana. As a result, only one region initially under Confederate jurisdiction was back in the Union before the end of the war. That region consisted of the heavily Unionist northwestern counties of Virginia brought under federal control early in the war. Through highly irregular if not downright illegal maneuvers, West Virginia entered the Union in June 1863.

The differences between Lincoln and Congress were substantial, but they should not be exaggerated. Both sides were united in their conviction that the slaves had to be freed and enlisted as soldiers in order to win the war and preserve the Union. Both realized that Reconstruction required an extension of federal power over the internal affairs of states that would have been unthinkable in 1860. The 13th Amendment freeing the slaves passed Congress in January 1865 only through the combined efforts of Lincoln and his Republican critics. In the final months of his life, Lincoln moved closer to the congressional position favoring federal supervision of black rights in the postwar South. In his last public speech on April 11, 1865, he endorsed the congressional call for some limited form of black suffrage in the South. Had he lived, there is every reason to believe that Lincoln and Congress would have reached a common ground on Reconstruction.

SEE ALSO

Proclamation of Amnesty and Reconstruction; Wade-Davis bill

FURTHER READING

Belz, Herman. *Reconstructing the Union: Theory and Practice during the Civil War.* Ithaca, N.Y.: Cornell University Press, 1969.
Harris, William C. *With Charity for All: Lincoln and the Restoration of the Union.* Lexington: University Press of Kentucky, 1997.

Weapons

SEE   Artillery; Rifles

Welles, Gideon

UNION POLITICIAN

- Born: July 1, 1802, Glastonbury, Conn.
- Political parties: Democrat, Republican
- Education: private academies
- Military service: none
- Government service: Connecticut House of Representatives, 1827–35; Connecticut comptroller of public accounts, 1835, 1842–43; Chief of the Bureau of Provisions and Clothing for the Navy, 1846–49; U.S. secretary of the navy, 1861–69
- Died: February 11, 1878, Hartford, Conn.

Although he had little prior experience in naval matters, Gideon Welles proved to be an extremely competent Union secretary of the navy. One of the most loyal and reliable of President Abraham Lincoln's cabinet members, he oversaw the expansion of the Union's small, outmoded navy into a large, modern force that operated effectively both as offensive weapons on the inland rivers of the Confederacy and as blockaders along its coastline.

Born into a wealthy Connecticut family whose roots stretched back to the founding of Hartford in 1635, Welles attended private academies and studied law before committing himself to a career in politics and journalism as a Jacksonian Democrat. He left the Democrats in opposition to their passage of the Kansas-Nebraska Act and joined the Republicans in 1855. From 1856 to 1864 he was a member of the Republican national executive committee. He joined Lincoln's cabinet in 1861 as its New England representative.

"When I took charge of the Navy Department," Welles wrote in his diary, "I found great demoralization and defection among the naval officers." In addition to restoring morale and deciding which officers he could trust, he quickly had to formulate a program to increase the size and combat effectiveness of the navy. Aided by his resourceful deputy, Assistant Secretary of the Navy Gustavus A. Fox, he commissioned new ships, had merchant vessels converted to military use, and increased the number of Union warships six times over by the end of 1861. He created a Navy Board in June 1861 that evolved from a task force on the Union blockade into a strategic planning center for naval policy and army-navy cooperation.

Welles was no radical innovator, but he had enough foresight to champion the creation of an Ironclad Board and to contract with Swedish inventor John Ericsson in October 1861 for the construction of an ironclad warship. Thus, when Washington was thrown into panic on March 9, 1862, at the spectacular initial success of the Confederate ironclad Virginia, the Union had a weapon in the ironclad Monitor that could reestablish its naval supremacy. By the summer of 1862, the Union had 21 more ironclads under construction, a number that the Confederacy could not hope to match. Armored cruisers and improved artillery and steam engines were among the other modernizing changes that Welles incorporated into the Union's naval war effort.

Although a conservative on both constitutional and racial issues, Welles supported Lincoln's Emancipation Proclamation as a necessary war measure. "The [Confederate] slaves must be with us or against us in the War," he noted in his diary. "Let us have them." Recognizing the navy's need for manpower, he had authorized the enlistment of runaway slaves as sailors as early as

September 1861. Still, he continually fretted that the zeal of radical Republicans for emancipation in all the states and for citizenship rights for the freed slaves might "destroy the great framework of our political governmental system" by trampling on states' rights.

Welles's innate conservatism led him to oppose the postwar program of Reconstruction favored by most of his fellow Republicans. After supporting President Andrew Johnson's more conservative program for the postwar South, Welles returned to the Democratic party in 1868, and he remained a Democrat until his death.

SEE ALSO
Blockade; Naval warfare

FURTHER READING
Niven, John. *Gideon Welles: Lincoln's Secretary of the Navy*. New York: Oxford University Press, 1973.
West, Richard S. *Gideon Welles: Lincoln's Navy Department*. Indianapolis: Bobbs-Merrill, 1943.

Whig party

Organized in the mid-1830s in response to the policies and ideology of the Jacksonian Democrats, the Whig party collapsed in the 1850s when the reaction in the North to the Kansas-Nebraska Act produced a major party realignment. Former Northern Whigs, including Abraham Lincoln, comprised the largest single bloc in the new antislavery coalition put together by the Republican party.

In contrast to the Democrats, the Whigs offered Americans a vision of progress anchored in the positive use of governmental power to promote economic development and regulate morality. Embodying the ideas of its most prominent leader, Henry Clay of Kentucky, the party called for protective tariffs, government sponsorship of a national bank, and federal funds for internal improvements. As the political voice of most Northern evangelical Protestants, the party also championed reforms such as temperance, public-supported education, and new asylums for the poor and mentally ill.

By 1840, once they had learned from the Democrats how to promote their candidates through massive rallies and a barrage of banners and slogans, the Whigs were fully competitive with the Democrats in all sections of the country. In 1840, and again in 1848, the Whigs captured the Presidency by running popular military heroes. The party, however, was never able to legislate its economic program into practice, and its Northern antislavery wing was always at odds with the proslavery planters and businessmen who headed the party in the Lower South.

Already gravely weakened by sectional divisions that had opened up over the Compromise of 1850, the Whigs disintegrated as a national organization in the wake of the Kansas-Nebraska Act. Northern fears of a Slave Power conspiracy intent on converting the Trans-Mississippi West into a vast slave territory were so great that the Whigs no longer appeared anti-Southern enough for angry Northern voters. Before joining the new Republican party, many former Whigs first flocked into a short-lived nativist party, the Know-Nothings, which attempted to restrict immigration (especially for Catholics) and deprive the foreign-born of the right to hold political office. By 1856, however, the Republicans had emerged as the major political alternative to the Democrats in the North.

This cartoon depicts the split in the Whig party between the supporters of Henry Clay and those of Zachary Taylor in the months leading up to the party's national convention in 1848. The rock that has jolted the party wagon is the "Wilmot Proviso," which would have prohibited slavery in any territory acquired in the Mexican War, an issue both Whigs and Democrats tried to avoid in the election of 1848.

Although the Whigs retained considerable strength in the Upper South, the party never recovered from the defections to the Republicans. Nonetheless, the party had provided a core of leaders for the Republicans, and its economic nationalism would serve as the basis for the sweeping economic changes inaugurated by the Republicans during the Civil War.

SEE ALSO

Compromise of 1850; Democratic party; Kansas-Nebraska Act; Republican party

FURTHER READING

Cole, Arthur C. *The Whig Party in the South.* Washington, D.C.: American Historical Association, 1913.
Holt, Michael F. *The Rise and Fall of the American Whig Party: Jacksonian Politics and the Onset of the Civil War.* New York: Oxford University Press, 1999.

Whitman, Walt

UNION POET

- *Born: May 31, 1819, West Hills, N.Y.*
- *Education: some schooling in lower grades*
- *Occupation: teacher, journalist, author*
- *Died: March 26, 1892, Camden, N.J.*

Author of the most moving wartime poetry produced in the North, Walt Whitman spent much of the war caring for wounded Union soldiers in the Washington hospitals. His experiences as a nurse deepened his mystic Unionism and inspired some of his best work.

Born in Long Island, Whitman grew up in Brooklyn, where his family moved in 1823. He attended public schools but derived most of his education from the bustling streets and cultural activities of America's most dynamic metropolitan center. After working as a printer's apprentice and a teacher, he entered the newspaper trade as a reporter and editor. While editing the *Brooklyn Daily Eagle* in the late 1840s, he declared himself a free-soiler—that is, an opponent of the extension of slavery into the territories. In 1855 he published, at his own expense, the first edition of his *Leaves of Grass,* a collection of sprawling, free-verse poems that celebrated the democratic individualism of the American people. Shocked by his experimental forms of poetic expression and his sexual imagery, most critics at the time denounced the work as indecent.

At the age of 42 when the Civil War began, Whitman was still young enough to fight, but he chose not to. "I had my temptations," he later told his friend, Horace Traubel, "but they were never strong enough to tempt. I could never think of myself as firing a gun or drawing a sword on another man." Instead, he served the Union cause by nursing its wounded (and many rebel soldiers as well) and distilling his experience in prose and in memorable poetry.

Whitman first went to Washington in December 1862 upon hearing that his brother George had been wounded at the battle of Fredericksburg. After finding George in good health, he began visiting the hospitals and convalescent camps. The conditions in the hospitals both appalled and moved him. "These hospitals," he wrote in the *New York Times* in February 1863, "so different from all others—these thousands, and tens and twenties of thousands of American young men, badly wounded, all sorts of wounds,... dying with fever, pneumonia, etc., open a new world somehow to me, giving closer insights, new things, exploring deeper mines than any yet."

For Whitman, the sick and maimed soldiers were "America brought to Hospital in her fair youth," and as long as his own health held out, he administered to them with affection, care, and what small gifts he could afford from his salary as a temporary government clerk. Physically and emotionally, the work was draining, but he persisted.

Although failing health forced Whitman to move back to Brooklyn in the summer of 1864, he continued to visit soldiers at the Brooklyn City Hospital. By the war's end, he estimated that he had seen more than 80,000 men on his more than 600 hospital visits. The poems in *Drum-Taps* (1865) and the war notes that he published as *Specimen Days* (1882–83) remain among the best sources for the underreported medical side of the war. He also authored the two most stirring poems inspired by President Abraham Lincoln's assassination: "O Captain! My Captain!" and "When Lilacs Last in the Dooryard Bloom'd."

The war touched Whitman more deeply than any other Northern writer. While living as an invalid in Camden, New Jersey, following a paralytic stroke in 1873, he told his friend Traubel: "I have never left [those] real, terrible, beautiful days." And he always believed, as he wrote in *Specimen Days,* that "the real war will never get in the books."

SEE ALSO

Literature; Medicine

FURTHER READING

Allen, Gay Wilson. *The Solitary Singer: A Critical Biography of Walt Whitman.* New York: New York University Press, 1967.

Lowenfels, Walter, ed. *Walt Whitman's Civil War.* New York: Knopf, 1971.

Morris, Roy. *The Better Angel: Walt Whitman in the Civil War.* New York: Oxford University Press, 2000.

Reynolds, David S. *Walt Whitman's America: A Cultural Biography.* New York: Knopf, 1995.

Walt Whitman's wartime writings are a valuable source of information about conditions in the Union's military hospitals. His frequent visits helped comfort thousands of the sick and wounded soldiers.

The Wilderness

SEE Grant's Virginia campaign

Wilmot Proviso

In August 1846, Democratic Representative David Wilmot of Pennsylvania introduced in Congress a rider to a military appropriations bill. Known as the Wilmot Proviso, the rider stipulated that slavery was to be prohibited in any territory acquired in the Mexican War. As praised in the North as it was condemned in the South, the proviso highlighted the issue of slavery's expansion that was instrumental in the coming of the Civil War.

In stressing that he had "no morbid sympathy for the slave," Wilmot made it clear that he was not an abolitionist. Instead—and this was the source of the proviso's popularity in the North—he was a free-soiler speaking for the growing numbers of Northern whites who did not want to be forced into competition with slave labor in the territories. For Wilmot, the territories were to be a land of opportunity "where the sons of toil, of my own race and own color, can live without the disgrace which association with negro slavery brings upon free labor."

Support for or against the Wilmot Proviso immediately broke down party lines in Congress. Just as Northerners rallied behind a call to reserve territorial acquisitions for free white labor, outraged Southerners opposed what they saw as an unconscionable exclusion from territories that Southern blood and treasure had helped conquer. To accept the proviso would be to consign the slave South to a permanent and declining minority position within the Union and to deny Southern whites avenues for social mobility and economic advancement.

The House, where the North had a comfortable majority, approved the proviso on several occasions, but the Senate repeatedly blocked its passage. Nevertheless, it revived the slavery issue, which all parties had tried to bury for a quarter of a century. Despite the efforts of the parties to defuse the issue, it continued to poison sectional relations until tensions finally boiled over in the outbreak of the Civil War.

SEE ALSO
Mexican War

FURTHER READING
Morrison, Chaplain W. *Democratic Politics and Sectionalism: The Wilmot Proviso Controversy.* Chapel Hill: University of North Carolina Press, 1967.

Woman's National Loyal League

SEE Anthony, Susan B.; Stanton, Elizabeth Cady

Women in the war

The Civil War challenged but did not overturn gender roles assigned to women within antebellum American society. In both the Union and the Confederacy, women seized new opportunities opened up by the war to express their patriotism and support their respective war causes. In most instances, however, the return of peace brought a

Working out of their homes, Southern women practically clothed Confederate troops in the first year of the war. A contemporary marveled: "Heaven only knows what the soldiers of the South would have done without the exertions of the women in their behalf."

return to traditional limits on women's participation in public affairs.

Deeply entrenched cultural values in the mid-19th-century United States held that woman's proper and God-ordained place was in the home, where she would naturally be dependent on her husband. What is often called the "Cult of Domesticity" divided life into private and public spheres segregated by gender. Only men were to engage in the aggressive, competitive world of politics and business. Women, deemed to be physically weaker but morally stronger then men, were to remain in the private sphere of home and family raising virtuous children and nurturing Christian values.

The Civil War, by mobilizing loyalties and energies that affected women fully as much as men, encouraged and, in some cases, demanded that women take on new public roles. As 19-year-old Sarah Morgan of Baton Rouge, Louisiana, exclaimed in her diary: "If I was only a man! I don't know a woman here who does not groan over her misfortune in being clothed in petticoats; why can't we fight as well as the men?" Some 400 women actually did fight in the Union or Confederate armies. In an era of obviously lax medical examinations, they disguised their gender and enlisted as soldiers. An illness or wound

requiring hospitalization soon revealed the true identity of most of these female soldiers. Six were unmasked when they had babies.

Comparatively very few women, of course, saw any active military service. Far more common was participation in relief and soldier-aid societies. In the North, 200,000 women volunteered to work in relief agencies that sent a stream of clothing, food packages, and hospital supplies to the front. Women's sewing skills were in particularly high demand early in the war, when the production of uniforms fell far short of what was needed.

The strong leadership of Clara Barton and Dorothea Dix helped break down barriers in the North against the employment of their sex in government service. Federal bureaus took the unprecedented step of hiring women as clerks and copyists, and, of some 20,000 women who served as nurses, more than 3,000 were army nurses filling positions that did not exist before the war. The absence of male workers due to their service in the Union army opened up 100,000 jobs for women in private business. By 1864, women made up one-third of the manufacturing workforce, increasing from one-quarter at the start of the war. To be sure, women still had to settle for wages that were considerably lower than those for men in comparable jobs, and the return of the soldiers after the war reduced women's manufacturing employment back to its prewar level. Involvement in war-related services and jobs nonetheless had raised the self-esteem of countless women. Participation in the war effort broadened the humanitarian concerns and organizational skills of thousands of women reformers and hastened the professionalization of nursing and teaching as careers for women.

Southern women also assumed

major new responsibilities that were crucial to the support of the war effort. If anything, they were even more fervid patriots than their Northern counterparts. They were the most active Confederate recruiters in encouraging, if not shaming, their menfolk into doing their duty by enlisting and defending the South. A popular Confederate slogan summed up their role: "Better a widow than married to a craven."

Within the first year of the war Southern women formed 1,000 relief associations and sewed thousands of items of clothing for the soldiers. While upper-class women were organizing fairs and giving dramatic readings to raise funds for soldiers' relief work, women in nonslaveholding families were laboring in the fields of farms stripped of a male workforce. Women became army nurses, although fears that they might transgress woman's proper sphere kept their numbers lower than in the Union. Daughters of the rural poor filled industrial jobs in textile factories and Confederate war plants.

Both psychologically and economically, Southern women made vital contributions to the Confederate cause in the first half of the war. However, their support waned as they faced problems unique to women in the South: mainly high prices, shortages of essential items, and the constant threat of invasion and enemy occupation. Women in the North never had to experience the trauma of the refugee experience.

As their sacrifice seemingly resulted only in greater suffering, Southern women increasingly became critics of the war or its management by Confederate authorities. Female factory workers went on strike for better wages and safer working conditions. They organized public protests against food shortages. Most important, and in a remarkable reversal from their attitudes at the start of the war, women wrote their sons and husbands in the army urging them to come home and save their families from utter destitution. By 1864, desertion rates in Confederate armies were climbing. Charles Fenton James of North Carolina explained why in a letter to his sister: "Desertion takes place because desertion is encouraged.... And though the ladies may not be willing to concede the fact, they are nevertheless responsible... for the desertion in the army and the dissipation in the country."

The burden of the war fell far more heavily on women in the South then those in the North. In both instances, however, the openings for a greater public expression of women's independence created by the war all but closed when the guns fell silent. Some women continued to carve out additional autonomy for themselves, but legal restrictions were still in place for all women. After the disruptions of the war years, most women settled for a return to their traditional and limited roles as housewives and mothers.

Dr. Mary Edwards Walker became the first female officer in the American military when she received a commission in the U.S. Army in 1864. Her attire of pants was also highly unusual for that era and shocked her contemporaries.

SEE ALSO

Barton, Clara; Dix, Dorothea L.; Government workers; Industrial workers; Refugees; Richmond Bread Riot; Wartime economies; Women's rights movement

FURTHER READING

Attie, Jeanie. *Patriotic Toil: Northern*

Few could have predicted from this obscure notice in a Seneca Falls newspaper that the most cele- brated conven- tion in the his- tory of the women's rights movement was about to con- vene.

Women and the American Civil War. Ithaca: Cornell University Press, 1998.

Clinton, Catherine and Nina Silber, eds. *Divided Houses: Gender and the Civil War.* New York: Oxford University Press, 1992.

Culpepper, Marilyn Mayer. *Trials and Tri- umphs: Women of the American Civil War.* East Lansing: Michigan State Uni- versity Press, 1991.

Faust, Drew Gilpin. *Mothers of Invention: Women of the Slaveholding South in the American Civil War.* Chapel Hill: Univer- sity of North Carolina Press, 1996.

Massey, Mary Elizabeth. *Bonnet Brigades: American Women and the Civil War.* New York: Knopf, 1966.

Rable, George C. *Civil Wars: Women and the Crisis of Southern Nationalism.* Urbana: University of Illinois Press, 1989.

Sigerman, Harriet. *Laborers for Liberty: American Women, 1865–1890.* Vol. 6 of *The Young Oxford History of Women in the United States,* ed. Nancy F. Cott. New York: Oxford University Press, 1994.

———. *An Unfinished Battle: American Women, 1848–1865.* Vol. 5 of *The Young Oxford History of Women in the United States,* ed. Nancy F. Cott. New York: Oxford University Press, 1994.

Silber, Nina. *Daughters of the Union: North- ern Women Fight the Civil War.* Cam- bridge: Harvard University Press, 2005.

Women's rights movement

Women were active in all phases of Northern reform in the antebellum period. Gaining self-confidence and organizational experience, some of these women began to question their subordi- nate social and legal position in Ameri- can life. Especially for women coming out of the abolitionist crusade, this new self-assertion produced the first orga- nized women's rights movement in American history.

In mid-19th-century America, women were denied the vote, deprived of property or control of their own

Women's Rights Convention.

A Convention to discuss the social, civil and religious condition and rights of Woman, will be held in the Wesleyan Chapel, at Sen eca Falls, N. Y., on Wednesday and Thurs day the 19th and 20th of July current, com mencing at 10 o'clock A. M.

During the first day, the meeting will be exclusively for Woman, which all are earn estly invited to attend. The public gener ally are invited to be present on the second day, when LUCRETIA MOTT, of Philadelphia, and others both ladies and gentlemen, will address the Convention.

wages after marriage, shut out of the business world, and generally barred from advanced education. Cultural con- ventions held that their God-ordained role was to serve society as wives and mothers within their homes. Women reformers, whose work was first seen as an extension of their domestic role as nurturers, challenged their assigned role as men's submissive followers when their efforts to be treated as equals in the cause of reform met resistance. In particular, women abolitionists began to draw parallels between the condition of the slaves and their own dependent status in Northern society. Abby Kelley, a Quaker abolitionist, made the point forcefully when she argued, "In striving to cut [the slave's] irons off, we found most surely that *we* were manacled *ourselves.*"

Women's demands that abolitionist societies treat them as equals were a major factor in the split that took place within the abolitionist movement by 1840. The same issue of the "woman question" also disrupted the 1840 World Anti-Slavery Convention in Lon- don. When the convention refused to seat the American female delegates, Lucretia Mott and Elizabeth Cady Stan- ton, two of those excluded, vowed to build a movement for women's equality.

Despite having to take a back seat to the abolitionist crusade, Stanton and

Mott succeeded in calling the Seneca Falls Convention in upstate New York in 1848. This was the first national convention ever devoted to women's rights. In their Declaration of Sentiments, the delegates called for full female equality. The linchpin of their push for political equality was the demand for the vote for women as a sacred and inalienable right of citizenship. By drawing upon ideas of equality and individual rights they first had learned to use in condemning slavery, these women were now addressing issues of male oppression in their own lives.

Although the politicians of the day scorned most of these demands, this first generation of feminists did gain some successes in the 1850s: they helped secure more liberal divorce laws and greater legal control for married women over their property. During the Civil War, feminist leaders suspended their drive for civil and political rights and threw their energies into the cause of Union victory.

The feminist-abolitionist alliance, one strained but not broken by the women's rights movement, achieved its greatest success in the petition campaign organized in 1863 by the Woman's National Loyal League. The 400,000 signatures collected by the league reflected a mass campaign of political mobilization that was instrumental in the passage of the 13th Amendment ending slavery. The feminist goal of a new Constitution guaranteeing liberty and equality to all Americans regardless of sex or race remained out of reach for the moment, however.

SEE ALSO

Abolitionism; Anthony, Susan B.; Stanton, Elizabeth Cady; 13th Amendment; Women in the war

FURTHER READING

Du Bois, Ellen Carol. *Feminism and Suffrage: The Emergence of an Independent Women's Movement.* Ithaca, N.Y.: Cornell University Press, 1978.

Hewitt, Nancy A. *Women's Activism and Social Change: Rochester, New York, 1822–1872.* Ithaca, N.Y.: Cornell University Press, 1984.

Yancey, William Lowndes

CONFEDERATE POLITICIAN

- *Born: August 10, 1814, Warren County, Ga.*
- *Political party: Democrat*
- *Education: private academies*
- *Government service: Alabama House of Representatives, 1841, 1843; U.S. House of Representatives, 1844–46; Confederacy: commissioner to England and France, 1861–62; Confederate Senate, 1862–63*
- *Died: July 27, 1863*

A fiery and eloquent orator, William Lowndes Yancey of Alabama was a leading secessionist credited with popularizing secessionist doctrines throughout the South. Along with other fire-eaters, men more adept at tearing down government than constructing a workable replacement, he played only a minor role in the Confederacy and soon became a harsh critic of Jefferson Davis's administration.

Yancey spent much of his youth in the North following the death of his father from yellow fever. His mother's second husband, the Reverend Nathan Beman, moved the family in 1823 to Troy, New York. Whether because of Beman's zeal for abolitionism or his frequent quarrels with his wife, Yancey came to hate his stepfather as the personification of all that was grasping and hypocritical in Northern society. In 1833 he left Williams College in Massachusetts before graduating and returned

William Lowndes Yancey was a spellbinding orator who successfully agitated for secession, but he was a poor choice as a Confederate commissioner to Europe. The British consul at Charleston accurately characterized him as "impulsive, erratic and hot-headed."

to his native South.

Yancey studied law in Greenville, South Carolina, under Benjamin F. Perry and, like Perry, was a Unionist in his early politics. He also acquired 35 slaves through marriage. But his career as a South Carolina lawyer-planter was cut short in 1839 when most of his slaves were accidentally poisoned. To rebuild his fortune—and perhaps to escape the notoriety he won by killing his wife's uncle in a brawl—he moved to Alabama and opened a law office.

When Yancey returned to politics in the 1840s, he was a committed states'-rights advocate. He served briefly in the Alabama House and in the U.S. Congress but had little of the compromising temperament needed for success in party politics. His fame and influence would rest on his oratory. Defending secession as a constitutional right, he delivered hundreds of speeches in an attempt, as he phrased it in 1858, to "fire the Southern heart" in defense of liberties allegedly being trampled by a hostile North. After agitating in 1860 to force a split in the national Democratic party over the issue of slavery, he championed secession once Abraham Lincoln was elected President. At the state convention in January 1861, he introduced the ordinance of secession that took Alabama out of the Union.

The man of the hour at the moment of secession, Yancey never held a commanding position in the new Confederacy. Too radical even to be chosen as a delegate to the Montgomery convention of seceding states in February 1861, he was sent off to Europe as part of a diplomatic team charged with gaining foreign recognition for the Confederacy. After the British rebuffed him, he returned to the South in early 1862 and accepted a seat as an Alabama senator in the Confederate Congress.

Although he was willing to support the raising of a national army and the levying of new taxes, Yancey continually clashed with President Jefferson Davis over the issue of executive powers. He attacked Davis's appointment policy for generals and his efforts to establish a Confederate Supreme Court as violations of states' rights. In opposing an administration measure to draft the civil officials of the states into the army, he warned that the Confederacy was in danger of subverting the constitutional freedoms it was pledged to defend. "The province of this government, its sole province," he proclaimed, "is to defend...the Constitutional liberties of States and of the people of States. There is no National life to defend."

Yancey did not live to see the end of the Confederacy he feared was giving way to a military tyranny. Suffering from bladder and kidney ailments, he died at his farmhouse in Alabama in the summer of 1863.

SEE ALSO
Fire-eaters; Secession

FURTHER READING
Dubose, John Witherspoon. *The Life and Times of William Lowndes Yancey.* 2 vols. New York: Peter Smith, 1942.
Walther, Eric H. *William Lowndes Yancey and the Coming of the Civil War.* Chapel Hill: University of North Carolina Press, 2006.

THE CIVIL WAR

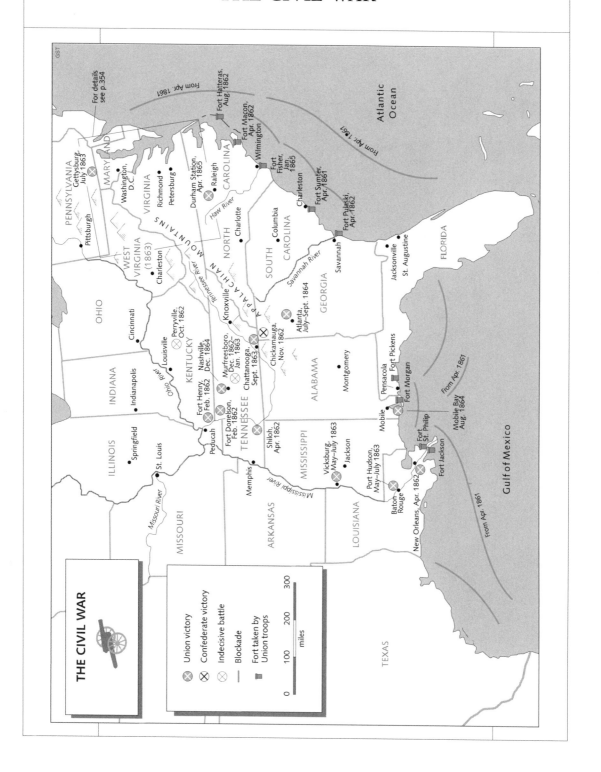

THE CIVIL WAR

- ⊗ Union victory
- ⊗ Confederate victory
- ⊗ Indecisive battle
- — Blockade
- ▪ Fort taken by Union troops

miles

0   100   200   300

MAP 2

THE VIRGINIA BATTLES

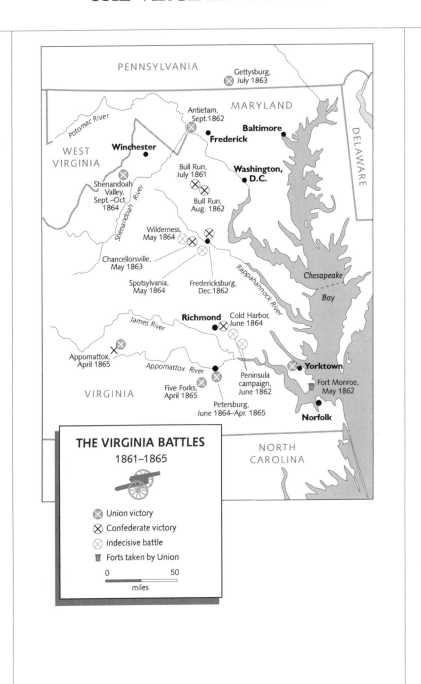

THE VIRGINIA BATTLES

1861–1865

⊗ Union victory
⊗ Confederate victory
⊗ Indecisive battle
🏰 Forts taken by Union

0   50
miles

APPENDIX 1

IMPORTANT DATES IN THE CIVIL WAR ERA

1820

Congress passes the Missouri Compromise on slavery in the Louisiana Purchase

1831

Abolitionist movement begins when William Lloyd Garrison starts publication of the *Liberator*

1832–33

Nullification crisis in South Carolina

1846

Wilmot Proviso is introduced in Congress but is defeated

1850

Congress passes the Compromise of 1850

1852

Harriet Beecher Stowe publishes *Uncle Tom's Cabin*

1854

Kansas-Nebraska Act repeals the Missouri Compromise

Republican party forms in opposition to the spread of slavery

1855

Violence erupts in "Bleeding Kansas"

1856

Congressman Preston Brooks of South Carolina canes Massachusetts senator Charles Sumner in the U.S. Senate

1857

Supreme Court issues *Dred Scott* decision

1858

Illinois senatorial candidates Abraham Lincoln and Stephen A. Douglas hold series of debates over slavery

1859

John Brown's raid at Harpers Ferry, Virginia

1860

Republican candidate Abraham Lincoln is elected President

South Carolina secedes from the Union

1861

January–February
Six additional states from the Lower South join South Carolina in leaving the Union

February
Delegates from seceded states establish the Confederate States of America in a convention at Montgomery, Alabama, and select Jefferson Davis as the president of the new Confederate government

March
Lincoln is inaugurated as President

April
The Civil War begins after Confederate forces bombard Fort Sumter

Lincoln proclaims the Union blockade

April–May
Virginia, North Carolina, Tennessee, and Arkansas secede from the Union

July
First Battle of Bull Run

November
Union navy seizes Port Royal, South Carolina

1862

February
Union forces gain the initiative in the western theater by capturing Forts Henry and Donelson

March
Peninsula campaign begins in Virginia

The *Monitor* and *Merrimack* clash in the first battle of ironclad ships

April
Battle of Shiloh

New Orleans falls to federal forces

July
The Peninsula campaign ends when Lincoln recalls McClellan to Washington

August
Second Battle of Bull Run

September
Bragg's Kentucky invasion

Battle of Antietam

December
Battle of Fredericksburg

Battle of Stones River

1863

January
Lincoln's Emancipation Proclamation takes effect

April
Grant launches his Vicksburg campaign

May
Battle of Chancellorsville

July
Battle of Gettysburg

Vicksburg surrenders to Union forces

New York City draft riots

Assault on Fort Wagner by the 54th Massachusetts Regiment establishes in the eyes of whites the bravery of black union troops

September
Battle of Chickamauga

November
Battle of Chattanooga

1864

May
Grant's Virginia campaign and Sherman's Atlanta campaign begin

September
Atlanta falls to Sherman's army

November
President Lincoln is reelected

Sherman begins his march to the sea through Georgia

1865

January
Congress passes the 13th Amendment, ending slavery

March
Confederate Congress authorizes the enlistment of black soldiers

April
Petersburg and Richmond fall to Grant's army

Lee surrenders to Grant at Appomattox Court House

John Wilkes Booth assassinates Lincoln

May
President Andrew Johnson announces his Reconstruction plan

December
Congress refuses to seat representatives from the former Confederate states

1866

Congress and President Johnson remain deadlocked over Reconstruction

Congress passes the 14th Amendment (ratified in 1868), granting the freed population national citizenship

1867

Congress launches its own plan of Reconstruction with the Military Reconstruction Act

New Republican parties, based on black suffrage, begin to organize in the South

1868

President Andrew Johnson is impeached and tried by the Senate

1869

Congress passes the 15th Amendment (ratified in 1870), on black suffrage

1873

A severe economic depression begins

1876

Disputed Presidential election between Rutherford B. Hayes and Samuel J. Tilden

1877

The Compromise of 1877 makes Hayes President and marks the formal end of Reconstruction

MUSEUMS AND HISTORIC SITES

There are many facilities of various kinds devoted, wholly or in part, to the Civil War. The first category listed below consists of exhibits, monuments and museums, and the second of selected battlefield sites and cemeteries, which often include military museums and displays, maintained by the National Park Service.

Museums and Exhibits

Abraham Lincoln Birthplace
2995 Lincoln Farm Road
Hodgenville, KY 42748
270-358-3137
www.nps.gov/abli

Andersonville National Historic Site
496 Cemetery Road
Andersonville, GA 31711
229-924-0343
www.nps.gov/ande

Andrew Johnson National Historic Site
101 North College St.
Greeneville, TN 37743
423-638-3551
www.nps.gov/anjo

Arlington House/The Robert E. Lee Memorial
George Washington Memorial Parkway
Turkey Run Park
McLean, VA 22101
703-235-1530
www.nps.gov/arho

Atlanta Cyclorama and Civil War Museum
800 Cherokee Avenue, SE
Atlanta, GA 30315
404-624-1071
www.atlantacyclorama.org

Beauvoir, Jefferson Davis Home and Presidential Library
2244 Beach Boulevard
Biloxi, MS 39531
228-388-4400
www.beauvoir.org

Belle Boyd Cottage
101 Chester Street
Front Royal, VA 22630
540-636-1446
www.warrenheritagesociety.org/belleboyd.php

Boston African American National Historic Site
14 Beacon Street, Suite 401
Boston, MA 02108
617-742-5415
www.nps.gov/boaf

Clara Barton National Historic Site
5801 Oxford Road
Glen Echo, MD 20812
301-320-1410
www.nps.gov/clba

Ford's Theatre National Historic Site
511 10th Street, NW
Washington, DC 20004
202-426-6924
www.nps.gov/foth

Fort Union National Monument
P.O. Box 127
Watrous, NM 87753
505-425-8025
www.nps.gov/foun

Frederick Douglass National Historic Site
1411 W Street, SE
Washington, DC 20020
202-426-5961
www.nps.gov/frdo

General Grant National Monument
Riverside Drive and West 122 Street
New York, NY 10027
212-666-1640
www.nps.gov/gegr

Hampton University Museum
Hampton University
11 Frissel Avenue
Hampton, VA 23668
757-727-5308
http://museum.hamptonu.edu

Harriet Tubman Home for the Aged
180-182 South Street
Auburn, NY 13021
315-252-2081
www.nps.gov/history/nr/travel/pwwmh/ny13.htm

Lincoln Home National Historic Site
413 South Eighth Street
Springfield, IL 62701-1905
217-492-4241, ext. 221
www.nps.gov/liho

The Museum of the Confederacy
1201 East Clay Street
Richmond, VA 23219
804-649-1861
www.moc.org

National Museum of American History, Smithsonian Institution
14th Street and Constitution Avenue, NW
Washington, DC 20560
202-633-1000
www.americanhistory.si.edu

National Museum of Civil War Medicine
48 East Patrick Street
Frederick, MD 21701
301-695-1864
www.civilwarmed.org

Penn Center Historic District
110 Martin Luther King Jr. Dr.
St. Helena Island, SC 29920
843-838-2432
www.penncenter.com

Ulysses S. Grant National Historic Site
7400 Grant Road
St. Louis, MO 63123
314-842-3298
www.nps.gov/ulsg

Valentine Richmond History Center
1015 East Clay Street
Richmond, VA 23219
804-649-0711
http://richmondhistorycenter.com

Women's Rights National Historical Park
136 Fall Street
Seneca Falls, NY 13148
315-568-0024
www.nps.gov/wori

National Park Service Battlefield Sites

For a complete listing of battlefield sites see *www.nps.gov/history/hps/abpp/civil.htm*

Antietam National Battlefield
P.O. Box 158
Sharpsburg, MD 21782
301-432-5124
www.nps.gov/anti

Appomattox Court House National Historical Park
Hwy. 24, P.O. Box 218
Appomattox, VA 24522
434-352-8987 ext. 26
www.nps.gov/apco

Arlington National Cemetery
Arlington, VA 22211
703-607-8000
www.arlingtoncemetery.org

Battleground National Cemetery
6625 Georgia Avenue, NW
Washington, DC 20240
202-426-6829
www.nps.gov/cwdw/historyculture/
    battleground-national-cemetery.htm

Brices Cross Roads National Battlefield Site
2680 Natchez Trace Parkway
Tupelo, MS 38804
800-305-7417
www.nps.gov/brcr

Chickamauga and Chattanooga National Military Park
P.O. Box 2128
Fort Oglethorpe, GA 30742
706-866-9241
www.nps.gov/chch

Fort Donelson National Battlefield
P.O. Box 434
Dover, TN 37058
931-232-5706
www.nps.gov/fodo

Fort Pulaski National Monument
P.O. Box 30757
Savannah, GA 31410
912-786-5787
www.nps.gov/fopu

Fort Sumter National Monument
1214 Middle Street
Sullivan's Island, SC 29482
843-883-3123
www.nps.gov/fosu

Fredericksburg and Spotsylvania County Battlefields Memorial National Military Park
120 Chatham Lane
Fredericksburg, VA 22405
540-371-6122
www.nps.gov/frsp

Gettysburg National Military Park
1195 Baltimore Pike
Gettysburg, PA 17325-2804
717-334-1124
www.nps.gov/gett

Harpers Ferry National Historical Park
171 Shoreline Drive
Harpers Ferry, WV 25425
304-535-6029
www.nps.gov/hafe

Kennesaw Mountain National Battlefield Park
900 Kennesaw Mountain Drive
Kennesaw, GA 30152
770-427-4686
www.nps.gov/kemo

Manassas National Battlefield Park
12521 Lee Highway
Manassas, VA 20109
703-361-1339
www.nps.gov/mana

Monocacy National Battlefield
4801 Urbana Pike
Frederick, MD 21704
301-662-3515
www.nps.gov/mono

Pea Ridge National Military Park
15930 E. Highway 62
Pea Ridge, AR 72732
479-451-8122 ext. 227
www.nps.gov/peri

Pecos National Historical Park
(includes the battlefield of Glorietta
Pass)
P.O. Box 418
Pecos, NM 87552
505-757-7200
www.nps.gov/peco

Petersburg National Battlefield
5001 Siege Road
Petersburg, VA 23803
804-732-3531 ext. 200
www.nps.gov/pete

Richmond National Battlefield Park
3215 East Broad Street
Richmond, VA 23223
804-226-1981 ext. 23
www.nps.gov/rich

Shiloh National Military Park
1055 Pittsburg Landing Rd
Shiloh, TN 38376
731-689-5696
www.nps.gov/shil

Stones River National Battlefield
3501 Old Nashville Highway
Murfreesboro, TN 37129
615-893-9501
www.nps.gov/stri

Tupelo National Battlefield
c/o Natchez Trace Parkway
2680 Natchez Trace Parkway
Tupelo, MS 38804
800-305-7417
www.nps.gov/tupe

Vicksburg National Military Park
3201 Clay Street
Vicksburg, MS 39183
601-636-0583
www.nps.gov/vick

Wilson's Creek National Battlefield
6424 West Farm Road 182
Republic, MO 65738
417-732-2662 ext. 227
www.nps.gov/wicr

FURTHER READING

Overviews

Boatner, Mark Mayo III. *The Civil War Dictionary*. New York: Vintage, 1991.

Burton, Orville Vernon. *The Age of Lincoln*. New York: Hill and Wang, 2007.

Catton, Bruce. *The Centennial History of the Civil War*. 3 vols. Garden City, N.Y.: Doubleday, 1961–1965.

Eicher, David J. *The Civil War in Books: An Analytical Bibliography*. Urbana: University of Illinois Press, 1997.

McPherson, James M. *Battle Cry of Freedom: The Civil War Era*. New York: Oxford University Press, 1988.

Nelson, Scott and Carol Sheriff, *A People at War: Civilians and Soldiers in America's Civil War, 1854–1877*. New York: Oxford University Press, 2008.

Roland, Charles P. *An American Iliad: The Story of the Civil War*. Lexington: University Press of Kentucky, 1991.

Seidman, Rachel Filene. *The Civil War: A History in Documents*. New York: Oxford University Press, 2001.

Sewell, Richard H. *The House Divided: Sectionalism and Civil War, 1848–1865*. Baltimore: Johns Hopkins University Press, 1988.

Sheehan-Dean, Aaron C. *Concise Historical Atlas of the U. S. Civil War*. New York: Oxford University Press, 2009.

Weigley, Russell F. *A Great Civil War: A Military and Political History, 1861–1865*. Bloomington: Indiana University Press, 2000.

Williams, David. *A People's History of the Civil War: Struggles for the Meaning of Freedom*. New York: Free Press, 2005.

The Coming of the War

Boritt, Gabor S., ed. *Why the Civil War Came*. New York: Oxford University Press, 1996.

Egnal, Marc. *Clash of Extremes: The Economic Origins of the Civil War*. New York: Hill and Wang, 2009.

Freehling, William W. *The Road to Disunion: Secessionists at Bay, 1776–1854*. New York: Oxford University Press, 1990.

——. *The Road to Disunion: Secessionists Triumphant*. New York: Oxford University Press, 2007.

Holt, Michael F. *The Political Crisis of the 1850s*. New York: Wiley, 1978.

Potter, David M. *The Impending Crisis, 1848–1861*. New York: Harper & Row, 1976.

Reid, Brian Holden. *The Origins of the American Civil War*. New York: Addison, Wesley, Longman, 1996.

Battles and Strategy

Boritt, Gabor S., ed. *Lincoln's Generals*. New York: Oxford University Press, 1994.

Foote, Shelby. *The Civil War: A Narrative*. 3 vols. New York: Random House, 1958–1974.

Gallagher, Gary W. *The Confederate War*. Cambridge: Harvard University Press, 1997.

Hattaway, Herman. *Shades of Blue and Gray: An Introductory Military History of the Civil War*. Columbia: University of Missouri Press, 1997.

Keegan, John. *The American Civil War: A Military History*. London: Hutchinson, 2009.

McMurry, Richard M. *Two Great Rebel Armies: An Essay in Confederate Military History*. Chapel Hill: University of North Carolina Press, 1989.

Royster, Charles. *The Destructive War: William Tecumseh Sherman, Stonewall Jackson, and the Americans.* New York: Knopf, 1991.

Stoker, Donald. *Grand Design: Strategy and the U. S. Civil War.* New York: Oxford University Press, 2010.

Symonds, Craig L. *A Battlefield Atlas of the Civil War.* Baltimore, Md.: Nautical & Aviation Pub. Co. of America, 1994.

Woodworth, Steven E. *Davis and Lee at War.* Lawrence: University Press of Kansas, 1995.

Work, David. *Lincoln's Political Generals.* Urbana: University of Illinois Press, 2006.

Soldiers

Daniel, Larry J. *Soldiering in the Army of Tennessee.* Chapel Hill: University of North Carolina Press, 1991.

Hess, Earl J. *The Union Soldier in Battle.* Lawrence: University Press of Kansas, 1997.

Linderman, Gerald F. *Embattled Courage: The Experience of Combat in the American Civil War.* New York: Free Press, 1987.

Manning, Chandra. *What This Cruel War Was Over.* New York: Knopf, 2007.

McPherson, James M. *For Cause and Comrades: Why Men Fought in the Civil War.* New York: Oxford University Press, 1997.

Mitchell, Reid. *Civil War Soldiers.* New York: Viking, 1988.

Robertson, James I., Jr. *Soldiers Blue and Gray.* Columbia: University of South Carolina Press, 1988.

Sheehan-Dean, Aaron C. *Why Confederates Fought: Family and Nation in Civil War Virginia.* Chapel Hill: University of North Carolina Press, 2007.

Photographic and Pictorial Works

Brother Against Brother: Time-Life Books History of the Civil War. New York: Prentice Hall Press, 1990.

Catton, Bruce. *The American Heritage New History of the Civil War, with an introduction by James M. McPherson.* New York: Viking, 1996.

Davis, William C., ed. *Touched by Fire: A Photographic Portrait of the Civil War.* 2 vols. Boston: Little, Brown, 1985–86.

Kagan, Neil, ed. *Eyewitness to the Civil War: The Complete History from Secession to Reconstruction.* Washington, D. C.: National Geographic, 2006.

Neely, Mark E. Jr., Harold Holzer, and Gabor S. Boritt. *The Confederate Image: Prints of the Lost Cause.* Chapel Hill: University of North Carolina Press, 1987.

Sears, Stephen W., ed. *The American Heritage Century Collection of Civil War Art.* New York: McGraw-Hill, 1974.

Zeller, Bob. *The Blue and Gray in Black and White: A History of Civil War Photography.* Westport, Conn.: Praeger, 2005.

Reconstruction

Abbott, Richard H. *The Republican Party and the South, 1855–1877.* Chapel Hill: University of North Carolina Press, 1986.

Belz, Herman. *Reconstructing the Union: Theory and Practice During the Civil War.* Ithaca, N.Y.: Cornell University Press, 1969.

Blum, Edward J. *Reforging the White Republic: Race, Religion, and American Nationalism, 1865–1898.* Baton Rouge: Louisiana State University Press, 2005.

Fitzgerald, Michael F. *Splendid Failure: Postwar Reconstruction in the American South*. Chicago: Ivan R. Dee, 2007.

Foner, Eric. *Reconstruction: America's Unfinished Revolution, 1863–1877*. New York: Oxford University Press, 1988.

Franklin, John Hope. *Reconstruction After the Civil War*. Chicago: University of Chicago Press, 1961.

Harris, William C. *With Charity for All: Lincoln and the Restoration of the Union*. Lexington: The University Press of Kentucky, 1997.

Keith, Lee Anna. *The Colfax Massacre: The Untold Story of Black Power, White Terror, and the Death of Reconstruction*. New York: Oxford University Press, 2008.

Perman, Michael. *Emancipation and Reconstruction, 1862–1879*. Arlington Heights, Ill.: Harlan Davidson, 1987.

Stampp, Kenneth M. *The Era of Reconstruction, 1865–1877*. New York: Knopf, 1966.

Stampp, Kenneth M. and Leon F. Litwack, eds. *Reconstruction: An Anthology of Revisionist Writings*. Baton Rouge: Louisiana State University Press, 1969.

African Americans

Berlin, Ira et al. *Slaves No More: Three Essays on Emancipation and the Civil War*. New York: Cambridge University Press, 1992.

Blassingame, John W., ed. *Slave Testimony: Two Centuries of Letters, Speeches, Interviews, and Autobiographies*. Baton Rouge: Louisiana State University Press, 1977.

Foner, Eric. *Nothing but Freedom: Emancipation and Its Legacy*. Baton Rouge: Louisiana State University Press, 1983.

Frankel, Noralee. *Break Those Chains at Last: African Americans, 1860–1880*. Vol. 5 of *The Young Oxford History of African Americans*, ed. Robin D. G. Kelley and Earl Lewis. New York: Oxford University Press, 1996.

Franklin, John Hope and Loren Schweninger. *Runaway Slaves: Rebels on the Plantation*. New York: Oxford University Press, 1999.

Hahn, Steven. *A Nation under Our Feet: Black Political Struggles in the Rural South from Slavery to the Great Migration*. Cambridge: Belknap Press of Harvard University, 2003.

Litwack, Leon F. *Been in the Storm So Long: The Aftermath of Slavery*. New York: Knopf, 1979.

O'Donovan, Susan E. *Becoming Free in the Cotton South*. Cambridge: Harvard University Press, 2007.

Miller, Randall M. and John Davis Smith, eds. *Dictionary of Afro-American Slavery*. Westport, Conn.: Praeger, 1997.

Rawick, George P., ed. *The American Slave: A Composite Autobiography*. 41 vols. Westport, Conn.: Greenwood Press, 1972–81.

Women

Attie, Jeanie. *Patriotic Toil: Northern Women and the American Civil War*. Ithaca, N.Y.: Cornell University Press, 1998.

Censer, Jane Turner. *The Reconstruction of White Southern Womanhood, 1865–1895*. Baton Rouge: Louisiana State University Press, 2003.

Clinton, Catherine and Nina Silber, eds. *Divided Houses: Gender and the Civil War*. New York: Oxford University Press, 1992.

Edwards, Laura F. *Scarlett Doesn't Live Here Anymore: Southern Women in the Civil War Era*. Urbana: University of Illinois Press, 2000.

Faust, Drew Gilpin. *Mothers of Invention: Women of the Slaveholding South in the American Civil War*. Chapel Hill: University of North Carolina Press, 1996.

Leonard, Elizabeth. *Yankee Women: Gender Battles in the Civil War*. New York: Norton, 1994.

Scott, Anne Firor. *The Southern Lady: From Pedestal to Politics, 1830–1930*. Chicago: University of Chicago Press, 1970.

Silber, Nina. *Gender and the Sectional Conflict*. Chapel Hill: University of North Carolina Press, 2008.

Whites, LeeAnn. *The Civil War as a Crisis in Gender: Augusta, Georgia, 1860–1890*. Athens: University of Georgia Press, 1995.

WEBSITES

There are hundreds of Civil War websites, many of which include valuable archives, bibliographies, and source guides. The sites listed below are good examples of the quality and quantity of information available.

Africans in America
www.pbs.org/wgbh/aia
A companion site to the PBS television series tracing the struggle against slavery.

American Civil War & Confederacy Library Guide
http://libguides.miami.edu/content .php?pid=13662&sid=93459
A portal to more than 40 websites and library collections on a variety of Civil War themes, many on African Americans in the war and digitized document collections. Compiled by the University of Miami Library.

The American Civil War: Dakota State University
www.homepages.dsu.edu/jankej/ civilwar/civilwar.htm
An index of websites divided into 60 Civil War topics, including everything from biographical sites to the Civil War in movies, compiled by Jim Janke, associate professor of finance, Dakota State University.

The American Civil War Homepage
http://sunsite.utk.edu/civil-war/ warweb.html
A superb source for hypertext links to all facets of the Civil War, sponsored by the University of Tennessee's School of Information Sciences.

American Memory Project at the Library of Congress
Archival resources for exploring the Civil War.

Photographs:
http://memory.loc.gov/ammem/ cwphtml/cwphome.html

Maps:
http://memory.loc.gov/ammem/ gmdhtml/cwmhtml/cwmhome.html

Sheet music:
http://memory.loc.gov/ammem/ cwmhtml/cwmhome.html

Civil War Era Collection at Gettysburg College
www.gettysburg.edu/library/ gettdigital/civil_war/civilwar.htm
Digital repository of artifacts, letters, lithographs, maps, battlefield paintings, pamphlets, photographs, political cartoons, and sheet music from Gettysburg College's Special Collections.

Civil War Music
www.civilwarmusic.net
Sources on music, from fife tunes to song lyrics to photographs of Civil War bands.

Civil War Soldiers and Sailors System
www.itd.nps.gov/cwss
Type the name of any Civil War soldier into the CWSS website and quickly pull up information on that soldier.

Civil War Treasures from the New-York Historical Society
*http://lcweb2.loc.gov/ammem/ndlp
coop/nhihtml/cwnyhshome.html*
Posted in collaboration with the Library of Congress, this digital repository of highlights from the New-York Historical Society includes photographs, sketches, posters, etchings, graphic designs, and letters from Walt Whitman and Sarah Blunt, a nurse in Maryland and West Virginia.

Crisis at Fort Sumter
www.tulane.edu/~sumter
Documentary resources for the study of events leading up to the Civil War.

Documenting the American South
http://docsouth.unc.edu
Primary-source materials documenting the cultural history of the American South from the viewpoint of Southerners. A special section is devoted to the Southern home front during the Civil War.

The Frederick Douglass Papers
*http://lcweb2.loc.gov/ammem/
doughtml/doughome.html*
Approximately 7,400 items related to all aspects of Douglass's life, from the Library of Congress.

Freedmen and Southern Society Project
www.history.umd.edu/Freedmen
Historical papers chronicling emancipation during the Civil War.

The Gilder Lehrman Institute of American History: The Civil War Era
*www.gilderlehrman.org/institute/era_
civilwar.php*
Podcasts, slideshows, curriculum modules, and a database of images and scans of historical documents from the Gilder Lehrman Institute.

Intelligence in the Civil War
*www.cia.gov/library/publications/
additional-publications/
civil-war/introduction.html*
A chronicle by the U.S. Central Intelligence Agency of the spy war within the Civil War, including information on the Confederacy's Signal Corps and the Union's Bureau of Military Information.

The Lot of the Civil War Sketch Artist
http://at.bc.edu/beckercollection
A multimedia presentation from *Boston College Magazine* about the sketches of Joseph Becker, a former errand boy for *Frank Leslie's Illustrated Newspaper*, who was sent to the Union front lines in 1863. Allows comparison of original sketches with published images.

Mathew Brady Civil War Photographs
*www.flickr.com/photos/usnational
archives/collections/721576224952
26723*
The National Archives' digital collection of 6,000 images from the Mathew Brady Photographs of Civil War-Era Personalities and Scenes collection. Browse on the flickr platform, or follow a link to the catalog record.

NYPL Digital Schomburg Images of 19th-Century African Americans
*http://digital.nypl.org/schomburg/
    images_aa19*
An extensive primary-source archive of photographs, woodcuts, and other images of 19th-century African Americans from the Schomburg Center for Research in Black Culture, New York Public Library.

Uncle Tom's Cabin and American Culture
*http://utc.iath.virginia.edu/
    sitemap.html*
A collection of images, mp3s, essays, and transcriptions of historical documents pertaining to the novel, including period reviews from the pro- and anti-slavery perspectives, preceding texts and cultural context, and *Uncle Tom's Cabin* in music, poetry, plays, and movies.

The United States Civil War
*www.fordham.edu/halsall/mod/
    modsbook27.html*
A source for online resources that deal with the war, its background, and Reconstruction, including contemporary narrative accounts, personal memoirs, songs, newspaper reports, and other documents.

The United States Civil War Center
www.cwc.LSU.edu
Over 2,000 links to such resources as documents, archives and manuscripts, historic places, games, Civil War round tables, and book reviews.

Valley of the Shadow
http://valley.lib.virginia.edu
Multimedia resources bring to life two Virginia communities divided by the Civil War.

The War of the Rebellion: A Compilation of the Official Records of the Union and Confederate Armies
*http://digital.library.cornell.edu/m/
    moawar/waro.html*
Part of the Cornell University Library Making of America collection, this site hosts the official records of the Union and Confederate armies and navies in full text.

Women and the Civil War
*http://library.duke.edu/special
    collections/bingham/guides/
    civilwar.html*
Duke University's Special Collections Library presents full text transcriptions and scans of diaries, reminiscences, and letter collections from women who experienced the Civil War, as well as links to similar projects on the web.

INDEX

PICTURE CREDITS

The American Numismatic Society: 189; Center for Popular Music, Middle Tennessee State University: 210, Cincinnati Museum Center: 286; Free Library of Philadelphia: 158; George Mason University: 173; Kansas State Historical Society, Topeka, Kans.: 183; From Morton Keller, *The Art and Politics of Thomas Nast* (New York: Oxford University Press, 1968): 212; Kentucky Historical Society: 46; From Charles Leland, *Ye Book of Copperheads* (Philadelphia: F. Leypoldt, 1863), 21: 101; The Lester S. Levy Collection of Sheet Music, Sheridan Libraries, The Johns Hopkins University: 240; The Library Company of Philadelphia: 60; Library of Congress, Prints & Photographs Division: 2 (B811-378), 8 (USZ62-30847), 10 (USZ62-2201), 15 (B815-552), 17 (USZ62-548), 19 (B811-2700), 21 (B8184-3630), 22 (BH82-4084), 24 (USZ62-19319), 25 (USZ62-34418), 31 (USZ62-7824), 33 (USZ62-127610), 34 (BH8201-5169), 36 (USZ62-92023), 37 (USZ62-127604), 39 (B811-482), 40 (USZ62-11193), 48 (USZ62-115350), 51 (USZ62-115350), 54 (USZ62-7020), 56 (USZ62-127602), 57 (USZ62-10556), 62 (USZ62-92043), 64, 65 (USZ62-4374), 70 (B8184-10011), 75 (USZ62-127597), 78 (USZ62-41178), 81 (USZ62-16616), 85 (B817-7122), 86 (BH82-4741), 88 (USZ62-127303), 91 (B811- 221A), 92 (B811-2663), 93 (USZ62-72955), 95 (USZ62-89719), 97 (USZ62-127600), 100 (B8171-8221), 103 (USZ62-9797), 104 (USZ62-1754), 106 (RB E449.D749 1849), 107 (USZ62-14827), 110 (B817- 7656), 112 (USZC4-4616), 119 (USZ62-52492), 123 (USZC4-4658), 125 (BH834-88), 128 (B8184-2908), 129 (USZ62-33811), 133 (BH 824-4754), 139 (USZ62-121633), 141 (USZ62-127601), 142 (USZ62-90750), 143 (BH8201-5004A), 146 (B8171-227), 149 (B817-7903), 150 (USZ62-51046), 152 (USZ61-909), 154 (USZ62-127605), 156 (BH 832-2492), 163 (USZ62-8276), 165 (USZ62-4373), 166 (B811-2651), 168 (B8184-10366), 175 (B811-3411), 176 (BH82101-5839), 178 (USZ62-127615), 184 (USZ62-18094), 187 (BH83101-562), 191 (BB171-7951), 193 (USZ62-7992), 195 (MS-18630-81), 196 (B8184-B82), 198 (B812-3185), 200 (USZ62-73632), 202 (B184-4099), 204 (B8151-10168), 207 (USZ62-2618), 208 (USZ62-127611), 213 (USZ62-90652), 215 (B811-2342), 217 (USZ62-127614), 222 (USZ62-127304), 224 (B8184-B198), 225 (B815-732), 227 (USZ62-1), 228 (USZ18423-048778), 229 (BH832-30276), 233 (USZ62-7005), 234 (WZ62-30837), 235 (B8184-B263), 237 (B8184-10037), 236 (B8171-4018), 239 (BH83-3754), 245 (B816-8218), 248 (B8171-7942), 250, 251 (USZ62-8788), 253 (USZ62-28044), 254 (USZ62-127608), 255 (B8171-173), 257 (USZ62-127606), 258 (USZ62-2747), 261 (B8171-657), 262 (USZ62-1794), 264 (USZ62-132302), 267, 269 (B812-2001), 271 (USZ62-90258), 275 (USZ62-154), 277 (USZ62-11191), 280 (BA1713), 281 (USZ62-110608), 284 (B8172-6454), 286 (USZ62-127598), 288 (USZ62-3581), 290 (USZ62-7014), 291 (USZ62-7014), 292 (B8171-2297), 293 (USZ62-10571), 296 (USZ62-117998), 299 (B815-763), 300 (USZ62-95984), 301 (USZ62-40603), 305 (B813-1430 A), 309 (USZ62-30830), 312 (USZ62-16820), 314 (USZ62-127603), 316 (USZ62-178), 317 (B8171-756), 324 (USZ62-7816), 325 (USZ62-15257), 326 (USZ62-5925), 327 (USZ62-127612), 329 (USZ62-117249), 335 (USZ62-100070), 340 (USZ62-127609), 345 (USZ62-1994), 346 (USZ62-8678), 348 (USZ62-15693), 352 (USZ62-127613); Library of Congress, Map Division: 12; Library of Congress, National Library of Medicine: 347; Library of Congress, Rare Book and Special Collections Division: 137; The Maryland Historical Society, Baltimore, Md.: 246; The Metropolitan Museum of Art, Rogers Fund, 1948 (48.80): 138; The Museum of the Confederacy, Richmond, Va., Photography by Katherine Wetzel: 127; National Archives: 135, 147, 181, 186, 232, 268, 280, 298, 330; Gift of Edgar William and Bernice Chrysler Barbisch, Photograph © 2000 Board of Trustees, National Gallery of Art, Washington: 113; New York Public Library, Astor, Lenox and Tilden Foundations: 113, 319; New York State Museum: 339; RIA Novosti: 272; Oberlin College Archives, Oberlin, Ohio: 260; Ohio Historical Society: 268; Courtesy Old State House Museum, Little Rock, Ark.: 127; Courtesy of the Seneca Falls Historical Society: 303, 350; Texas State Library and Archives Commission: 220; Gary Tong: 14, 42, 61, 63, 67, 73, 145, 277, 294, 299, 300, 334, 353, 355; U.S. Army Military History Institute, Carlisle, Pa.: 109, 220, 238; Julia Ward Howe, "Battle Hymn of the Republic," Clifton Waller Barrett Library of American Literature, Special Collections Department, University of Virginia Library: 169; Zebulon B. Vance Birthplace State Historic Site: 333; West Point Museum: 321; The Western Reserve Historical Society, Cleveland, Ohio: 283.

William L. Barney has taught U.S. history at the University of North Carolina at Chapel Hill since 1975. A specialist on the 19th century, in his research and writing he has focused on the Civil War era. His books include *The Road to Secession* (1972), *The Passage of the Republic* (1987), *Battleground for the Union* (1990), and *The Making of a Confederate: Walter Lenoir's Civil War* (1997). He is also a co-author of *The American Journey: A History of the United States* (1998; 2nd ed., 2000) and editor of *A Companion to 19th-Century America* (2001). He has lectured on the Civil War as a Fulbright scholar in Italy and as a consultant to Civil War roundtables and teacher workshops.